A Research Guide to Psychology

A Research Guide to Psychology

Print and Electronic Sources

Deborah Dolan

ROWMAN & LITTLEFIELD
Lanham • Boulder • New York • London

Published by Rowman & Littlefield
An imprint of The Rowman & Littlefield Publishing Group, Inc.
4501 Forbes Boulevard, Suite 200, Lanham, Maryland 20706
www.rowman.com

Unit A, Whitacre Mews, 26-34 Stannary Street, London SE11 4AB

British Library Cataloguing in Publication Information Available

Library of Congress Cataloging-in-Publication Data

Names: Dolan, Deborah, 1958– author.
Title: A research guide to psychology : print and electronic sources /
    Deborah Dolan.
Description: Lanham : Rowman & Littlefield, [2017] | Includes bibliographical
    references and indexes.
Identifiers: LCCN 2017046195 (print) | LCCN 2017055959 (ebook) | ISBN
    9781442276024 (electronic) | ISBN 9781442276017 (hardcover : alk. paper)
Subjects: LCSH: Psychology—Research. | Psychology—Sources.
Classification: LCC BF76.5 (ebook) | LCC BF76.5 .D6285 2017 (print) | DDC
    150.72—dc23
LC record available at https://lccn.loc.gov/2017046195

∞™ The paper used in this publication meets the minimum requirements of
American National Standard for Information Sciences—Permanence of Paper
for Printed Library Materials, ANSI/NISO Z39.48-1992.

Printed in the United States of America

To my parents and sister, Tom, Mary and Kathleen,

and

Jay, Kitty, and Jim—
I love you and miss you all

Contents

List of Figures

Foreword

Many years ago, as an undergraduate psychology major, I was seeking to fill a one-credit hole in my schedule when I stumbled upon a course entitled Introduction to Library Research. Figuring it would be a useful and easy course, I signed up. Little did I realize how much this five-week class would immediately benefit me as I pursued a senior research project. With ease, I understood how to navigate through (what seemed like hundreds of volumes of) *Psychological Abstracts* and learned to use a special thesaurus of psychological terms for searching the printed indexes. Later I learned to use other research tools, such as *Dissertation Abstracts International*, for both recent research not yet published and older, unpublished studies of merit and was fascinated at how one could determine the importance of an article's impact on research literature through the *Social Science Index*. I learned to use the serials index our library had to determine what journal holdings the library held and whether I needed to search a shelf for a printed journal, go to another academic library within a reasonable distance, or take a trip to the microforms room. My course taught me that many older journals were available in a variety of photographed and miniaturized forms, such as microfilm and microfiche. Each of the various technologies, and there were quite a few, required its own special machine. Some had the ability to print pages by inserting coins into the machine, while others required that you read the article and take good notes.

My library research skills served me well when I enrolled the following fall semester in a PhD program in clinical psychology and immediately was immersed in many research projects. However, library research was beginning to change due to technological innovations. The computer revolution of that time seemed to begin with universities having large, room-sized mainframe computers, often used for administrative functions and data-crunching purposes by those with large grants. As computers decreased in size to personal computers (PCs), new applications were being developed that today seem commonplace. I remember being one of the first students on campus to create my master's thesis using word processing, by typing hundreds of punch cards to enter the words. Two heavy stacks of these cards were then inserted into a special reading machine, which would produce a stack of paper, the thesis, that could be picked up the next day at the computer center.

It was around that time that the university introduced a specialized form of *Psychological Abstracts*. You had to make an appointment with the proper research librarian and come prepared with a list of key index terms to do your search. Your time with the librarian was limited, but if you were lucky you would find a number of key articles, for which the citations could immediately be printed out on a continuous sheet of paper, which could be ripped from the printer and taken with you. This was an amazing advancement!

Technology marches on, and today I can sit in front of any computer in the world, access my university's electronic resources, and search multiple databases, receiving results within seconds of pressing the enter key. Many articles are immediately available on-screen or can be easily obtained. Keeping up with these advances takes a lot of time and learning, but there is a secret to how it is done: Professor Deborah Dolan.

Deborah Dolan, MA, MLS, a Hofstra University research librarian extraordinaire, is my most important resource for library research in psychology. She deeply understands the field and has the knowledge to help users find what they need, and most important, she is an excellent educator. Professor Dolan's ability to explain the processes involved in library research have extended my capabilities well beyond that rudimentary library course all those years ago. She is a nonstop font of information, able to suggest the latest sources, guides, compendiums, encyclopedias, websites, and search engines depending upon your needs. Professor Dolan regularly gives a two-day orientation to all the entering doctoral students in our clinical psychology program. They seek her out for help and guidance through to the completion of their dissertation projects.

Now you have the opportunity to benefit from Professor Dolan's knowledge and skills as my students have. In this fine book, you will find well-organized information about psychology resources for all levels of study. Whether you are a newcomer to the field, considering a career in psychology, applying to graduate school, conducting research, or a professor yourself, I guarantee that you will find this volume a very useful resource. If you are seeking information on psychological tests or research measures for a project, trying to understand the intricacies of American Psychological Association style for a research assignment, researching a subfield for a general resource, looking for government resources, getting confused about a database, or looking for the correct graduate program, you will find guidance in this book. Professor Dolan's volume has an easy and logical table of contents that allows the reader to quickly narrow the search to the relevant question. This book is a unique source for research in and about the field of psychology that I know will serve you well.

Mitchell L. Schare, PhD, ABBP
Professor of Psychology
Hofstra University
Board Certified in Behavioral and Cognitive Therapy

Preface

I am so excited to write this book, which has been on my mind for over ten years! In 2006 we at the Hofstra University Library were doing a major renovation of our first floor, on which the reference collection was housed. The need for modern reference and circulation areas, particularly for more student computers, study areas, and comfortable seating, involved a thorough overhaul of the reference collection, which had grown out of its own room into the main area and onto part of another floor. During the weeding process I came across the 1982 *Research Guide for Psychology* by Raymond McInnis.

As McInnis's book was twenty-four years old at the time, I knew that many parts would be very outdated. I also knew that in the age of expanding electronic finding aids and texts, many viewed this type of work as no longer necessary. From my teaching and research consultations, however, I knew that this was not the case. In this era of an expanding number and type of publications, databases, access points, and formats, such a guide was perhaps *more* necessary than in the past. I kept that copy of the *Research Guide* in my office with the intention to write an updated version. (If your library still has McInnis's *Guide*, I suggest that you keep it.) Many finding aids mentioned in it have morphed into other products or been discontinued. It will be useful to researchers researching pre-1980 works in psychology. I have included it in chapter 6 because it covers tools not covered in this work.

Ten years flew by, and other projects took precedence, but I periodically took the *Research Guide* off my bookshelf, glanced through it, and reminded myself that I really wanted to write that updated version. Then, in the spring of 2016, I saw a solicitation from Charles Harmon, executive editor at Rowman & Littlefield, for authors to write research guides in the social sciences. Normally I would put such a solicitation in my "to-do" file, where it would gently age until it became irrelevant. In this case, however, I responded immediately, and voila!, here is my updated guide. (Actually,

it wasn't so much "voila!" as an extended series of periods of work and interruptions.)

The overall goal of this work is to guide the user to primarily recent works in various areas of psychology. As work and publication in psychology is uneven, so is coverage in this book. Most chapters begin with an introduction to their content. I have personally examined all works included, as well as hundreds of others that were not included, often because they were not research oriented. I have *no* doubt in my mind that there are works that I would have included had I encountered them, but time is a limited resource, publishers need to publish, and to maintain timeliness, this work needed to be published. In psychology terms, this book is subject to negative error (not including items that would be great additions) but hopefully no positive error (inclusion of items that should not be here).

My vision of this work is that it should be updated every five years or so, with a primary focus on materials published within the previous five years, and hopefully I will have the opportunity to do that.

I would like to thank my colleagues Howard Graves (currently director) and Annmarie Boyle (currently chair) for providing me the freedom to work on this project over the past year. Thank-you to them and to Georgina Martorella for their support and encouragement both in this endeavor and generally during my career at Hofstra. Thank-you also to Helen Hough, retired from the University of Texas at Arlington, who created the original online *Tests and Measures in the Social Sciences: Tests Available in Compilation Volumes*, which forms the basis of the section on collections of full-text tests. Thank-you also to my colleagues in the Psychology Department and Speech-Language-Hearing Department and their students. In addition to being fun and supportive, they have asked great questions and undertaken projects that prompted me to do what I love doing: research and learning. I would particularly like to thank Mitchell Schare of the Psychology

Department, who has been a great support since my arrival at Hofstra as psychology subject specialist and has also provided interesting conversations! Thank-you to Charles Harmon of Rowman & Littlefield for his patience with this project and with my many e-mails. Finally, thank-you to my daughter, Alexandra Dolan-Mescal, always the best thing in my life, for nudging me forward with this project when my energy was flagging.

Introduction

SCOPE OF PSYCHOLOGY

The primary characteristic of psychology is that it is the study of behavior, be it animal, individual human, group, or organizational. *Interest* in psychology as defined here can be traced back to antiquity. Psychology as a *science*, however, did not flourish until the mid- to late 1800s. What defines psychology as a science is its commitment to the development and use of the scientific method and empirical research methods to assess behavior or inferred internal workings. Psychology as a *profession* began to flourish after its development as a science and is defined by the application of psychological findings to the solutions of problems in real life. The discipline of psychology has expanded in leaps and bounds from the late 1800s to the present day, as have research and the types of sources used to identify and acquire useful research. These increases in the literature are not systematic across subdisciplines. More skill and effort may be required to uncover literature in some areas than others, and the research yield will be greater in some areas than others. In addition, some topics become "hot" during a specific period, with subsequent waning of interest and research as some other topic becomes "hot," so the researcher may find temporal unevenness in coverage.

One interesting and relatively recent paradox is how advances in brain and biology research have increased the focus on neuroscience, the brain-body relationship, and evolutionary psychology as related to internal psychological development, while at the same time external events such as mass shootings and terrorism have increased the focus on interpersonal, group, and influence development.

WHY THE FOCUS ON RESEARCH?

When teaching library sessions for undergraduate, master's, and doctoral students, I always advise them that the research tools they need to use can be their best friend or their worst enemy, and suggest that they develop intimate relationships with their resources! As some students plan to be or are already in applied fields, they sometimes don't understand why there is such an emphasis on research literacy. We then discuss the scholar-practitioner model and how psychology and other fields have faced increasing demands for accountability of practices, leading to the adoption of the "evidence-based practice" model. Indeed, it is the basing of practice on good evidence that differentiates the professional from the layperson.

The *goal of the researcher* is to discover appropriate, useful, and substantive resources efficiently and effectively. There are two requirements for conducting research: literature searching skills (how) and knowledge of the bodies of literature (what and where).

The *purpose of this volume* is to assist the researcher in meeting those requirements by gathering significant print and electronic resources in one place, with annotations to assist the user in determining if a particular resource will be of use to him or her. It is designed to solve unique research problems by providing general background information for the novice as well as enabling exhaustive searching by the advanced or expert researcher.

This book is organized with the goal of helping the individual researcher with a specific problem. Therefore, all the resources on a specific topic are grouped together. For example, the chapter on encyclopedias, handbooks, and dictionaries is divided into specific topical sections. Likewise, the section on eating disorders includes available and appropriate encyclopedias, handbooks, dictionaries, monographs, specific journals, websites, and other resources that specifically address eating disorders.

Sources that cover a broad range of topics, such as theses and dissertations, organizations, research methods and statistics, style manuals, biographical resources, book reviews, general psychology bibliographies, government agencies, and special collections, are addressed in chapters bearing those titles.

The book is designed such that any chapter can be used independently of other chapters. Materials included in one chapter often pertain to topics covered in another chapter. In such cases, the user would usually be directed to the primary annotations using cross-references. However, because this work will also be published in e-book format, and because of the difficulty involved in moving back and forth to cross-references, some entries are repeated in all relevant chapters. In addition, those titles that can be categorized under more than one heading within a chapter are repeated under each applicable heading.

The book's intended audience includes advanced-placement high school students, undergraduate and graduate students, faculty, advanced researchers.

Chapter 1 begins by identifying various types of works and what types of problems they are best suited for solving.

Chapter 2 provides an extensive, annotated list of specialized dictionaries, encyclopedias, and handbooks that provide background information, from definitions to deep and extensive coverage of major subjects. The chapter is divided by subject, and following the major comprehensive works on a given topic, works on assessment and bibliographies are included.

Chapter 3 focuses on current research, that is, journal articles and annual reviews. This chapter takes a more instructional than an informational tone, with illustrations on how small changes in one's search create large changes in one's results, how to use limiters, how to save results for future use, how to save searches or share them with another, and how to create reference lists from the database.

Chapter 4 focuses on commercial and research measures, the differences between them and their purposes, resources about testing in general and in specific areas, and resources that index and abstract tests and measures, as well as those that contain the full text of tests. The chapter is organized in a manner similar to chapter 2.

Chapter 5 addresses the various uses of theses and dissertations, current issues affecting their availability, and accessing them, and provides information on a variety of international sources that provide either full text of theses and dissertations or abstracts.

Chapter 6 reviews annotated and unannotated bibliographies organized by subject, similar to the organization of chapter 2. As noted in the chapter, fewer bibliographies appeared in journals indexed in PsycINFO from 1998 onward, but many were found using Google Scholar that were produced by government or nongovernmental organizations and often transcend disciplinary boundaries.

Chapter 7 covers *major* US federal agencies related to some aspect of psychology. Myriad smaller agencies are subsumed within larger agencies, and the best strategy for the researcher is to visit the major agency's website (provided) to determine which areas best suit his or her needs.

Chapter 8 focuses on biographical sources, which are very important because they are so intertwined with the history of psychology and illustrate the development of various schools of thought. Substantive works on both dead and living psychologists are included, as well as bibliographies on major figures in psychology.

Chapter 9 covers directories of both graduate programs and international organizations of psychology. Some organizations are based on region or geography, while others are based on topical interests. Items in this chapter are not annotated, as the content is self-evident from the title of the directory or organization.

Chapter 10 covers not only the *Publication Manual of the American Psychological Association* (6th ed., 2010), but also various other works that assist users at various levels in understanding and adhering to the style and requirements put forth in the manual.

Chapter 11 focuses primarily on the fifth edition of the *Diagnostic and Statistical Manual of Mental Disorders* (DSM-5) and other works intended to facilitate understanding and use of the manual. It also covers the *International Classification of Diseases and Related Health Problems* (ICD) and related materials, as well as the Research Domain Criteria (RDoC) developed by the National Institute of Mental Health (NIMH).

Chapter 12 includes a variety of materials covering undergraduate career and education options, employment with a bachelor's degree in psychology, graduate education and careers in various areas of psychology and related fields, graduate school directories, applying to graduate school, undergraduate and graduate practica, getting the most out of graduate school and navigating one's department, the dissertation, and life and career after graduate school.

Chapter 13 reviews where and how to find book reviews.

Chapter 14 focuses on major international museums and archives of psychology.

INCLUSIONS/EXCLUSIONS

Only the most recent editions of works are included in this volume. As indicated elsewhere, I have no doubt that I have missed some works that are valuable and would have been included if I had had unlimited time and resources. But in order to make this volume timely, the research must end and the publication must begin. Materials that are excluded include textbooks, self-help books, primarily practitioner-oriented works, and book-length works not available in the English language.

I hope the reader learns as much while using this book as I did writing it.

1
Research Problems and Their Solutions: Types of Resources

INTRODUCTION

There are many types of resources of use to researchers in psychology. This is a brief overview of the types of resources included in this volume and the research problems they address.

WHY EVEN WRITE THIS CHAPTER?

I sometimes teach a distance education course in information literacy. It is often a required course for freshmen taken in conjunction with an advanced psychology seminar restricted to freshmen. In the bustle of their first year at university, and with other face-to-face courses being more salient, it can be difficult for students to understand what the course is, its purpose, or why they are required to take it with the seminar. Knowing this, in addition to the course introduction, I start each weekly module with a section entitled "What is this and why do I need to know it?" Because that is, of course, the key question, and isn't everything on Google anyway?

In 2005, my colleague, Georgina Martorella, and I published an article entitled "Use of Technology in Research: Two Steps Forward, One Step Back" (https://www.academia.edu/34204732/Use_of_Technology_in_Research_Two_Steps_Forward_One_Step_Back). In it we addressed the issue of information access changing from being discipline or publication specific to being amorphous and constantly changing, putting the responsibility for distinguishing among types, formats, quality, and relevance directly on the user and examining the implications for users at the university level and beyond. The main points were that it is well-documented that undergraduate and graduate students have difficulty with the research process, including but not limited to disciplinary perspective; currency of materials (particularly regarding publication timelines); ability to distinguish among books, articles, dissertations, and websites; and where to search for various types of publications, and

that much of this confusion arises from the ahistorical nature of society, the multidisciplinary nature of aggregated databases and the multiple formats available. The brief version of our conclusions is that there is still a need to be able to distinguish among types of materials regardless of format, as the significance and utility of their information is often constrained by publication variables such as purpose, audience, and publication timeline.

Anecdotally, my personal experiences have included a student asking "Where are the books on 9/11?" on *the day after 9/11*, with no conception that there would not yet be any books published, and more recently, a graduate student asking if she would "really need to use any books because isn't anything important in peer-reviewed journals?"

Of course, the answer to the latter question is yes, but is one really going to be able to read *all* of the peer-reviewed literature? Or might a book or two reviewing, analyzing, and interpreting some of that literature come in handy?

Unfortunately, it does not appear that the situation has changed much since 2005; thus this chapter. Hopefully it will illuminate for the reader the *what* of material types and the *why* of using each. A big thank-you to the students who have let me know what they need to know!

Materials are usually defined as a *type* based on the information in them. The *format* is how the information is delivered (e.g., print, web-based, downloadable).

Traditionally, in a work such as this web-based resources were organized into their own chapter. That approach has not been taken in this work, for several reasons. First, researchers are typically interested in a topic and information type (e.g., article, book) rather than an information format. Second, relevant materials on a topic may be available in different formats; many of the resources in this volume are available in multiple formats. Materials are therefore organized by type, then by topic.

As the audience for this work is advanced undergraduates, graduate students, researchers, faculty, and to a lesser degree clinicians, it does *not* include literature that is considered "popular literature," which is aimed at the public; it may be high-brow (e.g., the *New York Times*) or low-brow (e.g., the *National Enquirer*), but it is aimed at a *nonscholarly* or *nonacademic* audience. Popular literature includes but is not limited to materials such as newspapers, magazines, trade papers, newsletters, popular books, essays, and many (though not all) publicly accessible websites.

Some trade papers and websites, such as the American Psychology Association's (APA's) *Monitor on Psychology* or the American Speech-Language-Hearing Association's (ASHA's) *Leader*, are primarily aimed at scholarly and academic audiences, but their content is not considered scholarly within those disciplines; the content is more news-oriented than research-oriented. In addition, trade papers/websites of professional advocacy organizations such as these typically aim part of their publication toward advanced undergraduates/graduate students/researchers/faculty/clinicians and part of it toward the public. These sections are usually clearly delineated according to their audience.

Just to complicate the picture a bit, scholarly and peer-reviewed publications often contain materials that are *not* scholarly or peer-reviewed. Most peer-reviewed journals, for example, contain book reviews, editorials, letters to the editor, and commentaries, all of which are important, but none of which are peer-reviewed articles.

With these issues and caveats in mind, let's move on to the types of sources and materials and the research problems they address.

PRIMARY, SECONDARY, AND TERTIARY RESOURCES

Primary sources are original materials upon which other materials (including research) are based. What exactly does that *mean*? Primary sources in psychology may include but are not limited to letters (such as those between Freud and his colleagues), objects such as laboratory equipment, photographs, illustrations, notes, clinical or other records, measurements, and diaries or journals. Autobiographies are primary sources on both the author and subject (who are the same person); biographies are secondary sources on the subject, but a primary source on the author.

The primary source most frequently referred to in psychology, however, is original research. This includes case studies and observational, correlational, and experimental research. It also includes interviews, self-reported, other-reported, direct behavioral measurement, and inferential research. Primary research in psychology includes any case in which there is recording of measurement or activity (i.e., data). When data are organized, they become a primary source of information. Information only becomes knowledge upon its consumption.

In psychology, when one refers to a primary research journal article, one is referring to an article in which the author(s) present (among other sections) a research methodology, organized data collected using that methodology (results), and analysis and interpretation of the results (discussion). Occasionally, research methodologies, results, and discussion are published in book form by the investigators; in this case the book would also be a primary research source. (New and original research is not required for an article to be a primary resource; an author(s) can present previous findings in an article the primary purpose of which is to present a new *theory* to explain prior research findings.)

Secondary sources are based on primary sources; they analyze and interpret the primary source information, and in doing so, they create new information. An example of this is a literature review in which the author reviews, synthesizes, and interprets the primary research done on a specific subject, typically for a defined time period (e.g., 2001–2010). In gathering, comparing, contrasting, and synthesizing the results of the prior primary research, the literature review author creates new information. Another example is a handbook or book that not only presents information gathered from primary sources, but may also interpret it in a new way or from alternate theoretical viewpoints, place it in historical or sociological perspective, evaluate methodologies and their impact on results, etc.

Tertiary sources are those that consolidate and summarize information from primary and secondary sources; they do not create new information. Examples of tertiary sources are traditional dictionaries and encyclopedias and collections of statistical tables.

DICTIONARIES AND ENCYCLOPEDIAS

Traditionally, dictionaries provided concise definitions of particular *terms*, and encyclopedias covered topics; encyclopedias provided lengthier entries including definitions, history, concepts, and facts. Currently, the word "dictionary" or "encyclopedia" in a scholarly title does not necessarily indicate the length of entries; there are "encyclopedias" with one-paragraph entries and "dictionaries" with multiple-page entries. What both have in common, however, is that they typically provide broad coverage of their discipline or topic and are arranged alphabetically. They are also usually considered reference items and are housed in the reference area of a library. They are considered reference items because one "refers" to them rather than reading them from cover to cover. Some encyclopedias also have a synoptic table of contents in which entries are arranged categorically. Entries in scholarly encyclopedias may be quite lengthy, typically identify the author, and include reference lists as well as further readings. Dictionaries and encyclopedias are tertiary sources.

Uses of Dictionaries and Encyclopedias

Encyclopedias are excellent sources of background information and organization of a topic. For example, in the case of psychological disorders, one can typically expect to find an encyclopedia entry organized by etiology, diagnosis, course, prognosis, treatments, and outcomes. While typically not useful to locate the most recent information on a topic, they are excellent sources not only for their content, but also for their reference lists, which can be quite extensive and include the most significant works on the topic. While I have known faculty to consult specialized psychology encyclopedias, undergraduates and graduate students in psychology often do not even consider encyclopedias or dictionaries unless they are specifically directed to them by their course instructors or a librarian. As I point out in library sessions and research consultations: "These are not your mamma's encyclopedias!" Because peer-reviewed articles are not written for a student audience (see the section on peer-reviewed articles), students sometimes have difficulty understanding such articles because they do not have enough background information to understand references being made or are unfamiliar with topic-specific terminology. Both dictionaries and encyclopedias can be very helpful to students in becoming familiar with terminology; encyclopedias are particularly helpful in gaining a broad understanding of their topics and selecting subtopics on which to do research.

HANDBOOKS

Like dictionaries and encyclopedias, handbooks were traditionally considered to be reference items that covered a single subject, typically narrower than the subject area of an encyclopedia, providing more in-depth treatment, and organized topically rather than alphabetically. Some handbooks are multivolume sets (e.g., Wiley's 12-volume *Handbook of Psychology*), and they may have entries that are a hundred pages long with approximately ten pages of references (e.g., Wiley's *Handbook of Child Psychology*, historically known as "Carmichael's"). In such sets, each volume usually covers a single subtopic in-depth and can be used independently of the other volumes. Like other reference works, this type of item is not intended to be read cover to cover. Recently there has been a plethora of works published with the term "handbook" in the title; many are published as individual volumes and provide information similar in style and depth to single volumes of multivolume sets, while others provide in-depth information but in a size and style suitable for cover-to-cover reading.

Uses of Handbooks

Like encyclopedias, handbooks are typically not the best source for the most recent research. Unlike encyclopedias, they are not the most useful tool for getting general background information or to understand the basic organization of a topic. Handbooks are hefty reading! They are most useful for the serious researcher (including students) seeking comprehensive and in-depth coverage of a topic, including historical perspectives, with extensive referencing.

BOOKS

Books may be edited volumes with chapters by various authors or monographs written by a single author. Books are more variable than dictionaries, encyclopedias, and handbooks. A book can be short or long, covering one topic or a number of related topics. While encyclopedias and handbooks by their very nature are comprehensive in scope, books are not necessarily so; the parameters of coverage are typically described in the introduction. Books may be highly research oriented, containing extensive documentation or a series of essays, providing ideas or arguments for the reader to ponder. Their content may be biographical, autobiographical, or historical. They may be collections of primary sources, such as letters between individuals. Some books contain discrete chapters, the understanding of which does not depend upon reading the other chapters. In other books, chapters are meant to be read sequentially, and the content is such that the whole is more than the sum of its parts, meaning that the book is most valuable when read in its entirety.

Uses of Books

Because books are so variable in their style and content, it is difficult to determine how they are best used in the research process; it is easier to indicate in what contexts they are not the best sources. Books are not the best sources for recent research, nor are they the most efficient sources of general background and organization of a topic. Beyond that, their value is best determined by the individual user.

JOURNAL ARTICLES

Journal articles are scholarly literature. *The authors are scholars and the audience is other scholars.* Journal articles are the medium for communication among scholars in a field and are not written for instructional purposes. I always point this out to students, for two reasons. The first is that they usually know they need to cite peer-reviewed articles in their papers, but have no idea why. The second is that I want to advise them that they are *budding* scholars, that knowledge of this literature is part of their scholarly development, and if they are really struggling with peer-reviewed articles, they should consult specialized dictionaries and encyclopedias, which will provide the background information necessary to understand the articles.

Some journals are scholarly, but not peer-reviewed or refereed. Articles in scholarly (but not peer-reviewed) journals undergo editorial review by an individual editor or editorial board. The editorial process is typically open;

the reviewer(s) know the identity of the author(s) and the author(s) know the identity of the reviewer(s). In peer-reviewed journals, the journal editor sends the submitted article to a panel of reviewers who are experts on the topic of the article. The reviewers evaluate the overall quality of the scholarship, methodology, presentation of findings, and discussion of results, including the appropriateness of conclusions based on the results. Reviewers may recommend acceptance as is, rejection, or acceptance pending specific revisions. The review process is usually double-blind, meaning that the reviewers do not know the identity of the author(s) and the author(s) do not know the identity of the reviewer(s) (at least in theory; in reality, reviewers may know that person X conducted Y research).

Uses of Journal Articles

Peer-reviewed journal articles are *the* source for finding recent research in psychology. Writing a final draft, submission, peer review, and the publication timeline can be quite variable and take well over a year, which in addition to the advantages of being "first" has led to "pre-pubs" during recent years. Pre-pub is the preliminary publication of research findings even though the article is not in final form.

In addition to keeping abreast of recent findings in one's area of interest, peer-reviewed literature also provides one with the basis for conducting one's own research. Research does not occur in a vacuum. In psychology, as in most, or perhaps even all disciplines, information and knowledge build incrementally. Following is a very simplified description of that process. Researcher A studies a particular phenomenon with methodology A and a particular population, reports his or her results and conclusions, discusses the limitations of the research, and makes suggestions for future research. Then researcher B replicates that study using the same methodology with a similar population, or perhaps using a different population. Researcher C, having read the articles by A and B, including their discussions of the limitations of their own research and suggestions for future research, uses an alternative method and another population. This process continues, building a body of literature on the topic.

Over time and with various methods, instruments, populations, and interpretations, some findings will show themselves to be fairly consistent, while others will not. This leads future researchers to address research limitations with their own investigations. This process leads to both convergent validity of one construct and divergent validity of that construct from another. It is through engagement with the peer-reviewed literature, including the most recent findings, that one develops a research project or research program of one's own.

In working with those who wish to be clinicians, I have pointed out that one cannot be an ethical practitioner without being a continual consumer of peer-reviewed literature in one's area of practice.

Finally, there are many different types of peer-reviewed articles, serving many purposes; these are addressed in more detail in chapter 3.

2
Definitions to Deep Background:
Encyclopedias, Handbooks, and Dictionaries

INTRODUCTION

Before writing this chapter, I gave great thought to its purpose and that of the materials in it. I determined that the encyclopedias and handbooks are most useful for users who want to learn about a topic in the broad sense (history, phenomenology, conceptualizations, theories, controversies, trends, etc.), learn about recent research findings supporting or refuting existing theories and concepts, and also learn about unanswered questions and future research directions. As the terminology of psychology expands and changes, specialized dictionaries are, of course, useful adjuncts in this learning process, and indeed, despite a broad and deep background in psychology, I have found them quite useful several times during this project. Given these considerations, the materials in this chapter were selected based on the following criteria:

- recency;
- authority;
- substantive topical information;
- most recent edition of the work;
- extensive reference lists, virtually always within the chapter, and usually comprising 10 to 20 percent of the chapter; and
- presence of an index to the work.

Materials are research oriented, either in terms of the content (reviewing research literature) or by virtue of extensive reference lists that will be useful to the researcher. For example, there are many beautifully written and informative books on *practice* in applied psychology (e.g., clinical, counseling, school, industrial, and organizational). These are included *only* if they provide extensive reference lists that would be of use to the researcher. The audience is primarily advanced undergraduates and graduate students through advanced researchers (and clinicians and policy makers as appropriate). Items that are only suitable for advanced graduate students and researchers are so noted.

As many are major edited research works, most have international authorship, even if "international" is not included in the title. All works are available in the English language.

Tests and measures are a major historical and current domain within the field of psychology and merit their own chapter. The same is true of bibliographies. However, materials included in those chapters often pertain to topics covered in this chapter. In such cases, the user would usually be directed to the main annotations using cross-references. As mentioned in the introduction, because this work will also be published in e-book format, and because of the difficulty involved in moving back and forth to cross-references, relevant entries from those chapters are included in this chapter following the dictionary/encyclopedia/handbook entries and under subheadings. Some titles can be categorized under more than one heading; these entries are repeated under each applicable heading.

Currently, many works are reprinted in various formats with different publication dates, despite being the same edition. For this reason, the earliest publication date of the particular edition is provided, so that the user will be aware that research published after that date is not included in the work. Earlier research guide publications included ISBNs and pricing, but because various formats made available by multiple vendors typically have different ISBNs and prices, this information is not included here. Bibliographic information (e.g., number of pages) has been taken from the hardcover publication wherever possible. The US Library of Congress (LOC) major subclass information is also provided.

Items were selected for this chapter using a multistep process. Beginning with the year 2017 and working backward through and including 2012, a search was conducted in WorldCat for "keyword = dictionary or encyclopedi* or handbook" and "subject = psychology." A similar process was followed in GOBI, using the same time period and searching relevant call numbers. Publication lists for major publishers in psychology were also generated for this time period. After examining the 2012–2017 titles, the same process was followed for 2007–2011 publications. Items are included from prior to 2007 only if they cover material not covered as well in a later publication. As resources are always limited, including pages in this book, items were restricted to those that I determined would benefit the most users or that cover newer, growing, or less well-covered areas of interest (e.g., hoarding and acquiring, fatigue). Although I searched for reviews of each item, lack of such a review (e.g., CHOICE, Doody's, PsycCRITIQUES) did not preclude inclusion in this book, for two reasons. First, the rationale for some books being reviewed and others not being reviewed is not transparent or systematic, and second, the focus on recently published items sometimes precludes a review being available, although one may be available later. Dissertations and theses are not included in this chapter; major sources of dissertation/thesis indexes, abstracts and full-text are covered in chapter 5.

To ensure that virtually all subdisciplines of this broad discipline were covered, I used the list of the fifty-four APA divisions as a guide (available at http://www.apa.org/about/ division/). Inevitably there is unevenness of coverage in this chapter because there is unevenness in research actually conducted, published, and compiled on these types of resources. There was also a bit of serendipity involved; as I was strolling aisles to find a particular title, occasionally another recent title that met the overall criteria would catch my attention. Any errors, omissions of titles, or omissions of special features or titles are mine—mea culpa!

So what can you, the user, generally expect from these resources? Encyclopedia entries are typically shorter than those in handbooks, generally ranging from two to five pages, and with significantly shorter reference lists or suggested readings. The purpose of these specialized encyclopedias generally is to provide an overview of topics included and serve as an early starting point in users' research, helping them focus on a specific area. Encyclopedias are usually published less frequently than handbooks; as their main purpose is to provide an overview and organizational scheme for a topic rather than cutting-edge research, this does not diminish their utility. They provide the basic launch pad from which the researcher can then take off into more in-depth research such as that found in handbooks. Because encyclopedias are often quite broad in their coverage, the annotations are often shorter than for handbooks, because only a more general description can be provided in a succinct manner.

Handbook chapters are generally twenty to thirty pages long and address fairly specific topics in depth. Most works have an easily apparent and consistent manner of presenting information (e.g., overview, history, theories, controversies, seminal and current research, future research) in each chapter. Most will critique the research presented and provide suggestions for further research. Many works (though not all) have tables, charts, or illustrations to better illuminate or organize the subject matter. All works will be well-referenced and well-indexed. When a work significantly deviates from these general features, that is noted in the annotation.

The number of pages is included to provide the user with an idea of the breadth/depth of the work. Only the general and specific subject area sections of call numbers have been presented, to give the user a general idea of the classification of the item. Publication year has not been included with the call number because the various renditions of a particular publication (hardcover, paperback, electronic) often contain different years in their call numbers despite being the same edition. I have leaned more toward inclusion of handbooks than of encyclopedias.

With the exception of the "General" category at the beginning and "Other" at the end, the categories are arranged alphabetically.

GENERAL

2.1. *APA dictionary of psychology* (2nd ed.). VandenBos, G. R. (2015). Washington, DC: American Psychological Association. 1204 pp. BF31. This second edition of what is now a standard work has been updated to remove obsolete entries, update existing entries, and add new entries reflecting changes that occurred during the eight years after the first edition. Biographical entries have been placed in their own separate section following the main section. There are several appendixes, which list the names of institutions and organizations; psychological tests and assessment instruments; and psychotherapeutic techniques, biological treatments, and other treatments for which there are entries in the body of the work. This work has been updated to incorporate DSM-V and ICD-10 diagnostic systems, while also maintaining DSM-IV-TR references. This work will be useful to all users engaging in research or general reading in psychology.

2.2. *Dictionary of psychology* (4th ed.). Colman, A. M. (2015). Oxford: Oxford University Press. 883 pp. BF32. This fourth edition of Colman's standard work has been updated to incorporate DSM-V terminology, reflect current usage of existing terms, and include new terms that may not originate within psychology but are frequently used in psychological works. As expected in a dictionary, entries are concise; where deeper explanation is required, however, entries are lengthier, occasionally reaching half a page. Appendix I presents and defines phobias and phobic stimuli. Appendix II lists abbreviations and symbols and references where they are used in the work. Appendix III provides a topically organized list of websites; as indicated in its introductory paragraph, the links to the websites can be found at http://oxfordreference.com/page/ psych. This work remains affordable to many and will be useful for all users researching unfamiliar territory.

2.3. *Handbook of psychology* (2nd ed.). Weiner, I. B. (Ed.). (2012). Hoboken, NJ: John Wiley and Sons. 8560 pp. BF121. Twelve-volume set. This set provides one-stop shopping for an authoritative review of long-standing and emerging topics in psychology, written by international experts. The twelve volumes are (1) *History of Psychology*, (2) *Research Methods*, (3) *Behavioral Neuroscience*, (4) *Experimental Psychology*, (5) *Personality and Social Psychology*, (6) *Developmental Psychology*, (7) *Educational Psychology*, (8) *Clinical Psychology*, (9) *Health Psychology*, (10) *Assessment Psychology*, (11) *Forensic Psychology*, and (12) *Industrial and Organizational Psychology*. Similar to other handbooks, individual chapters are approximately twenty-five pages long. Each volume can be used independently of the others.

ADDICTIONS

2.4. *APA addiction syndrome handbook.* Shaffer, H., LaPlante, D. A., & Nelson, S. E. (Eds.). (2012). Washington, DC: American Psychological Association. 879 pp. HV5801. Two-volume set. This work provides a comprehensive treatment of addiction, with a focus on evidence both supporting and refuting the concept of the addiction syndrome model, and with the goal of advancing research on addiction. Volume 1 (*Foundations, Influences, and Expressions of Addiction*) consists of three sections. Section I addresses historical perceptions of addictions, nosology, epidemiology, and individual dynamics of addiction. Section II covers neurobiology, psychiatric comorbidity, personality, and social and developmental factors. Section III covers universal characteristics and unique consequences of addiction. Volume 2 (*Recovery, Prevention, and Other Issues*) also has three sections. Section I covers diagnosis, physical and psychological treatments, relapse prevention, self-help programs, and short-term interventions. Section II covers prevention in schools, public health approaches, and addiction in the college setting. Section III covers technology, special populations, driving under the influence, externalizing spectrum, sexually transmitted diseases, and homelessness.

2.5. *Co-occurring addictive and psychiatric disorders: A practice-based handbook from a European perspective.* Dom, G., & Moggie, F. (Eds.). (2015). Heidelberg, Germany: Springer. 389 pp. RC564. This volume provides an overview of the diagnosis and treatment of dual disorders (substance and psychiatric), with a focus on clinical practice in European care systems. Although the title indicates that it is "practice-based," it covers research on practice. Part I ("General Aspects") covers epidemiology of comorbidity; pathogenesis of dual disorders; evolution of mental health and addiction care systems in Europe; integrated treatment; and similarities and differences among US, Canadian, and European care. Part II covers specific psychiatric disorders as they relate to comorbidity with substance abuse, including schizophrenia, mood disorders, personality disorders, anxiety disorders, stress disorders, ADHD, autism spectrum disorder, and mild intellectual disability. It also addresses substance-induced psychotic disorders and comorbidity of gambling and Internet addictions. Part III ("Topics of Interest") covers a variety of issues, including assessment strategies and instruments for dual diagnosis, psychosocial treatment, pharmacotherapy, comorbidity with smoking, violence and somatic problems, heroin and methadone maintenance, and adolescent populations. Each chapter begins with a detailed table of contents, making information location more manageable, and the volume has useful tables and figures.

Addictions: Tests and Measures

2.6. *Assessing alcohol problems: A guide for clinicians and researchers* (2nd ed.). Allen, J. P., & Wilson, V. B. (2003). Washington, DC: US Department of Health and Human Services, Public Health Service, National Institutes of Health, National Institute on Alcohol Abuse and Alcoholism. 571 pp. HV5279. Includes seventy-five full-text instruments related to diagnosis, treatment planning, and outcome evaluation. Pages 1–234 contain an overview, how to select instruments, quick-reference tables comparing instruments, and other information. The instruments and their individual information and permissions information start on page 235. An index to the full-text instruments included starts on page 667. This document can be downloaded from http://pubs.niaaa.nih.gov/publications/AssessingAlcohol/index.pdf.

2.7. *Can we measure recovery? A compendium of recovery and recovery-related instruments.* Vol. 1 of *A compendium of recovery measures.* Ralph, R. O., Kidder, K., & Phillips, D. (2000). Washington, DC: US Department of Health and Human Services/Evaluation Center @ HRSI. 227 pp. Includes twenty full-text instruments covering conceptualization and measurement of recovery. Concise charts of recovery measures are on pages 13–15 and recovery-related measures are on pages 24–28. Charts contain title, author/date, development, number of items and type of scaling, domains measured, reliability and validity data, and populations. Full-text instruments are in appendix B. Information and permissions contact information is provided for each measure. This document can be downloaded from http://www.hsri.org/publication/Can_We_Measure_Recovery_A_Compendium_of_Recovery_and_Recovery-Related_. A list of full-text documents in this work is located at http://libguides.hofstra.edu/TMdb/RalphKidderPhillips2000.

2.8. *Integrated treatment for dual disorders: a guide to effective practice.* Mueser, K. T. (2003). New York: Guilford Press. 470 pp. RC564. Contains twenty full-text instruments and sixteen educational handouts. Handouts are in appendix B, and instruments are in appendix C. Instruments cover substance use, functioning, treatment, relapse prevention, activities and lifestyle, and family awareness/involvement. See "limited photocopy license" on the verso for information on permissions. A list of full-text measures in this book is located at http://libguides.hofstra.edu/TMdb/Mueser2003.

2.9. *Measuring the promise: A compendium of recovery measures.* Vol. 2 of *A compendium of recovery measures.* Orde, T. C., Chamberlin, J., Carpenter, J., & Leff, H. S. (2005). Washington, DC: US Department of Health and Human Services/Evaluation Center @ HRSI. Contains fourteen full-text instruments. Includes measures of individual recovery and of recovery-promoting environments. Information about scales is on pages 24–91; scales are on pages 111–244. Scale summaries provide an introduction, development, stakeholders in development, alternate forms, item and domain information, populations, administration and scoring, psychometrics, utility, permission information, and references. Permission statements indicate if the measure is free to use without further permissions or provide publisher information. This document can be downloaded from http://www.hsri.org/publication/measuring-the-promise-a-compendium-of-recovery-measures-volume-ii/. A list of full-text measures in this document may be found at http://libguides.hofstra.edu/TMdb/OrdeChamberlinCarpenterLeff2005.

2.10. *Screening and assessing adolescents for substance abuse disorders.* Center for Substance Abuse Treatment. (2012/1998). Treatment Improvement Protocol (TIP) Series, No. 31. Rockville, MD: Substance Abuse and Mental Health Services Administration (SAMHSA). 165 pp. This document covers screening and assessment of adolescents, substance use disorders as related to adolescent development, and legal issues and juvenile justice settings for adolescents. It provides information on twenty-eight screening instruments, comprehensive assessment instruments, and general functioning instruments for use with substance-using adolescents. For each instrument, it provides title, purpose, type of assessment (e.g., interview, self-report), life areas/problems assessed, reading level if applicable, credentials required if any, commentary, pricing information if applicable, where item has been reviewed, and contact information.

2.11. *Treating alcoholism: Helping your clients find the road to recovery.* Perkinson, R. R. (2004). Hoboken, NJ: Wiley. 326 pp. RC565. Includes thirty-three full-text instruments measuring alcohol-related issues as well as fetal alcohol syndrome, gambling, sex addiction, obsessive-compulsive behavior, and social anxiety. As this book is also a treatment manual, it also addresses concepts of alcoholism, treatment planning, dual diagnosis, adolescent treatment, relapse prevention, and the recovery community. A list of full-text measures in this book is located at http://libguides.hofstra.edu/TMdb/Perkinson2004.

Addictions: Bibliographies

2.12. Alcohol and drug prevention, intervention, and treatment literature: A bibliography for best practices. Nissen, L. B. (2014). *Best Practices in Mental Health: An International Journal*, 10(1), 59–97. Comprehensive bibliography on best practices drawn from a variety of sources, perspectives, and ideologies.

2.13. *Annotated bibliography of behavior analytic scholarship outside of "Analysis of Gambling Behavior" 2013–2015.* Costello, M. S., Whiting, S. W., Hirsh, J. L., Deochand, N., & Spencer, T. (2016). Vol. 10(1). Annotated bibliography of scholarly literature published outside of this journal dedicated to gambling behavior. This open-access article is available at http://repository.stcloudstate.edu/agb/vol10/iss1/1.

2.14. *Annotated bibliography of measurement compendia: Reliable, valid, and standard measures of substance abuse and mental and behavioral health indicators and outcomes of interest.* Substance Abuse and Mental Health Services Administration (SAMHSA). Selected, annotated bibliography of seventeen compendia containing full text of instruments or describing available instruments. Most are compendia of measures used with individuals; several are for institutions to measure outcomes. This document is available online at https://www.samhsa.gov/capt/tools-learning-resources/annotated-bibliography-measurement-compendia.

2.15. Bibliography of literature reviews on drug abuse treatment. Prendergast, M., Podus, D., & McCormack, K. (1998). *Journal of Substance Abuse Treatment*, 15(3), 267–270. Bibliography of literature reviews on drug abuse treatment efficacy from articles and books. Covers categories of drug abuse treatment (general), opiate treatment, cocaine treatment, therapeutic communities, adolescent treatment, behavioral and cognitive treatment, family therapy, Minnesota model, relapse prevention, acupuncture, transcendental meditation, 12-step programs, and natural recovery.

2.16. Cultural identification and substance use in North America: An annotated bibliography. Beauvais, F. (1998). *Substance Use & Misuse*, 33(6), 1315–1336. Annotated bibliography on issues related to cultural identification and substance abuse. Includes items on ethnic identification in general, specific ethnic identities, and measurement issues. Reference list includes citations to related readings not annotated.

2.17. Primary prevention of alcohol misuse: Overview and annotated bibliography. Hittner, J. B., Levasseur, P. W., & Galante, V. (1998). *Substance Use & Misuse*, 33(10), 2131–2178. Comprehensive, annotated bibliography on alcohol misuse primary prevention literature, including a review of conceptual and methodological issues.

2.18. A select annotated bibliography: Illegal drug research in rural and suburban areas. Hunt, K., & Furst, R. T. (2006). *Journal of Psychoactive Drugs*, 38(2), 173–188. Annotated bibliography covering drug consumption, drug distribution, drug prices, and ethnography.

2.19. A tribute to Bunky at 125: A comprehensive bibliography of E. M. Jellinek's publications. Ward, J. H., & Bejarano, W. (2016). *Journal of Studies on Alcohol and Drugs*, 77(3), 371–374. This comprehensive bibliography of Jellinek, considered the father of alcoholism studies, includes 165 original publications published between 1912 and 1982. Many of his works have been reprinted; for these entries the reprint information follows that on the original work. Jellinek also published in other areas, and these works are included as well.

ALTRUISM/PROSOCIAL BEHAVIOR

2.20. *Oxford handbook of prosocial behavior*. Schroeder, D. A., & Graziano, W. G. (Eds.). (2015). Oxford: Oxford University Press. 787 pp. HM1146. This volume provides a comprehensive review of the literature on when and why people engage in behavior that benefits others. Its thirty-four chapters are divided into three major areas of prosocial behavior. The micro level covers evolutionary and comparative psychology, economics, development, and self-protective nature of prosocial behavior. The meso level covers the empathy-altruism hypothesis, functional motives and consequences, gender and race issues, and late-life behavior. The macro level covers volunteerism, community involvement, cooperation, tolerance, and inter- and intra-group cooperation. The fourth section covers new directions such as religion, environmental action, patient participation in clinical trials, peace psychology, and the prevention of mass violence. Chapters begin with an abstract and keywords and have useful diagrams, illustrations, and black-and-white photographs. This is an essential tool for researchers of prosocial behavior, and individual chapters will also be useful to students.

Altruism/Prosocial Behavior: Bibliographies

2.21. *Annotated bibliography: Altruism, empathy, and prosocial behavior (1998–2013)*. Yahner, E. (2014). Washington, DC: Humane Society of the United States Institute for Science and Policy. Annotated bibliography of books, chapters, and articles on the relationship of human/animal interaction and the development of altruism, empathy, and prosocial behavior in children. Document is downloadable from http://animalstudiesrepository.org/hum_ed_bibs/9/.

2.22. *Research on altruism and love: An annotated bibliography of major studies in psychology, sociology,* evolutionary biology and theology. Post, S. G. (Ed.). (2007/2003). Philadelphia, PA: Templeton Foundation Press. 202 pp. BJ1474 / Z5865. This volume is organized into five chapters covering altruism and helping behavior works from the disciplines of psychology, sociology, evolution, biology, and the religious love interface with science. It also contains a nonbibliographic, biographical chapter on major figures such as Gandhi, Martin Luther King Jr., and the Dalai Lama.

ANXIETY DISORDERS

2.23. *Anxiety and its disorders: The nature and treatment of anxiety and panic* (2nd ed.). Barlow, D. H. (2002). New York: Guilford Press. 704 pp. RC531. This comprehensive volume covers virtually all aspects of anxiety, including the experience of anxiety, fear and theories of emotion, anxious apprehension, phenomena of panic, biological aspects of anxiety and panic, conditioned anxiety, vulnerabilities, classification, agoraphobia, specific phobias, post-traumatic stress, social phobias, generalized anxiety disorder, and obsessive-compulsive disorder. Written in 2002, it does not provide the most recent information or include DSM-V guidelines but provides a very thorough overview of anxiety.

2.24. *Treatment resistant anxiety disorders: Resolving impasses to symptom remission*. Sookman, D., & Leahy, R. L. (Eds). (2010). New York: Routledge. 369 pp. RC531. Each chapter in this volume begins by presenting empirical evidence on treatment resistance of different types of anxiety disorders and various treatments for this resistance. It covers metacognitive therapy, specialized cognitive behavior therapies, treatments for complex post-traumatic stress disorder, emotional schemas, dialectical behavior therapy, motivational interviewing, acceptance and commitment therapy, treatment resistance in the context of substance abuse, and pharmacological therapies.

Anxiety Disorders: Tests and Measures

2.25. *Assessment scales in depression, mania, and anxiety*. Lam, R. W., Michalak, E. E., & Swinson, R. P. (2005). London: Taylor & Francis. 198 pp. RC537. Includes sixty-four full-text instruments; there are additional instruments for which full text is not included but that may have sample items. This book also includes a section on how to select an assessment scale. Instruments cover depression, mania, anxiety, related symptoms, side effects, functioning, quality of life, and special populations. For all instruments, there is a commentary on the instrument, scoring information, alternate forms, references, and author/publisher contact information. A list of full-text measures in this book is located at http://libguides.hofstra.edu/TMdb/LamMichalakSwinson2005.

2.26. *Practitioner's guide to empirically based measures of anxiety.* Antony, M. M., Orsillo, S. M., & Roemer, L. (Eds.). (2001). New York: Kluwer Academic/Plenum. 512 pp. RC531. Contains seventy-seven full-text instruments and reviews of more than 200 instruments. This book, published under the auspices of the Association for Advancement of Behavior Therapy (AABT), covers general issues in the assessment of anxiety disorders and strategies for assessing panic disorder and agoraphobia, generalized anxiety disorder, social phobia, acute stress disorder, post-traumatic stress disorder, specific phobias, and obsessive-compulsive disorder. Scale summaries include original citation, purpose, description, administration and scoring, psychometrics, alternative forms, and author/publisher information. Instruments are in appendix B. Each instrument is followed by a "permission" statement. A list of full-text measures in this book is located at http://libguides.hofstra.edu/TMdb/AntonyOrsilloRoemer2001.html.

ATTACHMENT

2.27. *Handbook of attachment: Theory, research, and clinical applications* (3rd ed.). Cassidy, J., & Shaver, P. R. (Eds.). (2016). New York: Guilford Press. 1068 pp. BF575. For this third edition, contributors were asked to compare the current state of theory and research on specific topics in attachment to earlier conceptualizations and research presented in the previous edition. New chapter topics include attachment and genetics, psychoneuroimmunology, adolescent sexuality, and school readiness. Part I provides an overview of attachment, including its nature, disruptions, loss, grief, psychopathology, new developments, and controversies. Part II covers biological issues, including evolutionary psychology, attachment in rhesus monkeys and infants, genetics, parenting, and psychoneuroimmunology. Parts III and IV cover attachment through the life span. Part V focuses on psychopathology and clinical applications through the life span. Part VI addresses culture and context of attachment, including universal and cultural dimensions, empathy and prosocial behavior, religion, child care policies, school readiness, and divorce. Part VII concludes with coverage of the place of attachment in development.

2.28. *Routledge handbook of attachment.* Holmes, P., & Farnfield, S. (Eds.). (2014). New York: Routledge. 610 pp. BF575. Three-volume set. Volume I is *Theory*, volume II is *Assessment*, and volume III is *Implications and Interventions*. Each volume may be used independently of the others. *Theory* provides an overview of current conceptions of attachment, not only in childhood but throughout the life span. It covers the ABC + D theory, the strange situation procedure as the gold standard of assessment, and the Dynamic-Maturational Model (DMM). It also covers disorganized attachment and reactive attachment disorders,

neurology, and nonattachment factors in developmental issues. *Assessment* provides an overview of assessment issues and provides information about specific measures and procedures for assessing attachment. *Implications and Interventions* addresses applications of attachment theory in areas such as child psychotherapy, parent psychotherapy, family interventions, and interventions in attachment in immigrant families and in foster care and adoption.

BEREAVEMENT AND GRIEF

2.29. *Grief and bereavement in contemporary society: Bridging research and practice.* Neimeyer, R. A., Harris, D. L., Winokuer, H. R., & Thornton, G. F. (Eds.). (2011). New York: Routledge. 442 pp. BF575. This volume takes a unique approach to its content. A researcher and a practitioner team (often from different countries) wrote each chapter together, integrating research and practice. Section I covers a two-track model of bereavement, integrating research and practice, meaning reconstruction in bereavement, attachment and implications for intervention, unresolved loss, task-based approaches in counseling, gender, and socialization issues in grieving style. Section II covers spousal bereavement in older people, parenting issues after loss of a child, bereavement in children and adults after loss of a sibling, and translation of research into treatment programs. Section III covers treatment of complicated grief; ambiguous loss; chronic sorrow; restorative retelling of violent death; and disaster-, terrorism-, and suicide-related bereavement. Section IV covers specific populations, specifically GLBT and military persons, and those experiencing pet loss. Section V covers specific treatment modalities, including family, art, bereavement rituals, and hospice models. Section VI takes a global perspective, focusing on culture and ethnicity in experiencing, policing, and handling grief; the role of religion; Internet support for grieving; and culturally conscious practice. Chapters are relatively brief (ten to fifteen pages long) but topic-specific and well-referenced.

2.30. *Handbook of bereavement research and practice: Advances in theory and intervention.* Stroebe, S., Hansson, R. O., Schut, H., & Stroebe, W. (Eds). (2008). Washington, DC: American Psychological Association. 658 pp. BF575. This volume is the third of a trilogy. It joins *The Handbook of Bereavement Research* (Stroebe, et al., 2001) and *Bereavement in Late Life* (Hansson & Stroebe, 2007). This volume synthesizes scientific knowledge about the phenomena and manifestations of bereavement, with an emphasis on theory and empirical findings. This volume was developed from questions and topics that emerged from the earlier volumes. In particular, it focuses on the relationship of bereavement research to contemporary social and practice issues. Parts I and II address the nature and causes of grief, past and present theories of grief, contemporary perspectives on bereavement research, grieving in contemporary society, attachment perspectives, relinquishment or maintenance of a bond with the deceased, and psychometric issues in the measurement of grief. Part III covers the case for inclusion of "prolonged grief disorder" and clinical aspects of a DSM "complicated grief" diagnosis in DSM-5 ("persistent complex bereavement disorder" is listed under "Other Specified Trauma- and Stressor-Related Disorder" in DSM-V). It also reviews grief in various cultures, disenfranchised grief in history and cultures, and public mourning. Part IV focuses on caregiving and bereavement, trajectories of grieving, post-traumatic growth after loss, the role of religion, and a biopsychological perspective on grieving related to romantic rejection. Part V focuses on consequences of grief over loss in close relationships, such as the loss of a child, parental death in childhood, partner loss in older couples, and grief in grandparents. Part VI addresses interventions, particularly following disasters; family therapy from palliative care into bereavement; family meaning-making; building resilience in children who've lost a parent; and Internet bereavement support. Part VII synthesizes current research and explores future research prospects.

Bereavement and Grief: Bibliographies

2.31. *Death and dying: A bibliographical survey.* Southard, S. (1991). New York: Greenwood Press. 514 pp. Z5725 or HQ1073. This work is an annotated bibliography containing citations and abstracts for more than 2,200 books, book chapters, articles, and reports. Covers ancient and modern thinking, philosophical theology, counseling the terminally ill, grief, caretaking professions, and education for death. Although it covers many areas, the major focus is on counseling the terminally ill and the grieving.

2.32. *Death and dying: An annotated bibliography of the thanatological literature.* Szabo, J. F. (2009). Lanham, MD: Scarecrow Press. 382 pp. Z5725. Covers more than 2,200 citations to monographs on the science and study of death and dying. Includes psychology, philosophy, and attitude issues; coping and dealing with caregiving and working in the helping professions; cultural differences in bereavement rituals and grief and mourning; childhood bereavement; mental health issues; and legal issues. Also covers death themes in literature, ethical and policy issues, and popular literature on death and dying. Only selected items are annotated.

BODY IMAGE AND APPEARANCE

2.33. *Encyclopedia of body image and human appearance.* Cash, T. (Ed.). (2012). London: Elsevier. 882 pp. BF697. Two-volume set. This set provides comprehensive coverage of issues in body image and human appearance. The 117 entries are arranged alphabetically. Both volumes contain a table of contents. In addition to a detailed index at the end of volume 2, there is also a subject classification index on pages 809–811 in volume 2, which classifies the entries by subject. Entries are typically five to ten pages long; start with a glossary of terms; and end with cross-references, a further reading list, and "relevant websites"

2.34. *Oxford handbook of the psychology of appearance.* Rumsey, N., & Harcourt, D. (Eds.). (2012). Oxford: Oxford University Press. 717 pp. BF697. This volume, part of the Oxford Library of Psychology, is important in that in addition to covering areas of physical appearance addressed in other works, it also covers unique areas of inquiry. Fifty chapters are divided into five major areas. Section 1 covers appearance and society, embodiment, cross-cultural influences, and health-care challenges in the United States, United Kingdom, and resource-poor countries as well as biomedical technologies and models and theories of appearance. Section 2 covers appearance concerns across the life span, individual differences by population (gender, GLBTQI, and culture/ethnicity), media influence, family and peer influences, adult adjustment to visible differences, appearance concerns, exercise, diet, eating disorders, and cosmetic procedures. It also includes a subsection on the experiences of those with visible differences, including congenital conditions, trauma-induced conditions with a focus on burns, and skin conditions associated with disease. Section 3 addresses what needs to be changed, including media; the public; health-care providers; regulation of cosmetic surgery; and school-based, therapeutic, and computer-based interventions. Section 4 addresses research issues, and section 5 suggests further research issues and ideas. Some chapters are shorter than usual in handbooks (ten to fifteen pages) but are focused on specific topics; similarly, some have substantial reference lists, while others have fewer references because they are newer areas of inquiry.

Body Image and Appearance: Tests and Measures

2.35. *Exacting beauty: Theory, assessment, and treatment of body image disturbance.* Thompson, J. K. (Ed.). (1999). Washington, DC: American Psychological Association. 396 pp. RC569. Includes thirty-six full-text instruments. Covers virtually all areas of body image disturbance with accompanying instruments. Instruments are in appendixes numbered according to corresponding chapter. A list of full-text measures in this book may be found at http://libguides.hofstra.edu/TMdb/Thompson1999.

CLINICAL AND COUNSELING

2.36. *Adult psychopathology and diagnosis* (7th ed.). Beidel, D. C., Frueh, B. C., & Hersen, M. (Eds.). (2014).

Hoboken, NJ: John Wiley & Sons. 848 pp. RC454. This is the seventh edition of this work, written to incorporate changes in the DSM-5. There are two major parts: "Overview" and "Specific Disorders." "Overview" covers discrete versus dimensional classifications of disorders, dual diagnosis, interviewing for differential diagnosis, and the roles of race ethnicity and culture in psychopathology. "Specific Disorders" chapters generally include a description; case study; epidemiology; clinical picture; etiological factors; diagnosis, course, and prognosis; and psychological and biological assessment. These chapters cover schizophrenia, mood, anxiety, and obsessive-compulsive disorders; trauma- and stress-related disorders; dissociative and somatic disorders; eating/feeding and sleep-wake disorders; sexual dysfunctions, paraphilias, and gender dysphoria; substance use disorders; and neurocognitive and personality disorders. Chapters are lengthy (thirty to seventy pages long), and reference lists are ten to fifteen pages long.

2.37. *APA dictionary of clinical psychology.* VandenBos, G. R. (2013). Washington, DC: American Psychological Association. 636 pp. RC467. This work, containing more than 11,000 entries, covers topics specific to clinical psychology. These include emotional and physiological states, clinical disorders, theories, assessment, diagnosis, prevention, training, supervision, psychopharmacology, and etymological information as well as the biological, cognitive, and sociopsychological bases of mental health. Typical entries are paragraph length. In addition to being cross-referenced, words in all uppercase letters indicate entries elsewhere in the book. There are two appendixes, which are simple alphabetical listings of major biographical figures and psychotherapeutic approaches. This volume is aimed at graduate students in clinical psychology, but will also be valuable to clinicians in a variety of disciplines, including medicine, law, and social work.

2.38. *APA handbook of counseling psychology.* Fouad, N. A., Carter, J. A., & Subich, L. M. (Eds.). (2012). Washington, DC: American Psychological Association. 1132 pp. BF636. Two-volume set. This set provides comprehensive coverage of counseling psychology. Volume 1 (*Theories, Research, and Methods*) is divided into two major sections. The first section covers the history of counseling psychology, its evolution in theory, research methods, role of evidence-based practice, assessment, and emerging trends in counseling psychology education and training. The second section covers process and outcome research in counseling psychology, theories of vocational psychology, supervision, positive psychology theory and research, prevention, gender and sexual orientation, race and ethnicity, aging, religion/spirituality, and social class in counseling psychology. Volume 2 (*Practice, Interventions, and Applications*) is divided into five major sections. The first section covers the role of counseling psychology regarding work, education, and work-family

balance. The second covers counseling psychology in partner violence, child maltreatment, and community violence. The third and fourth sections cover disparities in health and economics, homelessness, racism, sexism, and heterosexism and counseling psychology. The fifth section covers emerging trends in counseling psychology and forensics, religion/spirituality, immigration, older adults, consulting, and school settings.

2.39. *Bergin and Garfield's handbook of psychotherapy and behavior change* (6th ed.). Lambert, M. J. (Ed.). (2013). Hoboken, NJ: John Wiley & Sons. 851 pp. RC480. The sixth edition of this classic work continues the tradition of being the major reference for psychotherapy effectiveness research. While the major focus is still on empirical research using standard research designs, new chapters also incorporate qualitative research designs and methodologies and research in natural settings. Part I covers history of psychotherapy research, methodologies of evaluation, and qualitative research methods. Part II focuses on what components contribute to therapeutic efficacy, therapist effects, and process and outcome research. Part III focuses on particular modalities, including behavioral, cognitive, cognitive-behavioral, psychodynamic, and humanistic-experiential therapies. Part IV addresses special groups and settings, including children and adolescents, couples and families, small groups, behavioral medicine and clinical health psychology, and combining medication and psychotherapy for major mental disorders. The book ends with a chapter on training and supervision in psychology.

2.40. *Clinical handbook of psychological disorders: A step-by-step treatment manual* (5th ed.). Barlow, D. H. (2014). New York: Guilford Press. 768 pp. RC489. The fifth edition of this well-known work has been updated to incorporate changes related to the DSM-5. It contains eighteen chapters covering the most common disorders. Each chapter provides background on the disorder; common presenting symptoms; an overview of assessment and suggested measures; and a detailed treatment protocol, often session-by-session, of the treatment modalities most commonly used for the disorder and for which there is the most evidence of efficacy. Chapters are lengthy (thirty to fifty pages long), with extensive and generally up-to-date references. The primary audience for this work is graduate students and early-career practitioners who are seeking a detailed "how-to" on treating specific disorders, but the reference lists will be useful to researchers in this area.

2.41. *Diagnosis and treatment of mental disorders across the lifespan* (2nd ed.). Woo, S. M., & Keatinge, C. (2016). Hoboken, NJ: John Wiley & Sons. 1232 pp. RC454. The second edition of this work has been updated to incorporate DSM-5 criteria and classifications and to integrate cultural and diversity issues through all aspects of diagnosis and treatment for all disorders. Part I consists of three major chapters, on intake and interviewing, essentials of diagnosis, and fundamentals of treatment. Case conceptualizations now include identity issues, and treatment models now include crisis intervention. Part II covers disorders most commonly seen in practice (autism spectrum disorders; attention deficit hyperactivity disorder; schizophrenia and other psychotic disorders; depressive and bipolar disorders; anxiety; obsessive-compulsive and trauma disorders; eating, oppositional-defiant, and Conduct disorders; substance-related disorders; neurocognitive disorders; and personality disorders). Chapters demonstrate the application of the principles from part I and cover historical information, epidemiology, clinical presentation, onset, course, comorbidities, differential diagnosis, and medication. In addition to being a resource for researchers, this work was designed to be useful as a textbook in graduate courses in clinical psychology.

2.42. *Encyclopedia of clinical psychology.* Cautin, R. L., & Lilienfeld, S. O. (2015). Chichester, England: John Wiley and Sons. 3138 pp. BF31. Five-volume set. This set provides both historical perspective and newer empirical evidence related to seven major areas in psychology: historical, philosophical, and conceptual issues; methodological issues; classification/diagnosis and assessment (including DSM-V); psychological disorders (including culturally bound syndromes); treatment and prevention; legal and ethical issues; and professional issues. Where relevant, entry authors were asked to emphasize what is the best available scientific evidence in order to assist users in critical evaluation. Volume 1 contains both alphabetical and thematic lists of entries for all five volumes. Typical entries are eight to ten pages long.

2.43. *Handbook of adolescent behavioral problems: Evidence-based approaches to prevention and treatment* (2nd ed.). Gullotta, T. P., Plant, R. W., & Evans, M. A. (Eds.). (2015). New York: Springer. 697 pp. RJ503. Although primarily aimed at practitioners and policy makers, this book will also be useful to researchers, as it focuses on evidence-based prevention and treatment and also addresses particular topics not frequently covered in other handbooks. Part I provides an overview of primary prevention, adolescent mental health, family and community influences, and evidence-based treatment. Part II covers standard disorders: anxiety, post-traumatic stress, attention deficit hyperactivity, depressive, bipolar, suicidal, obsessive-compulsive, oppositional-defiant, eating, autism spectrum, and schizophrenic disorders. Part II covers both traditional and some less-frequently addressed areas of adolescent issues: media, school failure and success, cyberbullying, violence, gang behavior, substance abuse, homicide, gambling, dating violence, adolescent sex-offending, sibling incest, abuse and neglect, and self-injury. Chapters generally include introduction, definitions, prevalence rates, biological/genetic factors,

evidence-based treatment, conclusion, recommended best practice, and references.

2.44. *Handbook of comparative interventions for adult disorders* (2nd ed.). Hersen, M., & Bellack, A. S. (Eds.). (1999). New York: Wiley. 708 pp. RC480.5 .H275 1999. This book presents major treatment strategies for common disorders. Part I reviews four major treatment strategies: dynamic psychotherapy, behavior therapy, cognitive-behavior therapy, and pharmacotherapy. Subsequent parts cover depression, panic and agoraphobia, social phobia, obsessive-compulsive disorder, post-traumatic stress disorder, anorexia and bulimia, borderline personality disorder, and alcoholism and substance abuse, with chapters on two to four treatment approaches for comparison. Chapters on disorders contain theoretical formulation of each treatment modality, any diagnostic issues (based on DSM-IV), assessments and strategies, case examples, dialogues, and a summary. Although this work is primarily aimed at practitioners, the reference lists will be very useful to researchers in comparative interventions.

2.45. *Handbook of complementary and alternative therapies in mental health.* Shannon, S. M. (2002). San Diego, CA: Academic Press. 574 pp. RC480. This book describes a number of alternative treatment modalities, with specific focus on their application to mental health. It contains eight sections: overview, physical modalities, mind-body approaches, spiritual approaches, modern innovations, traditional medical systems, other approaches, and synthesis. Modalities within each section contain an overview, relevance for mental health, safety, compatibility with conventional care, contraindications, treatment, training, resources, and references. This book is useful to clinicians seeking more information about alternative practices that are increasingly in demand, students, and researchers interested in the depth of research support for these alternative practices and as a starting point for research.

2.46. *Handbook of evidence-based practice in clinical psychology.* Sturmey, P., & Hersen, M. (2012). Hoboken, NJ: John Wiley & Sons. 1476 pp. RC467. Two-volume set. Volume 1 covers child and adolescent disorders. Volume 2 covers adult disorders. The set documents research that identifies evidence-based practices (EPB) for many disorders. Part 1 of each volume consists of five chapters covering foundations of EBP, standards of evidence, professional issues, and limits and economics of EPB. Part 2 of each volume covers specific disorders. Chapters contain an overview, diagnostic criteria, demographics, treatment approaches, randomized controlled studies, conclusion, and references. Coverage of disorders varies with the amount of EBP-related research conducted on the disorder, but typical chapters are twenty-five to thirty pages long with five to six pages of references. This set is an excellent resource for practitioners, students, and researchers interested in research-supported clinical practices.

2.47. *Handbook of group counseling and psychotherapy.* DeLucia-Waack, J. L., Kalodner, C. R., & Riva, M. (Eds). (2014). Thousand Oaks, CA: Sage. 640 pp. RC488. The forty-six chapters of this volume cover a wide range of issues in group therapy, particularly focusing on research published during the past ten years. Parts I and II focus on current and historical perspectives and best practices of group therapy. Parts III, IV, and V are particularly useful to researchers as they focus on specific populations, settings, and therapeutic issues. Populations covered are native peoples, African Americans, Asian Americans, Latinos, LGBTQI, persons with disabilities, older people, and privileged and oppressed groups. Settings include schools, colleges/universities, and behavioral health and veterans' facilities. Special topics include depression, anxiety, complicated grief, addictions, violence, offenders and mandatory treatment, attachment, child sexual abuse, mindfulness, stress reduction, dialectical behavior therapy, eating disturbances, bullying, women's and men's groups, prevention groups, career and transitions, adventure therapy, children and adolescents, and postdisaster groups. Chapters are shorter than usual in a handbook (ten to twenty pages long), but each is highly focused, and references comprise approximately 20 percent of each chapter. This book is aimed at advanced researchers (graduate students and above) and practitioners and provides easy access to topic-specific research.

2.48. *Handbook of homework assignments in psychotherapy: Research, practice, and prevention.* Kazantzis, N., & L'Abate, L. (2007). New York: Springer. 464 pp. RC480. This book covers the use of homework in therapeutic and preventive practice as well as research on the use of homework assignments. Part I describes the use of homework in different therapeutic approaches; each chapter includes a brief description of the approach, description of the role of homework within that approach, and at least one case study. Part II examines homework with specific populations, and Part III examines homework with specific problems. Part IV covers directions for research on homework, for the integration of homework into practice, and for the use of homework in prevention. Chapters are relatively brief (ten to twenty pages long). This book will be most useful to novice and experienced practitioners seeking to incorporate homework assignments into their work.

2.49. *Handbook of mentalizing in mental health practice.* Bateman, A., & Fonagy, P. (2012). Washington, DC: American Psychiatric Association. 593 pp. RC480. This book provides an introduction to mentalizing (attending to our own and others' mental states in understanding of our own and others' actions) as a developmental and clinical concept and how to use mentalizing in clinical practice. It begins with a detailed introduction to the concept and how to assess mentalization, proceeds to techniques for using it in various treatment settings, and ends with chapters about using it with specific disorders. This book is most useful to practicing clinicians and those wanting to better understand the mentalization process.

2.50. *Handbook of mindfulness: Theory, research, and practice.* Brown, K. W., Creswell, J. D., & Ryan, R. M. (Eds.). (2015). 466 pp. BF327. The twenty-three chapters of this book provide a comprehensive review of current knowledge of mindfulness. The chapters are organized into five major sections: part I, "Historical and Conceptual Overview of Mindfulness"; Part II, "Mindfulness in the Context of Contemporary Psychological Theory"; part III, "The Basic Science of Mindfulness"; part IV "Mindfulness Interventions for Healthy Populations"; and part V, "Mindfulness Interventions for Clinical Populations." Chapters are approximately twenty pages long and include explanatory notes, useful illustrations and tables, and four to five pages of references. This book will be useful to both practitioners and researchers, bringing much of the key recent research together in one place.

2.51. *Handbook of preschool mental health: Development, disorders, and treatment* (2nd ed.). Luby, J. L. (Ed.). (2017). New York: Guilford Press. 416 pp. RJ499. This book provides an overview of mental health in two- to six-year-old children. Part I covers developmental psychopathology, risk, and resilience, particularly sensitive periods of development; protection and risk factors in the environment and early caregiving; and brain development during this age period. Part II addresses behavioral and emotional disorders, specifically oppositional defiant and conduct disorders, attention-deficit/hyperactivity, anxiety and depressive disorders, autism spectrum disorder, attachment, and sleep disorders in this age group. Part III focuses on empirically supported interventions, including parent-child interaction, cognitive-behavioral, and attachment-based parent-child therapies, as well as updates on early interventions for autism spectrum disorder and psychopharmacological treatment of preschoolers. The book ends with a chapter on integrating translational developmental neuroscience into a model intervention.

2.52. *Handbook of psychodynamic approaches to psychopathology.* Luyten, P., Mayes, L. C., Fonagy, P., Target, M., & Blatt, S. J. (Eds.). (2015). New York: Guilford Press. 578 pp. RC480. This book consists of twenty-five chapters on adult, child, and adolescent psychopathology, focusing on frequently encountered disorders for which there is empirical support for the effectiveness of psychodynamic treatment. Part I covers theoretical background of psychodynamic approaches, developmental perspective, and diagnostic issues. Parts II and III cover specific disorders in adults and children/adolescents respectively, with each chapter including case illustrations and formulations. Part IV addresses process and outcome of psychodynamic treatments, as well as the need for integrative theories, transdiagnostic approaches, integration with neuroscience, and a dynamic, life span-developmental approach. This book will be particularly useful to those interested in the relationship between psychodynamic theory and existing and future diagnostic systems, and the extensive references will be very useful to researchers interested in empirical evidence for the efficacy of psychodynamic approaches to treatment.

2.53. *Handbook of psychological assessment, case conceptualization, and treatment.* Hersen, M. (2008). Hoboken, NJ: Wiley. 1509 pp. RC454. Two-volume set. In anticipation of the publication of DSM-V, this set addresses its topics in a broad manner not specifically tied to the DSM-IV. The first part of volume 1 (*Adults*) covers an overview of behavioral assessment, diagnostic issues, behavioral conceptualization, an overview of behavioral treatment, medical and pharmacological issues, and ethical issues. Part 1 of volume 2 (*Children and Adolescents*) covers the same topics as volume 1, but also covers developmental issues and the role of family. Part II of the adult volume covers assessment, conceptualization, and treatment of specific disorders, namely specific phobias, panic and agoraphobia, social anxiety, obsessive-compulsive, post-traumatic, generalized anxiety and major depressive disorders, schizophrenia, personality disorders, bulimia, organic disorders, and alcoholism. Part III of the adult volume addresses special issues such as marital distress, sexual deviation, adults with intellectual disabilities, issues related to older adults, insomnia, health anxiety, and compulsive hoarding. Part II of the children and adolescent volume also covers depressive, anxiety, and post-traumatic stress disorders as well as oppositional defiant, conduct, learning, motor, and communication disorders; attention deficit/hyperactivity disorder; early-onset schizophrenia; and substance use disorders. Part III covers special topics such as neglect and abuse, neurological impairment, habit and sleep disorders, enuresis and encopresis, and firesetting. This set has useful tables comparing measures and set-off boxes with case descriptions, including assessment tools used and treatment.

2.54. *Humanistic psychotherapies: Handbook of research and practice* (2nd ed.). Cain, D. J., Keenan, K., & Rubin, S. (2016). Washington, DC: American Psychological Association. 556 pp. RC480. This volume presents recent studies investigating the evidence for the efficacy of humanistic psychotherapies. It begins with the historical and conceptual foundations of humanistic therapies, an overview of humanistic processes and outcomes, and research methodologies in this area. It then addresses major approaches (person-centered, gestalt, experiential, existential, and emotion focused) and empirically supported humanistic approaches with couples, families, and children. Chapters include transcripts from therapy sessions and substantial reference lists. As the major components of humanistic therapies are also found to be important factors in other therapy models, this book will be valuable to researchers in all therapeutic schools.

2.55. *Oxford handbook of social class in counseling.* Liu, W. M. (Ed.). (2013). New York: Oxford University Press. 569 pp. BF636. This work is unique in its dedication to the concept and issues of social class and "classism" as related to counseling and psychotherapy. Many other works address race and ethnicity, and these issues are also related to social class but do not address it as their major construct of interest. The first of the four major parts addresses definitions and theoretical and methodological issues of social class. The second part addresses social class as related to psychotherapy and assessment, particularly as they relate to psychotherapy process, positive psychology, crisis intervention, disasters, veterans, body image and eating disorders, rehabilitation, substance abuse and treatment, and social media. The third part addresses developmental issues such as parenting, attachment, school counseling, resilience, and geropsychology. The final part addresses how culture and identity intersect with social class and psychotherapy, particularly religion, racial and ethnic identity, rural populations, LGBTQI issues, international issues, men and women's issues, immigrant issues, and further research on the relationship of social class to other variables in psychotherapy.

2.56. *Practitioner's guide to evidence based psychotherapy.* Fisher, J. E., & O'Donohue, W. T. (2006). New York: Springer. 754 pp. RC480. This book provides concise and practical information about seventy-three disorders, each with its own chapter. Written in 2006, it is based on DSM-IV and ICD-10. Each chapter includes a definition and basic facts (e.g., prevalence, gender differentials if any, comorbidities), assessment methods, and evidence-based treatments. For some disorders, chapters include "rule out" and effective self-help treatments, including readings and websites. Chapters are relatively short (ten to fifteen pages long) and highly focused. This book is useful for clinicians needing a quick overview of evidence-based treatments and how to select among them and as a starting point for research on evidence-based treatments for specific disorders.

Clinical and Counseling: Tests and Measures

2.57. *Acceptance and commitment therapy measures package: Process measures of potential relevance to ACT.* http://integrativehealthpartners.org/downloads/ACTmeasures.pdf. Ciarrochi, J., & Bilich, L. (Comps.). (2006). 159 pp. RC489. Thirty-nine instruments measure various processes believed by the authors to be potentially relevant to acceptance and commitment therapy (ACT). Measures are organized into six areas: avoidance/acceptance, fusion/dysfunctional thinking, mindfulness/awareness of feelings, value clarification/goal striving/action orientation, measures for specific populations, and general ACT measures. The author, contact information, scoring, reliability and validity, references about development and use of the measure, and permission information are provided. A list of full-text measures in this book is located at http://libguides.hofstra.edu/TMdb/CiarrochiBilich2006.

2.58 *Assessment scales in child and adolescent psychiatry.* Verhulst, F. C., & Van Der Ende, J. (2006). Abingdon, England: Taylor and Francis. 220 pp. RJ503. Includes forty-six full-text measures used with children and adolescents and sample items from other measures. Contains general rating scales of behavior and symptoms, strengths, and difficulties. Also includes scales for specific problems, including anxiety, obsessive-compulsive disorder, depression, suicide, eating disorders, tics, ADHD, conduct disorders, substance abuse, and global impairment. For each scale there are commentary, information on alternate forms, properties of the scale and subscales, psychometric information, information on use, key references, and author/publisher contact information. Some scales are in the public domain, others are reproduced with permission, and some are commercial. An alphabetical list of measures is on pages 219–220. This work will be valuable to researchers of all levels, although some commercial tests may be restricted to those with professional credentials. A list of full-text measures in this book is located at http://libguides.hofstra.edu/TMdb/VerhulstVanDerEnde2006.

2.59. *Compendium of psychosocial measures: Assessment of people with serious mental illnesses in the community.* Johnson, D. L. (2010). New York: Springer. 545 pp. RC473. This volume provides information about 372 measures intended to be used in research with severely mentally ill individuals. The measures are divided into twenty-nine areas: general background information; functional assessment; community living; social functioning; global assessment; level of psychopathology; insight and judgment; stress; social problem solving and coping; social support; quality of life; consumer satisfaction; continuity of care; treatment adherence; substance abuse; environmental measures and group processes; housing; cultural issues; special purpose methods; agency performance evaluation; work behavior; family measures; premorbid adjustment; psychotic symptoms; depression; mania; anxiety; screening; and empowerment, recovery, and stigma. For each measure, the title, primary source(s), purpose, description, reliability, validity, measure source, and comments are provided. Because these measures are all intended for use with severe mental illness, it will be most useful to advanced graduate students and researchers working with that population.

2.60. *Handbook of assessment and treatment planning for psychological disorders* (2nd ed.). Antony, M. M., & Barlow, D. H. (2010). New York: Guilford Press. 706 pp. RC469. The purpose of this work is to provide detailed guidelines for assessing individuals with specific disorders, assessing results to select effective treatments,

and using standard assessment tools to measure treatment outcomes. The first section consists of four chapters, covering assessment in evidence-based practice (EBP), evaluating measures, specific brief screening and outcome measures, and specific structured and semistructured diagnostic interviews. Each of the remaining thirteen chapters reviews specific measures for specific disorders. Chapters are each thirty to forty pages long, including six to seven pages of references. This work will be particularly useful for graduate students, clinicians, researchers, and faculty who teach assessment courses.

2.61. *Handbook of clinical rating scales and assessment in psychiatry and mental health.* Baer, L., & Blais, M. A. (Eds.). (2010). New York: Humana Press. 320 pp. RC473. Includes forty-one full-text measures on a variety of mental health issues. In addition to the full-text instruments provided, this book covers other tests for each clinical issue and also indicates the "gold standard" test for that issue. It also addresses the purpose of each scale (e.g., diagnostic, screening, and treatment assessment) and provides psychometric and other information. Some tests may be copied directly without further permission; some indicate the need to contact the author/publisher for permission (if the latter, this information and contact information are usually provided immediately following the test). A list of full-text measures available in this book is located at http://libguides.hofstra.edu/TMdb/BaerBlais2010.

2.62. *Handbook of family measurement techniques.* Tsouliatos, J., Perlmutter, B. F., & Strauss, M. A. (Eds.). (2001). Thousand Oaks, CA: Sage. 1208 pp. HQ728. This three-volume set is a different item, rather than a second edition of the 1990 work with the same title and authors. Volume 1 of this set contains the contents of the entire 1990 edition. This includes an introductory chapter on family measurement principles and techniques, followed by detailed abstracts for 504 instruments measuring dimensions of marital and family interaction, intimacy and family values, parenthood, roles and power, and adjustment. Each topical chapter provides a discussion of the topic before the abstracts are presented. Detailed abstracts include availability information, variables measured, instrument type (e.g., self-report, projective), description, sample items (where permission was acquired), commentary, and references. All measures appear in their entirety in a published work (most measures), or permission was provided to deposit the entire instrument with the National Auxiliary Publication Service (NAPS 1-3). In addition to these 504 detailed abstracts, abbreviated abstracts are provided for another 472 instruments that met the same criteria (total of 976 instruments abstracted). These original abstracts from the 1990 work, now forming volume 1 of the 2001 set, are for instruments from the 1929–1986 literature, with the major focus being the 1975–1986 literature. Volume 2 of this three-volume set contains 367 additional abstracts for measures that were newly developed or substantially revised during 1987–1996. It begins with chapters on family measurement overview and developing, interpreting, and using family assessment techniques. Detailed abstracts in volume 2 cover family relations; marital relations; parent-child relations; family adjustment, health, and well-being; and family problems. Abstracts include variables measured, instrument type, samples measured, description, sample items (where permission was acquired), psychometrics, commentary, keywords, references, and availability information. Volume 3 contains the full text of 168 of the 367 instruments abstracted in volume 2. In addition to the actual instrument, scoring instructions are provided, as well as the original source of the instrument. This set will be highly valuable to clinicians, researchers, graduate students, and advanced undergraduates interested in measurement of numerous family issues. A list of full-text measures in volume 3 is located at http://libguides.hofstra.edu/TMdb/TsouliatosPerlmutterStrauss2001.

2.63. *Handbook of psychiatric measures* (2nd ed.). Rush, A. J., First, M. B., & Blacker, D. (Eds.). (2008). Washington, DC: American Psychiatric Association. 828 pp. RC473. Contains 136 full-text instruments on the accompanying CD. An alphabetical list of the full-text instruments is on pages 755–757. A list by chapter (topic) is on pages 757–761. Covers general psychiatric symptoms, mental health status, functioning, and disability; general health status, functioning, and disability; quality of life; adverse effects; patient perceptions of care; stress and life events; family risk factors; suicide risk; child and adolescent measures; symptom-specific measures for infancy, childhood, and adolescence; child and adolescent functional status; delirium and cognition; neuropsychiatric symptoms; substance use disorders; psychotic disorders; mood disorders; anxiety disorders; somatoform and factitious disorders and malingering; sexual dysfunction; eating disorders; sleep disorders; impulse control; personality traits and disorders; defense mechanisms; and aggression. Also covered are another 139 instruments for which full text is not included. The book provides a "practical issues" section for each instrument, including permission information and cost if any. A list of full-text measures in this book is located at http://libguides.hofstra.edu/TMdb/RushFirstBlacker2008.

2.64. *Integrated treatment for dual disorders: A guide to effective practice.* Mueser, K. T. (2003). New York: Guilford Press. 470 pp. RC564. Contains twenty full-text instruments and sixteen educational handouts. Handouts are in appendix B and instruments are in appendix C. Instruments cover substance use, functioning, treatment, relapse prevention, activities and lifestyle, and family awareness/involvement. See "limited photocopy license" on verso for information on permissions. A list of full-text measures in this book is located at http://libguides.hofstra.edu/TMdb/Mueser2003.

2.65. *Measures for clinical practice and research: A sourcebook* (5th ed.). Corcoran, K., & Fischer, J. (2013).

Oxford: Oxford University Press. 1628 pp. BF176. Two-volume set. Covers 500 full-text instruments for adults, children, couples, and families. Volume 1 contains measures for couples, family, and children. Volume 2 contains measures for adults. Frontmatter includes an alphabetical list and a topical list as well as guidance in test selection. Topics covered are abuse, acculturation, addiction, anger, hostility, assertiveness, beliefs, child behaviors/problems, client motivation, depression and grief, eating problems, ethnic identity, family functioning, geriatrics, guilt, general health, mental health, identity, impulsivity, interpersonal behavior, locus of control, loneliness, love, couple/marital relationships, obsessive-compulsive behavior, pain, family relations, perfectionism, phobias, post-traumatic stress, problem-solving, procrastination, rape, life satisfaction, schizotypal symptoms, self-concept, self-control, self-efficacy, sexuality, social functioning, social support, stress, suicide, substance abuse, and treatment issues. Psychometric and other necessary information is provided for each instrument, and at the end of each instrument's information profile, "availability" is indicated. Most instruments indicate "may be copied from book," some indicate "journal article" and indicate the primary reference citation, and some indicate the author/publisher's contact information. A list of full-text measures in this book is located at http://libguides.hofstra.edu/TMdb/CorcoranFischer2013.

2.66. *Practitioner's guide to empirically based measures of social skills.* Nangle, D. W., Hansen, D. J., Erdley, C. A., & Norton, P. J. (Eds.). (2010). New York: Springer. 538 pp. HM691. Includes twenty full-text measures; one hundred instruments are reviewed. Part of the Association for Behavioral and Cognitive Therapies (ABCT) Clinical Assessment Series, this volume covers a wide range of issues in the measurement of social skills in adults, children, and adolescents. It begins by addressing definitions and target skills, social-cognitive models, and learning theory. It then goes on to practical issues in assessment and interventions, as well as special factors in measuring social skills such as diversity, anger and aggression, social anxiety and withdrawal, intellectual disability, autism spectrum disorders, schizophrenia, and substance use. For measures discussed and included, the original citation is provided, as are the purpose, population, description, administration and scoring information, psychometrics, source, cost (if any), and alternative forms (if any). There is a "Quick-View Guide" appendix that facilitates identification and comparison by age level. Full-text measures are located in the reprints appendix. A list of full-text measures in this book is located at http://libguides.hofstra.edu/TMdb/NangleHansenErdleyNorton2010.

2.67. *Rating scales in mental health* (3rd ed.). Sajatovic, M., & Ramirez, L. F. (2012). Baltimore, MD: Johns Hopkins University Press. 502 pp. RC473. Includes 119 full-text tests. Copyright information is provided for each test;

some will indicate "N/A" or "public domain" and do not need further permission. In other cases, contact information is provided. Some tests are very long, so representative sample items are provided. Chapters are organized by condition and cover anxiety, mood disorders, psychosis, social functioning, general health, insight, involuntary movement, satisfaction with health care, quality of life, substance abuse, suicide risk, impulsivity, aggression, eating disorders, premenstrual dysphoria, sleep disorders, sexual disorders, and geriatric and childhood disorders. Scale summaries include overview, applications, psychometrics, copyright holder, administration, completion time, representative study, references, and the scale itself. A list of full-text measures in this book is located at http://libguides.hofstra.edu/TMdb/SajatovicRamirez2012.

2.68. *Sourcebook of adult assessment strategies*. Schutte, N. S., & Malouff, J. M. (2014/1995). New York: Plenum Press. 471 pp. RC473. Includes seventy-five full-text instruments organized around broad categories of psychopathology in DSM-IV. Scale summaries include purpose and development, administration and scoring, sample and cutoff scores, psychometrics, subscales, alternate forms and the scale itself. Scales cover disorders of delirium and dementia, substance use, schizophrenia and related psychosis, mood, anxiety, somatoform, pain and related phenomena, dissociation, sexual function, eating, sleep, impulse control, relationships, and other areas of clinical interest and global functioning. Instruments are reprinted with permission from the author/publisher and require author/publisher permission for use. A list of full-text measures in this book is located at http://libguides.hofstra.edu/TMdb/SchutteMalouff2014.

Clinical and Counseling: Bibliographies

2.69. *Annotated bibliography of measurement compendia: Reliable, valid, and standard measures of substance abuse and mental and behavioral health indicators and outcomes of interest*. Substance Abuse and Mental Health Services Administration (SAMHSA). Selected, annotated bibliography of seventeen compendia mostly containing full text of instruments; the others describe available instruments. Most are compendia of measures used with individuals, but several are for institutions to measure outcomes. Available online at https://www.samhsa.gov/capt/tools-learning-resources/annotated-bibliography-measurement-compendia.

2.70. A bibliography of articles relevant to the application of virtual reality in the mental health field. Rizzo, A. A., Wiederhold, B., Riva, G., & Van Der Zaag, C. (1998). *CyberPsychology & Behavior*, 1(4), 411–425. Bibliography containing more than 200 items on virtual reality and mental health. Items are classified into twelve categories general theory, spatial skills and navigation, memory, attention, neglect, traumatic brain injury, developmental and learning disabilities, neurological diseases, transfer of training, auditory virtual reality, brain imaging, human factors, and clinical psychology.

2.71. Bibliography of literature reviews on drug abuse treatment. Prendergast, M., Podus, D., & McCormack, K. (1998). *Journal of Substance Abuse Treatment*, 15(3), 267–270. Bibliography of literature reviews on drug abuse treatment efficacy from articles and books. Covers categories of drug abuse treatment (general), opiate treatment, cocaine treatment, therapeutic communities, adolescent treatment, behavioral and cognitive treatment, family therapy, Minnesota model, relapse prevention, acupuncture, transcendental meditation, 12–step programs, and natural recovery.

2.72. A bibliography of mental patients' autobiographies: An update and classification system. Sommer, R., Clifford, J. S., & Norcross, J. C. (1998). *An American Journal of Psychiatry*, 155(9), 1261–1264. Seven anthologies and forty-eight autobiographies of former psychiatric patients published between 1980 and 1998.

2.73. Bibliography of Michael Balint's related works. Hudon, M., & Haynal, A. (2003). *The American Journal of Psychoanalysis*, 63(3), 275–279. Bibliography of Michael Balint's related works, incorporating references from various sources, including The Balint Archives and the Balint Society website.

2.74. Carl Rogers bibliography of English and German sources. Schmid, P. F. (2005). *Person-Centered and Experiential Psychotherapies*, 4(3–4), 153–160. This bibliography lists all original publications of Carl Rogers from 1922 onward, including German translations. Following English-, German-, and Spanish-language introductory remarks, the chronological part lists unpublished papers and interviews, and, separately, films. The alphabetical part consists of both name and title indexes. The bibliography is also available online at http://www.pfs-online.at/1/indexbibliocrr0.htm, where it is updated.

2.75. Cognitive-behavioral therapy. https://nicic.gov/library/package/cbt. National Institute of Corrections (NIC). Links to reports on and evaluations of cognitive-behavioral therapy (CBT) and evidence-based practice (EBP), CBT and female offenders, CBT and mentally ill offenders, CBT and probation, CBT and sex offenders, CBT program evaluations, CBT effectiveness with youth, moral reconciliation therapy (MRT), "Thinking for a Change" CBT programs, and general CBT effectiveness reports.

2.76. *Jacques Lacan: An annotated bibliography*. Clark, M. (2014/1988). New York: Routledge. 893 pp. Z8469 or BF109. 2 vols. Covers primary and secondary works by and about Lacan, including books, essays, seminars, interviews, and dissertations. Incorporates (and corrects where appropriate) information from all earlier published bibliographies of Lacan's work, including Joel Dor's *Bibliographie des travaux de Jacques Lacan*. Also includes all information about Lacan's published work on record in the Bibliotheque de I'Ecole de la Cause Freudienne Includes items in English, French, Japanese, Russian, and five other languages.

2.77. Karen Horney: A bibliography of her writings. Paris, B. J. (2001). *American Journal of Psychoanalysis*, 60(2), 165–172. Bibliography of Karen Horney's books, articles, essays, lectures and talks, and other writings.

2.78. Managed behavioral health services: A bibliography of empirical studies, articles of interest, and books. Feldman, S., Cuffel, B., & Hausman, J. (1999). *Administration and Policy in Mental Health*, 27(1–2), 5–88. Selective bibliography on managed behavioral health services. Part I is annotated and focuses on benefit design and insurance arrangements, managed mental health's effects on cost and utilization, and managed care in the public sector. Parts II and III are not annotated; they focus on theory, policy, and analysis.

2.79. Mental health parity: A review of research and a bibliography. Feldman, S., Bachman, J., & Bayer, J. (2002). *Administration and Policy in Mental Health*, 29(3), 215–228. Summarizes the content of a 2001 meeting held to review existing research on the effects of mental health parity, identify what knowledge can be gleaned from research in progress, and identify knowledge gaps. Includes bibliography of materials on parity published from 1996 to 2001.

2.80. *Mental health services in criminal justice system settings: A selectively annotated bibliography, 1970–1997.* Van Whitlock, R., & Lubin, B. (1999). Westport, CT: Greenwood Press. 190 pp. Contains 1,264 citations to books and scholarly articles, about half of which are annotated. Most empirically based works are annotated; theoretical and practical works are annotated only if they are of major value. Items are from psychology, psychiatry, nursing, education, social work, and other related areas and are related to service provision to mentally ill and substance-abusing offenders in criminal justice settings.

2.81. MMPI-2 and MMPI-A research with U.S. Latinos: A bibliography. Corrales, M. L., Cabiya, J. J., Gomez, F., Ayala, G. X., Mendoza, S., & Velasquez, R. J. (1998). *Psychological Reports*, 83(3, pt. 1), 1027–1033. Comprehensive listing of research conducted on US Latinos, including Puerto Ricans, with the MMPI-2 and MMPI-A from 1989 through 1998.

2.82. Multilingual bibliography of the works of Michael Balint. Haynal, A., & Hudon, M. (2003). *The American Journal of Psychoanalysis*, 63(3), 257–273. Multilingual and chronologically arranged bibliography of the works of Michael Balint.

2.83. Principles of multicultural counseling and therapy: A selective bibliography. (pp. 419–432). In *Principles of multicultural counseling and therapy*. Gielen, U. P., Draguns, J. G., & Fish, J. M. (2008). New York: Routledge. 463 pp. RC455. Selective bibliography includes books, book chapters, and journal articles classified under

nineteen categories, covering multicultural therapy and counseling, special populations and issues, therapy with children and adolescents, family therapy, care of refugees and immigrants, history of psychological healing in the West, psychopathology and mental health across cultures, transcultural psychiatry, culture and assessment, shamanism, altered states of consciousness, indigenous North American healing traditions, indigenous healing traditions in Latin America and the Caribbean, Asian and Oceanic healing traditions, Western psychology and Asian traditions, and African and Islamic healing traditions.

2.84. *Psychiatry in Nigeria: A partly annotated bibliography.* Boroffka, A. (2006). Kiel, Germany: Brunswiker Universitätsbuchhandlung–Medizin. 560 pp. Bibliography of almost 2,500 papers, rare documents, articles, and books related to psychiatry and neighboring disciplines, written in and about Nigeria and other parts of Africa, including early history of psychiatry and related research, and covering most of the twentieth century. Approximately half of the items are annotated.

2.85 Seventy-five years of Kleinian writing, 1920–1995: A bibliography. Hinshelwood, R. D. (2000). *Kleinian Studies E-journal*. Bibliography of Kleinian writings by Melanie Klein and other authors from 1920 to 1995. Available online at http://ww.psychoanalysis-and-therapy.com/human_nature/ksej/hinbib.html.

2.86. Sixty years of client-centered/experiential psychotherapy and counseling: Bibliographical survey of books, 1940–2000. Lietaer, G. (2002). *Journal of Humanistic Psychology*, 42(2), 97–131. Bibliographical, three-part survey of books published from 1940 to 2000. Part one focuses on books about client-centered/experiential psychotherapy (1939–1989) in their original language. Part two contains books about client-centered/experiential psychotherapy (1990–2000); items pre-1989 that were revised after 1989; and subsections on publications in English, German, French, and Dutch. Part three focuses on books about related approaches published in 1990–2000. Includes existential, interpersonal, Gestalt, narrative-constructivist, feminist, and integrative/eclectic approaches.

2.87. The treatment of attention-deficit hyperactivity disorder: An annotated bibliography and critical appraisal of published systematic reviews and meta-analyses. Jadad, A. R., Booker, L., Gauld, M., Kakuma, R., Boyle, M., Cunningham, C. E., Kim, M., & Schachar, R. (1999). *Canadian Journal of Psychiatry* (*La Revue Canadienne de Psychiatrie*), 44(10), 1025–1035. Annotated bibliography of meta-analyses and systematic reviews on the treatment of attention deficit hyperactivity disorder (ADHD). Items cover various aspects of treatment, including nonpharmacological, pharmacological, and combination treatments for children and adults.

2.88. Work with older people: A bibliography. Kegerreis, P. (2012). *British Journal of Psychotherapy*, 28(1), 117–124. References to books and articles on psychodynamically oriented treatment covering general issues; individual, couples; and family, group, and creative therapies.

COGNITION, THOUGHT, AND LANGUAGE

2.89. *Cambridge handbook of cognitive science.* Frankish, K., & Ramsey, W. M. (2012). Cambridge, England: Cambridge University Press. 333 pp. BF311. Cognitive science is a cross-disciplinary (e.g., psychology, neurosciences, artificial intelligence, philosophy) perspective on understanding cognition and the mind. This volume focuses on a broad understanding of the approach rather than technical issues in order to provide a single-volume overview of diverse approaches to cognitive research and philosophical issues regarding such research. The book is divided into three major sections. Part I ("Foundations") covers history and core themes, representational theory of mind, and cognitive architectures. Part II ("Aspects of Cognition") focuses on perception, action, human learning and memory, reasoning and decision making, concepts, language, emotion, and consciousness. Part III ("Research Programs") covers types of programmatic research being done, including cognitive neuroscience; evolutionary psychology; embodied, embedded, and extended cognition; and animal cognition. There are many helpful tables and images, and each chapter ends with "further readings" in addition to references.

2.90. *Cambridge handbook of psycholinguistics.* Spivey, M., McRae, K., & Joanisse, M. F. (Eds.). Cambridge, England: Cambridge University Press. 745 pp. BF455. This work brings together decades of historical and current research into one comprehensive volume, with recent research incorporating the latest neuroimaging technologies for understanding psycholinguistics. Thirty-four topics are divided into ten major sections, covering speech perception, spoken word recognition, written word recognition, semantic memory, morphological processing, sentence comprehension, sentence production, figurative language, discourse and conversation, and language and thought. These topics are covered from behavioral, computational, cognitive, neuroscience, and developmental perspectives.

Cognition, Thought, and Language: Tests and Measures

2.91. *Handbook of cognition and assessment: Frameworks, methodologies, and applications.* Rupp, A. A., & Leighton, J. P. (2017). Chichester, England: John Wiley and Sons. 623 pp. LB1062. In a period when education, learning, and educational assessment are under serious scrutiny, this handbook seems to present some of the best current practices while also considering further ways of enhancing and keeping those practices at the cutting edge of educational assessment, incorporating psychometrics and cognition. Section I ("Frameworks") focuses on how various models of cognition inform assessment design, delivery, scoring, and validation. It covers learning and cognitive theories as they apply to assessment design, development, implementation, validation, automatic item generation, social models and socioemotional and self-management variables in learning and assessment, understanding and improving accessibility for special populations, and relationship of automatic scoring with validity. Section II ("Methodologies") covers item response, longitudinal, and diagnostic classification models; Bayesian networks; rule space and attribute hierarchy methods; and educational data mining and learning analytics. Section III ("Applications") focuses on large-scale standards-based assessments of educational achievement, educational survey assessments, professional certification and licensure examinations, in-task assessment framework for behavioral data, digital assessment environments for scientific inquiry practices, assessing constructs in video games, and conversation-based assessment, followed by a concluding chapter. This is an advanced work that will chiefly be of interest to psychometricians, educational measurement researchers, cognitive psychologists interested in assessment, assessment developers, and graduate students who want to learn more about the issues in assessment design.

COMMUNICATION

2.92. *APA handbook of intercultural communication.* Matsumoto, D. R. (2010). Washington, DC: American Psychological Association. 329 pp. HM1211. This work is a companion volume to the *APA Handbook of Interpersonal Communication.* Its focus is on communication among individuals from different cultures; the encoding and decoding of messages; and how even when the same language is used, it has different meanings to those of different cultures. The first part of the book covers theoretical issues, including cognition, social psychology of language, intercultural conflict, power, identity, and silence and taboo in intercultural communication. The second part covers applied intercultural communication in health-care settings, schools, intimate relationships, the workplace, and interpretation of media, and ending with training in intracultural communication. This book will be most valuable to advanced students and researchers interested in communication.

2.93. *APA handbook of nonverbal communication.* Matsumoto, D. R., Hwang, H. S., & Frank, M. G. (2016). Washington, DC: American Psychological Association. 626 pp. BF637. This volume reviews the state of the art methodologies for researching nonverbal communication and nonverbal behavior. It is organized into four major themes. The first addresses the history of the field. The second covers theoretical frameworks which inform research on nonverbal communication. The third covers factors such as appearance, facial expressions, voice, gesture, eye gaze, posture, gait, and haptics. The last theme covers the measurement and analysis of the above factors. This work is primarily addressed at advanced researchers in nonverbal communication and behavior.

Communication: Tests and Measures

2.94. *Sourcebook of nonverbal measures: Going beyond words.* Manusov, V. (2009/2005). New York: Routledge. 540 pp. P99. Includes twenty-seven full-text instruments. Covers social skills, affectionate communication, touch avoidance, perception, emotional expressiveness, visual affect, interactional synchrony, conversational equality, speech rate, expression of rapport, and other variables for individuals and dyads. Contains participant-completed measures, passive observation coding systems, and observational measures and methods for dynamic interactive behaviors. A list of full-text measures in this book is located at http://libguides.hofstra.edu/TMdb/Manusov2009.

COMMUNITY AND PREVENTION PSYCHOLOGY

2.95. *APA handbook of community psychology.* Bond, M. A., Garcia de Serrano, I., & Keys, C. (Eds.). (2016). Washington, DC: American Psychological Association. 1201 pp. HM1019. Two-volume set. This set covers traditional and emerging areas of interest in community psychology. Volume 1 (*Theoretical Foundations, Core Concepts, and Emerging Challenges*) begins with the history and paradigm of community psychology, then goes on to identify synergies with feminism, liberation psychology, and other psychology subdisciplines. It then discusses its core concepts of empowerment, prevention, social support, and participation and how diversity and multiculturalism interact with the opportunities and challenges of community psychology. Volume 2 (*Methods for Community Research and Action for Diverse Groups and Issues*) covers various research methods, such as action research and program evaluation and methods for creating community change in a variety of settings. It then addresses particular social issues, including immigration, health care, substance abuse, educational disparities, environmental issues, and disasters. The last sections cover working with different groups such as Asian Americans, Latinos/as, indigenous peoples, Arab Americans, LGBTQI, women and girls, and children and adolescents, and the education and careers of community psychologists.

2.96. *Cambridge handbook of international prevention science.* Israelashvili, M., & Romano, J. L. (Eds.). (2017). New York: Cambridge University Press. 1068 pp.

RA790. This work on prevention of mental health problems is unique in two aspects. The first is the breadth of the issues, risks, situations, and prevention methods and programs addressed. The second is the breadth of the geographic locations in which these phenomena are encountered and prevention methods and programs implemented. Part I begins by addressing issues in prevention such as policy development, economics and cost-effectiveness of prevention, international ethics of prevention, multicultural and social justice perspectives, and methodological and statistical issues in conducting reliable and valid longitudinal prevention research. It then addresses implementation in various settings: recreational nightlife, career management under economic uncertainty, victimization of racial/ethnic minorities and immigrants, childhood antisocial behavior and social exclusion, school counseling, parenting among immigrants, issues among international student populations, adolescent risk behaviors, disasters, social hatred, and violence. Part II addresses prevention efforts in various geographic areas: Internet addiction in South Korea; early intervention programs in Singapore; substance abuse in Bhutan, Spain, Hong Kong, and Latin America; coping skills in Australia; suicide in India; university counseling in Thailand; school shootings in the United States and Europe; childhood sexual abuse in the United States; adolescent programs in Mexico; early progress in Croatia; stress prevention in Germany; school interventions in Italy; parenting programs in Spain; youth risk prevention in Poland; prevention of HIV/AIDS spread; and stigma in Swaziland and Botswana.

Community and Prevention Psychology: Tests and Measures

2.97. *Assessing children in the urban community.* Mercer, B. L., Fong, T., & Rosenblatt, E (Eds). (2016). New York: Routledge. 245 pp. BF722. This work takes a community psychology approach to assessment, expanding traditional psychological assessment, which focuses on diagnosis and treatment, to include social and cultural contexts in the assessment process and the psychological report. Section I focuses on community psychology as it relates to managed care, policy, assessment settings, and interventions. Section II covers collaborative assessment, social justice, issues of undocumented immigrants, race and culture, cross-cultural supervision, vicarious trauma, and training. Section III presents case studies in community-based psychological assessment.

2.98. *Compendium of psychosocial measures: Assessment of people with serious mental illnesses in the community.* Johnson, D. L. (2010). New York: Springer. 545 pp. RC473. This volume provides information about 372 measures intended to be used in research with severely mentally ill individuals. The measures are divided into twenty-nine areas: general background information; functional assessment; community living; social functioning; global assessment; level of psychopathology; insight and judgment; stress; social problem solving and coping; social support; quality of life; consumer satisfaction; continuity of care; treatment adherence; substance abuse; environmental measures and group processes; housing; cultural issues; special purpose methods; agency performance evaluation; work behavior; family measures; premorbid adjustment; psychotic symptoms; depression; mania; anxiety; screening; and empowerment, recovery, and stigma. For each measure, the title, primary source(s), purpose, description, reliability, validity, measure source, and comments are provided. Because these measures are all intended for use with severe mental illness, it will be most useful to advanced graduate students and researchers working with that population.

Community and Prevention Psychology: Bibliographies

2.99. Families and communities: An annotated bibliography. Brossoie, N., Graham, B., & Lee, S. (2005). *Family Relations: An Interdisciplinary Journal of Applied Family Studies*, 54(5), 666–675. Resources for family social scientists focusing on the nexus of families and communities by highlighting recent theoretical, methodological, and empirical contributions.

2.100. La ricerca-azione in Italia: Spunti per una bibliografia (Action research in Italy: A bibliography). Galuppo, L., & Risorsa, U. (2006). *Rivista di Psicologia del Lavoro e dell' Organizzazione*, 12(2–3), 261–268. Brief Italian bibliography on action research published from the 1970s through 2006. Items are organized into methodological and epistemological studies, community psychology, educational psychology, and organizational studies.

COMPARATIVE PSYCHOLOGY

2.101. *APA handbook of comparative psychology*. Call, J. (Ed.). (2017). Washington, DC: American Psychological Association. 1830 pp. BF671. Two-volume set. This set provides one-stop shopping for both historical and current theories, methods, and research in comparative psychology. Volume 1 (*Basic Concepts, Methods, Neural Substrate, and Behavior*) covers the definition(s) of comparative psychology, trends and themes, methods (laboratory, field, observation, experimental), DNA population data, measurement tools, statistical models, methods for studying animal personality, and comparative cognition. It also covers evolution of behavior; adaptation; cognition; sociality, language, and domestication; instinct; behavioral genetics; attachment; neural substrates of emotions and behaviors; and biological rhythms. Finally,

it covers various forms of behavior, including communication; play; exploration; maternal, paternal, and alloparental behavior; courtship and mate choice; predator-prey interactions; territorial aggression; conflict resolution; friendship; and prosocial behavior. Volume 2 (*Perception, Learning, and Cognition*) covers sensation, hearing, vision, chemoreception, perceptual categorization, object and face perception, attention, and memory. It also covers conditioned learning, decision making, relational thinking, serial learning, social learning, animal culture, spatial cognition, homing and navigation, delayed gratification, innovation, inferential reasoning, empathy, self-recognition, and animal welfare science.

CONSUMER AND ECONOMIC PSYCHOLOGY

2.102. *Cambridge handbook of consumer psychology*. Norton, M. I., Rucker, D. D., & Lamberton, C. (2015). New York: Cambridge University Press. 767 pp. HF5415. The twenty-seven chapters of this timely volume provide comprehensive coverage of research in specific areas of consumer psychology, with a focus on research conducted within the past ten years. Part I ("Individual Consumer Decision-Making and Behavior") focuses on individual issues such as consumer well-being, persuasion, emotions, evolutionary perspectives, and neuroscientific and developmental approaches. Part II ("Interpersonal and Social Consumer Psychology") emphasizes interpersonal and social issues such as presence of others, signaling identity, social power and status, gift giving, and sharing of consumer information with others. Part III ("Societal Structures") focuses on how consumer behavior is influenced by their culture, economic constraints, political and moral alliances, and public and collective spending, and on how consumers can influence these factors through their consuming behavior. Each chapter also provides an agenda for future research in the particular area, making this volume of particular value to those pursuing research in this area.

2.103. *Cambridge handbook of psychology and economic behavior*. Lewis, A. (Ed.). Cambridge, England: Cambridge University Press. 565 pp. HB74. Interest in consumer and economic behavior has increased during the past decade, and this volume aims to address theories and research at the individual, group, and market levels. Following an introduction and discussion of theories and methods in part I, part II covers psychology of finance: the stock market, stock prices, saving and borrowing, household finances, and corporate social responsibility. Part III covers individual consumer behavior: consumption, identity, wealth, and happiness. Part IV addresses psychology of finance in the public sector: the size and role of government and tax evasion and avoidance. Part V examines how personal economic psychology is related to sustainable consumption, car ownership and use, and environmental values and morale. Finally, part VI addresses neuroscience and evolutionary psychology of economics and consumption.

CREATIVITY

2.104. *Cambridge handbook of creativity and personality research.* Feist, G. J., Reiter-Palmon, R., & Kaufman, J. C. (Eds.). (2017). Cambridge, England: Cambridge University Press. 427 pp. BF408. In contrast to *Handbook of Research on Creativity* (see below), which largely focuses on external factors influencing, facilitating, or blocking creativity, this volume focuses on factors within the individual related to creativity. Part I covers openness, intellect, curiosity, interests, creative self-concept, and environmental variability and dispositional plasticity. Part II covers creativity and mood, emotions, motivation, psychopathology, personality disorders, and creativity as positive and negative personality. Part III covers the relationship of creativity to the Big Five personality traits, sense of humor, individuality, creativity in teams, entrepreneurial innovation, and effects of creativity training programs on individual characteristics. It also addresses existing themes and future research directions.

2.105. *Handbook of research on creativity.* Thomas, K. (Ed.). (2013). Cheltenham, England: Edward Elgar. 559 pp. BF408. This work takes a multidisciplinary approach to creativity, with authors from psychology, sociology, philosophy, economics, history, and education. Part I provides an overview of creativity research, sources and conditions for creativity, and a critical analysis of what is and is not researched. Part II focuses on conceptualizations of creativity, including creativity and Marxism, creativity as designer capitalism, creativity in science and engineering, lived experience of creative identification, malevolent creativity, evaluating creativity, and sociological perspectives on social and national recognition of creativity. Parts III and IV focus on processes and practices of creativity, both individual and collaborative. Part V addresses factors that facilitate or create barriers to creativity and the role of copyright as a creativity incentive. Part VI covers leading and managing creativity, including European cultural policies, "creative industries," enhancing creativity of groups and teams, creativity in research and development, and the role of scientific leaders in creativity in the sciences.

Creativity: Bibliographies

2.106. Bibliography of recently published books on creativity and problem solving. Dutcher, A. J. (2004). *Journal of Creative Behavior*, 38(4), 282–284. Bibliography of published books on creativity and problem solving.

DEVELOPMENTAL PSYCHOLOGY

2.107. *APA dictionary of lifespan developmental psychology.* VandenBos, G. R. (2013). Washington, DC: American Psychological Association. 473 pp. BF712. Contains 7,500 entries specifically designed for those who study or conduct research in developmental psychology. Entries are listed alphabetically, and cover four areas: theories (e.g., Piagetian stages, learning theory), biosocial (e.g., heredity, sexual maturation), cognitive (e.g., memory, neuroscience), and psychosocial (e.g., family, education, employment) components of development throughout the life span. Entries range from one sentence to half a page in length and provide abbreviations and cross-referencing. An excellent reference to have nearby while reading scholarly literature.

2.108. *Attachment theory and research: New directions and emerging themes.* Simpson, J. A., & Rholes, W. S. (Eds.). (2015). New York: Guildford Press. 452 pp. BF575. This volume presents recent research on attachment theory. This research includes studies on the classic areas of interest (e.g., early attachment relationships as they relate to later relationships, attachment and dependence, and the impact of stress on attachment). It also includes research on neuroscience and attachment, regulation of relationships, sexuality, and parenting; how attachment plays out in organizational settings; health behavior; care of the aged; individual and couples therapy; and early interventions with at-risk infants and young children. In addition to presenting research findings, this work also indicates what questions were not answered, and each chapter ends with questions for future research.

2.109. *Cambridge handbook of environment in human development.* Mayes, L. C., & Lewis, M. L. (Eds.). (2012). Cambridge, England: Cambridge University Press. 723 pp. HQ767. The purpose of this volume is to address environment not as a peripheral factor in child development, but as a central factor. Part I (on the "environmental" variable) examines proximal and distal environments, risk and adversity, maternal care, and new assessment techniques to identify proximal and distal environmental risk factors. Part II ("Contemporary Themes") addresses the interaction of genetic and social factors, systems perspectives, new approaches in considering environmental risk, and the changeability of the environment over time. Part III ("Environments") covers a variety of environments, including parental care, family environment, early care, education and intervention programs, school, siblings and peers, neighborhoods, rural versus urban environments, poverty, social networks, marital health, parental psychopathology, illicit drug use environments, early exposure to domestic and community violence, child maltreatment, the cultural organization of the child's environments, and electronic media as environment. Part IV ("Measurement") covers measurement of parenting behavior, home environment, parental psychopathology and adaptive functioning, social support, networks and capital, child stress reactivity, and mixed model analyses for repeated-measures data.

2.110. *Child psychology: A handbook of contemporary issues* (3rd ed.). Balter, L., & Tamis-LeMonda, C. S. (Eds.). (2016). New York: Routledge. 505 pp. BF721. The third edition of this work includes updated research in development, including individual differences, dynamic systems and processes, and developmental contexts. The first three sections cover research that is organized by age—infancy, childhood, and adolescence—and covers self-regulation, attachment, language acquisition, cognition and social cognition, sibling and peer relationships, learning, decision making, morality, ethnic-racial identity, social aggression, and digital communication. The fourth section covers contextual issues, including family systems approaches to social development, neighborhood context, ethnically diverse families, risk and resilience, digital play contexts, and antipoverty programs. Chapters reflect a broad range of research methodologies.

2.111. *Handbook of child psychology and developmental science* (7th ed.). Lerner, R. M. (Ed.). (2015). Hoboken, NJ: John Wiley and Sons. 3969 pp. BF721. Four-volume set. First published in 1946, this long-standing set, now in its seventh edition, was known in former renditions as *Handbook of Child Psychology* and *Carmichael's Manual of Child Psychology*. This set provides one-stop shopping for authoritative and comprehensive treatments of long-standing and emerging topics in child psychology and developmental science. Volume 1 (*Theory and Methods*) covers topics such as dynamic systems, biology, human evolution, embodiment, agency, models of socialization, culture, emotional development and consciousness, personal and cultural identities, moral development, self-regulation, developmental psychopathology, positive development, systems, and various research methodologies. Volume 2 (*Cognitive Processes*) covers brain, cognitive, perceptual, and attentional development; symbolic representation; conceptual and language development; literacy; executive functioning and reasoning; memory; spatial and time sense; the development of play; gender; and cultural development. Volume 3 (*Social, Emotional, and Personality Development*) covers temperament; regulation; relationships; resilience; illness and disability; effects of discrimination, race, class, and ethnicity; maltreatment; prosocial development; achievement motivation and engagement; morality; concept of self; sexuality; gender; peer and romantic relationships; religion and spirituality; and violence and aggression. Volume 4 (*Ecological Settings and Processes*) covers development in time and place, family diversity, peer groups, school and organized activities, children at work, digital media, children in neighborhoods and economic status, children in war and disaster, and children in cultural context. Each volume and chapter can be used independently of the others.

2.112. *Handbook of children and youth studies*. Wyn, J., & Cahill, H. (Eds.). (2015). New York: Springer. 926 pp. HQ767. This volume is unique in that it approaches experiences of children and youths primarily from nontraditional and contemporary themes such as social justice, citizenship, labor, bodies, and spirituality. One of the premises is that the lines between childhood, adolescence, and adulthood are blurred, and research should reflect that. In addition, the research covered was conducted on numerous continents. A sample of the nontraditional topics addressed includes social geographies; gender-based violence in school classrooms; embodiment of sexuality; sexual health and well-being in a world of common pornography; young people's experiences of identity and social class; staying in or leaving rural places; citizenship participation, particularly in troubled areas; youth work identities; ideas of nationhood; rhythms and flows of digital daily life; online gaming culture; cell phone culture; educational aspirations; ideas of consumption; and religion/spirituality. This work contains many tables and charts and presents many alternative ways of thinking about the lives of children and adolescents in the rapidly changing social and economic environments in which they develop.

2.113. *Handbook of developmental psychopathology* (3rd ed.). Lewis, M., & Rudolph, K. D. (2014). New York: Springer. 852 pp. RJ499. This work provides a comprehensive examination of theory and research in the area of developmental psychology. Published in 2014, it incorporates DSM-5 diagnostic criteria and classifications and recently implemented research methodologies. In addition to addressing developmental psychopathology within the DSM-5 classification system, however, it provides multiple conceptual perspectives on the development of psychopathology. Part I addresses issues and theories, including nature/nurture integration, assessment issues, epidemiology, and resilience. Part II focuses on context such as family, schooling, peer relationships, stressors, and culture. Part III covers neuroscience issues such as behavioral genetics, MRI data, biology, temperament, and puberty changes. Part IV covers early childhood issues: attachment, early deprivation, prematurity and failure to thrive, and sleep issues. Part V covers disruptive disorders: ADHD, aggression and violence, and conduct disorder. Part VI addresses emotional disorders: depression, self-injury, borderline psychopathology, suicide risk, anxiety, and obsessive-compulsive behavior. Part VII covers problems of control: substance use, eating disorders, and elimination disorders. Part VIII covers chronic developmental disorders: autism spectrum disorders, intellectual disabilities, gender dysphoria, and personality pathology. Part IX covers trauma disorders: child maltreatment, PTSD, and dissociative disorders.

2.114. *Handbook of intraindividual variability across the life span.* Diehl, M., Hooker, K., & Sliwinski, M. J. (2015). New York: Routledge. 371 pp. BF697. This volume is unique in its coverage of intraindividual variability (IIV) over the life span. It provides comprehensive coverage of data collection and analysis methodologies. Topics covered include the history, nature, and meaning of IIV; IIV in motor skills; learning; mood; neuropsychological functioning; attention; personality; and health behavior. Key issues in research, such as vulnerability versus resilience, covariation, short-term versus long-term IIV, psychometrics, factor structures, discriminant validity, multiple-time scale design and analysis, and computational developmental science. Chapters include an introduction, review of existing research, new theoretical developments, conclusions and implications, suggestions for new research, and extensive reference lists.

2.115. *Handbook of pediatric psychology* (4th ed.). Roberts, M. C., & Steele, R. G. (2009). New York: Guilford Press. 808 pp. RJ47. This book contains fifty-one chapters on pediatric psychology (psychology practice with children having medical issues, particularly if they are ongoing and traumatic). Six major areas are covered: part I, "Professional Issues"; part II, "Cross-cutting Issues" (crossing medical/psychology boundaries); part III, "Medical, Developmental, Behavioral, and Cognitive-Affective Conditions"; part IV, "Public Health Issues"; part V, "Systems" (of which the child is part); and part VI, "Emerging Issues." Chapters are relatively short and highly focused as well as being heavily referenced, yet they are easy to read, providing explanations of terminology. This book will be especially useful to clinicians already working in medical settings and to those interested in doing so; the reference lists also make it a useful starting point for researchers interested in this area.

2.116. *Handbook of preschool mental health: Development, disorders, and treatment* (2nd ed.). Luby, J. L. (Ed.). (2017). New York: Guilford Press. 416 pp. RJ499. This book provides an overview of mental health in two- to six-year-old children. Part I covers developmental psychopathology, risk and resilience, particularly sensitive periods of development, protective and risk factors from the environment and early caregiving, and brain development during this age period. Part II addresses behavioral and emotional disorders, specifically oppositional defiant and conduct disorders; attention deficit hyperactivity, anxiety, and depressive disorders; autism spectrum disorder; and attachment and sleep disorders in this age group. Part III focuses on empirically supported interventions, including parent-child interaction, cognitive-behavioral and attachment-based parent-child therapies, and updates on early interventions for autism spectrum disorder and psychopharmacological treatment of preschoolers. The book ends with a chapter on integrating translational developmental neuroscience into a model intervention.

2.117. *Oxford handbook of the development of play.* Pellegrini, A. D. (2011/2015). Oxford: Oxford University Press. 377 pp. BF 717. Part of the Oxford Library of Psychology, this handbook provides comprehensive treatment of current theory, methods, and research on play from interdisciplinary perspectives. It covers definitions and cultural beliefs, theories, methods of conducting research, and the dimensions and functions of play throughout the life span, including tool use, locomotion, gender and temperament, social aspects of play with peers and other age groups, playground activity, social pretend play, technology and play, and the implications for learning and educational policy. Each chapter begins with an abstract and keywords and contains suggestions for further research.

2.118. *Routledge international handbook of young children's thinking and understanding.* Robon, S., & Quinn, S. F. (Eds.). (2015). London: Routledge. 505 pp. LB1139. This work brings together theory about, current research on, and case examples of young children's thinking in a variety of contexts. Part I addresses the development of play, creativity, social cognition, memory and thought, causal explanations, and narrative abilities. Part II covers children's understanding of social interactions, school readiness, private speech, metacognition and self-regulation, and sensitive periods. Part III covers how children make sense of the world, including working theories, shared understanding, pretend play, musical and mathematical thinking, and experiences with digital technologies. Part IV covers how researchers think about, measure, document, and reach conclusions from children's behavior.

Developmental Psychology: Tests and Measures

2.119 *Assessing adolescent psychopathology: MMPI-A / MMPI-A-RF* (4th ed). Archer, R. P. (2016). New York: Routledge. 459 pp. RJ503. The fourth edition of this work provides a strong historical foundation on the development of the MMPI-A and MMPI-A-RF. Aimed at both researchers and clinicians, it incorporates both developmental issues in assessment and the latest research on these MMPI forms. Topics covered include adolescent development and psychopathology, development of the forms, administration and scoring issues, psychometric issues, the basic clinical scale and codetype correlates for adolescents, and additional scales within each form.

2.120. *Assessing children's well-being: A handbook of measures.* Naar-King, S., Ellis, D. A., & Frey, M. A. (Eds.). (2004). Mahwah, NJ: Lawrence Erlbaum. 307 pp. RJ50. Contains twenty full-text instruments; an additional forty-four instruments are reviewed. Topics covered are health status and quality of life, adherence, pain management, child behavior, child development, child coping, cognition, attributions, attitudes, environment, and consumer satisfaction. Full-text measures are in the appendixes. A list of full-text measures in this book is located at http://libguides.hofstra.edu/TMdb/Naar-KingEllisFrey2004.

2.121. *Assessment scales in child and adolescent psychiatry.* Verhulst, F. C., & Van Der Ende, J. (2006). Abingdon, England: Taylor and Francis. 220 pp. RJ503. Includes forty-six full-text measures used with children and adolescents; also contains reviews and sample items from other measures. Contains general rating scales of behavior and symptoms, strengths, and difficulties. Also includes scales for specific problems, including anxiety, obsessive-compulsive disorder, depression, suicide, eating disorders, tics, ADHD, conduct disorders, substance abuse, and global impairment. For each scale there are commentary, information on alternate forms, properties of the scale and subscales, psychometric information, information on use, key references, and author/publisher contact information. Some scales are in the public domain, others are reproduced with permission, and some are commercial. An alphabetical list of measures is on pages 219–220. This work will be valuable to researchers at all levels, although some commercial tests may be restricted to those with professional credentials. A list of full-text measures in this book is located at http://libguides.hofstra.edu/TMdb/VerhulstVanDerEnde2006.

2.122. *Handbook of tests and measurements for black populations.* Jones, R. L. (Ed.). (1996). Hampton, VA: Cobb & Henry. 1205 pp. BF176. Two-volume set. Includes eighty-two full-text measures. Other measures for which full text is not provided in this set are also covered. Measures in this set were developed in response to concerns about measures developed and validated on white populations being administered to black populations. Underlying the work is the view that tests and measures should be based on African American history, characteristics, experiences, behaviors, and needs. Many of the constructs have applicability to other populations, but some are specific to African Americans or other racial/ethnic minorities (e.g., coping with racism, African American identity development, African self-consciousness). Rationale, development, and psychometrics are provided for all measures. Some of the measures are from theses and dissertations; they may have more and newer documentation since publication of this volume. With the exception of the introductory chapter, each chapter begins with an abstract, discusses its topic, presents full-text assessment tools and/or reviews them, and ends with a "for further information, contact" box. Volume 1 covers measures for infants, cognitive approaches and measures for children, self-esteem measures for children, race-related measures for children, a variety of measures for adolescents and young adults, language assessment and attitude measures, parental attitudes and values measures, and measures of family structure and dynamics. Volume 2 contains worldview measures, physiological measures, and neuropsychological assessment; measures of spirituality, acculturation, life experiences,

and values; race identity attitude measures; stress, racism and coping measures; mental health delivery measures; fair employment testing concepts and work environment and organizational assessment measures; research program–based measures; and a variety of other measures. In addition to the eighty-two full-text measures, chapters contain many useful tables and diagrams. A list of full-text measures in this book is located at http://libguides.hofstra.edu/TMdb/Jones1996.

2.123. *Measuring health-related quality of life in children and adolescents: Implications for research and practice.* Drotar, D. (1998). Mahwah, NJ: Lawrence Erlbaum Associates. 372 pp. RJ380. Contains four full-text instruments and reviews of other instruments covering a broad range of topics of conceptual, ethical, and practical issues in measuring health-related quality of life in children and adolescents. Also covers assessment related to specific health-related issues such as diabetes, asthma, low birth weight, cancer, cystic fibrosis, AIDS, growth problems, and Turner syndrome. A list of full-text measures in this book is located at http://libguides.hofstra.edu/TMdb/Drotar1998.

2.124. *Mirrors for behavior III: An anthology of observation instruments.* Simon, A., & Boyer, E. G. (Eds.). (1974). Wyncote, PA: Communication Materials Center. 758 pp. LB1131. Ninety-nine full-text instruments covering school-aged children are included; most are designed to be used in some type of educational setting. Covers affective and cognitive communication, psychomotor behavior, activity, content of communication, sociological structure, and physical environment. An overview and review of specific issues in observation is followed by summaries for each of the instruments. Summaries indicate subject of observation, number of subjects to be observed, collection methods, dimensions, settings, coding units, personnel required, and uses reported. The full-text instruments follow the summary section. A list of full-text measures in this book is located at http://libguides.hofstra.edu/TMdb/SimonBoyer1974.

2.125. *Oxford handbook of child psychological assessment.* Saklofske, D. H. Reynolds, C. R., & Schwean, V. L. (Eds.). (2013). Oxford: Oxford University Press. 860 pp. BF722. This book surveys the foundations, models, special topics, and practice of assessment for clinical and educational purposes. Its thirty-six chapters begin with abstracts and keywords and are organized into four major sections. Part 1 ("Foundations") covers theory, measurement, and statistical issues; psychometric versus actuarial interpretations of intelligence and aptitude; projective techniques; group assessments; cultural variation–adapting tests for cross-language use; diagnosis; classification and screening systems; the ICF-CY; and responsible use of tests. Part 2 ("Models") covers models of intelligence, aptitude and achievement, neuropsychological and personality assessment, behavioral assessment, and therapeutic assessments. Part 3 ("Practice") addresses history taking, clinical interviewing, the mental status exam, testing of cognitive ability, neuropsychology, memory, personality and affect, academic achievement, learning and study, creativity, and behavior. Part 4 ("Special and Emergent Topics") covers assessment alternatives, assessing mild intellectual disability, integration of models of dyslexia, testing accommodations, forensic assessment, subjective well-being, parenting style, and effective instruction. References are included; this book will be useful to graduate students and novice and experienced researchers who want to learn about or keep up-to-date on issues in child assessment.

2.126. *Pain in children: Nature, assessment, and treatment.* McGrath, P. A. (1990). New York: Guilford Press. 466 pp. RJ365. Contains twenty full-text instruments. This volume covers nature of children's pain experiences, assessment of pain, complexity of the nociceptive system, pharmacological interventions, nonpharmacological interventions, integrated pain management, acute pain, recurrent pain, and chronic pain. Instruments are in the appendix. A list of full-text measures in this book is located at http://libguides.hofstra.edu/TMdb/McGrath1990.

2.127. *Tests and measurements in child development: Handbook I.* Johnson, O. G., & Bommarito, J. W. (1976). San Francisco, CA: Jossey-Bass. 524 pp. BF722. This work covers tests for children aged birth to twelve years. It provides information on approximately 300 measures of cognition, personality and emotional characteristics, perceptions of environment (nonfamily), self-concept, environment (family), motor skills, brain injury, sensory perception, physical attributes, miscellaneous attitudes and interests, social behavior, and other variables. For each measure, it provides title, author, population for use, variable measured, type of measure, source from which measure may be obtained (frequently an item in the bibliography), description of the measure, reliability and validity information, and a bibliography referencing works on the measure. It also contains a useful test title index as well as other indexes. **NOTE:** See *Tests and Measurements in Child Development: Handbook II* for tests for children twelve to eighteen years old.

2.128. *Tests and measurements in child development: Handbook II.* Johnson, O. G. (1976). San Francisco, CA: Jossey Bass. 1327 pp. BF722. Two-volume set. This work covers tests for children twelve to eighteen years old. It provides information on approximately 900 measures of cognition, personality and emotional characteristics, perceptions of environment (nonfamily), self-concept, environment (family), motor skills, brain injury, sensory perception, physical attributes, miscellaneous attitudes and interests, social behavior, vocational interests, and other variables. For each measure, it provides title, author, population for use, variable measured, type of measure, source from which measure may be obtained (frequently an item in the bibliography), description of the measure,

reliability and validity information, and a bibliography referencing works on the measure. It also contains a useful test title index as well as other indexes. **NOTE:** See *Tests and Measurements in Child Development: Handbook I* for tests for children aged birth to twelve years.

Developmental Psychology: Bibliographies

2.129. *An annotated bibliography on children's development of social inclusion and respect for diversity.* Romero, M. (2010). New York: Columbia University—National Center for Children in Poverty. 8 pp. Annotated bibliography of books, articles, reports, and other resources on how children aged birth to ten years develop concepts related to social inclusion and respect for diversity. This document is available at https://academiccommons.columbia.edu/catalog/ac:135666.

2.130. Annotated bibliography supporting high-risk foster youth in transition: Research findings. Martinez, N. I. (2010). *Illinois Child Welfare*, 5(1), 169–183. Annotated bibliography of articles addressing the following in high-risk foster youth: mental health outcomes, such as symptoms of depression or post-traumatic stress disorder; educational outcomes (e.g., short term such as attendance and long term such as graduation); placement stability (reunification, adoption, or preventing premature placement disruption); independent living or independence upon aging out of foster care; and reduction in risk of violence or delinquency.

2.131. *Annotated bibliography: The impact of deployment on children; A review of the quantitative and qualitative literature.* Borden, L. M., et al. (2011?). Tucson: Arizona Center for Research and Outreach (AZ REACH). 101 pp. Detailed, annotated bibliography on the impact of parental deployment on child and family functioning during Operation Enduring Freedom (OEF) and Operation Iraqi Freedom (OIF). Annotations cover works on internalizing behavior problems, externalizing behavior problems, academic adjustment, family problems (family violence and other family problems), peer problems and physical health. This document is available online at https://reachmilitaryfamilies.umn.edu/sites/default/files/upload_material/Compiled Annotated Bibliography_Impact of Deployment on Children_AZ REACH.pdf.

2.132. Bibliography: Current world literature. (no authorship indicated). (2003). *Current Opinion in Psychiatry*, 16(4), 473–493. Bibliography of literature published in *Current Opinion in Psychiatry* between early 2002 and early 2003. Items cover child and adolescent psychiatry and services research and outcomes.

2.133. Bibliography: Current world literature. (no authorship indicated). (2008). *Current Opinion in Psychiatry*, 21(4), 422–437. Bibliography of articles on child and adolescent psychiatry, services research and outcome, and medical comorbidity.

2.134. Pediatric psychosomatic medicine: An annotated bibliography. Pao, M., Ballard, E. D., Raza, H., & Rosenstein, D. L. (2007). *Journal of Consultation and Liaison Psychiatry*, 48(3), 195–204. Not represented as exhaustive or comprehensive, this bibliography covers clinical issues relevant to children and adolescents with medical illnesses; includes developmental issues, familial interactions, diagnostic categories, and pharmacologic concerns.

DISSOCIATIVE DISORDERS

2.135. *Dissociation and the dissociative disorders: DSM-V and beyond.* Dell, P. F., & O-Neil, J. A. (Eds.). (2009). New York: Routledge. 864 pp. RC553. This is a comprehensive volume of what was known about dissociative disorders at the time of publication. It begins with an overview of dissociation, followed by developmental approaches, including attachment, relational context, adaptive functions of dissociation, and attachment trauma and dissociation. The next two parts address the issue of normal versus abnormal dissociations. Part V addresses chronic pathological dissociation, including trauma-related dissociation of the personality, somatoform dissociation, and psychoanalytic viewpoints. Part IV covers the neurobiology of dissociation. Other topics covered include multiple personality disorder, dissociative amnesia and fugue, depersonalization disorder, dissociation in post-traumatic stress, borderline personality disorder and substance abuse, and dissociation and psychosis, including hallucinosis. The final chapters address assessment and treatment of dissociation and developing a further delineation of pathological dissociation and a research agenda for the future.

EATING DISORDERS AND OBESITY

2.136. *Night eating syndrome: Research, assessment, and treatment.* Lundgren, J. D., Allison, K. C., & Stunkard, A. J. (2012). New York: Guilford Press. 299 pp. RC552. This is one of the few books on night eating syndrome (NES), first declared a diagnosis by researchers in 1955 and classified under "Other Specified Feeding or Eating Disorder." There are five major sections: part I, "Introduction and History"; part II, "Biology"; part III, "Relation to Other Clinical Syndromes"; part IV, "Assessment"; and part V, "Treatment." Chapters are relatively brief (ten to twenty pages long), but highly focused and referenced. Research on this syndrome is relatively new and limited in terms of sample size and population, but the authors do an excellent job of presenting what is available. They also include actual assessment tools for NES. This book would be useful to clinicians encountering this disorder, and particularly to researchers seeking assessment tools and previous research on NES.

2.137. *Oxford handbook of eating disorders.* Agras, W. S. (2010). Oxford: Oxford University Press. 499 pp. RC552. Part of the Oxford Library of Psychology, this book is aimed at beginning and experienced clinicians, with the goal of helping them better understand specific aspects of eating disorders, related medical and sociological issues, and evidence-based practices in treatment of eating disorders. The book has four major sections: part 1, "Phenomenology and Epidemiology"; part 2, "Approaches to Understanding Eating Disorders"; part 3, "Assessment and Comorbidities of Eating Disorders"; and part 4, "Prevention and Treatment." Chapters include an abstract, keywords, literature review, conclusions, and suggestions for further research. Although written before the DSM-V was issued, it addresses diagnostic issues with suggestions for the DSM-V. An excellent resource for graduate students in clinical areas and practicing clinicians.

2.138. *Wiley handbook of eating disorders.* Smolack, L., & Levine, M. P. (Eds.). (2015). Chichester, England: John Wiley and Sons. 986 pp. RC552. Two-volume set. This set provides one-stop shopping for research on eating disorders. Volume 1 (*Basic Concepts and Foundational Research*) contains thirty-seven chapters in six major sections. One of the great features of this set is that section I (definitions and history) covers unusual eating behaviors throughout early history, a table indicating in which countries and in what years articles were published about disordered eating behaviors in medical and psychiatric journals between the last quarter of the 1800s and the first half of the 1900s, and how eating disorders have been conceptualized and classified in each edition of the *Diagnostic and Statistical Manual of Mental Disorders* (DSM) from its first edition up to and including DSM-5. Section II covers epidemiology (prevalence and incidence) of eating disorders, not only in Western societies, but also in Asian and underrepresented countries as well. Section III covers diagnosis, including psychiatric comorbidity and ethnic/cultural issues. Section IV covers biopsychiatric, cognitive-behavioral, feminist, psychodynamic, and sociocultural theories. Section V covers risk and protective factors, including body image; cultural issues; dieting; familial and gender issues; media and peer influences; and personality, stress, and trauma factors. Section VI covers particular populations, including athletes, dancers, boys and men, and life span periods. Volume 2 (*Assessment, Prevention, Treatment, Policy, and Future Directions*) contains thirty-one chapters in five major sections. Section VII covers screening, clinical interviews, and research tools for assessing eating disorders (including a chart of studies in which measures have been used). Section VIII covers various approaches to prevention, including school-based, feminist, cognitive and behavioral, media, ecological, and social policy approaches. Section IX covers treatment issues, including team care, medical complications, psychiatric comorbidity, and the "natural course" of eating disorders. Section X covers various treatment approaches, including various therapies, psychopharmacology, medical and family approaches. Section XVI covers controversies such as measurement of outcome and whether obesity is a disorder, as well as social policy and future research. Chapters are relatively short (approximately fifteen pages long) but topic-specific and with extensive referencing on the topic. This work will be valuable to all researchers from advanced undergraduates through faculty and researchers.

Eating Disorders and Obesity: Tests and Measures

2.139. *Handbook of assessment methods for eating behaviors and weight-related problems: Measures, theory, and research* (2nd ed.). Allison, D. B., & Baskin, M. L. (2009). Los Angeles, CA: Sage. 701 pp. RC552. Contains forty-five full-text instruments. Covers quality of life in obesity and eating disorders; attitudes toward obese people; body image; restrained eating; physical activity; food intake; hunger and satiety; binge-eating and purging; eating-disordered thoughts, feelings, and behaviors; and eating and weight-related problems in children. Instruments are in appendixes organized by chapter. Psychometric and administration/scoring information is provided, as well as author/publisher contact information. A list of full-text measures in this book is located at http://libguides.hofstra.edu/TMdb/AllisonBaskin2009.

2.140. *Obesity assessment: Tools, methods, interpretations (A reference case: The RENO Diet-Heart Study).* St. Jeor, S. (Ed.). (1997). New York: Chapman & Hall. 932 pp. RC628. Includes forty-four full-text instruments. Based on the RENO Diet-Heart Study, this book examines diagnosis and treatment of obesity. Instruments can be used in normal weight and obese adults and cover physical activity, dietary intake, attitudes, eating and dieting behaviors, personality and psychological factors, emotions and stress, genetics, and lifestyle. A list of full-text measures in this book is located at http://libguides.hofstra.edu/TMdb/StJeor1997.

EDUCATIONAL AND SCHOOL PSYCHOLOGY

2.141. *APA educational psychology handbook.* Harris, K. R., Graham, S., & Urdan, T. C. (2012). Washington, DC: American Psychological Association. 1843 pp. LB1051. Three-volume set. This set provides comprehensive coverage of education as it stands in the twenty-first century. Volume 1 (*Theories, Constructs, and Critical Issues*) contains twenty chapters in four major sections, covering the boundaries of educational psychology, research design, critical current topics, and emerging issues. Volume 2 (*Individual Differences and Cultural and Contextual Factors*) contains twenty-one chapters in five

major sections. These cover individual differences in intelligence(s), learning styles, motivation, and achievement; instructional influences on motivation; engagement and moral development; ethnic and racial identity; racial achievement gaps; peer relations; prevention of bullying and sexual harassment; parental involvement; class size; and teacher beliefs, characteristics, and practices. Volume 3 (*Application to Learning and Teaching*) contains twenty-three chapters in five sections covering applications throughout the life span; individual assessments for teaching and learning and large-scale assessments for accountability; accommodations for students with disabilities; teaching in core educational areas such as reading, writing, math and science; and instructional methods and teaching special populations.

2.142. *Handbook of educational psychology* (3rd ed.). Corno, L., & Anderman, E. M. (Eds.). (2016). New York: Routledge. 481 pp. LB1051. This third edition is sponsored by Division 15 of the American Psychological Association. Its thirty chapters integrate new developments in theory and research methods with previous theories and research. Part I ("Psychological Inquiry in Education") addresses philosophical issues in theory and research. Part II ("Functional Processes for Learning") addresses cognition, emotion, and motivation. Part III ("Learner Readiness and Development") addresses learner issues, while part IV ("Building Knowledge and Subject Development") addresses educator issues. Finally, part V ("The Learning and Task Environment") addresses learning environments inside and outside of school, sociocultural issues, and assessment. Chapters are short (ten to fifteen pages long), highly focused, and heavily referenced. This volume will be useful to a wide audience, including education researchers, teacher educators, teachers, policy makers, and students of educational psychology.

2.143. *Handbook of learning disabilities* (2nd ed.). Swanson, H. L., Harris, K. R., & Graham, S. (2013). New York: Guilford Press. 716 pp. LC4704. The second edition of this work provides a comprehensive and timely treatment of research on learning disabilities (LDs). Chapter authors make instructional recommendations based on synthesis of years of empirical field-based research. Part I provides a history of the learning disabilities field, definitions and classifications, and instruction and methodology, as well as addressing issues of linguistically diverse students, adults with LDs, legal issues, and the state of current science. Part II addresses causes and manifestations, including attention deficit hyperactivity, executive functions, basic cognitive processes, memory issues, language processing, social cognition, behavior genetics, and diagnosing and treating specific disabilities. Part III covers domain-specific instruction interventions for reading, mathematics, writing, science, social studies, and history. Part IV covers a number of general instructional models, and part V covers methods and measures, including experimental and quasi-experimental methods, single-case design, meta-analysis, neurobiological and qualitative research methods, and findings.

2.144. *International handbook of emotions in education.* Pekrun, R., & Linnenbrink-Garcia, L. (2014). New York: Routledge. 698 pp. LB1072. This work provides an interdisciplinary treatment of theory and research on the role of emotions in educational environments. Part I covers basic concepts of affect and emotions, goal pursuit, motivations, attributions, and emotional intelligence and regulation in educational contexts. Part II covers emotions and their regulation: interest, enjoyment, curiosity, shame, anxiety, confusion, boredom, and emotions as they relate to testing. Part III covers specific education subjects, family and cultural influences on emotion/emotion regulation in school, and teacher emotions. Part IV covers measurement: self-report and observation, as well as other sources of input.

2.145. *International handbook of research on teachers' beliefs.* Fives, H., & Gill, M. G. (2015). New York: Routledge. 502 pp. LB2840. This work covers a broad range of teacher beliefs and the impact of those beliefs on educational practice. Its twenty-seven chapters cover six areas. "Foundations of Teachers' Beliefs Research" reviews historical and theoretical perspectives, the development of teachers' beliefs, and how those beliefs affect teaching practices. "Studying Teachers' Beliefs" covers research rationale and methodologies. "Teachers' Identity, Motivation and Affect" covers the intersection of those factors with politics and self-efficacy beliefs. "Contexts and Teachers' Beliefs" covers beliefs about learning, classroom climate, assessment, and shared norms. "Teachers' Beliefs about Knowing and Teaching within Academic Domains" covers beliefs about teaching and learning of specific academic subjects. "Teacher's Beliefs about Learners" addresses beliefs about development and learning, cultural diversity, English-language learning, special needs students, and inclusion. Chapters are topic specific (fifteen to twenty pages long), with useful reference lists. This book will be useful to school psychology researchers interested in research on teachers and how their beliefs affect their and others' behavior in schools.

2.146. *Handbook of pediatric psychology in school settings.* Brown, R. T. (Ed.). (2015/2004). Mahwah, NJ: Lawrence Erlbaum. 819 pp. LB1027. This volume focuses on pediatric psychology services (psychology practice with children having medical issues, particularly if they are ongoing and traumatic) delivered within school settings. Typically, pediatric psychology is first experienced in a medical setting, but children still need these services when they return to school, whether delivered by a pediatric psychologist or a school psychologist. This work begins with an overview of pediatric psychology and collaboration with schools in providing services, followed by areas of prevention and health promotion (e.g., injury

prevention, early identification, medical adherence) and illnesses encountered in schools, such as asthma, diabetes, pediatric HIV/AIDS, seizure disorders, sickle cell anemia, hemophilia, cancer, gastrointestinal disorders, traumatic brain injury, and cystic fibrosis; elimination disorders; and developmental disorders such as fetal alcohol syndrome, ADHD, autism spectrum disorders, and mental retardation. It then addresses interventions within schools, including behavioral and group interventions, psychoeducational and pharmacological approaches, and consultation with school personnel and family/caregivers. It finishes with discussion of professional, ethical, and legal issues pertaining to pediatric psychology in the school setting. This work will be of benefit to graduate students, researchers, and practitioners interested in this topic.

2.147. *Routledge international handbook of social psychology of the classroom.* Rubie-Davies, C. M., Stephens, M. M., & Watson, P. (Eds.). (2015). New York: Routledge. 367 pp. LB3013. This work is a comprehensive and integrated presentation of theory and research on social cohesion in the classroom, organized into the major areas of motivation, self-concept, engagement, student-teacher relationships, teacher expectations, classroom management, culture, and identities. Part I covers student motivation. Parts III and IV cover student racial/ethnic identity, stigma, in-school and online discrimination, social status, and stereotype threat. Part IV covers teacher-student relationships and their influence on motivation, competence, engagement, achievement, social withdrawal, and barriers to teacher-student relationships. Part V addresses classroom climate and management, including observation and student report methodologies and teacher authority. Parts VI and VII cover teacher expectations, judgment, motivations, emotions, emotional skills and self-efficacy, and professional boundaries as they relate to student and teacher well-being.

Educational and School Psychology: Tests and Measures

2.148. *Handbook of psychoeducational assessment: Ability, achievement, and behavior in children.* Andrews, J., Janzen, H. L., & Saklofske, D. H. (Eds.). (2001). San Diego, CA: Academic Press. 512 pp. LB3051. This handbook provides a brief summary of some of the major tests for assessing ability, achievement, and behavior in children and adolescents. Data from other review publications are included, as well as reliability and validity findings. The case studies and references will be particularly useful to graduate students, faculty, and practitioners in school psychology.

2.149. *Handbook of tests and measurement in education and the social sciences* (3rd ed.). Lester, P. E., Inman, D., & Bishop, L. K. (2014). Lanham, MD: Rowman & Littlefield. 343 pp. LB3051. Includes 126 full-text instruments covering forty domains in education and social sciences, particularly industrial and organizational psychology. Most are from published (but noncommercial) sources; several are from dissertations. Test summaries include comments, test construction, sample(s), psychometrics, references, and the measure itself. There is also a chapter with information on related commercial instruments. A list of full-text measures in this book is located at http://libguides.hofstra.edu/TMdb/LesterInmanBishop2014.

2.150. *Handbook of tests and measurements for black populations*. Jones, R. L. (Ed.). (1996). Hampton, VA: Cobb & Henry. 1205 pp. BF176. Two-volume set. Includes eighty-two full-text measures. Other measures for which full text is not provided in this set are also covered. Measures in this set were developed in response to concerns about measures developed and validated on white populations being administered to black populations. Underlying the work is the view that tests and measures should be based on African American history, characteristics, experiences, behaviors, and needs. Many of the constructs have applicability to other populations, but some are specific to African Americans or other racial/ethnic minorities (e.g., coping with racism, African American identity development, African self-consciousness). Rationale, development, and psychometrics are provided for all measures. Some of the measures are from theses and dissertations; they may have more and newer documentation since publication of this volume. With the exception of the introductory chapter, each chapter begins with an abstract, discusses its topic, presents full-text assessment tools and/or reviews them, and ends with a "for further information, contact" box. Volume 1 covers measures for infants, cognitive approaches and measures for children, self-esteem measures for children, race-related measures for children, a variety of measures for adolescents and young adults, language assessment and attitude measures, parental attitudes and values measures, and measures of family structure and dynamics. Volume 2 contains worldview measures, physiological measures, and neuropsychological assessment; measures of spirituality, acculturation, life experiences, and values; race identity attitude measures; stress, racism and coping measures; mental health delivery measures; fair employment testing concepts and work environment and organizational assessment measures; research program–based measures; and a variety of other measures. In addition to the eighty-two full-text measures, chapters contain many useful tables and diagrams. A list of full-text measures in this book is located at http://libguides.hofstra.edu/TMdb/Jones1996.

2.151. *Measuring bullying victimization, perpetration, and bystander experiences: A compendium of assessment tools.* Hamberger, M. E., Basile, K. C., Vivolo, A. M. (Comps. and Eds.). (2011). Atlanta, GA: Centers for Disease Control and Prevention (CDC), National Center for Injury Prevention and Control. 119 pp. SUDOC HE 20. Includes thirty-three full-text instruments. There are four sections, containing "bully only" scale, "victim only" scales, "bully and victim" scales, and "bystander, fully, and/or victim" scales. Most, though not all, scales are Likert-type scales. They are available online at http://www.cdc.gov/violenceprevention/pub/measuring_bullying.html. A list of full-text measures in this book is located at http://libguides.hofstra.edu/TMdb/HambergerBasileVivolo2011.

2.152. *Mirrors for behavior III: An anthology of observation instruments.* Simon, A., & Boyer, E. G. (Eds.). (1974). Wyncote, PA: Communication Materials Center. 758 pp. LB1131. Ninety-nine full-text instruments covering school-aged children are included; most are designed to be used in some type of educational setting. Covers affective and cognitive communication, psychomotor behavior, activity, content of communication, sociological structure, and physical environment. An overview and review of specific issues in observation is followed by summaries for each of the instruments. Summaries indicate subject of observation, number of subjects to be observed, collection methods, dimensions, settings, coding units, personnel required, and uses reported. The full-text instruments follow the summary section. A list of full-text measures in this book is located at http://libguides.hofstra.edu/TMdb/SimonBoyer1974.

2.153. *Practitioner's guide to empirically based measures of school behavior.* Kelley, M. L., & Noell, G. (Eds.). New York: Kluwer Academic/Plenum. 231 pp. RJ503. This volume reviews approximately one hundred tests used to measure child and adolescent behaviors in the school setting, focusing particularly on functional behavior assessment (FBA) and curriculum-based assessment (CBA). Topics covered include ADHD, oppositional defiant disorder, conduct disorder, adjustment, interpersonal relations, attention, personality, home situations, school situations, self-concept, social behavior, and social skills, among others. For each test, the guide includes the purpose, population, description, administration and scoring, psychometrics, clinical utility, strengths and limitations, and author/publisher information. Most, but not all, of the measures reviewed are commercial and require a fee, and some may also require professional credentials for purchase. This volume will be of use to advanced graduate students and beginning and advanced researchers in school psychology.

2.154. *Special educator's comprehensive guide to 301 diagnostic tests* (rev. ed.). Pierangelo, R., & Giuliani, G. (2006). San Francisco, CA: Jossey-Bass. 484 pp. LC 4019. This volume provides an overview of assessment in special education, including how a child is recommended for assessment, the role of the family, the role of the evaluator, understanding the student's behavior during testing, and reporting test results. It provides one to two pages of information for each of 301 tests in 25 domains. The chapter for each domain begins with a brief introduction to issues in that domain, followed by information for each test, which includes author/ publisher contact information, administration time, type of administration (group, individual), age/grade level, purpose of the test, subtest information, and strengths of the test. Virtually all of the tests are commercial tests that have undergone extensive psychometric evaluation. Tests cover academic achievement; anxiety and depression; aptitude; attention-deficit/hyperactivity; auditory processing; autism spectrum; behavioral disorders; deafness and hearing impairments; emotional disturbance; English as a second language and bilingual education; gifted and talented; infants, toddlers, and preschoolers; intelligence; learning disabilities; mathematics; mental retardation; neuropsychology; occupational therapy; personality; other psychological issues; reading; speech and language; visual processing; and written language. There is also an appendix containing referral forms commonly used in the special education process. **NOTE:** This is the revised edition of the 1998 *Special Educator's Complete Guide to 109 Diagnostic Tests*.

Educational and School Psychology: Bibliographies

2.155. La ricerca-azione in Italia: spunti per una bibliografia (Action research in Italy: A bibliography). Galuppo, L., & Risorsa, U. (2006). *Rivista di Psicologia del Lavoro e dell' Organizzazione*, 12(2–3), 261–268. Brief Italian bibliography on action research published from the 1970s through 2006. Items are organized into methodological and epistemological studies, community psychology, educational psychology, and organizational studies.

2.156. Schoolyard bullying: Peer victimization; An annotated bibliography. Renfrow, T. G., & Teuton, L. M. (2008). *Community and Junior College Libraries*, 14(4), 251–275. Annotated bibliography of scholarly articles, books, and websites aimed at psychologists, teachers, school administrators, and parents. Materials cover statistics, attitudes toward school bullying, prevention, intervention, and research methodologies.

ETHICS

2.157. *APA handbook of ethics in psychology*. Knapp, S. (2012). Washington, DC: American Psychological Association. 1008 pp. BF76.4 .A635 2012. This two-volume set takes a "positive ethics" or "active ethics" approach, encouraging psychologists not merely to avoid misconduct and consequences, but also to think about professional and research ideals. Volume 1 (*Moral Foundations and Common Themes*) covers ethical foundations, codes, social justice ideals, ethical decision making in clinical settings, and institutional ethical conflicts. It also covers ethical issues in professional practice, such as competence, emotional well-being of the practitioner, compe-

tence with diverse populations, boundaries, spiritual and religious issues, sexual relationships, informed consent, confidentiality, dealing with dangerous clients, patients at risk of treatment failure, termination, regulation, risk management, and business issues for professional psychologists. Volume 2 (*Practice, Teaching, and Research*) begins by addressing issues related to practice such as treating children and adolescents, older adults, multiple-person therapy, assessment, forensic issues, school and industrial/organizational practice, and the newer fields of life and executive coaching and telehealth. It then addresses ethical issues in academic and training programs such as creating ethical climates within programs, supervision issues, and teaching professional ethics. It ends by discussing research ethics, including conducting ethical research, research with vulnerable populations, deception, animal research, and research ethics in animal research.

2.158. *Handbook of professional and ethical practice for psychologists, counsellors and psychotherapists* (2nd ed.). Tribe, R., & Morrissey, J. (Eds.). Hove, England: Routledge. 341 pp. BF76. This volume provides an overview of ethical concerns that may arise in therapeutic practice. Five major areas are covered: professional practice and ethical considerations, legal considerations and responsibilities, clinical considerations and responsibilities, practice and ethical considerations when working with diverse populations, and research supervision and training. Chapters address the particular subject matter, provide useful vignettes and analysis, and end with reference lists. This is a British publication, so some of the legal details may apply only to that system.

Ethics: Bibliographies

2.159 *Annotated bibliography: Attitudes toward animal research (1998–2013)*. Yahner, E. (2014). Washington, DC: Humane Society of the United States Institute for Science and Policy. Annotated bibliography of books, chapters, and articles on attitudes toward animal research from a variety of disciplines. Downloadable from http://animalstudiesrepository.org/hum_ed_bibs/8/.

2.160. A four-part working bibliography of neuroethics. Part 1: Overview and reviews: Defining and describing the field and its practices. Buniak, L., Darragh, M., & Giordano, J. (2014). *Philosophy, Ethics, and Humanities in Medicine*, 9(9). Part 1 of a four-part bibliography. This part includes a repository of international papers, books, and chapters that address the field in general and present discussion(s) of more particular aspects and topics of neuroethics. This first installment lists reviews and overviews of the discipline, as well as broad summaries of basic developments and issues of the field. This open-access article is located at https://www.ncbi.nlm.nih.gov/pmc/articles/PMC4047768/.

2.161. A four-part working bibliography of neuroethics. Part 2: Neuroscientific studies of morality and ethics. Darragh, M., Buniak, L., & Giordano, J. (2015). *Philosophy, Ethics, and Humanities in Medicine*, 10(2). Part 2 of a four-part bibliography. This part covers works from 2002 through 2013 addressing the "neuroscience of ethics"—studies of putative neural substrates and mechanisms involved in cognitive, emotional, and behavioral processes of morality and ethics. Covers 397 articles, 65 books, and 52 book chapters that present empirical/experimental studies, overviews, and reviews of neural substrates and mechanisms involved in morality and ethics, and/or reflections upon such studies and their implications. This open-access article is located at https://www.ncbi.nlm.nih.gov/pmc/articles/PMC4334407/.

2.162 A four-part working bibliography of neuroethics. Part 3: "Second tradition neuroethics"—Ethical issues in neuroscience. Martin, A., Becker, K., Darragh, M., & Giordano, J. (2016). *Philosophy, Ethics, and Humanities in Medicine*, 11(7). Part 3 of a four-part bibliography. This part includes 1,137 papers, 56 books, and 134 book chapters published from 2002 through 2014, covering ethical issues in neuroimaging, neurogenetics, neurobiomarkers, neuropsychopharmacology, brain stimulation, neural stem cells, neural tissue transplants, pediatric-specific issues, dual-use, and general neuroscience research issues. This open-access article is located at https://www.ncbi.nlm.nih.gov/pmc/articles/PMC5028939/.

2.163. A four-part working bibliography of neuroethics. Part 4: Ethical issues in clinical and social applications of neuroscience. Becker, K., Shook, J. R., Darrah, M., & Giordano, J. (2017). *Philosophy, Ethics, and Humanities in Medicine*, 12(1). Part 4 of a four-part bibliography, a work in progress. This part focuses on clinical and social applications of neuroscience, including treatment-enhancement discourse; issues arising in neurology, psychiatry, and pain care; neuroethics education and training; neuroethics and the law; neuroethics and policy and political issues; international neuroethics; and discourses addressing "trans-" and "post-" humanity. This open-access article is located at https://www.ncbi.nlm.nih.gov/pmc/articles/PMC5452349/.

2.164. *Scientific misconduct: An annotated bibliography.* http://www.teachpsych.org/resources/Documents/otrp/resources/keith-spiegel94.pdf. Keith-Spiegel, P., Aronson, K., & Bowman, M. (1994). Statesboro, GA: Society for the Teaching of Psychology (APA Division 2), Office of Teaching Resources in Psychology (OTRP), Department of Psychology, Georgia Southern University. Annotated bibliography of scholarly and popular articles and books on scientific misconduct, created as a resource for teaching in psychology.

EXPERIMENTAL PSYCHOLOGY

2.165. *Stevens' handbook of experimental psychology and cognitive neuroscience* (4th ed.). Wixted, J. T. (Ed.).

(2018). New York, John Wiley and Sons. Five volumes. BF181. Previous editions of this five-volume set were entitled Stevens' Handbook of Experimental Psychology. The title change reflects changes in the field, in which theories of mind and neuroscience have been incorporated into virtually every area of what was traditionally considered experimental psychology. Volume I (Learning & Memory) covers virtually all areas of memory, including working memory, memory and attention, aging, motivation, and education; also includes autobiographical memory and eyewitness memory. Volume II (Sensation, Perception & Attention) covers attention, vision research, taste, touch, olfaction, motor control, and spatial perception among other topics. Volume III (Language & Thought) covers discourse, bilingualism concepts and categories, culture and cognition, creativity, reasoning, sentence processing and other cognitive and perceptual processing. Volume IV (Developmental & Social Psychology) covers topics such as development of attention, language development, implicit social cognition, moral development, and development of executive function. Volume V (Methodology) covers hypothesis testing, inference, model comparison, response time modeling, neural networks and neurocomputational modeling, neural time series, convergent methods, and open science. This set provides one-stop shopping for all users, from advanced undergraduates through advanced researchers.

FAMILY PSYCHOLOGY

Family Psychology: Tests and Measures

2.166. *Handbook of family measurement techniques.* Tsouliatos, J., Perlmutter, B. F., & Strauss, M. A. (Eds.). (2001). Thousand Oaks, CA: Sage. 1208 pp. HQ728. This three-volume set is a different item, rather than a second edition of the 1990 work with the same title and authors. Volume 1 of this set contains the contents of the entire 1990 edition. This includes an introductory chapter on family measurement principles and techniques, followed by detailed abstracts for 504 instruments measuring dimensions of marital and family interaction, intimacy and family values, parenthood, roles and power, and adjustment. Each topical chapter provides a discussion of the topic before the abstracts are presented. Detailed abstracts include availability information, variables measured, instrument type (e.g., self-report, projective), description, sample items (where permission was acquired), commentary, and references. All measures appear in their entirety in a published work (most measures), or permission was provided to deposit the entire instrument with the National Auxiliary Publication Service (NAPS 1-3). In addition to these 504 detailed abstracts, abbreviated abstracts are provided for another 472 instruments that met the same criteria (total of 976 instruments abstracted). These original abstracts from the 1990 work, now forming volume 1 of the 2001 set, are for instruments from the 1929–1986 literature, with the major focus being the 1975–1986 literature. Volume 2 of this three-volume set contains 367 additional abstracts for measures that were newly developed or substantially revised during 1987–1996. It begins with chapters on family measurement overview and developing, interpreting, and using family assessment techniques. Detailed abstracts in volume 2 cover family relations; marital relations; parent-child relations; family adjustment, health, and well-being; and family problems. Abstracts include variables measured, instrument type, samples measured, description, sample items (where permission was acquired), psychometrics, commentary, keywords, references, and availability information. Volume 3 contains the full text of 168 of the 367 instruments abstracted in volume 2. In addition to the actual instrument, scoring instructions are provided, as well as the original source of the instrument. This set will be highly valuable to clinicians, researchers, graduate students, and advanced undergraduates interested in measurement of numerous family issues. A list of full-text measures in volume 3 is located at http://libguides.hofstra.edu/TMdb/TsouliatosPerlmutterStrauss2001.

2.167. *Handbook of measurements for marriage and family therapy*. Fredman, N., & Sherman, R. (1987). New York: Brunner/Mazel. 218 pp. RC488. Contains twenty-four full-text measures; also includes reviews of other measures. The full-text measures in this volume cover marital satisfaction, adjustment, agendas, trust, jealousy, conflict, and instability. Also included are measures of attitudes toward feminism and working women. Family-oriented measures include tests of family feeling, cohesion, strength, and adaptability. There are also quality-of-life scales for parents and adolescents and a family therapist rating scale. Entries for full-text measures typically contain an introduction, description, subscale descriptions, psychometrics, administration and scoring information, and a brief discussion. Some measures are longer than suitable for a book; for these items, samples are included and the location of the entire measure is identified. A list of full-text measures in this book is located at http://libguides.hofstra.edu/TMdb/FredmanSherman1987.

2.168. *Marriage and family assessment: A sourcebook for family therapy*. Filsinger, E. E. (Ed.). (1983). Beverly Hills, CA: Sage. 338 pp. HV697. Includes six full-text instruments. Also reviews other instruments. Full-text instruments include measures for marital adjustment, communication, agendas, and conflict, as well as family events and change, adaptability, and cohesion. There is also an entire section on observation in marriages, as well as discussion and review of other marriage and family measures. A list of full-text measures in this book is located at http://libguides.hofstra.edu/TMdb/Filsinger1983.

2.169. *Measuring intimate partner violence, victimization and perpetration: A compendium of assessment tools.*

Thompson, M. P., Basile, K. C., Hertz, M. F., & Sitterle D. (2006). Atlanta, GA: Centers for Disease Control and Prevention, National Center for Injury Prevention and Control. 163 pp. HV6626. Contains forty-two full-text instruments. Scales measure physical victimization, sexual victimization, psychological/emotional victimization, stalking victimization, physical perpetration, sexual perpetration, psychological/emotional perpetration, and stalking perpetration. Available at https://stacks.cdc.gov/view/cdc/11402. A list of full-text measures in this book is located at http://libguides.hofstra.edu/TMdb/ThompsonBasileHertzeSitterle2006.

FORENSIC PSYCHOLOGY

2.170 *APA handbook of forensic psychology*. Cutler, B. L., & Zapf, P. A. (Eds.). (2015). Washington, DC: American Psychological Association. 1139 pp. RA1148. "Forensic Psychology" refers to the application of both the science and practice of psychology to law, legal systems, and issues. This comprehensive work consists of two volumes. Volume 1 (*Individual and Situational Influences in Criminal and Civil Contexts*) has eighteen chapters in three sections: "Forensic Evaluation and Treatment in Criminal Cases," "Individual and Situational Predictors of Criminal Behavior," and "Applications of Forensic Psychology in Civil Cases." Volume 2 (*Criminal Investigation, Adjudication, and Sentencing Outcomes*) consists of seventeen chapters in three sections: "Victim and Offender Groups," "Criminal Investigations and Jury Trials," and "Sentencing and Incarceration." For consistency, each chapter has five major sections, addressing the importance of the problem, relevant psychological theory and principles, research review, practice and policy issues, and summary and conclusions. Topics particular to specific chapters are included in further subsections. This work provides a wealth of information for researchers and practitioners in forensic psychology.

2.171. *APA handbook of psychology and juvenile justice*. Heilbrun, K. (Ed.). (2016). Washington, DC: American Psychological Association. 735 pp. HV9104. This handbook consists of thirty-one chapters covering the legal, psychological/scientific, and applied issues involved in dealing with juvenile offenders. Individual chapters address very specific topics, which fall under broader topics such as legislation and legal theory of preventive justice for adolescents; adolescent social and intellectual development; patterns of offending, including desistance and persistence into adulthood; risk factors such as juvenile psychopathy, substance abuse, gang membership, and trauma; forensic assessment community and residential placement; and training and ethics in the particular issues pertaining to this population. This work provides a solid base for researchers in this area as well as practitioners with this population.

2.172. *Criminal psychology.* Helfgott, J. B. (Ed.). (2013). Santa Barbara, CA: Praeger. 1689 pp. HV6080. Four-volume set. This set provides a comprehensive treatment of the nature of criminality and its relationship to psychology. Volume 1 (*Theory and Research*) has three major sections. Section I provides an overview of criminal psychology and criminal behavior. Section II covers theoretical perspectives on development and desistance and psychophysiology and neuroanatomy of criminality, sociological and psychological perspectives, and personality and criminality. Section III covers predatory and affective aggression, female criminality, and substance abuse and psychiatric disorder as they relate to criminality. Volume 2 (*Typologies, Mental Disorders, and Profiles*) also contains three major sections. The first focuses on criminal typologies and criminal profiling. The second addresses types of crimes, including violent crimes, sex crimes, profit-driven crimes, political crime, terrorism, cybercrime, and copycat crimes. The third section details the many issues of psychopathy: conceptualization, assessment, psychopathic sex offending, sex differences in psychopathy, and domestic violence. Volume 3 (*Implications for Forensic Assessment, Policing and the Courts*) also covers three major areas. Section I focuses on forensic assessment, classification of juvenile offenders, and controversies around the evaluation of sexually violent predators. Section II addresses law enforcement interactions with individuals who are mentally ill, hostage negotiation, serial murder, profiling in serial homicide cases, and forensic evaluation of police officers. Section III covers law and the courts, including competency to stand trial, the insanity defense, sentencing, and mental health courts. Volume 4 (*Implications for Juvenile Justice, Corrections, and Reentry*) contains two major sections. The first covers the development of antisocial and criminal behavior in children and adolescents, correctional and treatment programs, bullying and callousness, psychopathy, juvenile homicide, and childhood trauma and justice. The second part addresses rehabilitation, risk reduction, therapeutic relationships in and out of prison, consequences of incarceration, women's prisons, and prisoner reentry into society. Throughout the set, empirical findings are related to practice and implications for future research and practice.

Forensic Psychology: Bibliographies

2.173 *Annotated bibliography: Juvenile justice risk/need assessment & juvenile justice websites.* National Institute of Corrections Information Center (NICIC). (2013). Aurora, CO: NICIC. Annotated bibliography of articles, reports, and websites on juvenile risk assessment, including recidivism risk, gender- and ethnicity-related risk, case studies of evidence-based juvenile justice programs, and risk factors related to various types of offenses. Also includes links to scales for juvenile risk assessment. Available at https://info.nicic.gov/nicrp/system/files/027615.pdf.

2.174. An annotated bibliography for the testifying child and adolescent psychiatrist. Ash, P., & O'Leary, P. J. (2011). *Child and Adolescent Psychiatric Clinics of North America*, 20(3), 577–590. Citing scholarly literature is often important in persuading fact finders that professional opinion has a scientific basis. This work is not comprehensive, but provides examples of literature that may be cited to bolster testimony.

2.175. Bibliography: Current world literature. (no authorship indicated). (2004). *Current Opinion in Psychiatry*, 17(5), 423–431. Selected bibliography of articles on forensic psychiatry, scientific communication, and developmental intellectual disorders, published from mid-2003 through mid-2004.

2.176. *Cognitive-behavioral therapy.* https://nicic.gov/library/package/cbt. National Institute of Corrections (NIC). Links to reports on and evaluations of cognitive-behavioral therapy (CBT) and evidence-based practice (EBP), CBT and female offenders, CBT and mentally ill offenders, CBT and probation, CBT and sex offenders, CBT program evaluations, CBT effectiveness with youth, moral reconciliation therapy (MRT), "Thinking for a Change" CBT programs, and general CBT effectiveness reports.

2.177. *Mental health services in criminal justice system settings: A selectively annotated bibliography, 1970–1997.* Van Whitlock, R., & Lubin, B. (1999). Westport, CT: Greenwood Press. 190 pp. Includes 1,264 citations to books and scholarly articles, about half of which are annotated. Most empirically based works are annotated; theoretical and practical works are annotated only if they are of major value. Items are from psychology, psychiatry, nursing, education, social work, and other related areas and are related to service provision to mentally ill and substance-abusing offenders in criminal justice settings.

GEROPSYCHOLOGY

2.178. *APA handbook of clinical geropsychology.* Lichtenberg, P. A., Mast, B. T., Carpenter, B. D., & Wetherell, J. L. (Eds.). (2015). Washington, DC: American Psychological Association. 1343 pp. RC451. Two-volume set. This set provides comprehensive coverage of both normative and non-normative issues in aging, using a scholar-practitioner approach. It takes a strength-based approach, reviewing empirical issues and indicating applications for practice. Volume 1 (*History and Status of the Field and Perspectives on Aging*) traces the history of geropsychology from the time of Plato onward and focuses on normative issues such as healthy aging, grandparenting, same- and different-sex relationships, and spirituality. Volume 2 (*Assessment, Treatment, and Issues of Later Life*) addresses non-normative issues such as depression, anxiety, substance abuse, cognitive impairments, reduced mobility, elder neglect, and other issues. Many of the empirical findings are also summarized in useful tables. Research is provided on both foundational issues and assessment and intervention. The fifty chapters of this work meet the goal of providing a treasure of research findings for researchers and indicating applications of those findings to practice for clinicians.

Geropsychology: Tests and Measures

2.179. *Assessing older persons: Measures, meaning and practical applications*. Kane, R. L., & Kane, R. A. (Eds.). (2000/2004). Oxford: Oxford University Press. 542 pp. HQ1061. Includes one hundred full-text instruments, as well as information on other instruments for which the full text is not included. This volume is a sequel to, rather than a second edition of, Kane and Kane's 1981 book *Assessing the Elderly: A Practical Guide to Measurement* (see below). It addresses the areas of assessment in the 1981 volume (function, health, emotion, cognition, and social well-being) and also addresses new areas such as assessment of family caregivers, physical environments, values and preferences, spirituality, and satisfaction. In addition to the full-text measures, this book provides information on selecting and using instruments, psychometric information, and caveats about their use. The section on applications of assessment covers comprehensive assessment and management, care planning for those in health-care settings, long-term case management, mandated assessments, and assessment of older adults who cannot communicate. A list of full-text measures in this book is located at http://libguides.hofstra.edu/TMdb/KaneKane2000.

2.180. *Assessing the elderly: A practical guide to measurement*. Kane, R. A., & Kane, R. L. (1981). Lexington, MA: Lexington Books. 301 pp. RC954.3 .K36. Contains thirty-three full-text instruments and reviews of other measures not included. This book covers the assessment of older people in long-term care, particularly physical functioning, activities of daily living, cognitive and affective functioning, general mental health, and social functioning. Chapters are thirty to sixty pages long; present a discussion of the issues; cover measures not included; present administration, scoring, and interpretation information for the included full-text measures, and have references. This book will be useful to researchers interested in the status and functioning of older people who are in long-term care. A list of full-text measures in this book is located at http://libguides.hofstra.edu/TMdb/KaneKane1981.

2.181. *Handbook of geriatric assessment* (4th ed.). Gallo, J. J. (2006). Sudbury, MA: Jones and Bartlett. 473 pp. RC953. Contains thirty-eight full-text instruments; also provides information on other measures not included in the book. The goal of this book is to enable multidimensional assessment by discussing the domains that are significant in the lives of older people and providing some full-text measures of those domains. Domains covered include cognition, depression, substance use and abuse, activities of daily living, social issues (support, care, mistreatment, economic, health, environment, spiritual), physical, pain, health, home, nursing homes, hospitalization, adherence to medical regime, interdisciplinary teamwork, and disaster preparedness and response. Chapters are ten to thirty pages long and contain a discussion of the issue; description of measures not included; actual measures with administration, scoring, and interpretation information; and references. Measures are reprinted with permission. This book will be valuable to researchers interested in any of the domains covered, as well as to practitioners. A list of full-text measures in this book is located at http://libguides.hofstra.edu/TMdb/Gallo2006.

2.182. *Research instruments in social gerontology*. Mangen, D. J., & Peterson, W. A. (1982–1984). Minneapolis: University of Minnesota Press. 1664 pp. HQ1061. Three-volume set. Contains 298 full-test instruments. Also reviews other instruments for which full text is not included. Volume 1 (*Clinical and Social Psychology*) covers intellectual functioning, personality, adaptation, morale and life satisfaction, self-concept and self-esteem, death and dying, environments, ethnic group identification, subjective age identification, life phase analysis, and perceptions of old people. Volume 2 (*Social Roles and Social Participation*) covers social participation roles, dyadic relations, parent-child relations, kinship relations, work and retirement, socioeconomic status and poverty, religiosity, friends, neighbors and confidants, voluntary associations, and leisure activities. Volume 3 (*Health, Program Evaluation, and Demography*) covers functional capacity, health, utilization of health services, individual needs and community resources, social program tracking and evaluation, effectiveness of long-term care, evaluating of cost of services, organizational properties, indexes for the aging of populations, demographic characteristics, and geographic mobility. A list of full-text measures in this book is located at http://libguides.hofstra.edu/TMdb/MangenPeterson1984.

Geropsychology: Bibliographies

2.183. *Bibliography of research and clinical perspectives on LGBT aging*. David, S., Asta, L., Cernin, P., & Miles, J. (2006). Washington, DC: American Psychological Association. 43 pp. Comprehensive bibliography of books and articles on aging in the LGBT community. Available at http://www.apadivisions.org/division-44/resources/advocacy/aging-bibliography.pdf.

2.184. Work with older people: A bibliography. Kegerreis, P. (2012). *British Journal of Psychotherapy*, 28(1), 117–124.

References to books and articles on psychodynamically oriented treatment covering general issues and individual, couples, family, group, and creative therapies.

HAPPINESS/WELL-BEING/QUALITY OF LIFE

2.185. *Oxford handbook of happiness.* David, S. A., Boniwell, I., & Conley Ayers, A. (2013). Oxford: Oxford University Press. 1097 pp. BF575. This volume provides one-stop shopping for researchers interested in happiness. It is comprehensive not only on the topics covered, but in disciplinary perspectives as well. Section I covers various conceptualizations of happiness, including broaden-and-build theory of positive emotions, endowment-contrast model, flow, emotional intelligence, religious engagement, self-regulation, and reward. Section II covers definitions of happiness, including the good life, well-being, eudaimonia, and autonomy. Sections III and IV cover philosophical and religious/spiritual approaches to happiness. Sections V and VI focus on geographical and societal issues and teaching of happiness. Section VII addresses happiness in organizations, including work design, psychological capital, work engagement and identity, encouragement of employee happiness, and executive well-being. Section VIII addresses issues on happiness in relationships, including attachment and social support. Sections IX and X cover the development and stability of happiness, and happiness interventions. A particularly interesting feature is located in chapter 14, which recommends what measures should not be used and those that should be used and the rationale for each.

Happiness/Well-Being/Quality of Life: Tests and Measures

2.186. *Assessing children's well-being: A handbook of measures.* Naar-King, S., Ellis, D. A., & Frey, M. A. (Eds.). (2004). Mahwah, NJ: Lawrence Erlbaum. 307 pp. RJ50. Includes twenty full-text instruments; an additional forty-four instruments are reviewed. Topics covered are health status and quality of life, adherence, pain management, child behavior, child development, child coping, cognition, attributions, attitudes, environment, and consumer satisfaction. Full-text measures are in the appendixes. A list of full-text measures in this book is located at http://libguides.hofstra.edu/TMdb/Naar-KingEllisFrey2004.

2.187. *KIDSCREEN questionnaires: Quality of life questionnaires for children and adolescents.* KIDSCREEN Group Europe. (2006). Berlin: Pabst Science. 231 pp. BF722. Includes six full-text instruments. The Health-Related Quality of Life (HRQoL) questionnaire is available in fifty-two-, twenty-seven-, and ten-item formats; one set (three) is for the child/adolescent and one set (three) is for the proxy (parent/caregiver). The fifty-two-item questionnaire was designed for research purposes and measures physical well-being, psychological well-being, moods and emotions, self-perception, autonomy, parent relation and home life, financial resources, social support and peers, school environment, and social acceptance (bullying). The twenty-seven-item version is designed for epidemiological studies and screening and measures a subset of the constructs measured by the fifty-two-item version. The ten-item version results in one global health-related quality of life score and is recommended for use in large epidemiological studies. This volume covers theoretical background and development of the instruments; psychometrics; administration and scoring; and norms for children, adolescents, and parents. The measures are presented in the book in English; the accompanying CD contains the measures in Czech, Dutch, French, German, Greek, Hungarian, Polish, Spanish, and Swedish. A list of full-text measures in this book is located at http://libguides.hofstra.edu/TMdb/KIDSCREENEuropeGroup2006.

2.188. *Measuring health: A review of quality of life measurement scales* (3rd ed.). Bowling, A. (2005). Maidenhead/Berkshire, England: Open University Press. 221 pp. RA407. Contains three full-text instruments. Reviews concepts of functioning, health, well-being, and quality of life and methodologies of measurement, including for psychological well-being, social networks and social support, subjective well-being, and broad quality of life. A list of full-text measures in this book is located at http://libguides.hofstra.edu/TMdb/Bowling2005.

2.189. *Measuring health-related quality of life in children and adolescents: Implications for research and practice.* Drotar, D. (1998). Mahwah, NJ: Lawrence Erlbaum Associates. 372 pp. RJ380. Contains four full-text instruments; also includes reviews of other instruments covering a broad range of topics of conceptual, ethical, and practical issues in measuring health-related quality of life in children and adolescents. Also covers assessment related to specific health-related issues such as diabetes, asthma, low birth weight, cancer, cystic fibrosis, AIDS, growth problems, and Turner syndrome. A list of full-text measures in this book is located at http://libguides.hofstra.edu/TMdb/Drotar1998.

2.190. *Quality of life: The assessment, analysis, and reporting of patient-reported outcomes* (3rd ed.). Fayers, P. M., & Machin, D. (2016). Chichester, England: John Wiley & Sons. 626 pp. R852. This book provides a comprehensive treatment of measuring quality of life as reported by patients. When addressing specific domains, the focus is on quality of life as it pertains to health outcomes. In its entirety, however, it is an excellent resource for all researchers interested in quality of life. Part 1 focuses on the development and validation of instruments for assessing quality of life and patient-reported outcomes. It addresses questions such as the definition of quality of life, why it should be measured, and how to measure it; principles of measurement scales; developing questionnaires; psychometrics; item response theory; item banks; and computer-adaptive tests. Part 2 focuses on assessing, analyzing, and reporting patient-reported outcomes and quality of life. This section covers choosing and scoring questionnaires, sample sizes, cross-sectional analysis, longitudinal data, death and quality-adjusted survival, reporting bias and response shift, meta-analysis, and interpretation. Each chapter ends with a conclusion and further readings. The appendix contains samples of generic quality-of-life instruments, disease-specific instruments, and domain-specific instruments (i.e., anxiety, pain, fatigue, disability).

Happiness/Well-Being/Quality of Life: Bibliographies

2.191. *Well-evolved life: Well-being, evolution and person-hood; An annotated bibliography*. Moore, K., & Minchington, L. (2014). Canterbury, NZ: Lincoln University. 186 pp. This annotated bibliography of 347 sources focuses on the overlap in the literature on human well-being, evolutionary (including biological) perspectives on human behavior, and person (including "the self"). It includes articles, books, and reports.

HEALTH PSYCHOLOGY

Health Psychology: Tests and Measures

2.192. *Assessment in health psychology*. Benyamini, Y., Johnston, M., & Karademas, E. C. (Eds.). (2016). Boston: Hogrefe. 345 pp. R726. This volume addresses key issues and reviews measures in health psychology assessment. Topics include social cognition and health behavior, self-efficacy and outcome expectancies, illness representations, health behavior, patient-physician communication and patient satisfaction, adherence to medical advice, stress and stressors, coping, social support, pain and pain behavior, functional status, self-rated health, quality of life, psychological adjustment, neuropsychological assessment, biological and physiological measures in health psychology, and assessment methods. Many useful tables listing and comparing measures are included.

2.193. *Designing and conducting health surveys: A comprehensive guide*. Aday, L. (1989). San Francisco: Jossey-Bass. 535 pp. RA408. Includes four full-text instruments (sections A–D at the end of the book) and lists other measures. Provides information on designing and conducting health surveys, including selecting topics; matching survey design to survey objectives; defining variables; selecting data collection methods; sample selection and size; formulation of questions about health, behavior, demographics, knowledge, and attitudes; data analysis; and research reporting. A list of full-text mea-

sures in this book is located at http://libguides.hofstra.edu/TMdb/Aday1989.

2.194. *Measuring health: A review of quality of life measurement scales* (3rd ed.). Bowling, A. (2005). Maidenhead/Berkshire, England: Open University Press. 221 pp. RA407. Contains three full-text instruments. Reviews concepts of functioning, health, well-being, and quality of life and methodologies of measurement, including for psychological well-being, social networks and social support, subjective well-being, and broad quality of life. A list of full-text measures in this book is located at http://libguides.hofstra.edu/TMdb/Bowling2005.

HISTORY

History: Bibliographies

2.195. *History of psychology: A guide to information sources*. Viney, W., Wertheimer, M. & Wertheimer, M. L. (1979). Detroit, MI: Gale Research. 502 pp. Z7204 or BF81. Selectively annotated bibliography of materials useful to scholars researching the history of psychology. It includes general works on history, major periodicals, development of psychology in specific countries and regions of the world, archives and manuscripts, historiography, systems and schools of psychology, specific content areas, and histories of related fields such as psychiatry, philosophy, sociology, and biology.

2.196. *History of psychology and the behavioral sciences: A bibliographic guide*. Watson, R. I. (1978). New York: Springer. 241 pp. Z7201 or BF81. Annotated bibliography includes guides to the literature, encyclopedias, bibliographies, biographical collections, archives, manuscript collections, and oral histories. Also included are historical accounts of psychology in general, branches, national psychology, school psychology, science, philosophy, psychiatry, psychoanalysis, physiology, neurology, anatomy, biology, medicine, anthropology, sociology, and readings. This work also covers methods of historical research, historiographic fields in psychology and other behavioral sciences, and historiographic theories.

History: Websites

2.197. *Chronology of noteworthy events in American psychology: Book sources*. https://www.cwu.edu/~warren/sources.html. Warren Street wrote the book *A Chronology of Noteworthy Events in American Psychology* in 1994 (American Psychological Association). The book is a general academic book, which lists significant dates and events from before 1892 through the early 1990s. This website is the bibliography of books, most of which are scholarly works in themselves, used in Street's research to create his book.

IDENTITY

2.198. *Oxford handbook of identity development*. McLean, K. C., & Syed, M. U. (2015). New York: Oxford University Press. 590 pp. BF697 .O94 2015. Part of the Oxford Library of Psychology, this work's aim is to apply Erik Erikson's developmental theory to current issues and research in identity development. The first five of eight sections have titles that begin with "Debate . . ." and address identity development over the life span; processes of identity development; narrative perspectives on identity development; internal, external, and interactional approaches; and culture and development. The following two chapters address applications and extensions to culture and education, work, political conflict, psychotherapy, internalization, body image, parenting, divorce, resilience, and social networking. The final chapter focuses on the state of current research and suggestions for future research. The thirty-four chapters focus on specific topics; each begins with a boxed abstract and keywords and ends with up-to-date references. This work will be valuable to advanced undergraduates, graduate students, researchers, and practitioners.

INDUSTRIAL AND ORGANIZATIONAL PSYCHOLOGY

2.199. *APA handbook of human systems integration*. Boehm-Davis, D. A., Durso, F. T., & Lee, J. D. (2015). Washington, DC: American Psychological Association. 625 pp. TA166. A basic tenet of this work is that one must go beyond a single focus on the worker, the tools, the task, or the environment, and examine them together—thus "human systems integration" (HSI). Part 1 examines the history of HSI, which arose from the university, engineering, and the military, and then discusses various perspectives and considerations in HSI, including cognitive work analysis; anthropometry; digital modeling of physical constraints; strength, endurance, and movement; neuroergonomics; sleep and fatigue; physical stressors; and slips and falls. Part II examines perceptual and cognitive issues, including auditory perception, attention, multitasking, workload, situation awareness, decision making, and augmented cognition; political and social considerations; and economic aspects of HSI. Part III examines displays and controls, including visual-spatial displays and automation; personnel issues such as selection, training, motivation, and the implications of aging; and team and organizational factors such as effectiveness, macroergonomics, and organizational culture. Individual chapters cover very specific topics and are fifteen to twenty pages long; reference lists are not that lengthy but contain a combination of major works and up-to-date references on the specific topic. Of use to researchers and designers in human factors research and application.

2.200. *APA handbook of industrial and organizational psychology*. Zedeck, S. (Ed.). (2011). Washington, DC: American Psychological Association. 2300 pp. HF5548. Three-volume set. This set addresses behavioral and structural issues that industrial and organizational psychologists deal with both theoretically and practically in both academic and applied settings. Volume 1 (*Building and Developing the Organization*) contains twenty chapters in three major sections: foundational issues, designing organizations and human resource systems, and designing work and structuring experiences. Volume 2 (*Selecting and Developing Members for the Organization*) consists of nineteen chapters in five major sections: foundations of selection and development, selection strategies and issues, evaluating individuals, evaluating systems, and developing members. Volume 3 (*Maintaining, Expanding, and Contracting the Organization*) contains twenty-four chapters in five major sections: relationships with work, fostering a positive environment and relationships, managing problems and politics, planning for change, and the societal context. Chapters are ten to forty pages long, with extensive references. This set will be most useful to graduate students, researchers, and practitioners.

2.201. *Deviant and criminal behavior in the workplace*. Elias, Steven M. (2013). New York: New York University Press. 259 p. HF5549. This timely book provides unique coverage of a spectrum of deviant and criminal behaviors in the workplace. It contains ten chapters covering topics such as the aftermath of workplace crime, fraud, human resource management, job stress, organizational deviance, perceived and actual injustice, personality, prevention, revenge-seeking, sexual harassment, workplace culture, workplace discrimination, and workplace violence. Each chapter begins with a case study. This book will be valuable to workplace professionals and particularly to researchers interested in this topic of growing concern.

2.202. *International handbook of work and health psychology* (3rd ed.). Cooper, C. L., Quick, J. C., & Schabracq, M. (2009/2015). Chichester, England: Wiley-Blackwell. 491 pp. HF5548. This book addresses how organizational issues in the workplace affect health. In addition to covering psychosocial workplace issues and sources of stress, it specifically focuses on individual and organizational intervention and prevention. The book is comprised of twenty-one chapters in five parts: Part I covers contextual issues as they relate to health, the "psychological contract," social context, job strain, and attendance pressure. Part II is on individual differences. Part III discusses the role of workplace factors. Part IV covers supporting individuals at work. Part V is on organizational approaches to health and well-being. This book would be particularly useful to researchers interested in intervention and prevention in the workplace and to those within an organization tasked with those duties.

2.203. *Oxford handbook of work engagement, motivation, and self-determination theory.* Gagne, M. (2014). New York: Oxford University Press. 444 pp. HF5549.5.M63 2014. This book provides unique, in-depth coverage of a very specific area of industrial/organizational psychology: self-determination theory and how it relates to work engagement and motivation. There are twenty-six chapters in five sections: part 1, "Conceptual Issues"; part II, "Individual Considerations"; part III, "Organizational and Contextual Considerations"; part IV, "Outcomes of Work Motivation"; and part V, "Domains of Application." Chapters begin with an abstract, are brief (ten to fifteen pages with three to five pages of references), and focus on how self-determination theory applies to specific workplace issues. While primarily an explication of the theory, chapters do reference empirical studies related to the rationale. This book will be particularly useful to those interested in developing a deeper understanding of this theory and also provides sufficient research references to provide a good grounding for researchers interested in working on this subject.

Industrial and Organizational Psychology: Tests and Measures

2.204. *Handbook of tests and measurement in education and the social sciences* (3rd ed.). Lester, P. E., Inman, D., & Bishop, L. K. (2014). Lanham, MD: Rowman & Littlefield. 343 pp. LB3051. Includes 126 full-text instruments covering forty domains in education and social sciences, particularly industrial and organizational psychology. Most are from published (but noncommercial) sources; several are from dissertations. Test summaries include comments, test construction, sample(s), psychometrics, references, and the measure itself. There is also a chapter with information on related commercial instruments. A list of full-text measures in this book is located at http:// libguides.hofstra.edu/TMdb/LesterInmanBishop2014.

2.205. *Measuring bullying victimization, perpetration, and bystander experiences: A compendium of assessment tools.* Hamberger, M. E., Basile, K. C., Vivolo, A. M. (Comps. and Eds.). (2011). Atlanta, GA: Centers for Disease Control and Prevention (CDC), National Center for Injury Prevention and Control. 119 pp. SUDOC HE 20. Includes thirty-three full-text instruments. There are four sections, containing "bully only" scale, "victim only" scales, "bully and victim" scales, and "bystander, fully, and/or victim" scales. Most, though not all, scales are Likert-type scales. They are available online at http://www.cdc.gov/violence prevention/pub/measuring_bullying.html. A list of full-text measures in this book is located at http://libguides .hofstra.edu/TMdb/HambergerBasileVivolo2011.

2.206. *Oxford handbook of personnel assessment and selection.* Schmitt, N. (Ed.). (2012). New York: Oxford University Press. 973 pp. BF431. This volume provides a comprehensive treatment of issues in and measurement in personnel assessment and selection. Part 1 provides an overview of the main topic, followed by the history and social context of personnel selection in part 2. Part 3 addresses research strategies, including concept and process of validation, job analysis, predictor measures, performance outcomes, organizational strategy and staffing, and meta-analysis. Part 4 focuses on constructs of individual differences, including cognitive abilities, personality, person-environment fit, physical capabilities, and use of composite predictors in selection. Part 5 covers predictor constructions, including selection interview, background data, simulations, individual psychological assessment, self-reports, predictive bias, and web-based assessments. Part 6 focuses on performance and outcomes assessment, including supervisor ratings, objective measures, organizational citizenship, voluntary turnover, trainability, and occupational safety. Part 7 covers societal and organizational issues such as applicant reaction to testing, legal constraints, time, diversity, team selection, globalization, "retooling," layoff selection, and contingent workers. Parts 8 and 9 cover implementation and sustainability of selection systems, conclusions, and future directions. Each chapter begins with an abstract and keyword box.

2.207. *Pfeiffer's classic inventories, questionnaires, and surveys for training and development.* Gordon, J. (2004). San Francisco, CA: Pfeiffer. 549 pp. HF5549. Includes thirty-seven full-text instruments. This work covers beliefs about working people and the management role; views of manager" current behavior, both self-rated and other-rated; and climate factors that shape organizations" practices and will help or hinder desired changes in management behavior. It includes measures of supervision, motivation, work values, locus of control, barriers to creativity and innovation, time management, mentoring, collaboration, leadership, communication, cross-cultural issues, trust, leadership, conflict management, and organizational type. Each measure is contained within its own chapter, each of which is fifteen to twenty pages long and typically includes a summary and discussion of the topic to be measured; the theory underlying the measure; existing research findings, with the questionnaire, administration, scoring, and interpretation information; and references. Measures have been reproduced with permission. This work will be useful to industrial/organizational psychologists and others conducting research in the workplace as well as for practitioners engaging in organizational and personnel assessment and development. A list of full-text measures in this book is located at http:// libguides.hofstra.edu/TMdb/Gordon2004.

2.208. *Taking the measure of work: A guide to validated scales for organizational research and diagnosis.* Fields, D. L. (2013). Charlotte, NC: Information Age Publishing. 326 pp. HM786. Includes 137 full-text measures. Measures in this work cover job satisfaction, organizational commitment, job characteristics, job stress, job roles, organizational justice, work-family conflict, person-organization fit, work behaviors, and work values. With few exceptions, measures are those asking employees to choose one or more preselected responses (i.e., close-ended questions). Each chapter begins with a brief discussion of the construct addressed within, followed by the relevant measures. For each measure, the following information is provided: title, description, reliability, validity, source/availability, items, and scoring. A list of full-text measures in this book is located at http://libguides.hofstra .edu/TMdb/Fields2013.

Industrial and Organizational Psychology: Bibliographies

2.209. *Gender-based violence in the world of work: Overview and selected annotated bibliography.* Cruz, A., & Klinger, S. (2011). Geneva, Switzerland: International Labor Organization. 80 pp. Working paper aimed at understanding gender-based violence in the workplace. Defines "gender-based violence" and "world of work" and presents human rights and business rationales for prevention initiatives. Includes risk factors for victims and perpetrators and covers child laborers, forced and bonded laborers, migrant workers, domestic workers, health services workers, and sex workers. The bibliography is on pages 23–69 and is organized by geography—international works, regional and country-based works—and tools, measures, and guides. Available at http://www.ilo.org/gender/Informa tionresources/WCMS_155763/lang-en/index.htm.

2.210. La ricerca-azione in Italia: spunti per una bibliografia (Action research in Italy: A bibliography). Galuppo, L., & Risorsa, U. (2006). *Rivista di Psicologia del Lavoro e dell' Organizzazione*, 12(2–3), 261–268. Brief Italian bibliography on action research published from the 1970s through 2006. Items are organized into methodological and epistemological studies, community psychology, educational psychology, and organizational studies.

2.211. Police performance measurement: An annotated bibliography. Tiwana, N., Bass, G., & Farrell, G. (2015). *Crime Science: An Interdisciplinary Journal*, 4(1). Annotated bibliography includes works on overviews, methodological issues, and performance management in other industries; national, international, and cross-national studies; frameworks; criticisms (particularly unintended consequences); crime-specific measures; practitioner guides; performance evaluation of individual staff; police department plans and evaluations; and annotated bibliographies in related areas. This open-access article

is available at https://crimesciencejournal.springeropen .com/articles/10.1186/s40163-014-0011-4.

2.212. Selected bibliography on diversity consulting: Supplement to the special issue on culture, race, and ethnicity in organizational consulting psychology. Leong, F. T. L., Cooper, S., & Huang, J. L. (2008). Special issue of *Culture, Race, and Ethnicity in Organizational Consulting Psychology*, 215–226. This bibliography is neither exhaustive nor comprehensive, but rather a collection of references that have been found to be helpful in multicultural consultation practice.

2.213. Sources and bibliography of selected human factors and ergonomics standards. Rodrick, D., & Karwowski, W. (2006). In W. Karwowski (Ed.), *Handbook of standards and guidelines in ergonomics and human factors* (pp. 569–589). Mahwah, NJ: Lawrence Erlbaum. Bibliography of selected human factors and ergonomics standards as of 2004 and books and articles on theoretical and empirical research on the standards.

INTELLIGENCE, MEMORY, AND CREATIVITY

2.214. *Handbook of intelligence: Evolutionary theory, historical perspective, and current concepts.* Goldstein, S., Princiotta, D., & Naglierii, J. A. (2015). New York: Springer. 498 pp. BF431. This work consists of thirty chapters in six sections. Parts I and II, "Introduction" and "Background," cover intelligence in nonprimates, nonhuman primates, the evolution of language, and the development of intelligence as a construct. Part III, "Theories of Intelligence," covers Wundt, James, Cattell, Thorndike, Goddard, Yerkes, Piaget, Binet, Wechsler, and Luria as well as newer concepts such as multiple intelligences, social and emotional intelligence, and creativity as intelligence. Part IV, "Assessment of Intelligence," covers assessments ranging from traditional models to models assessing emotional intelligence. Part IV, "Applications of Intellectual Theory," addresses applications such as success, executive functioning, and education. Part VI, "Conclusion," addresses past, current, and future concepts of intelligence and testing. Chapters are ten to twenty pages long, with two to five pages of references, making this an excellent resource for researchers investigating the social and conceptual development of intelligence.

2.215. *Wiley-Blackwell handbook of individual differences.* Chamorro-Premuzic, T., von Stumm, S., & Furnham, A. (Eds.). (2011). Malden, MA: Wiley Blackwell. 820 pp. FB69. This work provides a comprehensive treatment of individual differences in the traditional areas of "intelligence" and personality, and expands on those to address how such differences pertain to broader aspects of functioning. The first three sections provide a historical and methodological overview of the topic, followed by an explanation of structure and development and biological factors in intelligence and personality. The next three sections address individual differences and how they are related to work, health, longevity, antisocial behavior, social inequality, motivation, vocational interests, exceptional talents, creativity, happiness, and self-esteem among other topics.

LEARNING

2.216. *Cambridge handbook of the learning sciences* (2nd ed.). Sawyer, K. (Ed.). (2014). New York: Cambridge University Press. 776 pp. LB1060. Learning sciences is an interdisciplinary field, including cognitive science, educational psychology, sociology, computer science, and neuroscience, among others. This volume covers theoretical issues, methodologies, empirical evidence, and application to schools and classrooms. It focuses on the best ways to write textbooks, design educational software, prepare teachers, organize classrooms, and use the Internet to enhance student learning. Part I covers the foundations of the learning sciences, scaffolding, metacognition, cognitive apprenticeship, and learning in activity. Part II covers design-based research, microgenetic methods, analyzing collaboration, digital video research, learning sciences perspective on educational assessment, data mining, and learning analytics. Part III focuses on practices that foster learning, including project-based and problem-based learning, complex systems and learning, tangible and full-body interfaces, embodied design, and videogames and learning. Part IV covers collaborative learning, arguing to learn, learning in museums, computer-supported collaborative learning, mobile learning, and learning in virtual worlds. Part V covers research in disciplinary learning. Part VI covers application of learning sciences research to the classroom.

2.217. *Handbook of social and emotional learning: Research and practice.* Durlak, J. A., Domitrovich, C. E., & Weissberg, R. P. (Eds.). New York: Guilford Press. 634 pp. LB1072. This handbook covers virtually all aspects of social and emotional learning (SEL) in academic settings, a topic of increasing interest in education reform. Its thirty-seven chapters are divided into four sections and address specific issues in SEL. Part I ("Foundations") addresses the conceptual and empirical bases of SEL and how it relates to other prevention and youth development approaches. Part II ("Evidence-based Programming") presents school-based SEL programs at all grade levels; programs are evaluated and sorted into "What Works," "What Does Not Work," and "What Is Promising." Part III ("Assessment") presents methods for continuous evaluation of SEL, such as planning improvements, monitoring implementation, and making adjustments to improve programming. Part IV ("Toward Widespread Practice and Policy") addresses the roles and school leadership at various levels, federal and state policies, teacher and principal

training, and future uses of technology. Chapters are short (twelve to sixteen pages long), focused on specific issues of SEL, and include two to three pages of references. This book will be useful to anyone working toward school reform, program planning, or researching these issues in academic settings.

MEMORY

2.218. *Wiley handbook on the cognitive neuroscience of memory.* Addis, D. R., Barense, M., & Duarte, A. (Eds.). Hoboken, NJ: Wiley-Blackwell. 462 pp. QP406. As its title indicates, this book focuses solely on the cognitive neuroscience of memory and presents the most recent research in this area. After reviewing various aspects of memory, it launches into specifics of neuroscience research. This includes MRI research on encoding and retrieval, temporal lobe functions, and event-related potentials (ERPs) in episodic memory; the frontal cortex and retrieval; neuroimaging of false memories; neural correlates of autobiographical memory; degenerative disorders and rehabilitation of neurological patients; effects of sleep; perception; and episodic memory across the life span. Includes useful charts and color plates of neural activity. **NOTE:** For graduate students and researchers.

MOOD/AFFECT/EMOTIONS AND THEIR DISORDERS

2.219. *Anhedonia: A comprehensive handbook.* Ritsner, M. S. (2014). Dordrecht, Netherlands: Springer. 680 pp. RC541.This unique work is a two-volume, comprehensive treatment of anhedonia (inability or decreased ability to experience pleasure), considered both as a personality trait and as a symptom of several psychiatric and physical disorders. Volume I includes fourteen chapters that cover two major areas: conceptual issues and neurobiological advances. Volume II contains fifteen chapters covering three major areas: anhedonia in psychotic disorders, anhedonia in mood and personality disorders, and anhedonia in neurological and physical disorders. Each chapter begins with an abstract, keywords, and list of abbreviations. Chapters range from approximately twenty to sixty pages in length, and approximately 20 percent of each chapter consists of up-to-date references. This work is for an advanced research audience of researchers in mental health and neurologically related areas, as well as practitioners.

2.220. *Handbook of emotion regulation* (2nd ed.). Gross, J. J. (2015). New York: Guilford Press. 669 pp. BF531. This volume provides a comprehensive and up-to-date review of the theoretical and empirical literature on emotion regulation. It begins with an overview of emotion regulation processes and then moves on to biological and neurological underpinnings, cognitive bases and issues, developmental processes, social and cultural issues, personality and individual differences, involvement in psychopathology, clinical interventions, and health implications. Various perspectives, including comparative psychology, neuropsychology, and developmental psychology, are incorporated throughout the book. The thirty-six chapters are fifteen to twenty-five pages long and include useful figures, illustrations, and critiques, as well as extensive reference lists. This book will be highly useful to researchers in this area, and individual chapters can be of use to students as well.

2.221. *Integrative therapies for depression: Redefining models for assessment, treatment and prevention.* Greenblatt, J. M., & Brogan, K. (Eds.). (2016). Boca Raton, FL: CRC Press. 531 pp. RC537. The first two-thirds of this unique work focuses primarily on biological factors in depression, such as inflammation, the gut-brain axis and other gastrointestinal tract issues, mitochondrial dysfunction, micronutrient deficiencies, vitamin and mineral deficiencies, the role of essential fats and amino acids, sex steroids, the hypothalamic-pituitary-adrenal axis, thyroid issues, exposure to toxic chemicals, dietary peptides, genetic biomarkers, the effects of nonpsychiatric medications on mood, and the role of stress and trauma. It then relates these factors to various treatment modalities, including mineral and vitamin therapies, amino acids, other nutrients, and botanical therapies; exercise, sleep, and light therapies; the role of spirituality and religion in therapy; yoga, meditation, and mindfulness-based cognitive approaches; narrative therapy; and integrative approaches to psychotherapeutic healing of the mind and body. There are also specific chapters on perinatal, adolescent, and geriatric depression. With more than 3,000 citations to research, the chapters are relatively short (ten to twenty pages long), topic specific, and very well-documented. Chapters can be read independently of each other and are clearly written, but assume some knowledge of biology and neurotransmitters.

Mood/Affect/Emotions and Their Disorders: Tests and Measures

2.222. *Assessment of depression.* Sartorius, N., & Ban, T. A. (Eds.). (1986). Berlin: Springer-Verlag. 376 pp. RC537. Contains thirteen full-text instruments. Reviews self-report and clinical interview assessments of depression used around the world. A list of full-text measures in this book is located at http://libguides.hofstra.edu/TMdb/Sartorius Ban1986.

2.223 *Assessment scales in depression, mania, and anxiety.* Lam, R. W., Michalak, E. E., & Swinson, R. P. (2005). London: Taylor & Francis. 198 pp. RC537. Includes sixty-four full-text instruments; there are additional instruments for which full text is not included, but sample items may be included. This book also includes a section

on how to select an assessment scale. Instruments cover depression, mania, anxiety, related symptoms, side effects, functioning, quality of life, and special populations. For all instruments, there are commentary on the instrument, scoring information, alternate forms, references, and author/publisher contact information. A list of full-text measures in this book is located at http://libguides.hofstra.edu/TMdb/LamMichalakSwinson2005.

2.224. *Measurement of affect, mood, and emotion: A guide for health-behavioral research.* Ekkekakis, P. (2013). Cambridge, England: Cambridge University Press. 206 pp. BF511. This volume addresses issues researchers deal with (or worse, don't deal with) when selecting measures of affect, mood, and emotion. It begins by documenting the problems and distinguishing among the three concepts. The author then outlines a three-step process: deciding which construct to study, deciding which theoretical model one is using, and deciding which measure one might use among those available and which fits the theoretical model being used. The book then reviews a number of measures of distinct states, dimensional measures, and domain-specific measurement and addresses issues related to each. The nine chapters are twenty to thirty pages long and contain illustrations that are useful in understanding the points being made. This book will be most useful to graduate students and new and experienced researchers interested in the measurement of affect, mood, and emotion; problems with such measurement; and how best to measure these constructs.

2.225. *Practitioner's guide to empirically based measures of depression.* Nezu, A. M. (Ed.). (2000). New York: Kluwer Academic/Plenum. 353 pp. RC537. Contains twenty-four full-text instruments; ninety measures of depression are reviewed. Full-text measures are in appendix B. Scale summaries include original citation, purpose, description, administration and scoring, psychometrics, alternative forms, and author/publisher information. Appendix A contains "Quick-View Guide" to instruments, which allows quick comparison of measures on target population, type of measure, measurement focus, time to complete, norm(s) availability, whether a fee is required, and availability of alternate forms. Each instrument is followed by a permission statement. Unless the statement indicates that the instrument may be copied freely, permission from the author/publisher is required. A list of full-text measures in this book is located at http://libguides.hofstra.edu/TMdb/Nezu2000.

Mood/Affect/Emotions and Their Disorders: Bibliographies

2.226. *Emotion and religion: A critical assessment and annotated bibliography.* Corrigan, J., Crump, E., & Kloos, J. (2000). Westport, CT: Greenwood Press. 242 pp. Annotated bibliography containing more than 1,200 entries from the scholarly literature in psychology, sociology, anthropology, history, theology, and philosophy. Contains an extensive introductory essay and covers various disciplinary methods.

MOTIVATION

2.228. *Oxford handbook of human motivation.* Ryan, R. M. (Ed.). (2012). New York: Oxford University Press. 579 pp. BF503. This volume, part of the Oxford Library of Psychology, provides one-stop shopping for the researcher interested in both traditional research in motivation and emerging areas of application. Parts 1 and 2 provide an overview of motivation and various theories, including social cognitive, cybernetic control, self-regulation, existential, and self-determination theories. Part 3 covers processes of ego depletion, flow, implicit and explicit motive congruence, curiosity, and interest. Part 4 covers achievement goals, goal pursuit, conscious and unconscious goal motivation, orientation, and focus. Part 5 addresses motivation in relationships, including self-enhancement and self-protection, objectification theory, child and parent relations, and close relationships. Part 6 covers evolution and biology as they pertain to motivation, and part 7 focuses on applications such as psychotherapy, education, exercise, physical activity, work, sport, and future areas of application of motivation research.

MULTICULTURAL PSYCHOLOGY

2.229. *APA handbook of multicultural psychology.* Leong, F. T. L. (2013). Washington, DC: American Psychological Association. 1275 pp. HM1271. Two-volume set. This set provides one-stop shopping for important information in both the existing research in this area and evolving areas of research. Volume 1 (*Theory and Research*) contains twenty-nine chapters with five major sections: "Conceptual and Professional Issues," "Ethnic Minority Research and Methods," "Individual Differences," "Social and Developmental Processes," and "Community and Organizational Perspectives." Volume 2 (*Applications and Training*) contains thirty-seven chapters in seven parts: "Historical and Professional Perspectives"; "Stress, Adjustment, and Positive Psychology"; "Diagnosis and Assessment"; "Psychopathology"; "Clinical Interventions"; "Applied and Preventive Psychology"; and "Training and Supervision." Individual chapters are relatively short (fifteen to twenty pages long) and cover very specific topics, with extensive references.

2.230. *Handbook of mental health in African American youth.* Breland-Noble, A. M., Al-Mateen, C. S., & Singh, N. N. (Eds.). (2015). New York: Springer. 326 pp. RC451. This volume focuses on the "unique chal-

lenges and resiliencies" of African American children and adolescents. Part I covers epidemiology of mental disorders in this population and the importance of culturally competent assessment and diagnosis. Part II covers treatment modalities—pharmacotherapy, cognitive-behavioral, dialectical, interpersonal, mindfulness based, inpatient hospitalization, and community approaches to promoting mental health and well being—and their effectiveness with this population. Part III covers treatments of specific disorders—conduct and oppositional defiant, anxiety and obsessive-compulsive, depressive eating, substance use, post-traumatic stress, schizophrenia, learning disabilities, autism spectrum disorder, and attention deficit hyperactivity disorders. It includes studies on the application and effectiveness of the treatment modalities discussed in part II with this population.

2.231. *Psychology of black boys and adolescents.* Vaughans, K., & Spielberg, W. (Eds.). (2014). Santa Barbara, CA: Praeger. 615 pp. E185. Two-volume set. Written over a ten-year period, this set presents both a phenomenological approach to the experiences of black boys and adolescents and empirical evidence related to their lives. Part I ("Development and Identity") addresses "invisibility" syndrome and racial identity development in counseling African American men, minimization of discriminatory experiences, attachment disorders, peer group influences, gender-nonconforming black boys, and racism-related stress. Part II ("Education") addresses social and cultural forces on academic achievement, black boys in special education, single-sex schools, urban independent schools, shame as an accelerator for underachievement, and perceptions of masculinity. Part III ("Community Issues") covers engagement of hip-hop generation youth, race and trauma, gang involvement, relations with police, and protective factors against delinquency. Part IV ("Health") covers health risk behavior, paternal health socialization, and racial discrimination in health care. Part V ("Parenting") addresses fatherhood in black communities, single mothers raising sons, poverty among black fathers, and familial influences on academically successful black children. Part VI ("Treatment") focuses on African-centered therapeutic interventions, African-centered rites of passage, the hurting child within the young black male, intergenerational trauma transmission from slavery, and nihilism as a treatment issue in black adolescents. Phenomenology of the experiences of black children and adolescents is interwoven in many chapters, and several chapters are essays written by individuals about their own experiences.

Multicultural Psychology: Tests and Measures

2.231. *Handbook of tests and measurements for black populations.* Jones, R. L. (Ed.). (1996). Hampton, VA: Cobb & Henry. 1205 pp. BF176. Two-volume set. Includes eighty-two full-text measures. Other measures for which full text is not provided in this set are also covered. Measures in this set were developed in response to concerns about measures developed and validated on white populations being administered to black populations. Underlying the work is the view that tests and measures should be based on African American history, characteristics, experiences, behaviors, and needs. Many of the constructs have applicability to other populations, but some are specific to African Americans or other racial/ethnic minorities (e.g., coping with racism, African American identity development, African self-consciousness). Rationale, development, and psychometrics are provided for all measures. Some of the measures are from theses and dissertations; they may have more and newer documentation since publication of this volume. With the exception of the introductory chapter, each chapter begins with an abstract, discusses its topic, presents full-text assessment tools and/or reviews them, and ends with a "for further information, contact" box. Volume 1 covers measures for infants, cognitive approaches and measures for children, self-esteem measures for children, race-related measures for children, a variety of measures for adolescents and young adults, language assessment and attitude measures, parental attitudes and values measures, and measures of family structure and dynamics. Volume 2 contains worldview measures, physiological measures, and neuropsychological assessment; measures of spirituality, acculturation, life experiences, and values; race identity attitude measures; stress, racism and coping measures; mental health delivery measures; fair employment testing concepts and work environment and organizational assessment measures; research program–based measures; and a variety of other measures. In addition to the eighty-two full-text measures, chapters contain many useful tables and diagrams. A list of full-text measures in this book is located at http://libguides.hofstra.edu/TMdb/Jones1996.

2.232. *Measuring race and ethnicity*. Davis L. E., & Engel, R. J. (2011). New York: Springer. 198 pp. HT1523. Contains sixty-one full-text instruments. Scales measure how individuals from various racial/ethnic groups think about themselves and about members of other racial/ethnic groups. Measures identity and acculturation for Asian and Pacific Islanders, Hispanic Americans, African Americans, Caucasian Americans, and Native Americans. Some scales are for administration to members of specific groups, while others are designed to be used with members of all groups. A list of full-text measures in this book is located at http://libguides.hofstra.edu/TMdb/DavisEngel2011.

2.233. *Psychological testing of Hispanics: Clinical, cultural, and intellectual Issues* (2nd ed.). Geisinger, K. F. (2015). Washington, DC: American Psychological Association. 336 pp. E184. The second edition of this work incorporates new assessment research as well as changes within the Hispanic communities of the United States. The first chapter addresses the existence and use of *Pruebas Publicadas en Espanol* for expanded test selection. It also addresses differences among various Hispanic and Latino/a populations. Other topics covered are issues pertaining to intelligence testing and learning disabilities evaluation with Spanish speakers; neuropsychological testing; clinical interviews; personality assessment; assessment of ADHD; anxiety, depression, and cultural issues related to stress assessment; sexual orientation; and gender identity.

NEURODEVELOPMENTAL DISORDERS

2.234. *Controversial therapies for autism and intellectual disabilities: Fad, fashion, and science in professional practice* (2nd ed.). Foxx, R. M., & Mulick, J. A. (Eds.). (2016). New York: Routledge. 568 pp. RC570. This is a truly unique work in that it addresses treatments for autism and intellectual disabilities that lack theoretical rationale, acceptable research methodologies, and evidence of effectiveness; treatments for which theories have been disproven or acceptable research methodologies have found no effect are also included. Topics include the origins and appeal of fad treatments, history from 1800 to the present, delusion of full inclusion, gullibility of providers, paranormal theories, fads in special education, and speech-language pathology. Specific interventions are also addressed, including sensory integration, facilitated communication, positive behavior support, gentle teaching, rapid prompting, and dietary interventions. Ethical, legal, and political concerns are also covered, as is "Why Applied Behavior Analysis (ABA) Is Not a Fad." The thirty chapters are each ten to thirty pages long and include two to eight pages of references. This well-documented work provides one-stop shopping for researchers interested in controversial and scientifically unsupported treatments and will also be of great value to beginning and experienced providers, particularly the chapters on susceptibility of providers regarding such treatments. **NOTE:** This title is the revision of the 2005 *Controversial Therapies for Developmental Disabilities*.

2.235. *Dictionary of developmental disabilities terminology* (3rd ed.). Accardo, P. J., Whitman, B. Y., & Accordo, J. A. (Eds.). (2011). Baltimore, MD: Paul H. Brookes. 512 pp. RJ135. The third edition of this work contains more than 4,000 entries, 800 of which are new since publication of the second edition in 1996, many arising in the areas of genetics, pharmacology, and technology. Entries range from a brief sentence to half a page, covering virtually all areas of developmental disabilities. It does an excellent job of cross-referencing, particularly where terms are commonly known by their acronyms. This dictionary will be useful to users from undergraduates through professionals in many areas, including psychology, speech-language pathology, special education, medicine, and rehabilitation.

2.236. *Handbook of assessment and diagnosis of autism spectrum disorder*. Matson, J. L. (2016). New York: Springer. 477 pp. RC553. This volume addresses assessment and diagnosis of autism spectrum disorder, including developmental considerations and comorbidities with other psychiatric and medical disorders. It addresses the purposes and types of assessment for preschool, early childhood, adolescents, and adults. It also addresses stress, intelligence, and intellectual functions in assessment, as well as the implications of the ICD and DSM on screening, assessment, and monitoring and report writing.

2.237. *Handbook of autism and pervasive developmental disorders* (4th ed.). Volkmar, F. R., Rogers, S. J., Paul, R., & Pelphrey, K. A. (2014). Hoboken, NJ: Wiley. 1305 pp. RC553. Two-volume set provides comprehensive coverage of autism and autism spectrum disorder (ASD). Volume 1 (*Diagnosis, Development, and Brain Mechanisms*) consists of three major parts. Part I covers diagnostic concepts of autism and ASD, epidemiology, and course and outcomes through adulthood. Part II covers development and behavior in infants and toddlers, school-aged children, adolescents, and adults, as well as social, language, and communication development; play; imitation; emotion; sensory and motor issues; play; and neuropsychological characteristics. Part III covers genetics, environmental factors, biochemical markers, neuropathology, social neuroscience, and medical care and psychopharmacology of autism disorders. Volume 2 (*Assessment, Interventions, and Policy*) also consists of three major parts. Part I covers screening in young children, diagnostic instruments, clinical evaluation, communication, and behavioral assessment. Part V covers interventions for at-risk infants and toddlers, comprehensive treatment models for children and youth, targeted communication interventions, augmentative and alternative communication (AAC), behavioral interventions, educational mainstreaming, recreation and social skill interventions, college success, employment for adults with ASD, adult independence support for high-functioning individuals, and supporting families of those with ASD. Part VI covers social policies across cultures, practice guidelines, forensic issues, alternative treatments, preparation of teachers and carers, economic issues, and translating research into more effective policy. Each chapter begins with a table of contents.

2.238. *Handbook of intellectual disability and clinical psychology practice* (2nd ed.). Carr, A., Linehan, C., O'Reilly, G., Walsh, P. N., & McEvoy, J. (Eds.). (2016). Hove, England: Routledge. 863 pp. RC570. This volume is aimed at clinicians working with those with intellectual disabilities. It is included here because it is an up-to-date publication incorporating changes in classifications and criteria in the DSM-V and the eleventh edition of the *American As-*

sociation on Intellectual and Developmental Disabilities Manual, with substantial references on each topic. Topics covered include diagnosis, classification, epidemiology, and life span development; assessment of intelligence; adaptive behavior; quality of life; interviewing and report writing; intervention frameworks, including active support; applied behavior analysis (ABA) and cognitive behavior therapy; family support; life skills training, relationships, and sexuality; and residential, vocational, and aging issues. This volume will be useful to graduate students, researchers, and clinicians interested in the assessment and treatment of those with intellectual disabilities.

2.239. *Neurodevelopmental disorders: Research challenges and solutions*. Van Herwegen, J., & Riby, D. (Eds.). (2015). London: Psychology Press. 298 pp. RJ506. This volume contains fourteen chapters divided into three areas pertaining to conducting research in neurodevelopmental disorders. The first part ("General Research Issues") addresses the importance of development in neurodevelopmental disorders, brain-behavior links, researching the brain, causal modeling, and a tool for visual modeling of causes and outcomes. Part II ("Neurodevelopmental Disorders and Their Challenges for Researchers") covers variability in autism spectrum disorders, development related to primary language impairment, comorbidity, genetic disorders as models of neurocognitive risk, experimental difficulties, and eye-tracking methodologies. Part II focuses on use of new technologies by those with developmental disorders and the role of anxiety, its assessment, and intervention. A nice feature is that at the end of each chapter, before the references, there is a "Practical Tips" section, which provides tips on the particular type of research under discussion.

Neurodevelopmental Disorders: Tests and Measures

2.240. *Measures for children with developmental disabilities: An ICF-CY approach*. Majnemer, A. (Ed.). (2012). London: Mac Keith Press. 538 pp. RM930. This volume contains information on assessment tools and outcome measures based on the International Classification of Functioning, Disability and Health—Children and Youth (ICF-CY) framework. It is not exhaustive, but covers what experts in each area consider to be the best measures available. It covers a wide range of measurement, including body functions, intellectual and interpersonal functioning, behavior, learning, communication, self-care, environmental, health, quality of life, and global development. Chapters contain a description of the construct; information on measurement within the particular domain; and a description of the best measures, including an outline of their purpose, content, and psychometric properties. There is also a table providing a capsule summary for each instrument, information on how to acquire it, and key references. Chapters are ten to twenty pages long, with reference lists.

NEUROPSYCHOLOGY

2.241. *Handbook of biobehavioral approaches to self-regulation.* Gendolla, G. H. E., Tops, M., & Koole, S. L. (2015). New York: Springer. 421 pp. QP360. While many books on self-regulation focus on its behavioral aspects, this volume focuses on physiology and self-regulation. Part II ("Integrative Perspectives") covers evolutionary perspectives on regulation, neural mechanisms, muscle physiology metaphor, and protective inhibition. Part II ("Interactions between Affect and Cognition in Self-Regulation") covers error monitoring, pupillometry and memory, and distraction and mindfulness. Part III ("The Central Nervous System and Self-Regulation") addresses the brain reward circuit, neural foundations of motivation, neural foundations of self-insight and the medial prefrontal cortex, and decision making. Part IV ("Self-Regulation of Effort") covers brain and autonomic factors in health and disease, psychobiology of perceived physical effort, bounded effort automaticity, cardiovascular intensity, self-focused attention, and future thought and energization. Part V ("Self-Regulatory Problems and Their Development") covers effort-related cardiovascular reactivity and depression, perinatal origins, consequences and mechanisms of rumination, biological aspects of self-esteem and stress, and a basic and applied model of the body-mind system overall. In addition to the references, this volume contains many useful tables, diagrams, and images.

Neuropsychology: Tests and Measures

2.242. *Compendium of neuropsychological tests: Administration, norms, and commentary* (3rd ed.). Strauss, E., Sherman, E. M. S., & Spreen, O. (2006). New York: Oxford University Press. 1216 pp. RC386. Includes sixteen full-text instruments. Although this work does contain some full-text measures, it has two other main purposes. It was designed to provide an overview of basic and advanced issues critical to neuropsychological assessment, develop a strong working knowledge of the strengths and weaknesses of instruments, and present information necessary to empirically based assessment. This is covered in chapters on psychometrics, norms selection, history taking, preparation of the patient, report writing and feedback, and assessment of premorbid functioning. The second purpose, which forms most of the volume, is to provide an easy-to-use tool in which the user would find the major highlights of commonly used neuropsychological tests. The authors' mantra is "Know Your Tools." Instruments included in earlier editions but no longer commonly used have been removed, and many newer instruments have been added. Test reviews follow a fixed format with purpose, source, age range, description, administration, administration time, scoring, demographic effects, normative data, reliability, validity, and commentary. Major domains covered are achievement, executive functions, attention, memory, language, visual perception, somatosensory function, olfactory function, body orientation, motor function, mood, personality and adaptive functions, and response bias and suboptimal performance. In the introduction to each domain, there is a table that summarizes important features such as age range, tasks, administration time, key processes, test-retest reliability, and other features. Following the standard information and commentary for each test, there is a reference list of major articles and books on the test. This work is aimed at clinicians and researchers using neuropsychological measures. A list of full-text measures in this book is located at http://libguides.hofstra.edu/TMdb/StraussShermanSpreen2006.

2.243. *Compendium of tests, scales and questionnaires: The practitioner's guide to measuring outcomes after acquired brain impairment.* Tate, R. L. (Ed.). (2010). Hove, England: Psychology Press. 746 pp. RC386. Includes 107 full-text instruments. Scales of consciousness and orientation; general and specific cognitive functions; regulation of behavior, thought, and emotion; sensory, ingestion, and motor functions; activities of daily living (ADLs); participation and social role; environmental factors; and quality of life. Information on each measure includes the source, purpose, scale development, administration and scoring, psychometrics, commentary, references, and the scale itself. Permission information is generally located immediately following the instrument. This work will be of greatest use to researchers and clinicians interested in measuring outcomes of rehabilitation from traumatic brain injury. A list of full-text measures in this book is located at http://libguides.hofstra.edu/TMdb/Tate2010.

2.244. *Handbook of neurologic rating scales* (2nd ed.). Herndon, R. M. (Ed.). (2006). New York: Demos Medical. 441 pp. RC348. Contains 130 full-text measures; also includes reviews of other measures. This handbook covers neurological rating scales frequently used in clinical trials and practice. Entries include a description, original purpose and current use, psychometrics, administration and scoring, advantages and disadvantages of particular measures, key references, and in most cases the measure itself. There are also a link and password at the end of the table of contents that enables one to access PDFs of the scales in the book. Although one can access the measures online as well as in the book itself, the true value of this volume is in the discussion and assessment of the measures. Measures cover general neuropsychological symptoms, pediatric development, pediatric neurologic and rehabilitation, amyotrophic lateral sclerosis (ALS), movement disorders, multiple sclerosis and other demyelinating diseases, dementia, stroke, peripheral neuropathy, pain, headache, ataxia, traumatic brain injury, epilepsy, HIV-related cognitive impairment, rehabilitation outcome, and quality of life. This volume will be very useful to researchers involved in clinical trials or outcome studies measuring neuropsychological symptoms and outcomes. A list of full-text measures in this book is located at http://libguides.hofstra.edu/TMdb/Herndon2006.

2.245. *Measurement in neurological rehabilitation.* Wade, D. T. (1992). Oxford: Oxford University Press. 388 pp. RC386. Contains 141 full-text instruments. This volume begins by presenting a useful model of thinking about pathology, impairment, disability, and handicap, followed by classifications; suggestions on how to choose the most appropriate measure(s); and discussion of measuring motor and sensory impairments, cognitive and emotional impairments, physical disability, social interaction, quality of life, specific diseases, specific circumstances, and miscellaneous. It then presents actual measures of cognitive impairment; motor impairment; focal disabilities; activities of daily living (ADLs); global measures of disability; handicap and quality of life; emotions and social interactions; and specific measures for multiple sclerosis, stroke, head injury, Parkinson's disease, and other movement disorders. Instructions, comments, psychometrics, and references are provided. This work will be most useful to those conducting research in clinical settings. A list of full-text measures in this book is located at http://libguides.hofstra.edu/TMdb/Wade1992.

2.246. *Neuropsychological assessment* (5th ed.). Lezak, M. D. (Ed.). (2012). Oxford: Oxford University Press. 1161 pp. RC386. The fifth edition of this now-classic work provides a comprehensive review of major neurobehavioral disorders and a detailed treatment of assessment practices and issues. There are two main divisions. Part I ("Theory and Practice of Neuropsychological Assessment") covers basic concepts, behavioral geography of the brain, rationale of deficit measurement, procedures and interpretation of the neuropsychological exam, etiology of symptoms, and diagnostic issues. Part II ("A Compendium of Tests and Assessment Techniques") covers assessments of orientation, attention, perception, memory, language, motor performance, concept formation and reasoning, executive functions, emotional functioning, and effort, as well as assessment batteries, observational methods, rating scales, and inventories. Publisher or citation, test characteristics, and neurological findings are provided for each test. Appendix A is a neuroimaging primer providing images and explanations; appendix B contains publisher information. The twenty chapters are each twenty-five to fifty pages long and contain test images, samples, and references.

OBSESSIVE-COMPULSIVE
AND RELATED DISORDERS

2.247. *Oxford handbook of hoarding and acquiring.* Frost, R. O., & Steketee, G. (Eds.). (2014). New York: Oxford University Press. 404 pp. RC569. As hoarding has only recently been recognized in the DSM system as a disorder (in the "Obsessive-Compulsive and Related Disorders" section), this is the first comprehensive work on this topic. As such, it covers empirical research on phenomenology, etiology, assessment, and intervention. Part 1 provides an overview of hoarding, its history over the past 5,000 years. Part 2 covers phenomenology, diagnosis, comorbidity, animal hoarding, and severe domestic squalor. Part 3 covers etiology, including genetics and family models, neurobiology, hoarding in animals, psychological models, and the economics of hoarding. Part 4 addresses assessment, insight and motivation, cognitive and behavioral treatments, pharmacotherapy, family and community interventions, and alternative interventions. Part 5 covers hoarding in children and older adults, and part 6 focuses on future research directions. Each chapter begins with an abstract and keywords, and this work also includes a number of measures specifically designed to assess hoarding and acquiring.

PERSONALITY AND PERSONALITY DISORDERS

2.248. *APA handbook of personality and social psychology.* Mikulincer, M., & Shaver, P. R. (Eds.). (2015). Washington, DC: American Psychological Association. 2974 pp. BF698. Four-volume set. This 3,000-page set provides one-stop shopping for current and relevant research on virtually all areas of personality and social psychology. Each chapter begins with an introduction, often presenting a real-life example of the topic and outlining the contents and organization of the chapter. Each chapter addresses a core topic, presenting a theoretically integrated review of the research literature, summary and conclusion, and suggestions for further research. Volume 1, *Attitudes and Social Cognition*, covers human nature, the specific role of conscious thought processes in judgment and behavior, subjective experience of the world, motivated cognition, and motivation. Volume 2, *Group Processes*, selectively addresses group and intergroup processes that are of current interest and illustrate the relevance of work in the area to other areas such as social justice, immigration, and collective action. Volume 3, *Interpersonal Relations*, includes major theoretical approaches, biological-health, attraction-relationship development, motivation-emotion, communication-support-power, friendship and love-sexuality, and relationship maintenance-dissolution. Volume 4, *Personality Processes and Individual Differences*, covers myriad topics organized into broad areas of biology and temperament, motivation and dynamics, individual differences, and the person as a whole. Each volume contains approximately thirty chapters on very specific topics; chapters are twenty to seventy pages long, and references comprise approximately 20 percent of (four to fifteen pages) of each chapter. Individual chapters in this work will serve as excellent reading for students of personality, and the extensive and up-to-date references will be valuable to advanced researchers as well.

2.249. *Cambridge handbook of creativity and personality research.* Feist, G. J., Reiter-Palmon, R., & Kaufman, J. C. (Eds.). (2017). Cambridge, England: Cambridge University Press. 427 pp. BF408. In contrast to *Handbook of Research on Creativity*, which largely focuses on external factors influencing, facilitating, or blocking creativity, this volume focuses on factors within the individual related to creativity. Part I covers openness, intellect, curiosity, interests, creative self-concept, and environmental variability and dispositional plasticity. Part II covers creativity and mood, emotions, motivation, psychopathology, personality disorders, and creativity as positive and negative personality. Part III covers the relationship of creativity to Big Five personality traits, sense of humor, individuality, creativity in teams, entrepreneurial innovation, and effects of creativity training programs on individual characteristics. It also addresses existing themes and future research directions.

2.250. *Comprehensive handbook of personality and psychopathology.* Hersen, M., & Thomas, J. C. (Eds.). (2006). Hoboken, NJ: John Wiley & Sons. 1519 pp. RC456. Three-volume set. This set is unique in that it focuses on the link between personality and psychopathology, as well as the impact of psychopathology on family, peer relations, work, school, and daily environment. Volume 1 (*Personality and Everyday Functioning*) contains four major sections, on foundations, broad-range theories, mid-range theories, and special applications. The twenty-three chapters follow a general format that includes a statement of the theory, developmental considerations, biology/physiology, boundaries of the theory, evidence supporting and refuting the theory, and predictions for everyday functioning. Volume 2 (*Adult Psychopathology*; thirty chapters) and volume 3 (*Child Psychopathology*; twenty-seven chapters) each contain three major sections, on general issues, major disorders and problems, and treatment approaches. Each chapter in volumes 2 and 3 generally follows a format of description of the disorder; epidemiology; clinical picture; etiology; course, complications, and prognosis; assessment and diagnosis; impact on the social environment; and treatment implications. The volume on adult psychopathology also included personality development and psychopathology as well as implications for future personality development. Chapters throughout are approximately twenty pages long and contain extensive reference lists. This set is an excellent resource for undergraduate and graduate students and provides the major references for more experienced researchers and clinicians who are interested in the interaction of personality and psychopathology.

2.251. *Handbook of self-regulation: Research, theory, and applications* (3rd ed.). Vohs, K. D., & Baumeister, R. F. (2016). New York: Guilford Press. 640 pp. BF632. The 2016 third edition of this handbook has greatly expanded the 2011 edition, adding nineteen chapters on topics not previously included. Part I covers self-regulation basic processes as related to action, affect, social cognition, desire, and habits. Part II covers neuroscience, physiology, sleep, goal pursuit, and failures of self-regulation. Part III addresses social and cultural issues, including trusting others, romantic relationships, religion, and emotional labor. Part IV focuses on personality issues, including impulsivity, positive emotion dysregulation, and "grit." Part V covers development, including self-regulation training, executive functioning, effortful control, and aging. Part VI focuses on self-regulation challenges such as attention deficit hyperactivity disorder, nonpersistence, problems with positive thinking, addiction, and financial well-being. Two chapters found in the second edition but not in the third ("Self-Efficacy Beliefs and the Architecture of Personality: On Knowledge, Appraisal, and Self-Regulation" and "Promotion and Prevention Systems: Regulatory Focus Dynamics within Self-Regulatory Hierarchies") are available at no charge at http://www.guilford.com/vohs2-materials, with free Guilford registration through that web page.

2.252. *Measures of personality and social psychological constructs.* Boyle, G. J. (Ed.). (2015). Amsterdam: Academic Press. 776 pp. BF698. Includes 123 full-text measures; many more are reviewed, and sample items are provided. The focus is on frequently used and cited measures, particularly those developed in recent years to assess constructs of current interest. Five major areas of personality and social-psychological assessment are covered. Part I covers core issues in assessment, including response bias, malingering, and impression management. Part II ("Emotional Dispositions") covers hope, optimism, anger, hostility, life satisfaction, self-esteem, confidence, and affect. Part III ("Emotion Regulation") covers alexithymia, empathy, resiliency, well-being, sensation seeking, ability, and emotional intelligence. Part IV ("Interpersonal Styles") covers adult attachment, public image, social evaluation, and forgiveness. Part V ("Vices and Virtues") covers values, morality, religiosity, dark personality, and perfectionism. Part VI ("Sociocultural Interaction and Conflict") covers cross-cultural values and beliefs, intergroup contact, stereotyping and prejudice, and sexual orientation. For each measure, it provides a description, the sample populations, psychometrics, location of scale, original study or publisher, and results and comments. A list of full-text measures in this book is located at http://libguides.hofstra.edu/TMdb/Boyle2015.

2.253. *Oxford handbook of personality and social psychology.* Deaux, K., & Snyder, M. (2012). Oxford: Oxford University Press. 858 pp. BF131. This handbook, part of the Oxford Library of Psychology, is based on field theory, meaning that personality cannot be studied without studying the social domain as well. It consists of thirty-three chapters divided into three major areas. Part 1 covers the histories of personality and social psychologies, including conceptual and methodological perspectives, situation and behavior assessment, neuroscience and evolutionary approaches, dyadic and group issues, and the cultural psychology approach. Part 2 covers traditional research areas such as self and identity in situations, motivation and goal pursuit, emotions, initial impressions of others, attitudes and persuasion, helping behavior and belongingness, antisocial behavior in individuals and groups, attachment theory and relationships, personality influences on group behavior, and prejudice/positive relations among groups. Part 3 covers areas of more recent investigation, such as individual and group well-being, multiculturalism, change and continuity over the life span, leadership, work and work organizations, health behavior, forensic psychology, collective action, and social policy. Chapters cover specific topics and are twenty-five to thirty pages long, with approximately 20 percent of each chapter devoted to references. This book will be most useful to graduate students and researchers.

2.254. *Personality disorders: Toward theoretical and empirical integration in diagnosis and assessment.* Huprich, S. K. (Ed.). (2015). Washington, DC: American Psychological Association. 452 pp. RC473. This book covers existing and emerging models of personality and suggests future directions for research. It reviews the controversy over dimensional versus categorical models of personality and provides an in-depth critique of DSM-5's retaining the existing categorical model. There are three major sections: part I, "Current Issues in the Diagnosis and Assessment of Personality Disorders," lays out the major issues and controversies in diagnosis of personality disorders. This lays the groundwork for part II, "Research and Assessment Strategies," and finally part III, "Moving Toward Integrated and Unified Models of Personality Disorders and Pathology." This last section addresses psychodynamic, attachment, interpersonal, evolutionary, and cognitive affective processing theories of personality as well as how theory relates to treatment. Chapters are twenty to thirty pages long with four to five pages of up-to-date references. While references are not exhaustive, they provide broad representation of issues. This book is an excellent, up-to-date resource for personality researchers as well as clinicians working with personality disorders.

2.255. *Wiley-Blackwell handbook of individual differences.* Chamorro-Premuzic, T., von Stumm, S., & Furnham, A. (Eds.). (2011). Malden, MA: Wiley Blackwell. 820 pp. FB69. This work provides a comprehensive treatment of individual differences in the traditional areas of "intelligence" and personality, and expands on those to address how such differences pertain to broader aspects of functioning. The first three sections provide a historical and methodological overview of the topic, followed by an explanation of structure and development and biologi-

cal factors in intelligence and personality. The next three sections address individual differences and how they are related to work, health, longevity, antisocial behavior, social inequality, motivation, vocational interests, exceptional talents, creativity, happiness, and self-esteem among other topics.

Personality and Personality Disorders: Tests and Measures

2.256. *Measures of personality and social psychological constructs.* Boyle, G. J. (Ed.). (2015). Amsterdam: Academic Press. 776 pp. BF698. Includes 123 full-text measures; many more are reviewed, and sample items are provided. The focus is on frequently used and cited measures, particularly those developed in recent years to assess constructs of current interest. Five major areas of personality and social-psychological assessment are covered. Part I covers core issues in assessment, including response bias, malingering, and impression management. Part II ("Emotional Dispositions") covers hope, optimism, anger, hostility, life satisfaction, self-esteem, confidence, and affect. Part III ("Emotion Regulation") covers alexithymia, empathy, resiliency, well-being, sensation seeking, ability, and emotional intelligence. Part IV ("Interpersonal Styles") covers adult attachment, public image, social evaluation, and forgiveness. Part V ("Vices and Virtues") covers values, morality, religiosity, dark personality, and perfectionism. Part VI ("Sociocultural Interaction and Conflict") covers cross-cultural values and beliefs, intergroup contact, stereotyping and prejudice, and sexual orientation. For each measure, it provides a description, the sample populations, psychometrics, location of scale, original study or publisher, and results and comments. A list of full-text measures in this book is located at http://libguides.hofstra.edu/TMdb/Boyle2015.

2.257. *Wiley handbook of personality assessment.* Kumar, U. (Ed.). (2016). Chichester, England: John Wiley & Sons. 437 pp. BF698. This handbook presents current trends in personality assessment, both conceptual and methodological. The first section focuses on emerging conceptual trends; it begins with a presentation of its agenda, which is to integrate trait and process approaches to personality and theories of personality assessment. It addresses situational perception, temperament in personality development, integrity tests, network analysis, emotional intelligence, assessing the darker side of personality, advances in use and interpretation of the MMPI-2, diversity in assessment, and an African perspective on future directions for personality research. The second section focuses on emerging assessment perspectives and methodological issues; it begins with the international adaptability of the MMPI-2. It then addresses a combination of issues and use of particular measures, covering precision assessment using temporally dynamic data, situational judgment tests versus traditional personality tests, self-report versus conditional reasoning problems, therapeutic assessment in counseling and clinical practice, assessment via virtual reality, correlates of military suicide, assessment of sexual and gender minorities, user reactions to assessment, applicant faking behavior, ethical issues, and issues and challenges in assessment paradigms.

POSITIVE PSYCHOLOGY

2.258. *Handbook of mindfulness: Theory, research, and practice.* Brown, K. W., Creswell, J. D., & Ryan, R. M. (Eds.). (2015). 466 pp. BF327. The twenty-three chapters of this book provide a comprehensive review of current knowledge of mindfulness. The chapters are organized into five major sections: part I, "Historical and Conceptual Overview of Mindfulness"; part II, "Mindfulness in the Context of Contemporary Psychological Theory"; part III, "The Basic Science of Mindfulness"; part IV, "Mindfulness Interventions for Healthy Populations"; and part V, "Mindfulness Interventions for Clinical Populations." Chapters are approximately twenty pages long and include explanatory notes, useful illustrations and tables, and four to five pages of references. This book will be useful to both practitioners and researchers, bringing much of the key recent research together in one place.

2.259. *Oxford handbook of positive psychology and disability.* Wehmeyer, M. L. (Ed.). (2014). Oxford, England: Oxford University Press. 544 pp. BF204. Part of the Oxford Library of Psychology, this timely resource covers the application of positive psychology to those dealing with disabilities. Part 1 includes a historical analysis of positive psychology and disability and the benefits of using a strengths-based approach. Part 2 covers quality of life, optimism, social well-being and friendship, exercise, leisure, coping, adaptive behavior, self-determination, hope, resilience, problem solving and decision making, self-regulation, gratitude, and career development. Part 3 covers supported employment, family quality of life, education, and aging with disability. Part 4 covers specific populations: those with physical disabilities, cognitive and developmental disabilities, autism spectrum disorders, severe multiple disabilities, and emotional and behavioral difficulties. Chapters begin with an abstract, keywords, and introduction, and end with future directions, conclusion, and reference list. Useful tables and figures also clarify the text. This book will be most useful to beginning and advanced researchers studying these areas as well as teaching faculty.

Positive Psychology: Tests and Measures

2.260. *Positive psychological assessment: A handbook of models and measures.* Lopes, S. J., & Snyder, C. R. (Eds.). (2003). Washington, DC: American Psychological Association. 495 pp. BF176. Contains nineteen full-text instruments; many others are reviewed in chapters covering positive psychological assessment through measures of optimism, hope, locus of control, creativity, positive emotions, self-esteem, forgiveness, gratitude, positive coping, and quality of life, among other constructs. A list of full-text measures in this book is located at http://libguides.hofstra.edu/TMdb/LopesSnyder2003.

RESEARCH METHODS AND STATISTICS

2.261. *APA dictionary of statistics and research methods.* Zedeck, S. (Ed.). (2014). Washington, DC: American Psychological Association. 434 pp. BF76. This work, containing more than 4,000 entries, covers statistical and research methods used in all areas of psychology. Entries are typically paragraph length, and more than a hundred of them also include tables, graphs, or illustrations. In addition to being cross-referenced, words in all uppercase letters indicate entries elsewhere in the book. There are several appendixes containing listings of abbreviations and acronyms, entries containing illustrations, and symbols. Because there are many high-level entries that contain other terms with which the novice will not be familiar, this work is most suitable for advanced undergraduates through professional researchers.

2.262. *Case study research: Design and methods* (5th ed.). Yin, R. K. (2014). Los Angeles, CA: Sage. 282 pp. H62. The fifth edition of this well-known work explains the appropriate use of the case study and identifies sources of evidence for case studies (documentation, archival records, interviews, physical artifacts, participant observation, and direct observation), including data collection from social media. It covers the role of the case study in psychology and how to design data protocols, presents five analytic techniques (pattern matching, explanation building, time-series, analysis, logic models, and cross-case synthesis), and explains how to compose a case study report. The book also contains seven tutorials and numerous examples of case studies and their generalizations. This book is aimed at graduate students and beginning researchers.

2.263. *Handbook of research design & social measurement* (6th ed.). Miller, D. C., & Salkind, N. J. (2002). Thousand Oaks, CA: Sage. 786 pp. H62. Includes thirty-three full-text instruments covering social status, group structure and dynamics, social indicators, organizational structure, community, social participation, leadership, morale and job satisfaction, attitudes, values, norms, family, and marriage. Also provides extensive references to instruments for which full text is not included in this book. A list of full-text measures in this book is located at http://libguides.hofstra.edu/TMdb/MillerSalkind2002.

2.264. *Quantitative applications in the social sciences (QASS) aka "the little green books."* Various authors (serial, 1987–). Thousand Oaks, CA: Sage. This ongoing series currently consists of 175 titles, available in print and online. The titles cover virtually all aspects of quantitative methods and analysis. Typically, an individual volume is fifty to one hundred pages long, covering a specific topic in detail. A list of the "little green books" is available at https://us.sagepub.com/sites/default/files/qass_2017_flyer.pdf.

2.265. *Quantitative research in psychology.* Miles, J., & Stucky, B. (Eds.). (2015). Los Angeles, CA: Sage. 1912 pp. BF76.5. Five-volume set. This set contains seventy-three major articles and chapters on quantitative research dating from 1925 to 2011. All materials have been reproduced exactly as they were published. The set integrates concepts and methodological techniques in quantitative research. The five volumes are (1) *Statistical Hypothesis Testing and Power*, (2) *Measurement*, (3) *Research Design and Sampling*, (4) *Statistical Tests*, and (5) *Complex Models*. Each volume begins with an introductory chapter that provides an overview of the volume's subject and how established theories and techniques are continuing to develop.

2.266. *Sage handbook of qualitative research in psychology* (2nd ed.). Willig, C., & Rogers, W. S. (2017). Thousand Oaks, CA: Sage. 664 pp. BF76. This handbook consists of three major sections: "Methods," "Perspectives and Techniques," and "Applications." Topics covered include but are not limited to thematic analysis, ethnography, action research, conversation analysis, discourse analysis, Q methodology, grounded theory methods, qualitative methods in feminist and postcolonialism psychology, interpretation of images, and applications in various subdisciplines of psychology.

2.267. *Sage handbook of social media research methods.* Sloan, L., & Quan-Haase, A. (Eds.). (2016). Thousand Oaks, CA: Sage. 679 pp. HM742. This volume provides a comprehensive treatment of using social media for research. It has seven major sections. Part I introduces the topic itself and addresses issues such as what social media are, questions that social media research can help answer, big data, building social media research teams, social media users' views on the ethics of social media research, online reputation management, trolling, and personality traits in social media. Part II covers developing data collection approaches, data processing, data sampling, data storage, curation, and preservation, and designing studies with the Qualitative E-Research Framework. Part III covers qualitative research, including trace-based social media research, researching images, circulations, and practices, coding of nontext data, using Twitter as a research tool, and small stories research. Part IV focuses on quantitative research, including geospatial analysis, network centrality, predictive analytics, and deception detection and rumor debunking. Part V covers site specificity and the role of place

in social media, social rhythms, and social location-aware services for cell phones. Part VI covers analytical tools, including COSMOS, Social Lab, social media analysis, GATE, Netlytic, theme detection, and sentiment analysis. Part VII covers various social media platforms, including Twitter, Instagram, Weibo, Foursquare, and Facebook. The volume contains many helpful illustrations and diagrams.

Research Methods and Statistics: Tests and Measures

2.268. *Handbook of research design & social measurement* (6th ed.). Miller, D. C., & Salkind, N. J. (2002). Thousand Oaks, CA: Sage. 786 pp. H62. Includes thirty-three full-text instruments covering social status, group structure and dynamics, social indicators, organizational structure, community, social participation, leadership, morale and job satisfaction, attitudes, values, norms, family, and marriage. Also provides extensive references to instruments for which full text is not included in this book. A list of full-text measures in this book is located at http://libguides.hofstra.edu/TMdb/MillerSalkind2002.

SENSATION AND PERCEPTION

2.269. *Cambridge handbook of applied perception research.* Hancock, R. R., Scerbo, P. A., Parasuraman, M. A., Szalma, R., & Hoffman, J. L. (Eds.). (2015). New York: Cambridge University Press. 612 pp. BF311. Two-volume set. This set has and meets two major goals: to present up-to-date basic research and methodology on perception and to relate that research to applied research in and application to real-world environments, primarily the workplace. Part I ("Background and Methodology") covers basic methods such as signal detection, eye-tracking, and neuroergonomics. Part II ("Attention and Perceptual Processes") covers human performance modeling, attention plasticity, working memory, visual attention, visual search, sustained attention, vigilance, and psychology of time. Part III ("Perception and Modality") covers multimodal and multisensory displays for perceptual tasks, audition, haptic perception, visual information, guidelines for vibrotactile display design, and olfactory interfaces. Part IV ("Perception in Context") covers biological motion perception, perceptual segmentation of natural events, visual attention in complex environments, perception of trust in automation, applied acoustics, affordance perception, nesting of affordances, perception of collision, and hazard awareness in driving. Part V ("Perception and Design") covers virtual training systems, design and evaluation of interfaces, triadic meaning processing, ecological interface design, comprehension of animations, and cartographic displays. Part VI ("Perception and Domains of Work and Professional Practice") covers perceptual learning and expertise, noticing events in the visual workplace, sustained attention, perceptual challenges in health care, color vision in aviation, human-robot interaction, military applications, detection of explosive hazards, situational awareness, spatial orientation and motion perception, motion sickness, perceptual anticipation, option generation, and expertise. Part VII ("Individual and Population Differences") covers attention in infants and children, gender differences, processing abnormalities in schizophrenia and autism spectrum disorder, older adults, and working dogs. Part VIII covers pedagogical and professional issues. Chapters contain useful diagrams and photographs and references. This handbook will be valuable to undergraduates, graduate students, and beginning and experienced researchers interested in current research and future directions in experimental research.

SEXUALITY AND GENDER

2.270. *APA handbook of men and masculinities.* Wong, Y. Joes, & Wester, S. R. (Eds.). Washington, DC: American Psychological Association. 799 pp. BF692. This volume provides a comprehensive examination of how men's and boys' lives are affected by bio/psycho/socio/cultural factors as well as various meanings associated with male biological sex status. It covers theoretical, empirical, and practical issues in the study of masculinities, focusing not only on existing literature, but also on new and emerging scholarship. The volume contains thirty-four chapters divided into four major sections. Part I ("Historical, Conceptual, and Methodological Issues") covers history of the study of masculinities, gender paradigms and ideologies, gender role conflict, social norms, positive and feminist masculinities, biological and evolutionary factors, and enhancing research methods in the study of masculinities. Part II ("Specific Populations") covers racism; gay, bisexual, and transgender men; specific racial/ethnic groups; and masculinities across the life span. Part III ("Topics"), covers social class, emotion, careers, fathering, pornography, socialization, friendship and romantic relationships, body image, violence, education, and sport. Part IV ("Applications") covers men's help-seeking patterns, health behaviors, mental health, and men in therapy. This work will be highly valuable to graduate students and researchers interested in this topic.

2.271. *APA handbook of sexuality and psychology.* Tolman, D. L., & Diamond, L. M. (Eds.). (2014). Washington, DC: American Psychological Association. 1288 pp. BF692. Two-volume set. This work provides one-stop shopping in a deep and broad compilation of empirical research on virtually all aspects of sexuality. Volume 1 (*Person-Based Approaches*) focuses on the individual. It provides an overview of sexuality theory and gender over time, methodologies of sexuality research (survey, experimental, psychophysiological, and phenomenological methods), sexuality development and dimensions of

sexuality, (biology, desire, pleasure, diversity, well-being, and violence), same-sex sexuality (including theories of sexual orientation and identity), sexual health, HIV/AIDS prevention, reproductive health, and transgender identity development. Volume 2 (*Contextual Approaches*) covers commodification of sex (pornography, sex work, technologies), sexuality and culture, social movements and communities, social policy, sex education, sex and entertainment media, and sex and religion.

2.272. *Palgrave handbook of the psychology of sexuality and gender.* Richards, C., & Barker, M. J. (2015). New York: Palgrave Macmillan. 476 pp. HQ21 2015. This work is organized into five sections. Part I ("Sexuality") covers asexuality, bondage/discipline, dominance/submission, sadism/masochism (BDSM), bisexuality, further sexualities, gay men, heterosexuality, lesbian psychology, and transsexualities. Part II ("Gender") covers cisgender, further genders, intersex, and transgender. Part III ("Relationships") covers monogamy and open nonmonogamies. Part IV ("Psychological Areas") covers clinical and counseling psychology, health psychology, qualitative and quantitative methods, and sex therapy. Part V ("Intersections") covers aging, class, disability, ethnicity, and religion. Each chapter has the same organization, which includes an introduction, key theory, research and current debates, implications for applied psychology and the wider world, future directions, and a summary. This work will be useful for students, researchers, and practitioners; the chapters include boxes with "important information for the student" and "important information for applied professionals" as well as other useful tables.

Sexuality and Gender: Tests and Measures

2.273. *Gender roles: A handbook of tests and measures.* Beere, C. A. (1990). Westport, CT: Greenwood Press. 575 pp. HM253. Covers scales of gender roles, children and gender, gender stereotypes, marital and parental roles, employee roles, multiple roles, and attitudes toward gender roles. Provides test title, authors, publication date, variables measured, description, psychometrics, extensive notes and comments, author/publisher contact information, and a reference list of works in which the scale was used. A very useful feature is the "Index of Variables Measured by Scales."

2.274. *Handbook of gender and sexuality in psychological assessment.* Brabender, V., & Mihura, J. L. (Eds.). (2016). New York: Routledge. 704 pp. BF176. This volume addresses six areas pertaining to gender and sexual identity. Part I addresses terminology, construction of identity, issues needing theoretical and empirical attention, competent respectful practice, and how gender and sexual identities intersect with other identities of the individual. Part II addresses how to broach the topic of gender and sexuality and how gender and sexuality variables influence performance on psychological tests and the implications of such, particularly regarding the MMPI-2, MCMI-III, PAI, the Rorschach, narrative, and drawing assessment. Part III addresses gender and sexual identity in terms of assessing attachment, personality, psychosis, affective and anxiety disorders, feeding and eating disorders, and suicide assessment. Part IV provides case illustrations of assessments. Part V addresses life span developmental issues, and part VI addresses practitioner training and ethical conundrums regarding assessment and gender and sexual identity. This book is aimed at and will be most useful to graduate students, researchers, and practitioners of clinical, counseling, and school psychology.

2.275. *Handbook of sexuality-related measures* (3rd ed.). Fisher, T. D. (2011). New York: Routledge. 656 pp. HQ60. Contains 209 full-text instruments covering topics including, but not limited to, abuse, aging, anxiety, arousal, assault attitudes, attraction, behavior, beliefs, body image, coercion, communication, compulsion, contraception, consent, double-standard, dysfunction, education, fantasy, functioning, harassment, homophobia, GLBTQI, knowledge, masturbation, orgasm, motivation, risk, STDs, and more. A description, reliability and validity data, and author/publisher contact information are provided for each instrument. A list of full-text measures in this book is located at http://libguides.hofstra.edu/TMdb/Fisher2011.

2.276. *Sex and gender issues: A handbook of tests and measures.* Beere, C. A. (1990). New York: Greenwood Press. 605 pp. BF692. This handbook provides information and citations on availability of 197 scales on heterosexual relations, sexuality, contraception and abortion, pregnancy and childbirth, somatic issues, homosexuality, rape and sexual coercion, family violence, body image and appearance, and eating disorders. For each test, the following information is provided: author(s), earliest date in a publication, variables examined, format (e.g., true/false, multiple-choice, forced choice, observational, semantic differentials, physiological), description, sample items, development of measure, previous subjects who have completed the measure, "appropriate for," administration (most are self-administered), scoring information, reliability and validity information, "available from," and "used in" (reference list of studies in which each measure was used). "Notes and Comments" are also provided as appropriate for the particular measure. Most of the measures are available in journal articles; some are available in ETS *Tests in Microfiche* (TIM), books, dissertations, dissertations, and National Auxiliary Publication Service (NAPS); and others may be commercial tests for which publisher information is provided.

2.277. *Women and women's issues: A handbook of tests and measures.* Beere, C. A. (1979). San Francisco, CA: Jossey-Bass. 550 pp. HQ1180.B43. This volume reviews 235 instruments on a broad spectrum of issues pertaining to women. Measures cover sex roles, sex stereotypes, sex-role prescriptions, children's sex roles, gender knowledge, marital and parental roles, employee roles, multiple roles, attitudes toward women's issues, somatic and sexual issues, and some miscellaneous women-related topics. Descriptions of measures follow a standard format, which includes the title and author, year it first appeared in the literature, characteristics of respondents who have competed the measure, respondents for which the instrument is appropriate, a description of the instrument, psychometric information, information about alternate forms, availability and acquisition information, and references to studies in which the measure has been used. This book will be valuable to undergraduates, graduate students, and beginning and experienced researchers interested in the measurement of issues related to women.

Sexuality and Gender: Bibliographies

2.278. Annotated bibliography for the mini-series on lesbian, gay, bisexual, transgender, and questioning youth: Their interests and concerns as learners in school. (no authorship indicated). (2000). *School Psychology Review*, 29(2), 231–234. [Special issue, Mini-series: Lesbian, gay, bisexual, transsexual, and questioning youths]. Annotated bibliography of twenty-two printed works and websites on the interests and concerns of lesbian, gay, bisexual, transgender, and questioning youth.

2.279. *Bibliography of research and clinical perspectives on LGBT aging.* David, S., Asta, L., Cernin, P., & Miles, J. (2006). Washington, DC: American Psychological Association. 43 pp. Comprehensive bibliography of books and articles on aging in the LGBT community. Available at http://www.apadivisions.org/division-44/resources/advocacy/aging-bibliography.pdf.

2.280. Gifted gay, lesbian, bisexual, and transgender annotated bibliography: A resource for educators of gifted secondary GLBT students. Treat, A. R., & Whittenburg, B. (2006). *Journal of Secondary Gifted Education*, 17(4), 230–243. A comprehensive resource for information regarding gifted youths who are gay, lesbian, bisexual, transgender, or questioning their sexual orientation and/or gender identity. It includes articles, brochures, books, lesson plans, staff development, video media, and web resources.

2.281. HIV/AIDS prevention through changing risky sexual behavior among heterosexual college students: A 1990s bibliography. Livingston, M. M. (1998). *Psychological Reports*, 83(3, pt. 1), 781–782. Bibliography of 126 citations to works on AIDS prevention among college students.

2.282. *An interdisciplinary bibliography on language, gender and sexuality (2000–2011).* Motschenbacher, H. (2012). Amsterdam, Netherlands: John Benjamins. 294 pp. P120. Comprehensive bibliography covering recent research activity in the field of language, gender, and sexuality. The main part of the bibliography lists 3,454 relevant publications (books, book chapters, and journal articles) that were published from 2000 to 2011.

2.283. A selective bibliography of transsexualism. Denny, D. (2002). *Journal of Gay & Lesbian Psychotherapy*, 6(2), 35–66. Transsexualism, codified in DSM-IV-TR as Gender Identity Disorder, first appeared in DSM-III in 1980 with the name Gender Dysphoria, but its history in the psychiatric profession dates back more than a hundred years. This article discusses the history of influential publications, treatment centers, and paradigms, including the sex reassignment of Christine Jorgensen, the Johns Hopkins University–affiliated clinic, and other gender clinics, their closure, transsexual support groups, literature written by transsexuals, and diverse conceptions of transsexuality and treatments, as well as alternative, nonpathological models of transsexualism.

2.284. *Sexual violence and individuals who identify as LGBTQ: Annotated bibliography*. Enola, PA: Pennsylvania Coalition Against Rape and (PCAR) and Pennsylvania Coalition Against Rape and the National Sexual Violence Resource Ctr (NSVRC). Annotated bibliography of articles, reports, and films that explore sexual violence against individuals who identify as LGBTQ from a variety of angles, including lifetime sexual victimization, intimate partner violence, sexual violence as hate/bias crimes, and service provisions for survivors. Available at http://nsvrc.org/sites/default/files/Publications_NSVRC_Bibliographies_Sexual-Violence-LGBTQ.pdf.

2.285. Sexuality and disability: A SIECUS annotated bibliography. (no authorship indicated). (2002). *Sexuality and Disability*, 20(3), 209–231. SIECUS (Sexuality Information and Education Council of the United States) annotated bibliography on issues of sexuality, physical and mental disabilities, and chronic illness.

SOCIAL PSYCHOLOGY

2.286. *APA handbook of personality and social psychology*. Mikulincer, M., & Shaver, P. R. (Eds.). (2015). Washington, DC: American Psychological Association. 2974 pp. BF698. Four-volume set. This 3,000-page set provides one-stop shopping for current and relevant research on virtually all areas of personality and social psychology. Each chapter begins with an introduction, often presenting a real-life example of the topic and outlining the contents and organization of the chapter. Each chapter addresses a core topic, presenting a theoretically integrated review of the research literature, summary and conclusion, and suggestions for further research. Volume 1, *Attitudes and Social Cognition*, covers human nature, the specific role of conscious thought processes in judgment and behavior, subjective experience of the world, motivated cognition, and motivation. Volume 2, *Group Processes*, selectively addresses group and intergroup processes that are of current interest and illustrate the relevance of work in the area to other areas such as social justice, immigration,

and collective action. Volume 3, *Interpersonal Relations*, includes major theoretical approaches, biological-health, attraction-relationship development, motivation-emotion, communication-support-power, friendship and love-sexuality, and relationship maintenance-dissolution. Volume 4, *Personality Processes and Individual Differences*, covers myriad topics organized into broad areas of biology and temperament, motivation and dynamics, individual differences, and the person as a whole. Each volume contains approximately thirty chapters on very specific topics; chapters are twenty to seventy pages long, and references comprise approximately 20 percent of (four to fifteen pages) of each chapter. Individual chapters in this work will serve as excellent reading for students of personality, and the extensive and up-to-date references will be valuable to advanced researchers as well.

2.287. *Cambridge handbook of the psychology of prejudice*. Sibley, C. G., & Barlow, F. K. (Eds.). (2017). Cambridge, England: Cambridge University Press. 671 pp. BF575. This work aims to answer three questions: Why is prejudice so persistent? How does it affect those exposed to it? What can be done to reduce it? To answer these questions, the book has three major corresponding sections. Part I provides an introduction to the psychology of prejudice, followed by chapters on theories of prejudice, including evolutionary approaches, social identity, in-group love and out-group hate, intergroup emotions theory, intergroup threat, social dominance theory, the dual process motivational model, and heritability models. Part II addresses specific domains, including the traditional areas of racism, sexism, and religion, as well as newer domains such as weight bias, prejudice against immigrants, and a new perspective on general prejudice. Part III focuses on prejudice reduction in applied contexts; covering affect; group status and contact valence in intergroup contact; collective action; self-regulation; stereotype biases in the criminal justice system; prejudice, stigma, and discrimination in health care; delegitimization; use of media to promote intergroup reconciliation in Africa; and identification with all humanity efforts.

2.288. *Handbook of prejudice, stereotyping, and discrimination* (2nd ed.). Nelson, T. D. (Ed.). 2016. New York: Routledge. 516 pp. BF575. The second edition of this work incorporates new research on many of the traditional areas of inquiry in social psychology. Part 1 presents a history of research on stereotyping, prejudice, and discrimination, including definitions; measurement; etiology; prediction; and reduction of related beliefs, attitudes, and behaviors. Part 2 focuses on cognitive, affective, and neurological processes, including upward and downward intergroup interactions, perceived threat, terror management, attributions, intentions, magnetic resonance imaging (MRI) research, and measurement tools. Part 3 covers targets of prejudice, including sexism, ageism, and sexual orientation. Unfortunately, it does not cover prejudice related to disabilities, religion, or obesity, among other topics. Part 4 covers methods of reducing prejudice, including self-regulation, intergroup experiences, and workplace and school interventions. As indicated above, this volume does a thorough job incorporating new research on many of the traditional areas, but misses some other areas of interest.

2.289. *Handbook of socialization: Theory and research* (2nd ed.). Grusec, J. E., & Hastings, P. D. (Eds.). New York: Guilford Press. 718 pp. HM686. This handbook provides a comprehensive treatment of socialization for early childhood through old age. Part I provides a historical review of socialization theory and research. Part II addresses socialization across the life span. Part III covers socialization in various relationships and settings, such as parent-child, siblings, the family, peers, school settings, media, and new employee socialization. Part IV addresses biological aspects such as evolutionary approaches, genetic and social factors, temperament, biological and psychological processes relating chronic family stress to substance abuse and obesity, and caregiver socialization. Part V focuses on cultural issues of everyday routines, emotional socialization, and acculturation. Part VI addresses areas that are particular targets of socialization, such as gender, cognition, emotional competence, achievement motivation, prosocial behavior, and morality.

2.290. *Praeger handbook of social justice and psychology.* Johnson, C., & Friedman, H. L. (Eds.). (2014). Santa Barbara, CA: Praeger. 875 pp. RC455. Three-volume set. This set is the initial work in the Social Justice and Psychology series. It is based on the idea that psychology is never value neutral and that work in psychology (what avenues are explored, methods used, and applications of findings) has implications for social justice. The objective is to bridge theoretical and applied psychology. Volume 1 (*Fundamental Issues and Special Populations*) covers the history of psychology and social justice, psychological framework for social justice praxis, social justice ideology in therapy, ideology and political mobilization, false consciousness, and maintenance of injustice and liberation psychology. It also covers special populations of American Indians, Alaska natives, gender and sexual orientation minorities, people with disabilities, the elderly, the poor, and those in the criminal justice system. Volume 2 (*Well-Being and Professional Issues*) covers stress and race/ethnicity, sustainability and environmental justice, mental illness and dignity, justice in the workplace, community empowerment and health promotion, community-based veterans services, disasters, jurisprudence, humans rights violations, socially engaged spiritual psychology, pedagogical tools, integration of social justice thinking in doctoral education, and social justice research methods. Volume 3 (*Youth and Disciplines in Psychology*) covers human rights for children; social justice in education and schools; and social justice issues in counseling and clinical, school, community, and industrial and organizational psychology. The authors acknowledge that social justice issues are often ambiguous and that there is legitimate disagreement about what should be done to remediate injustice, but also that social justice thinking can and should be incorporated into the many areas of psychology.

2.291. *Routledge international handbook of social psychology of the classroom.* Rubie-Davies, C. M., Stephens, M. M., & Watson, P. (Eds.). (2015). Abingdon, England: Routledge. 397 pp. LB3013. This work is a comprehensive and integrated presentation of theory and research on social cohesion in the classroom, organized into the major areas of motivation, self-concept, engagement, student-teacher relationships, teacher expectations, classroom management, culture, and identities. Part I covers student motivation. Parts II and III cover student racial/ethnic identity, stigma, in-school and online discrimination, social status, and stereotype threat. Part IV covers teacher-student relationships and their influence on motivation, competence, engagement, achievement, social withdrawal, and barriers to teacher-student relationships. Part V addresses classroom climate and management, including observation and student report methodologies and teacher authority. Parts VI and VII cover teacher expectations, judgment, motivations, emotions, emotional skills and self-efficacy, and professional boundaries as they relate to student and teacher well-being.

2.292. *Social psychology of good and evil* (2nd ed.). Miller, A. G. (Ed.). (2016). New York: Guilford Press. 542 pp. HM1116. This volume covers traditional areas of inquiry regarding good and evil, but focuses on topics in good and evil that are currently receiving the most attention. Part I addresses conceptual perspectives on evolutionary aspects, free will, intent and harm done, and demonization. Part II covers issues of harming others: racism among the well-intentioned, effects of media violence, dehumanization, genocide and mass atrocities, and objectification. Part III focuses on self-concept: false moral superiority, "evil person" versus "evil deed," and immoral behavior among "moral" people. Part IV addresses group issues such as bystander effects, intergroup conflict escalation and reduction, good and evil in organizations, and globalization and terrorism. The work winds up with part V, covering possibilities for kindness such as empathy-induced altruism, volunteerism, and heroism.

Social Psychology: Tests and Measures

2.293. *Handbook of research design & social measurement* (6th ed.). Miller, D. C., & Salkind, N. J. (2002). Thousand Oaks, CA: Sage. 786 pp. H62. Includes thirty-three full-text instruments covering social status, group structure and dynamics, social indicators, organizational structure, community, social participation, leadership, morale and job satisfaction, attitudes, values, norms, family, and marriage. Also provides extensive references to instruments for which full text is not included in this book. A list of full-text measures in this book is located at http://libguides.hofstra.edu/TMdb/MillerSalkind2002.

2.294. *Handbook of tests and measurements for black populations.* Jones, R. L. (Ed.). (1996). Hampton, VA: Cobb & Henry. 1205 pp. BF176. Two-volume set. Covers eighty-two full-text measures. Other measures for which full text is not in this set are also covered. Measures in this set were developed in response to concerns about measures developed and validated on white populations being administered to black populations. Underlying the work is the view that tests and measures should be based on African American history, characteristics, experiences, behaviors, and needs. Many of the constructs have applicability to other populations, but some are specific to African Americans or other racial/ethnic minorities (e.g., coping with racism, African American identity development, African self-consciousness). Rationale, development, and psychometrics are provided for all measures; some of the measures are from theses and dissertations, and they may have more and newer documentation since publication of this volume. With the exception of the introductory chapter, each chapter begins with an abstract, discusses its topic, presents full-text assessment tools and/or reviews them, and ends with a "for further information, contact" box. Volume 1 covers measures for infants, cognitive approaches and measures for children, self-esteem measures for children, race-related measures for children, a variety of measures for adolescents and young adults, language assessment and attitude measures, parental attitudes and values measures, and measures of family structure and dynamics. Volume 2 contains worldview measures; physiological measures and neuropsychological assessment; measures of spirituality, acculturation, life experiences, and values; race identity attitude measures; stress, racism and coping measures; mental health delivery measures; fair employment testing concepts and work environment and organizational assessment measures; research program–based measures; and a variety of other measures. In addition to the eighty-two full-text measures, chapters contain many useful tables and diagrams. A list of full-text measures in this book is located at http://libguides.hofstra.edu/TMdb/Jones1996.

2.295. *Measurement of attitudes toward people with disabilities: Methods, psychometrics and scales.* Antonak, R. F., & Livneh, H. (1988). Springfield, IL: Charles C. Thomas. 306 pp. HV1553. Includes twenty-four full-text measures; discussions and sample items from other measures are also provided. This volume addresses direct and indirect methods of attitude measurement; multidimensional scaling; psychometric guidelines for attitude scales; and twenty-four full-text measures of general attitudes toward people with disabilities, attitudes toward physical disabilities, psychiatric disabilities, the mentally retarded, and societal responsibilities toward people with disabilities. Tables and charts enhance the text; this volume will provide valuable information in addition to the measures for any researcher interested in the measurement of attitudes toward disabled persons. A list of full-text measures in this book is located at http://libguides.hofstra.edu/TMdb/AntonakLivneh1988.

2.296. *Measures of personality and social psychological constructs.* Boyle, G. J. (Ed.). (2015). Amsterdam: Academic Press. 776 pp. BF698. Includes 123 full-text measures; many more are reviewed, and sample items are provided. The focus is on frequently used and cited measures, particularly those developed in recent years to assess constructs of current interest. Five major areas of personality and social-psychological assessment are covered. Part I covers core issues in assessment, including response bias, malingering, and impression management. Part II ("Emotional Dispositions") covers hope, optimism, anger, hostility, life satisfaction, self-esteem, confidence, and affect. Part III ("Emotion Regulation") covers alexithymia, empathy, resiliency, well-being, sensation seeking, ability, and emotional intelligence. Part IV ("Interpersonal Styles") covers adult attachment, public image, social evaluation, and forgiveness. Part V ("Vices and Virtues") covers values, morality, religiosity, dark personality, and perfectionism. Part VI ("Sociocultural Interaction and Conflict") covers cross-cultural values and beliefs, intergroup contact, stereotyping and prejudice, and sexual orientation. For each measure, it provides a description, the sample populations, psychometrics, location of scale, original study or publisher, and results and comments. A list of full-text measures in this book is located at http://libguides.hofstra.edu/TMdb/Boyle2015.

2.297. *Measures of social psychological attitudes.* Robinson, J. P., Shaver, P. R., & Wrightsman, L. S. (1969). Ann Arbor, MI: Survey Research Center, Institute for Social Research. 662 pp. JA74 or HM. Includes 149 full-text measures of life satisfaction/happiness; self-esteem and related constructs; alienation and anomie; authoritarianism, dogmatism, and related constructs; other sociopolitical attitudes; values; general attitudes toward people; religious attitudes; and methodologies. **NOTE:** This individual volume is appendix B of Robinson et al., *Measures of Political Attitudes*; volumes may be located together in JA or separated by topic to JA and HM. A list of full-text measures in this book is located at http://libguides.hofstra.edu/TMdb/RobinsonShaverWrightsman1969.

2.298. *Measuring bullying victimization, perpetration, and bystander experiences: A compendium of assessment tools.* Hamberger, M. E., Basile, K. C., & Vivolo, A. M. (Comps. and Eds.). (2011). Atlanta, GA: Centers for Disease Control and Prevention (CDC), National Center for Injury Prevention and Control. 119 pp. SUDOC HE 20. Includes thirty-three full-text instruments. There are four sections, containing "bully only" scale, "victim only" scales, "bully and victim" scales, and "bystander, fully, and/or victim" scales. Most, though not all, scales are Likert-type scales. They are available online at http://www.cdc.gov/violenceprevention/pub/measuring_bullying.html. A list of full-text measures in this book is located at http://libguides.hofstra.edu/TMdb/HambergerBasileVivolo2011.

2.299. *Scales for the measurement of attitudes.* Shaw, M. E., & Wright, J. M. (1967). New York: McGraw-Hill Books. 604 pp. BF378. Includes 186 full-text instruments. This work begins with a discussion of the nature, conceptualizations, and definitions of attitudes and methods of scaling and measurement. Each chapter begins with a brief discussion of the topic, then discusses why some measures are and others are not included, followed by measures in that area. Topics for which measures are provided include social practices and social issues and problems (family, education, religious, health, economics), international issues (political relations, conflict, economics), abstract concepts (education, law), political and religious issues, ethnic and national groups, significant others, and social institutions. For each measure, the title, source, and description are provided, as well as administration and scoring information, psychometrics, and comments. Items, directions for use, and scale values and/or response alternatives are provided. A list of measures included is in the frontmatter. This work will be valuable to undergraduates, graduate students, and beginning and experienced researchers. A list of full-text measures in this book is located at http://libguides.hofstra.edu/TMdb/ShawWright1967.

STRESS AND TRAUMA

2.300. *Assessing psychological trauma and PTSD* (2nd ed.). Wilson, J. P., & Keane, T. M. (2004). New York: Guilford Press. 668 pp. RC552. This volume provides both an in-depth discussion of issues in assessing psychological trauma and PTSD and information on various measures that have been developed for assessing these issues. It contains twenty-one chapters in six major sections. Part I ("Understanding and Assessing Trauma and PTSD") provides an overview of symptoms, syndromes, diagnoses, and the assessment of acute stress. Part II ("Assessment Methods") covers standardized self-report measures of civilian trauma and PTSD, structured clinical interview techniques, a questionnaire on dissociative experiences, impact of event, projective techniques, epidemiological measurement, and measurement of military-related PTSD. Part III ("Psychobiology") covers psychophysiological assessment, neuropsychological symptoms, and neuroimaging studies. Part IV ("Physical Health, Substance Use Disorder, and Bereavement") covers assessment instruments for those areas. Part V ("Psychosocial Development and Gender Issues") covers assessment of

trauma and PTSD in children and adolescents, assessment of childhood trauma sequelae in adulthood, and gender issues in the assessment of PTSD. Part IV ("Assessing Traumatic Injury in Litigation") covers forensic as well as clinical assessment and also contains a wealth of information on assessment of malingering. Each section reviews multiple instruments for the specific topic, covering development, overview, purpose, population, reliability and validity, and how the instrument complements other instruments. This volume will be of particular value to graduate students, researchers, and clinicians.

2.301. *Handbook of stressful transitions across the lifespan.* Miller, T. W. (Ed.). (2010). New York: Springer. 691 pp. RC455. This work addresses life-span stressful transitions from the viewpoint of Erik Erikson's theory of psychosocial development. Thirty-four chapters are organized into seven categories: processing transitions in the life span; education and career; marriage, family, and sexual life cycle; legal, ethical, and financial; life-threatening transitions in maturation and health; cultural, religious, and spiritual influences; and directions and interventions in stressful life transitions. Broad coverage includes normal age-related transitions (e.g., education, retirement), history-related (e.g., 9/11 terrorist attack), and nonnormative (e.g., auto accidents). Chapters range from fifteen to fifty pages long, covering underlying principles, historical research, and current approaches to fostering successful transitions, and end with two to five pages of references. This book would be very useful to practicing clinicians in understanding the significance of their clients' transitions, as well as to students and researchers, for whom both the chapters and the reference lists will be particularly useful.

2.302. *Resilience handbook: Approaches to stress and trauma.* Davis, M. C., & Reich, J. W. (2013). New York: Routledge. 318 pp. BF698. This book focuses on resilience as a process, particularly on the initiation and progression of that process. It does not focus on outcomes as the authors indicate that there is already a large body of literature on resilience as an outcome. The book is organized into two main areas: empirical studies of resilience as a process and of resilience interventions. Within each of these areas, the initiation of resilience, intra- and interpersonal factors, and social factors is covered. Initiation areas include executive attention, anticipation and preparation, and approaches that support agency. Intra- and interpersonal areas include attentional flexibility, emotion regulation, positive emotion resources, affiliation, attachment, caregiving and volunteering, and approaches that increase resources such as forgiveness, meaning making, and interpersonal skills training. Resilience interventions at the group level are primarily under research and are not covered unless there is empirical evidence to present. Chapters are relatively short (ten to fifteen pages long), are focused, and include up-to-date reference lists.

Stress and Trauma: Tests and Measures

2.303. *Assessing psychological trauma and PTSD* (2nd ed.). Wilson, J. P., & Keane, T. M. (2004). New York: Guilford Press. 668 pp. RC552. This volume provides both an in-depth discussion of issues in assessing psychological trauma and PTSD and information on various measures that have been developed for assessing these issues. It contains twenty-one chapters in six major sections. Part I ("Understanding and Assessing Trauma and PTSD") provides an overview of symptoms, syndromes, diagnoses, and the assessment of acute stress. Part II ("Assessment Methods") covers standardized self-report measures of civilian trauma and PTSD, structured clinical interview techniques, a questionnaire on dissociative experiences, impact of event, projective techniques, epidemiological measurement, and measurement of military-related PTSD. Part III ("Psychobiology") covers psychophysiological assessment, neuropsychological symptoms, and neuroimaging studies. Part IV ("Physical Health, Substance Use Disorder, and Bereavement") covers assessment instruments for those areas. Part V ("Psychosocial Development and Gender Issues") covers assessment of trauma and PTSD in children and adolescents, assessment of childhood trauma sequelae in adulthood, and gender issues in the assessment of PTSD. Part IV ("Assessing Traumatic Injury in Litigation") covers forensic as well as clinical assessment and also contains a wealth of information on assessment of malingering. Each section reviews multiple instruments for the specific topic, covering development, overview, purpose, population, reliability and validity, and how the instrument complements other instruments. This volume will be of particular value to graduate students, researchers, and clinicians.

Stress and Trauma: Bibliographies

2.304. Bibliographie française sur l'expérience post-traumatique (French bibliography on post-traumatic stress). Brillon, P., & Martin, M. (2002). *Revue Québécoise de Psychologie*, 23(3), 271–279. List of French-language articles on post-traumatic stress. Citations are classified into ten categories: neurobiological aspects of post-traumatic stress, comorbidity, theoretical concepts, description of symptoms, epidemiological factors, evaluation, trauma experience in children, factors associated with the development of post-traumatic stress, reports on post-intervention in the field, and intervention strategies and treatment. A list of book chapters, books, and specialty reviews on post-traumatic stress is also included.

SUICIDE

2.305. *Routledge international handbook of clinical suicide research.* Cuttcliffe, J. R., Santos, J. C., Links, P. S.,

Zaheer, J., Harder, H. G., Cambell, F., McCormick, R., Harder, K., Gergmans, Y., & Eynan, R. (Eds.). (2014). Abingdon, England: Routledge. 408 pp. RC480. This work addresses a wide range of research and suicide, with a strong focus on research on suicide survivors and suicide prevention. The first four sections cover suicide research from disciplinary perspectives: nursing, psychiatry, psychology, and social work and allied health. These sections cover the provider perspective on working with suicidal patients; risk of suicide after discharge; genetics; means restriction as prevention strategy; suicide-related behavior in Canada, China, India, and the United States; epidemiology; impact of suicide on treatment providers; intervention with repeat suicide-attempters; and risk of conducting research with suicidal patients. Parts 5 and 6 focus on research with "the other" survivors of suicide (i.e., family, peers) and research with indigenous populations. This work is filled with tables and charts summarizing research results and extensive references and will be very useful to users interested in the impact and prevention of suicide, ranging from advanced undergraduates to researchers and practitioners.

TEACHING OF PSYCHOLOGY

2.306. *The Oxford handbook of undergraduate psychology education.* Dunn, D. (Ed.). (2015). New York: Oxford University Press. 927 pp. BF77. Part of the Oxford Library of Psychology, this comprehensive handbook covers the spectrum of what one needs to develop excellence as an instructor of undergraduate psychology. In addition to covering such pedagogical and practice issues as syllabi, readings, assignments, first and last days of class, teaching critical thinking, evaluating learning, class management, incorporating diversity, service learning, student research, online courses, and nontraditional students, the book also devotes twenty-five chapters to best practices in teaching specific topics. After covering the pedagogical areas, this volume also addresses preparing students for life after graduation (internships, graduate school guidance, preparation for the workforce) and departmental career and administrative issues. This book is a treasure trove for anyone involved in the teaching of undergraduate psychology.

Teaching of Psychology: Bibliographies

2.307. Annotated bibliography on *The Teaching of Psychology*. Johnson, D. E., Schroder, S. I., Erickson, J. P., & Grimes, K. N. (2007). *Teaching of Psychology*, 35(4), 376–384. The thirty-fifth and last version of this title to be published, it is an annotated bibliography of the year's publications on the teaching of psychology. Numbering is continued from previous bibliographies, and there are also some articles from 2006 that were not included in the previous year's bibliography. This annual bibliography was ended due to widespread use of database searching on the topic and fewer requests for reprints.

2.308. Behavioral contributions to *Teaching of Psychology*: An annotated bibliography. Karsen, A. M., & Carr, J. E. (2008). *The Behavior Analyst*, 31(1), 23–37. Summarizes behavioral contributions to the journal *Teaching of Psychology* from 1974 to 2006. Includes 116 articles of potential utility to college-level instructors of behavior analysis and related areas that have been annotated, and organized into nine categories.

2.309. A bibliography of articles of interest to teachers of psychology appearing in *Psychological Reports, 1955–2010*. Abramson, C. I., Curb, L. A., & Barber, K. R. (2011). *Psychological Reports*, 108(1), 182–212. A bibliography of 605 articles classified into twenty-one sections, including, among others, history, psychology of the scientists, teaching tips, textbook evaluation, and evaluation of students and professors.

2.310. *Scientific misconduct: An annotated bibliography*. http://www.teachpsych.org/resources/Documents/otrp/re sources/keith-spiegel94.pdf. Keith-Spiegel, P., Aronson, K., & Bowman, M. (1994). Statesboro, GA: Society for the Teaching of Psychology (APA Division 2), Office of Teaching Resources in Psychology (OTRP), Department of Psychology, Georgia Southern University. Annotated bibliography of scholarly and popular articles and books on scientific misconduct, created as a resource for teaching in psychology.

VIOLENCE

2.311. *Gun violence and mental illness*. Gold, L., & Simon, R. I. (2016). Arlington, VA: American Psychiatric Association. 434 pp. HV7436. This work provides a well-organized, timely, and well-referenced information on a topic of immediate interest. Part I addresses the nature of the issues relating to gun violence and mental illness: serious mental illness, suicide, urban youth, mass shootings, school shootings, criminal background checks, involuntary commitment, and access to mental health care. Part II is entitled "Moving Forward" and covers risk assessment, reducing suicide mortality, access to mental health services, civil commitment reform, reducing access to firearms during times of crisis, restoring firearms rights to persons who have been denied access due to mental health prohibitions, and social and public health interventions. A particularly nice feature of this volume is that each chapter begins with sections entitled "Common Misperceptions" and "Evidence-Based Facts."

2.312. *Psychology of radicalization and terrorism*. Koomen, W., & Van Der Pligt, J. (2016). Abingdon, England: Routledge. 274 pp. HV6431. This handbook consists of very timely and well-referenced chapters on a topic of immediate interest. Topics include stereotypes, prejudice, economic deprivation and discrimination, threats and their consequences, culture, social climate and catalyst events, individual factors of personality, demographics, social identity, polarization and collective action, social identity, ideology and religion, movement from extremism to violence via small group processes, social support and justification, and paths to and from violent extremism.

2.313. *Wiley handbook of mass shootings*. Wilson, L. C. (Ed.). (2016). Chichester, England: Wiley-Blackwell. 414 pp. HM866. This volume is the first book-length examination of mass shootings from an academic psychological perspective. It addresses patterns, prevalence, and types of mass shootings in the United States; the psychology of perpetrators; the role of the media following mass shootings; and psychological issues for those affected by mass shootings, including incident victims, family and friends, rescue workers and journalists. It also addresses clinical interventions, prevention, ethics, and further directions for research and applications in this area.

Violence: Tests and Measures

2.314. *Assessment of partner violence: A handbook for researchers and practitioners*. Rathus, J. H., & Feindler, E. L. (2004). Washington, DC: American Psychological Association. 392 pp. RC560. This volume addresses various issues in the assessment of partner violence, such as assessment modalities, assessment in clinical practice, research considerations in scale development, psychometrics, measuring treatment outcomes, and research issues and challenges particular to the assessment of partner violence. It covers interview measures and self-report measures specific to partner violence, as well as measures of general relationship functioning, anger and hostility, and other correlates of partner violence. For each measure it provides a description and the development of the method, target population, format, administration and scoring, psychometrics, advantages and limitations, primary reference to the scale, scale availability information, and related references. There is a list of measures reviewed in the beginning of the book, organized according to chapter.

2.315. *Measuring bullying victimization, perpetration, and bystander experiences: A compendium of assessment tools*. Hamberger, M. E., Basile, K. C., & Vivolo, A. M. (Comps. and Eds.). (2011). Atlanta, GA: Centers for Disease Control and Prevention (CDC), National Center for Injury Prevention and Control. 119 pp. SUDOC HE 20. Includes thirty-three full-text instruments. There are four sections, containing "bully only" scale, "victim only" scales, "bully and victim" scales, and "bystander, fully, and/or victim" scales. Most, though not all, scales are Likert-type scales. They are available online at http://www.cdc.gov/violence

prevention/pub/measuring_bullying.html. A list of full-text measures in this book is located at http://libguides.hofstra.edu/TMdb/HambergerBasileVivolo2011.

2.316. *Measuring intimate partner violence, victimization and perpetration: A compendium of assessment tools.* Thompson, M. P., Basile, K. C., Hertz, M. F., & Sitterle, D. (2006). Atlanta, GA: Centers for Disease Control and Prevention, National Center for Injury Prevention and Control. 163 pp. HV6626. Contains forty-two full-text instruments. Scales measure physical victimization, sexual victimization, psychological/emotional victimization, stalking victimization, physical perpetration, sexual perpetration, psychological/emotional perpetration, and stalking perpetration. Available at https://stacks.cdc.gov/view/cdc/11402. A list of full-text measures in this book is located at http://libguides.hofstra.edu/TMdb/ThompsonBasileHertzeSitterle2006.

2.317. *Measuring violence-related attitudes, behaviors and influences among youth: A compendium of assessment tools.* Dahlberg, L. L., Toal, S. B., Swahn, M., & Behrens, C. B. (2005). Atlanta, GA: Centers for Disease Control and Prevention, National Center for Injury Prevention and Control. 373 pp. Includes 167 actual instruments on many components of issues related to violence. Broad categories include attitude and belief assessments (aggression/delinquency, couple violence, education and school, employment, gangs, gender roles, guns, and television), psychosocial and cognitive assessments (aggressive fantasies, attachment to role models, attributional bias, psychological distress, ethnic identity, fatalism, future aspirations, hopelessness, hostility, moral reasoning, self-perception, personal safety, citizenship, self-efficacy, impulse control, coping, self-esteem, sense of caring and support, and social consciousness), behavioral assessments (aggressive and violent behavior, concentration, conflict resolution skills, dating violence, delinquent and disciplinary behavior, drug and alcohol use, exposure to gangs, handgun access, impulsivity, leisure activity, parental control, safety and threats, social competence, social problem-solving skills, victimization, and weapon carrying), and environmental assessments as they relate to violence (disciplinary practices, family communication, family conflict and hostility, parent/child relationships, parental attitudes, involvement, and supervision, quality of life, collective efficacy, community resources, exposure to violence, fear of crime, and neighborhood characteristics). Each of the four sections begins with a chart of the measures to follow, indicating the construct being measured, number of items, target groups, psychometric data if available, and citation to the original source (reference list follows each section). Document is available at http://www.cdc.gov/violenceprevention/pdf/yv_compendium.pdf. A list of full-text measures in this book is located at http://libguides.hofstra.edu/TMdb/DahlbergToalSwahnBehrens2005.

OTHER

2.318. *Abuse: An encyclopedia of causes, consequences, and treatments.* Skaine, Rosemarie (Ed.). (2015). Santa Barbara, CA: Greenwood. 330 pp. HV6625. Entries are one-half to two pages long and cover forms of abuse, the abusers, the abused, causes, consequences, prevention, and treatment of abuse as well as agencies and legislation that address abuse. An alphabetical list of entries is provided in "Contents." Forms of abuse covered include animal abuse; abduction; imprisonment; physical, sexual, mental, and emotional abuse; trafficking; domestic violence; hate speech crimes; bullying; brainwashing; sexual harassment at school and work; road rage; and stalking. Coverage of the abused includes men, women, children, the elderly, immigrants, and homosexual and transgender people. Entries include cross-references and "further readings" (books, articles, websites, and laws). Excellent as a quick reference or as a starting point for research.

2.319. *APA handbook of behavior analysis.* Madden, G. J., & Dube, W. V. (2013). Washington, DC: American Psychological Association. 1174 pp. BF199. Two-volume set. The term "applied behavior analysis" (ABA) refers to the application of behavior principles to developing interventions for individuals deficient in adaptive behaviors. This two-volume set focuses on both the basics of behavior analysis and its application. Volume 1 (*Methods and Principles*) focuses on basic principles of behavior as and methods of data collection and analysis, including single-case research design, observation and measurement, quantification of behavior, classical and operant conditioning, punishment and negative reinforcement, response persistence, generalization, and time series analysis. It also addresses specific topics such as attention, remembering and forgetting, self-control, and behavioral pharmacology. Volume 2 (*Translating Principles into Practice*) focuses on the translation of behavior analysis to areas such as clinical behavior therapy, elimination of undesirable behavior, behavioral economics, consumption and choice, health, public health, intellectual and developmental disabilities, attention deficit hyperactivity disorder, reading, sleep, and substance abuse disorders.

2.320. *APA handbook of career intervention.* Hartung, P. J., Savickas, M., & Walsh, W. B. (Eds.). 2015. Washington, DC: American Psychological Association. 1013 pp. HF5381. This two-volume set is unique in the depth and breadth of its coverage of virtually all aspects of career planning (occupational exploration, decision making, job entry, work adjustment, retirement). Volume 1 (*Foundations*) covers historical, contemporary, theoretical, demographic, assessment-based, and professional foundations of career intervention. Volume 2 (*Applications*) covers specific career intervention models, methods, and materials and how they are applied to facilitate career transitions. This book provides one-stop shopping for researchers, practitioners, educators, consultants, policy makers, and students in psychology, counseling, education, and business and industry who seek a solid background and up-to-date research in the area of careers. Volumes 1 and 2 have twenty-three and thirty-nine topic-specific chapters respectively; chapters are fifteen to twenty pages long, are topic specific, and have extensive references.

2.321. *APA handbook of psychology, religion, and spirituality.* Pargament, K. I. (2013). Washington, DC: American Psychological Association. 1449 pp. BF51. Two-volume set. This work provides a theoretical and empirical foundation for the integration of religion/spirituality and psychology. Volume 1 (*Context, Theory and Research*) contains forty-one chapters in four major sections: themes, measures, and methodology; explanatory models of why people are religious/spiritual; expressions and experiences of religiosity/spirituality; and specific religious/ spiritual populations. Volume 2 (*An Applied Psychology of Religion and Spirituality*) contains thirty-four chapters in five major sections: introduction to applied psychology of religion/spirituality, major orientations to change, application to religion/spirituality to specific problems, applications to specific contexts, and future directions for research and clinical applications. Chapters are fifteen to thirty pages long and contain extensive references. This set will be valuable to users ranging from advanced undergraduates to researchers and practitioners in a variety of fields, particularly clinical and counseling psychology.

2.322. *Attention-deficit hyperactivity disorder: A handbook for diagnosis and treatment* (4th ed.). Barkley, R. A. (2015). New York: Guilford Press. 898 pp. RJ496. The fourth edition of this comprehensive handbook provides one-stop shopping for both clinicians and researchers. Thirty-five chapters addressing specific ADHD issues are divided into four major sections: part I, "The Nature of ADHD," part II, "Assessment of ADHD," part III, "Treatment of Children and Adolescents with ADHD," and part IV, "Treatment of Adults with ADHD." Chapters are twenty to thirty pages long and include two to fifteen pages of up-to-date references. This book is very readable, can be used by anyone interested in ADHD, and will be highly useful to beginning and experienced practitioners as well as researchers.

2.323. *Behind the badge: A psychological treatment handbook for law enforcement officers.* Freeman Clevenger, S. M. (2015). New York: Routledge. 296 pp. HV7936. This book provides comprehensive coverage of the psychological aspects of law enforcement work. Topics covered include personality characteristics of good law enforcement officers, health consequences of stress and trauma, critical incident stress debriefing (CISD), law enforcement within the military and correctional facilities, hostage negotiation, undercover work, sex crimes work, first responder issues, as well as assessment and evaluation for treatment planning. Chapters are relatively short (fifteen to twenty pages long), highly focused, and heavily referenced. This book will be valuable to practitioners treating and researchers interested in the treatment of this special population.

2.324. *Cambridge handbook of the psychology of aesthetics and the arts.* Tinio, P. P. L., & Smith, J. K. (Eds.). (2014). Cambridge, England: Cambridge University Press. 620 pp. BH301. The psychology of aesthetics and the arts refers to the study of our experiences of the visual arts, music, literature, film, performances, architecture, and design. This volume begins by examining basic theories and empirical studies of perception, including psychophysics, Gestalt theory and experiments, psychobiological and drive theories and studies, neural network theory and research, and information-processing theories and research. Part I presents concepts, theories, and methods of investigation into the psychology of aesthetics. Part II covers various approaches, including information processing, psychodynamics, and evolutionary theory. Part III examines specific arts, including paintings, photography, music, theater and dance, literary fiction, and the built environment, as well as arts education, academic achievement and cognitive ability, and facial attraction. Part IV addresses contemporary debates regarding descriptive versus experimental approaches to neuroaesthetics, and emotions and personality as related to aesthetics. As necessary for this topic, the volume has many images to illustrate the points being made.

2.325. *Dictionary of hallucinations.* Blom, J. D. (2010). New York: Springer. 553 pp. RC553. This work covers five major topical areas related to hallucinations, illusions, and sensory distortion: individual hallucinatory symptoms, medical conditions and substances associated with hallucinations, definitions of the terms "hallucination" and " illusion" by important historical authors, historical individuals who are known to have experienced hallucinations, and miscellaneous other issues. Entries on hallucinatory symptoms include the definition, etymological origin, initial year of use if available, author(s) of term if available, current usage, etiology and pathophysiology if known, and references to related terms and to literature. Entry length ranges from a half-page to several pages; entries are cross-referenced and there are more than one hundred images to accompany relevant text. This is a specialized item most useful to researchers on this specific topic.

2.326. *Handbook of critical psychology.* Parker, I. (2015). Hove, England: Routledge. 477 pp. BF39. A key theme of critical psychology is that traditional research methodologies of the subdisciplines of psychology constrain measurement to selected social constructs and fail to address other important aspects of human phenomena. This work contains forty-six chapters in three major sections. The first section briefly reviews and critiques the major subdisciplines of psychology. The second section presents particular schools of critical psychology, including activity theory, Marxist psychology and the dialectical method, psychology from the viewpoint of the subject, deconstruction approaches, Deleuzian perspectives, and discursive psychology. The third section presents various perspectives on psychology and critical psychology, including feminist, liberation, and indigenous psychologies; queer theory; and postcolonial theory, and addresses psychology in specific locales such as Africa, the American continent, Asia, and Europe. Chapters are specific and brief (approximately ten pages long), and contain references. Most useful to graduate students, faculty, and researchers.

2.327. *Handbook of jealousy: Theories, research, and multidisciplinary approaches.* Hart, S. L., & Legerstee, M. (Eds.). (2010). Chichester, England: Wiley-Blackwell. 581 pp. BF575. This volume is unique in its topic: jealousy. Part I of this work addresses jealousy in Western history, loss and emotional development, and jealousy and romantic love. Part II examines sociobiological bases, beginning with infancy and a theory of jealousy as a biological dimension of temperament and neural structures involved in infants' experiences of social exclusion with caregivers and peers. It also addresses comparative species' jealousies, including sibling rivalry. Part III covers cognitive bases, including social bonds, triadic relationships, jealousy in autism spectrum disorders (ASD), and jealousy as an emotion. Part IV covers jealousy specifically within the parent-child-sibling context, including protest theory, attachment in the case of twins, sibling jealousy, and the socialization of sibling rivalry. Part V covers other contexts for the potential of jealousy, including triangular family interactions, culture and parenting, social class, competition and parental jealousy in children's sports, child and adolescent jealousy of friends having other friends, and finally jealousy in adulthood.

2.328. *Handbook of solitude: Psychological perspectives on social isolation, social withdrawal, and being alone.* Coplan, R. J. (Ed.). Hoboken, NJ: Wiley Blackwell. 588 pp. BF637. This work is unique in both its coverage of solitude and the broad array of perspectives from which it is addressed within psychology (e.g., developmental, clinical, social, and cultural psychology) and other disciplines (e.g., sociology, anthropology, religious studies, biology). It is divided into five major sections. Part I covers various theoretical perspectives on withdrawal and isolation among peers, loneliness, shyness, and experiences of solitude. Part II covers solitude through the life span, including playing alone, childhood peer rejection, preference for solitude in adolescence, social withdrawal, social approach and avoidance, ostracism, and social isolation among older people. Part III addresses solitude in various contexts, including school, college, status as a single, and Internet use. Part IV covers clinical perspectives such as anhedonia, social anxiety, social isolation in

autism spectrum disorders, and personality disorders. Part V covers various disciplinary perspectives, including biology (animal aloneness), anthropology (urban anomie), sociology (social crises), computer science (online gaming), political theory (subjectivity), and religious studies (solitude and spirituality). Chapters are relatively short (fifteen to twenty pages long), highly topic specific, and heavily referenced.

2.329. *Handbook of temperament.* Zentner, M., & Shiner R. L. (Eds.). (2012). New York: Guilford Press. 750 pp. BF798. This volume on temperament arose from a confluence of three factors: the development of tools to assess temperament, increased ability to measure biological factors in temperament, and understanding the role of temperament in later life behavior (e.g., school failure, depression, anxiety, and antisocial behavior) and the importance of intervention. Thus, part I covers history, concept, models, and measures of temperament from infancy through adulthood. Part II covers basic temperament traits such as behavioral inhibition, activity, positive emotionality, anger and irritability, effortful control, empathy, and prosocial behavior. Part III addresses measurement of temperament, and part IV covers biological issues such as temperament in animals, evolution, prenatal factors, genetics, and neurobiology and neurochemistry of temperament. Part V examines context and temperament, focusing on attachment, differential susceptibility, parenting, peer relationships, culture, gender, and personality traits. Part VI focuses on clinical issues such as vulnerability and resilience, internalizing and externalizing disorders, and physical health, and part VII addresses classroom and psychotherapy interventions and the response-to-intervention framework. The final chapter reviews fifty years of research in temperament, focusing on major themes and integrating findings.

2.330. *Psychology of fatigue: Work, effort and control.* Hockey, R. (2014). Cambridge, England: Cambridge University Press. 272 pp. BF482. This book is unique in that it covers sixty years of research focused specifically on fatigue. Topics include concept and working definition of fatigue, social history, work, stress, energy, work and effort, exercise physiology, neuroscience, sleep as they relate to fatigue, and psychopathology of fatigue. Based on existing research, a motivational control theory of fatigue is put forth as well as an agenda for future research in this area. Approximately forty pages of references are included, providing a focused collection of research for the advanced or beginning researcher.

2.331. Rand health surveys. http://www.rand.org/health/surveys_tools.html. Free-to-use scales on aging and health, homelessness, health economics, HIV/STDs/sexual behavior, maternal/child/adolescent health, mental health, military health, quality of care, quality of life, and managed health care.

3
Current Research: Journal Articles and Annual Reviews

INTRODUCTION

Psychology as a discipline is focused heavily on data and good methodology. How recent findings are is particularly important in the applied fields, such as clinical, counseling, and school psychology; neuropsychology; and industrial/organizational psychology. As health care and other services have become more expensive, the demand for evidence supporting the efficacy and efficiency of professional practice has also increased, hence the recent focus on evidence-based practice (EBP).

Generally, research results are most rapidly published and disseminated to academic and professional readers via peer-reviewed journals from established publishers. More recently, and particularly in the sciences, researchers have also been pre-publishing, that is, publishing their research findings even if the accompanying text is not in its final publishable form. There are several factors driving this trend: the ability to publicize one's work promptly; the recognition associated with being "first" to make a finding or propose a theory; the ability to get pre-publication commentary from fellow scholars; and in the case of the sciences, patent issues. In addition, the combination of easy setup on the Internet and the open-access movement has led to a plethora of open-access journals, creating more publishing and access opportunities.

The most effective method of searching for scholarly articles is to use a database. *Most of the long-standing and largest databases are index/abstract only and do not contain any full text.* Many students (some of whom later become faculty!) are totally unaware of this. The development of link-resolvers gives the impression that the full text is available in the database being searched and leads to the never-ending question, "Why isn't everything full text?" For those who are reading this and are not familiar with this subject, a link-resolver is a product that links a source (e.g., a citation/abstract in a database) to a target (e.g., the full text of an article in another database or at the publisher's website). The institution holding the "source" database must also have

access (typically by paid subscription) to the target product in order for the index/abstract source database to access the full-text article in the target database or publisher site. The more seamless this process is, the better for the user, but it does create a bit of confusion.

A number of key databases are used in psychology. As psychology is such a broad field, it is helpful, when selecting a particular database, to think first about the class of database that will yield the most fruitful results (see figure 3.1). This image is not to scale. It does not imply that psychology is more important than the other disciplines; the magnitude of overlap of these is not reflected in the size of the overlap in the image; and these are not the only disciplines that overlap with psychology. This image is intended to provide the researcher (particularly students) with a preliminary starting point for thinking about in what class(es) of database(s) he or she wants to begin searching.

Why is it important to think about classes of databases rather than using PsycINFO exclusively? Because virtually every database indexes/abstracts a limited number of publications. Large databases such as PsycINFO typically index 2,000–3,000 journals. In addition, only some of these journals are indexed completely, with others indexed only selectively (more about this in the PsycINFO section). Depending on one's topic, searching in one database may lead one

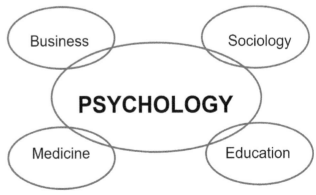

Figure 3.1. Psychology and related disciplines. Created by author

to miss important articles that are in journals not indexed in that database. (A mitigating factor is that articles identified in one database may index previous articles identified through another database.) It is this same issue of limitations of database coverage that makes topical bibliographies valuable—the bibliography may have been developed by searching across databases and book catalogs, thus including materials not found in a single database.

Selected databases in psychology, medicine, education, and language are reviewed below. This list is not exhaustive, but rather includes some of the more commonly used databases.

PSYCHOLOGY-SPECIFIC DATABASES

PsycINFO

3.1. PsycINFO. http://www.apa.org/pubs/databases/psyc info/. Washington, DC: American Psychological Association. (188?–present). PsycINFO is *the* premier database for research in psychology. Previously known in its database form as PsycLIT, in its earlier annual print format it was known as *Psychological Abstracts* (1927–1967) and *Psychological Index* (late 1800s–1927). It is a fee-based subscription database; coverage extends back to the eighteenth century. At this time PsycINFO contains over 9 million citations and 4.1 million records and adds more than 4,000 records each week. It is a subscription database and is currently available via the DIMDI, EBSCO, Ovid, ProQuest, ProQuest Dialog, and APA PsycNET platforms. PsycINFO and its former renditions cover not only psychology, but also related areas such as neuroscience, business, nursing, law, and education. It is professionally indexed, but more recent records also include keywords provided by authors. As of May 2017, PsycINFO covers 2,435 journals. A list of covered journals, as well as other coverage information, can be found at http://www.apa. org/pubs/databases/psycinfo/coverage.aspx. Of the 2,435 journals, 1,820 journals are included cover to cover. A list of complete-coverage journals can be found at http://www. apa.org/pubs/databases/psycinfo/coverage-full.aspx. Journal article records comprise approximately 80 percent of the records, with authored/edited books, book chapters, and dissertations comprising approximately 3, 8, and 12 percent, respectively. PsychINFO includes journals from more than fifty countries published in twenty-nine languages (non-English titles from 1978 through the present). *PsycINFO is an index/abstract database and contains NO full text.* Link-resolvers link to full text contained in other databases to which an institution subscribes.

PsycARTICLES

3.2. PsycARTICLES. http://www.apa.org/pubs/databases/psycarticles/. Washington, DC: American Psychological Association (200?–present). PsycARTICLES is a subscrip-

tion database in which all articles are full text. At this time, it covers 110 journals, many going back to the first volume, and includes more than 200,000 articles dating from 1894 to the present. It includes journals from the American Psychological Association, the Canadian Association, Hogrefe, the Educational Publishing Foundation, and the National Institute of Mental Health. A list of journals and their coverage dates is available at http://www.apa.org/pubs/databases/psycarticles/coverage-list.aspx.

While PsycARTICLES is valuable for its full-text content, it is not the best database for *searching* on a topic due to the limitations in journal coverage. All full-text materials in PsycARTICLES are available via PsychINFO when institutions subscribe to both databases.

PsycEXTRA

3.3. PsycEXTRA. http://www.apa.org/pubs/databases/psyc extra/. Washington, DC: American Psychological Association (200?–present). PsycEXTRA is a subscription database of "grey" or "fugitive" literature in psychology, behavioral sciences, and health. It indexes and provides full text for many items that are spread throughout the literature, various agencies, and websites, making identification an onerous process. Materials include items such as research reports, conference presentations and abstracts, policy statements, and standards, many of which are full text. It also indexes many magazines; it does not provide full text for magazines, as the text is typically available via other databases. A list of the magazines indexed can be found at http://www.apa.org/pubs/databases/psycextra/magazine.aspx.

MEDICALLY ORIENTED DATABASES

CINAHL (Cumulative Index to Nursing and Allied Health Literature)

3.4. CINAHL was first published as *Cumulative Index to Nursing Literature* (*CINL*) in 1960 and changed to its current title in 1977 when it expanded to include allied health journals. CINAHL indexes more than 3,100 journals, contains over 3.7 million records, and although originally started as an index, also now contains the full text of more than 70 journals. CINAHL, like other index/abstract databases, also works with link-resolvers. There is now a variety of related CINAHL products available via Ebsco, which acquired the database in 2003. These related products can be found at https://health.ebsco.com/products/the-cinahl-database.

Health Source: Nursing/Academic

3.5. Health Source: Nursing Academic is a primarily full-text database published by Ebsco. It indexes/abstracts approximately 830 journals and contains full text of 330 journals, 260 of which are peer reviewed. Both indexing/abstracting and full-text coverage range primarily from the 1990s to the present. A title list and subject list is available in Excel and HTML formats from https://www.ebsco.com/products/research-databases/health-source-nursing-academic-edition.

Embase

3.6. Embase. http://www.Elsevier.com/Embase. Amsterdam, Netherlands: Elsevier Publishing. Embase is a biomedical subscription index/abstract database. It indexes and abstracts articles from more than 8,500 peer-reviewed journals and contains over 30 million records at this time. According to its website, it indexes/abstracts 6 million records from 2,900 journals that are not included in Medline. Areas included in its coverage include pharmacology and pharmacovigilance; clinical and experimental human medicine; basic biological sciences related to human medicine; and biotechnology, biomedical engineering, and medical devices. Also indexed/abstracted are over 2.4 million conference papers from more than 7,000 biomedical, drug, and medical device conferences held from 2009 to the present. Embase is particularly suitable for identifying drug interactions and adverse effects. One can download journal coverage lists, conference coverage lists, information about Embase indexing, and other topics from https://www.elsevier.com/solutions/embase-biomedical-research/embase-coverage-and-content.

Medline

3.7. Medline is the journal citation database of the US National Library of Medicine (NLM). It is an index/abstract database containing *no* full text of its own. It was started in the 1960s, and coverage extends back to 1946. Indexing over 24 million items from more than 5,600 journals, Medline also has added value in its use of the NLM controlled vocabulary Medical Subject Headings (MESH) to index citations. Medline is available as a subset of PubMed (see below) and is also available through a variety of commercial vendors who add value by extending their own features (e.g., combining searches with other databases, use of accounts in which citations may be saved from multiple databases). One can restrict one's search within PubMed to Medline by using MESH headings. Medline, like most other index/abstract databases, works with link-resolvers to link to full text in other databases.

PubMed

3.8. PubMed. https://www.ncbi.nlm.nih.gov/pubmed/. (1996–). Its largest component is the contents of Medline, but with approximately 3 million additional citations that include in-process works, works outside the scope of Medline, works that precede the Medline date range, pre-1966 works that have not yet been assigned MESH, citations to manuscripts published by NIH-funded researchers, and the majority of books available on the National Center for Biotechnology Information (NCBI) Bookshelf. In addition, PubMed also often includes links to full text on publisher websites or PubMedCentral (PMC; see below). PubMed, like most other index/abstract databases, works with link-resolvers to link to full text in other databases.

PubMedCentral (PMC)

3.9. PubMedCentral (PMC). https://www.ncbi.nlm.nih.gov/pmc/. (2000–). A free archive of full-text biomedical and life science journal articles. It is a repository for participating publishers and for author manuscripts submitted in compliance with policies for government-funded research.

EDUCATION-ORIENTED DATABASES

Education Full Text

3.10 Education Full-Text is an H. W. Wilson product, formerly known as Education Index and Education Abstracts. Education Full-Text indexes/abstracts more than 1,000 journals, with full text for over 530 journals. Indexing began in the 1980s and full-text coverage in the 1990s. Like most other databases, Education Full-Text works with link-resolvers.

3.11. ERIC (Education Resources Information Center) (https://eric.ed.gov/) is a digital library of education-related information sponsored by the Institute of Education Sciences (IES) of the US Department of Education. ERIC was developed in 1966 as an indexing/abstracting resource, but over time many publishers have given ERIC the right to publish their materials. In addition to indexing articles from more than 1,000 journals, ERIC also contains records for books, research reports, technical reports, policy papers, conference papers, and other education-related materials. ERIC contains over 1.6 million records and links to more than 631,000 full-text documents. Like most indexing/abstracting databases, ERIC also works with link-resolvers. ERIC is available to the public using the URL above and is also available via several vendors, which add value in terms of creating accounts, combining results with those from other databases, and so forth.

3.12. Professional Development Collection is an Ebsco database that is primarily but not completely full text. It indexes/abstracts more than 750 journals and contains the full text of 470 journals, almost 300 of which are peer reviewed. It also contains educational reports. Like most other databases, it works with link-resolvers to retrieve full text from other sources.

SELECTED OTHER DATABASES

Annual Reviews

3.13 Annual Reviews. http://www.annualreviews.org/action/showPublications. There are two Annual Reviews directly related to psychology: Annual Review of Psychology and Annual Review of Clinical Psychology. The purpose of Annual Reviews is to provide comprehensive coverage of important topics researched in the field during the previous year or so, address the significance to society and practical applications of that research, and address the likely course of future research in the area. Articles are typically 25–35 pages long.

Google Scholar

3.14. What can one say about Google Scholar (https://scholar.google.com/)? One advantage of Google Scholar is that unlike most other databases, it does not restrict the range of journals indexed. This is also a disadvantage. Yes, the same point is both an advantage and a disadvantage. The advantage is obvious; the disadvantage is that one cannot restrict the disciplinary perspective or type of material. Google Scholar is primarily an indexing/abstracting database with a substantial body of full text. Full text is available for various types of materials and is made available via various routes. Some items in Scholar are organizational papers for which the organization provides open access. Some are articles from open-access journals. Some are papers that faculty or students make available full text. In addition to these open-access routes, there is the authentication route to subscription products. Typically, if one is on campus or has authenticated into an institution's database list, Google Scholar is on that list and so recognizes the institutional authentication. Under these circumstances, one will also see links indicating the item is available via a particular database, and clicking on the link will bring one to the article, or at least to the journal where one can browse or search for the article. Another advantage of Google Scholar is that one can enter a "target" article in one's search, and the result will provide a link indicating how many others have cited that article and bring one to the list of citing articles. A disadvantage of Scholar is that even its advanced search mechanism (available via drop-down arrow on the upper right of screen) is fairly primitive.

Linguistics and Language Behavior Abstracts (LLBA)

3.15. Linguistics and Language Behavior Abstracts (LLBA) is an indexing/abstract database of more than 1,500 journals as well as books, book chapters, and dissertations. Major areas of interest to psychology researchers include interpersonal behavior and communication, normal and pathological language, learning disabilities, nonverbal communication, psychometrics, and special education. It is international in scope and adds approximately 1,400 records monthly. More information on LLBA can be found at http://proquest.libguides.com/llba. Like other major databases, LLBA works with link-resolvers to retrieve full text from other sources.

SEARCHING DATABASES

The purpose of this section on databases is to provide information on efficient and effective search strategies to optimize their use. I decided to do an instructional section for several reasons. First, as I point out to my students, they know how to search and get results but are often unhappy with their results because they are not effective searchers. Second, faculty who attend library sessions with their students almost always leave stating, "I always learn something new when I come to these sessions." Third, in my contacts with faculty from various departments throughout the university, when we discuss research they are often surprised when I tell them, "You can do that in X database."

Detailed information is presented here only on the premier database for psychology, PsycINFO. This is because of space considerations and also because once one has a solid grasp of the multitude of features available in one database, one can user that knowledge with other databases.

As my institution subscribes to PsycINFO via the Ebscohost platform, illustrations reflect that fact; the concepts and strategies, however, remain the same regardless of the interface. One should be aware, however, that there are some field differences as well as some "behind the interface" differences among vendors. These differences may result in differences around the edges of the results but do not change the principles and strategies outlined below. Unlike the rest of this work, this chapter is written in the first person plural because it is instructional rather than solely informational and so is presented as it would be in a class.

3.16. Searching Strategy and Managing Results

Let's use the following as an example:

> Our research interest is the evaluation of antisocial behavior in adolescents

Our research interest has been presented using natural language—that is, the way we normally speak. When we search a database, however, we need to translate natural language into search terms.

Why? Because as a general rule, databases read words entered together as a single search term. This means the phrase is read as if it had parentheses or quotation marks around it—the search function looks for all of those words in exactly the order that they were entered.

But we don't care about the order of the words; we care about the *three concepts* in our research interest. Using a form similar to the "search strategizer" in figure 3.2 is a useful way to clarify various steps of the search process. The first step is to identify the concepts of the research topic.

Axinn Library Information Literacy Program - Search Strategizer

Write your research question here:

[Evaluation] of [antisocial behavior] in [adolescents]

1. Circle the 2 or 3 most important concepts in the sentence above.
2. Write the first concept on the first line of "Concept 1" below. Write synonyms/broader/narrower terms below that
3. Do the same for the second and/or third concept in your research question in "Concept 2" and "Concept 3" below.

Concept 1	Concept 2	Concept 3
Evaluation	*Antisocial Behavior*	*Adolescents*

Use various combinations from C1, C2, and C3 terms in your search strategy.

Remember, "keyword" or "default field" searching will broaden your results (more hits, less relevant)

"Subject" search will narrow your results (fewer hits, more relevance). (Examine item records for 'subject' terms)

Figure 3.2. Identifying main concepts from natural language research topic. Created by author

Having determined our three concepts or search terms, we can begin searching. We want to start with a very broad and exhaustive search on the area of interest and use various limiters to narrow it later.

> Enter one search term and examine the number of results to determine if they make sense before adding another search term.

Why enter only one term at a time? The answer is to examine the number of results to see if they make sense.

Why? Let's think about this. PsycINFO indexes millions of articles in thousands of journals going back over approximately 200 years. Given this, if we enter "antisocial behavior" as our first search term, there should be *a lot* of results. If there are not, we would be alerted to examine what had been entered to see if it had been spelled incorrectly, or perhaps a limiter was entered without realizing it. For example, in one class a student was searching for articles on aggression. Her result list contained only thirty-three items. This result makes no sense, so we examined her search. She had spelled "aggression" incorrectly, with only one "g." One might wonder why there were *any* results. I suggest that in a database with millions of records, there could be a few typos, and also that because PsycINFO indexes journals in more than twenty-five languages, perhaps "aggression" is spelled with one "g" in one of those languages.

As seen in figure 3.3, searching only "antisocial behavior" with no limiters results in 88,099 items.

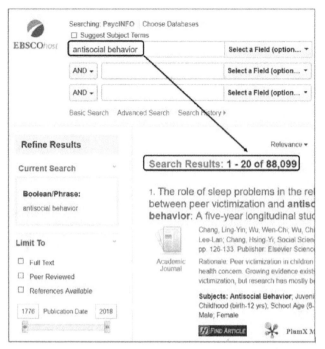

Figure 3.3. Entering first major search term. The PsycINFO® Database screen shot is reproduced with permission of the American Psychological Association, publisher of the PsycINFO database, all rights reserved. No further reproduction or distribution is permitted without written permission from the American Psychological Association. Screen shots also reproduced courtesy of EBSCO Information Services.

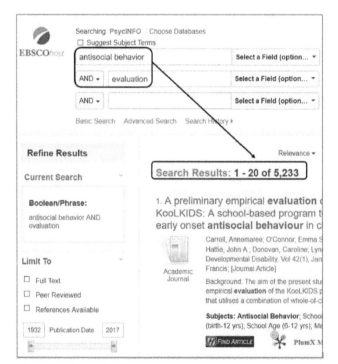

Figure 3.4. Adding another search term narrows results. The PsycINFO® Database screen shot is reproduced with permission of the American Psychological Association, publisher of the PsycINFO database, all rights reserved. No further reproduction or distribution is permitted without written permission from the American Psychological Association. Screen shots also reproduced courtesy of EBSCO Information Services.

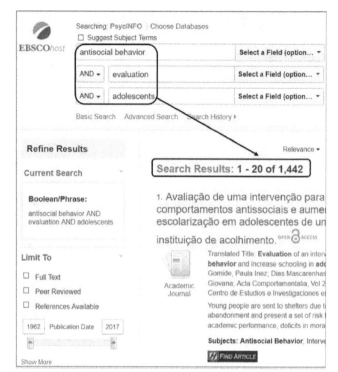

Figure 3.5. Adding third search term further narrows results. The PsycINFO® Database screen shot is reproduced with permission of the American Psychological Association, publisher of the PsycINFO database, all rights reserved. No further reproduction or distribution is permitted without written permission from the American Psychological Association. Screen shots also reproduced courtesy of EBSCO Information Services.

This makes sense in a database of this depth and breadth, so we can now add in another of our search terms: "evaluation." We are now telling the database that we want results that include both the term "antisocial behavior" *and* the term "evaluation." Notice in figure 3.4 that requiring both terms be present has reduced the results to 5,233.

We can now enter our third search term, "adolescents." Figure 3.5 shows how requiring all three terms (antisocial behavior *and* evaluation *and* adolescents) further reduces the results to 1,442.

This number of results is more than any researcher wants to begin with, but at least we know that our search terms are on target. We have not yet limited by document type or date. But before we begin narrowing our search with those limiters, we need to address another two "hidden" limiters—what I refer to as the "word form" problem and the "alternate terms/synonyms" problem.

3.17. Addressing the "Word Form" Problem

The "word form" issue pertains to terms such as "evaluation" in our sample. What if the author or indexer used any of the following terms: "evaluate," "evaluates," "evaluated," or "evaluating?" The word form does not essentially change our search, but it *does* change our results.

Years ago, when researchers paid by the minute for searching, they would spend preliminary time organizing their searches so that they knew exactly what they would enter.

HOFSTRA
UNIVERSITY.

Axinn Library Information Literacy Program - Search Strategizer

Write your research question here:

[Evaluation] of [antisocial behavior] in [adolescents]

1. Circle the 2 or 3 most important concepts in the sentence above.
2. Write the first concept on the first line of "Concept 1" below. Write synonyms/broader/narrower terms below that
3. Do the same for the second and/or third concept in your research question in "Concept 2" and "Concept 3" below.

Concept 1	Concept 2	Concept 3
Evaluation	*Antisocial Behavior*	*Adolescents*
OR		OR
Evaluat*	"	*Adolescen**

Use various combinations from C1, C2, and C3 terms in your search strategy.

Remember, "keyword" or "default field" searching will broaden your results (more hits, less relevant)

"Subject" search will narrow your results (fewer hits, more relevance). (Examine item records for 'subject' terms)

Figure 3.6. Example of thinking through word forms before searching. Created by author

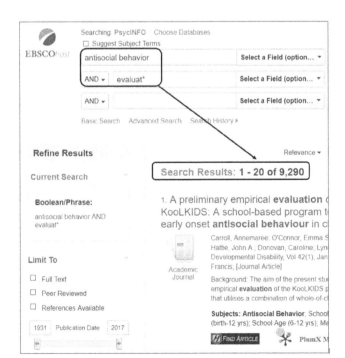

Figure 3.7. Searching using truncation to eliminate word form problem. The PsycINFO® Database screen shot is reproduced with permission of the American Psychological Association, publisher of the PsycINFO database, all rights reserved. No further reproduction or distribution is permitted without written permission from the American Psychological Association. Screen shots also reproduced courtesy of EBSCO Information Services.

Those days, thankfully, are gone. However, my experience, particularly with students, is that once the clicking starts, the thinking stops. Given this, it is good practice to write down search strategies before starting to search, which also gives one the opportunity and place to take notes on search results, subject headings, and so forth. Most platforms use the asterisk as the truncation symbol or "wild card" symbol. Figure 3.6 illustrates the thinking before clicking approach.

Figure 3.7 shows what happens to our results when we truncate "evaluation" to capture its various forms.

Notice that while the search for "antisocial behavior" and "evaluation" yielded 5,233 results (figure 3.4), truncating "evaluation" to "evaluat*" yields 9,290 results. Not truncating would have caused us to miss more than 3,000 citations on this topic. This is important *not* because we need more results, but because at this point we are trying to capture all of the literature relating in some way to our topic. We will narrow the results later.

The word form issue also pertains to the term "adolescents." What if the author or indexer used "adolescence" or "adolescent?" Figure 3.8 indicates what happens to our results when we search all three terms, truncating evaluation and adolescents (i.e., evaluat* *and* antisocial behavior *and* adolescen*) to capture the various word forms.

Our results increased from 1,442 (figure 3.5) with all three terms and no truncation to 2,902 with all three terms and "evaluation" and "adolescence" being truncated. Again,

the goal is *not* to increase the number of results, but to create an exhaustive search.

3.18. Addressing the "Alternate Terms/Synonyms" Problem

Our second "hidden" limiter is the failure to use alternate words or synonyms. In the case of our example, one alternate word for "evaluation" would be "assessment." An alternate word for "adolescents" would be "teenagers" or "youth." Again, we would want to truncate these terms to "assess*" and "teenage" to capture the various forms (i.e., assessing, assess, assessed, teen, teenage, teenaged). Figure 3.9 indicates how the number of results increases by using alternate words and synonyms and truncating those terms.

Changing our second search field from "evaluat*" to "evaluate* or assess*" while leaving our third search term "adolescen*" created an increase in results from 2,902 to 9,401. When we change our third search field from "adolescen*" to "adolescen* or teen*," the number of results increases only slightly. When we further add the term "youth," the results again increase only slightly. These changes indicate that researchers and/or indexers frequently use some variation of the word "assessment" instead of "evaluation," but use variations of "teen" and "youth" less frequently than some variation of the term "adolescents." I'd like to note here that one can't know any of this until one actually conducts the searches, which is

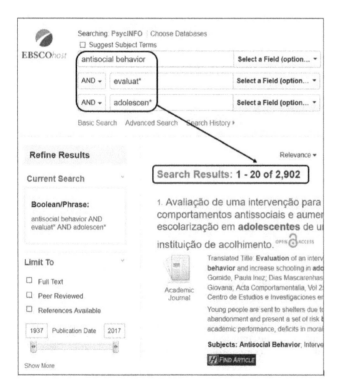

Figure 3.8.   Another sample of truncation eliminating word form problem. The PsycINFO® Database screen shot is reproduced with permission of the American Psychological Association, publisher of the PsycINFO database, all rights reserved. No further reproduction or distribution is permitted without written permission from the American Psychological Association. Screen shots also reproduced courtesy of EBSCO Information Services.

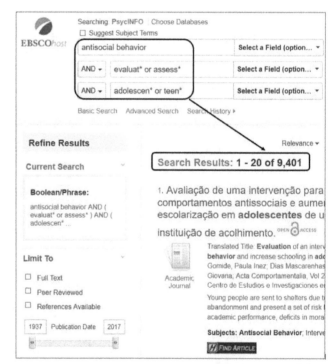

Figure 3.9.   Example of using "or" statement for alternate search terms. The PsycINFO® Database screen shot is reproduced with permission of the American Psychological Association, publisher of the PsycINFO database, all rights reserved. No further reproduction or distribution is permitted without written permission from the American Psychological Association. Screen shots also reproduced courtesy of EBSCO Information Services.

"OR" CAVEAT: Although there are boxes to the left of the search terms boxes that allow one to select "and" or "or" or "not," using these boxes to indicate "or" relationships only works under limited conditions such as "A (box 1) or B (box 2)" or "A (box 1) or B (box 2) not C (box 3)."

When combining "and" and "or" search terms as in our example, it is best to put "or statements" in a single box, as illustrated. This makes it clear that the search is A (box 1) and (B or C).

Basically, it is an order of operations problem—remember PEMDAS from high school—the order of operations? Parenthetical operations are done first—in this case, having "or" terms in a single box is equivalent to them being in parentheses, so that operation occurs first, regardless of which box is used.

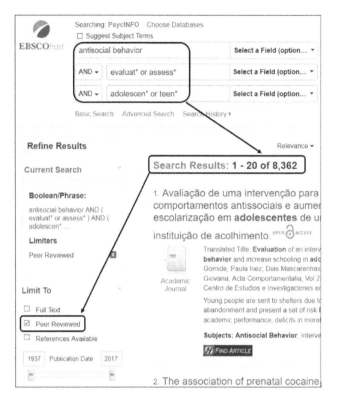

Figure 3.10. Limiting search to peer-reviewed articles. The PsycINFO® Database screen shot is reproduced with permission of the American Psychological Association, publisher of the PsycINFO database, all rights reserved. No further reproduction or distribution is permitted without written permission from the American Psychological Association. Screen shots also reproduced courtesy of EBSCO Information Services.

why it is so important to have something like the "search strategizer" at hand to plan one's searches and upon which to take notes.

At this point we can feel fairly confident that we have captured most of the literature relating to our topic. It is now time to narrow our results.

In the Ebscohost version, and probably other versions of PsycINFO, one can enter limiters from the search page or from the main advanced search page. We address each of these methods here. First, notice in the images above that one can check one or more boxes for "full-text," "peer-reviewed," and "references available." In our example, we want to see only peer-reviewed articles, so we will check the "peer-reviewed" box.

On the advanced search screen, one has the option of selecting "peer-reviewed journals" or "peer-reviewed." There are many items in peer-reviewed journals that are *not* peer reviewed, such as book reviews, commentaries, editorials, and letters to the editor. Selecting "peer-reviewed" limits the results to peer-reviewed articles.

An explanation of why we don't check the other boxes (e.g., "full-text") follows later in this chapter. As seen in figure 3.10, this reduces our results to 8,362. The eliminated items are some combination of book chapters, dissertations, editorials, commentaries, and so forth.

Notice that the next limiter is the date range bar. If we compare figures 3.3 through 3.5 and figures 3.7 and 3.8, we notice that the date range bar changes to indicate the period during which items that meet all the search criteria were published. Generally, when starting to search on a topic in psychology, we want to start with the most recent five years, expecting that anything significant from early periods will be cited in those articles. Manually sliding the bar to 2012 or entering "2012" in the first date box reduces the results from 8,362 to 3,161 items from 2012 through and including 2017 (the present).

Again, we've already checked "peer-reviewed," so we do not need to check "academic journals" or any other link/box

to limit to a journal type. To reiterate an earlier point, when presented with a choice of selecting "peer-reviewed" or "peer-reviewed journal," one should select "peer-reviewed." This is because peer-reviewed journals contain many items that are not peer-reviewed articles, including book reviews, editorials, letters to the editor, and commentaries.

Some of the other limiters available on the left sidebar are shown in figure 3.11.

Clicking on any of the limiters in figure 3.11 will provide the opportunity to further narrow your search. The sublimiters vary based on the existing search. Some of the sublimiters for our sample search can be seen in figure 3.12.

The option for major subject headings will indicate the major subject headings for the items in the result list with the number of items with each subject heading if one wants

3.19. KEYWORDS V. SUBJECTS

In recent years, authors have been asked to supply keywords with their articles. As individual authors, they may use different and idiosyncratic terms for the same topic.

Subject headings, on the other hand, are controlled vocabulary assigned by professional indexers employed by the database in question. Thus, multiple articles on the same topic, but for which the various authors have assigned different keywords, will be assigned the same subject headings by professional indexers.

WHY ARE SUBJECT HEADINGS SO IMPORTANT?

As indicated previously, subject headings are important because they pull together articles on the same topic but with different author-assigned keywords.

Another reason subject headings are important is that sometimes the researcher has no adequate phrasing for what he or she is seeking. For example, a student in class was interested in parental expectations when their child was the first person in the family to go to college. "Parental expectations" was fairly simple, but the second concept, "child is first person in family to go to college," is, to say the least, a clear concept but verbally awkward. I suspected that there would be a body of literature on this topic, but neither the student nor I had any good search ideas. She entered the phrase we have used, and the result was three items. We then opened the record for one of the items, and there was a subject heading "first-generation college student." When we searched using that subject heading, we found the body of literature she was seeking.

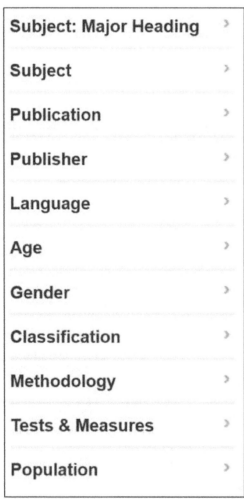

Figure 3.11. Fields that can be limited from left sidebar. The PsycINFO® Database screen shot is reproduced with permission of the American Psychological Association, publisher of the PsycINFO database, all rights reserved. No further reproduction or distribution is permitted without written permission from the American Psychological Association. Screen shots also reproduced courtesy of EBSCO Information Services.

Subject ⌄

☐ adolescent development (321)

☐ risk factors (310)

☐ victimization (219)

☐ human females (217)

☐ antisocial behavior (192)

☐ at risk populations (185)

Show More

Publication ⟩

Publisher ⟩

Language ⟩

Age ⟩

Gender ⟩

Classification ⟩

Methodology ⌄

☐ empirical study (7,178)

☐ quantitative study (5,209)

☐ longitudinal study (1,406)

☐ interview (1,189)

☐ followup study (565)

☐ prospective study (409)

Figure 3.12. Selected field limitation options. The PsycINFO® Database screen shot is reproduced with permission of the American Psychological Association, publisher of the PsycINFO database, all rights reserved. No further reproduction or distribution is permitted without written permission from the American Psychological Association. Screen shots also reproduced courtesy of EBSCO Information Services.

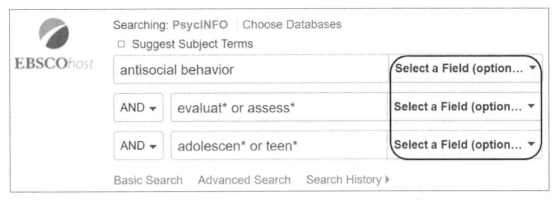

Figure 3.13. "Select a Field"; i.e., no search field selected. The PsycINFO® Database screen shot is reproduced with permission of the American Psychological Association, publisher of the PsycINFO database, all rights reserved. No further reproduction or distribution is permitted without written permission from the American Psychological Association. Screen shots also reproduced courtesy of EBSCO Information Services.

to narrow the results. Each of the other options on the sidebar works in much the same way, indicating the journals and how many result items are in each journal, the methodologies used and how many result items use that methodology, and so forth. Major classification codes are also available.

As mentioned previously, many limiters on the left sidebar of the search page are also available, along with others, on the main advanced search page. Typically, beginning researchers begin with searching, then limiting, and this is actually a good strategy for most beginners. More sophisticated researchers, however, may want to begin by setting their limiters first, using the main advanced search page, which is typically the page to which the database opens. If one is already on the search/results page, clicking "advanced search" beneath the search boxes will return one to the original opening screen.

We have not yet addressed "field" selection, which is related to both the advanced search page and the PsycINFO record. As seen in figure 3.13, the default field setting is "Select a Field."

The equivalent of "Select a Field" may be "Any Field," "keyword," or similar terms in other platforms and other databases. Clicking on "Select a Field" will result in a drop-down menu, as illustrated in figure 3.14.

Search terms are "what" is being searched. *Fields* are "where" the terms are being searched.

Thus far, searching and some limiters have been addressed, but not the crucial question of precisely *where* the search terms are being searched for (this is when I always get the deer-in-the-headlights look in class). With rare exception, what is being searched is the PsycINFO record. Figure 3.15 is an example of a PsycINFO record.

Note that many of the fields in the PsycINFO record correspond to the fields listed in figure 3.19. When one does *not* select a field (i.e., does not select from the drop-down menu to the right of the search terms), one is searching the entire

Figure 3.14. Fields to which one can limit search term(s). The PsycINFO® Database screen shot is reproduced with permission of the American Psychological Association, publisher of the PsycINFO database, all rights reserved. No further reproduction or distribution is permitted without written permission from the American Psychological Association. Screen shots also reproduced courtesy of EBSCO Information Services.

Interrelationships and **continuities** in symptoms of oppositional defiant and conduct disorders from age 4 to 10 in the community. ᴼᴾᴱᴺ ACCESS

Authors:	Husby, Silje Merethe. Department of Psychology, Norwegian University of Science and Technology, Trondheim, Norway, silje.husby@ntnu.no Wichstrøm, Lars. Department of Psychology, Norwegian University of Science and Technology, Trondheim, Norway
Address:	Husby, Silje Merethe, silje.husby@ntnu.no

Source:	Journal of Abnormal Child Psychology, Vol 45(5), Jul, 2017. pp. 947-958.
NLM Title Abbreviation:	J Abnorm Child Psychol
Page Count:	12
Publisher:	Germany : Springer
ISSN:	0091-0627 (Print) 1573-2835 (Electronic)
Language:	English
Keywords:	Oppositional defiant disorder, Conduct disorder, Longitudinal, Diagnostic interview, Early onset

Abstract:	Childhood oppositional defiant disorder (ODD) has commonly been thought to increase the risk of conduct disorder (CD) in late childhood and adolescence. However, symptoms of CD may also emerge during preschool and middle childhood. The few studies that have examined whether ODD increases the risk of such early onset CD have produced equivocal results, potentially due to methodological issues. In this study, a community sample of Norwegian 4-year-olds (n = 1042, 49.9 % males) was examined bi-annually over four waves of data collection. Symptoms of ODD, CD, attention-deficit/hyperactivity disorder (ADHD), anxiety and depressive disorders were measured through interviews with parents and children using the Preschool Age Psychiatric Assessment and the Child and Adolescent Psychiatric Assessment. The results showed that at all ages, more symptoms of ODD predicted more symptoms of CD at the next age of examination even after adjusting for previous CD and comorbid conditions. The effect of previous ODD on CD two years later did not differ according to gender, SES, or parental cohabitating status at any point in time. There was modest homotypical **continuity** in symptoms of CD and moderate homotypical **continuity** in symptoms of ODD. Symptoms of ODD increased from age 4 to 8 and declined to age 10. In conclusion, symptoms of ODD increase the risk of early onset symptoms of CD. The **continuity** in symptoms of ODD, and to some extent CD, combined with an increased risk of early symptoms of CD forecasted by symptoms of ODD, underscore the importance of detection, prevention and treatment of behavioral disorders already in early childhood. (PsycINFO Database Record (c) 2017 APA, all rights reserved)

Document Type:	Journal Article
Subjects:	*Child Psychopathology; *Conduct Disorder; *Oppositional Defiant Disorder; *Symptoms
PsycINFO Classification:	Behavior Disorders & Antisocial Behavior (3230)
Population:	Human Male Female
Location:	Norway
Age Group:	Childhood (birth-12 yrs) Preschool Age (2-5 yrs)
Tests & Measures:	Strengths and Difficulties Questionnaire-4–16 Version Child and Adolescent Psychiatric Assessment Preschool Age Psychiatric Assessment DOI: 10.1037/t39097-000
Grant Sponsorship:	Sponsor: Research Council of Norway, Norway Grant Number: 228685; 202478 Recipients: No recipient indicated
Methodology:	Empirical Study; Interview; Quantitative Study
Format Covered:	Electronic
Publication Type:	Journal; Peer Reviewed Journal
Publication History:	First Posted: Oct 25, 2016
Release Date:	20161031
Correction Date:	20170706
Copyright:	This article is published with open access at Springerlink.com.. The Author(s). 2016
Digital Object Identifier:	http://dx.doi.org/10.1007/s10802-016-0210-4
PMID:	27783258
Accession Number:	2016-52193-001

Figure 3.15.   Example of a PsycINFO record. The PsycINFO® Database screen shot is reproduced with permission of the American Psychological Association, publisher of the PsycINFO database, all rights reserved. No further reproduction or distribution is permitted without written permission from the American Psychological Association. Screen shots also reproduced courtesy of EBSCO Information Services.

record. One is essentially saying "Retrieve all results that contain my search terms *anywhere* in the record." When one uses the limiters on the left sidebar (shown in figure 3.12), one is selecting sublimiters within a field (i.e., subject, methodology). An advantage of using the sidebar limiters after searching is that the sublimiters are those that apply to the search conducted, and one can see the number of items that match that sublimiter. Classification codes are one of the limiters; major classifications are listed on the sidebar and on the advanced search page. A more detailed list of subcodes is available at http://www.apa.org/pubs/databases/training/class-codes.aspx, and these subcodes can be entered in the search box with "classification code" in the field box. An advantage of using limiters from the main search page is that the limiters "stick" even when one modifies one's search. Because the left sidebar limiters apply to the search conducted, when one modifies the search, they are often reset. Whether using the advanced search screen or the left sidebar, for novice users it is usually best to apply limiters after the search has been constructed so that one knows that one's search terms are on target.

As mentioned previously, one first wants to capture all relevant results, then weed out more tangential results. One does this by searching in particular fields and using other limiters such as those indicated above. The subjects under which the results fall are indicated on the left sidebar, and subject searching is usually an effective limiter. In addition, limiting one's major search term(s) to the "title" field will greatly reduce the number of results. For example, requiring that "antisocial behavior" be in the title field reduces our results to 348 (see figure 3.16) from the original 2,902 illustrated in figure 3.8.

Using the publication date slider on the left sidebar to restrict our results to the last five years further reduces the results to 78. This number of, and even 348, results can be easily scanned to identify items of interest to the researcher.

3.20. Saving Results

As indicated previously, one can manage to scan 78 or even 348 results to identify items of interest. But what to do with them? Virtually all major databases now have a folder function that enables one to save items of interest for future retrieval. In Ebsco, this is called the "folder." The folder is always available, and can be seen in figure 3.17.

Notice also that there is a link to "Sign In." While the folder is always available, one can only retrieve it and its contents if one has created an Ebsco account with which to retrieve it. Often users think they sign in with their institutional credentials; this is not the case. The Ebsco account resides

These accounts are *not* PsycINFO accounts.

They are vendor accounts (e.g., Ebsco, Proquest), which typically work with all databases from a particular vendor to which the institution subscribes.

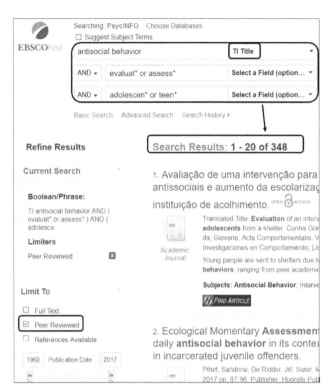

Figure 3.16. Narrowing results by limiting one search term to "Title" field. The PsycINFO® Database screen shot is reproduced with permission of the American Psychological Association, publisher of the PsycINFO database, all rights reserved. No further reproduction or distribution is permitted without written permission from the American Psychological Association. Screen shots also reproduced courtesy of EBSCO Information Services.

on Ebsco's server and must be *created*. When one clicks on "Sign In," one will be able to sign in or create an account.

Once one has created an account, one will be returned to the home screen, where one can create folders for various projects by first clicking on the folder at the top of the search screen and then clicking "new," as shown in figure 3.18.

One can create as many folders as one wishes and nest folders within each other. One can delete, move, and copy items among folders. To place items in a folder for future use, while in the results page one clicks on the folder icon, as shown in figure 3.19.

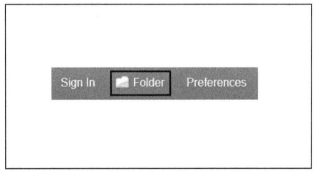

Figure 3.17. Generic folder. Screen shot reproduced courtesy of EBSCO

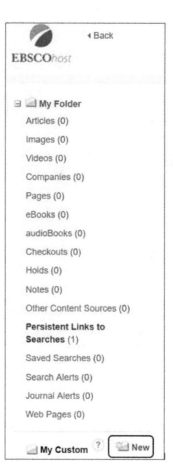

Figure 3.18. Creating folders in Ebsco account. Screen shot reproduced courtesy of EBSCO

Figure 3.19. Adding items in result list to account folder(s). The PsycINFO® Database screen shot is reproduced with permission of the American Psychological Association, publisher of the PsycINFO database, all rights reserved. No further reproduction or distribution is permitted without written permission from the American Psychological Association. Screen shots also reproduced courtesy of EBSCO Information Services.

You will only be able to place items in and retrieve them from *your* folder(s) if you are logged into your account. You should develop the habit of logging in when you begin work. If you are gone from the computer for a while, you may be timed out; check and log in again. If you forgot to log in when you started working, your work will be saved if you log in before exiting.

If you have more than one folder in your account, you will get a drop-down menu of folders from which to select. The folder icon will then turn yellow, indicating that the item has been placed in a folder.

3.21. Saving Searches

You have created some really sophisticated searches with many limiters that have yielded great result lists. This is for a long-term project or research program, and you know you will want to return and re-create your searches. UGH!! But voila!! You do not need to take copious notes on your search terms, fields, and limiters. You simply need to save your searches to be rerun at a later date. Reruns will conduct an identical search, but also pull in the most recent items that meet the search criteria, be it a month, six months, or two years later.

In Ebscohost, one saves searches by clicking on "Share" at the top of the results list, then adding the current search to the folder, as shown in figure 3.20. One can also share the search with another person with access to the same database and vendor by cutting, pasting, and sending the permanent URL to that person.

3.22. Creating Reference Lists from Databases

Many databases allow one to create reference lists in various citation formats from result lists or folder lists. In Ebsco, one enters one's folder at the top of the search screen; clicks on the folder of interest; and clicks on "Articles," which will cause the articles in the folder to appear in the main screen. On the right sidebar, one clicks on the "Print" link to be taken to a screen similar to that in figure 3.21, then can follows the instructions on how to create citations only in APA style.

Clicking "Print" will result in a list of citations that can be printed (see figure 3.22).

Your interest, however, is not in printing a separate page of citations, but in entering those citations into the reference

A few caveats: As noted at the top of the list, Ebsco refers users to one of its websites and also advises them to check their own publication manual requirements. Citations from virtually any citation manager often have errors. In this list, the citations are not in alphabetical order, and there are several places where the author and article title are in all capital letters. So a knowledge of APA formatting is still required. It seems, however, that it is easier to work with an existing list and check for formatting errors than to type the list letter by letter.

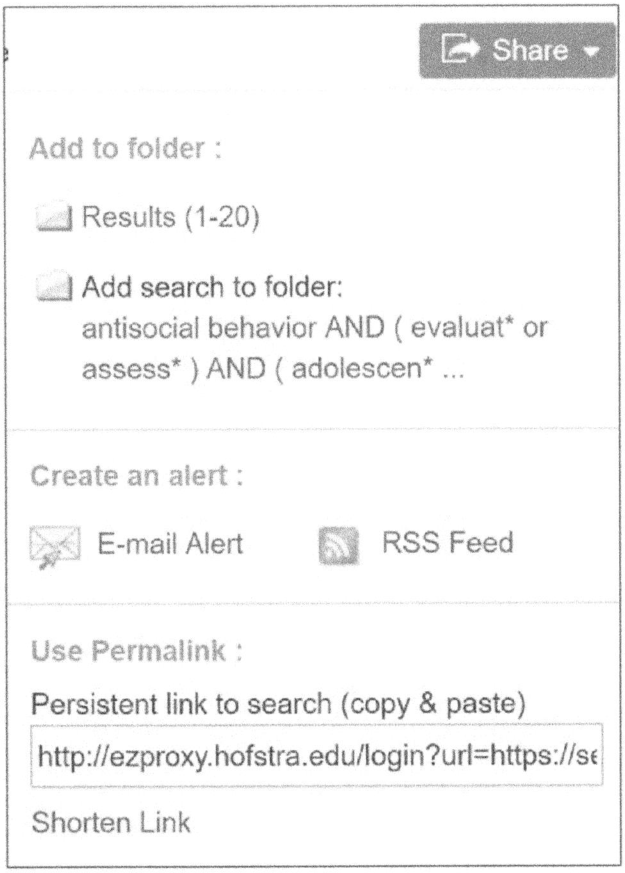

Figure 3.20.   Saving searches for further use. Screen shot reproduced courtesy of EBSCO

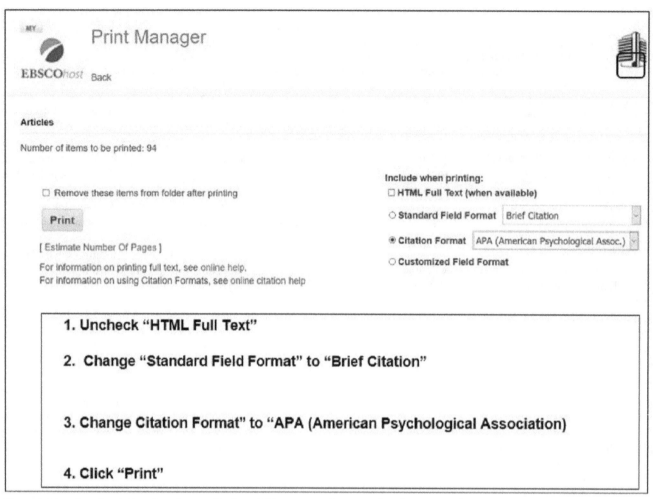

Figure 3.21.   Creating APA-style reference list from folder. Screen shot reproduced courtesy of EBSCO

NOTE: Review the instructions at http://support.ebsco.com/help/?int=ehost&lang=&feature_id=APA and make any necessary corrections before using. **Pay special attention to personal names, capitalization, and dates.** Always consult your library resources for the exact formatting and punctuation guidelines.

References

Brännström, L., Kaunitz, C., Andershed, A., South, S., & Smedslund, G. (2016). Aggression replacement training (ART) for reducing antisocial behavior in adolescents and adults: A systematic review. *Aggression And Violent Behavior*, 2730-41. doi:10.1016/j.avb.2016.02.006

Samek, D. R., Elkins, I. J., Keyes, M. A., Iacono, W. G., & McGue, M. (2015). High school sports involvement diminishes the association between childhood conduct disorder and adult antisocial behavior. *Journal Of Adolescent Health*, 57(1), 107-112. doi:10.1016/j.jadohealth.2015.03.009

Raine, A., Fung, A. C., Portnoy, J., Choy, O., & Spring, V. L. (2014). Low heart rate as a risk factor for child and adolescent proactive aggressive and impulsive psychopathic behavior. *Aggressive Behavior*, 40(4), 290-299. doi:10.1002/ab.21523

DiLallo, J. J., Jones, M., & Westen, D. (2009). Personality subtypes in disruptive adolescent males. *Journal Of Nervous And Mental Disease*, 197(1), 15-23. doi:10.1097/NMD.0b013e318192770c

Klahr, A. M., & Burt, S. A. (2014). Practitioner review: Evaluation of the known behavioral heterogeneity in conduct disorder to improve its assessment and treatment. *Journal Of Child Psychology And Psychiatry*, 55(12), 1300-1310. doi:10.1111/jcpp.12268

Manders, W. A., Deković, M., Asscher, J. J., van der Laan, P. H., & Prins, P. M. (2013). Psychopathy as predictor and moderator of multisystemic therapy outcomes among adolescents treated for antisocial behavior. *Journal Of Abnormal Child Psychology*, 41(7), 1121-1132. doi:10.1007/s10802-013-9749-5

Liu, M., Ming, Q., Yi, J., Wang, X., & Yao, S. (2016). Screen time on school days and risks for psychiatric symptoms and self-harm in mainland Chinese adolescents. *Frontiers In Psychology*, 7

Figure 3.22.   Sample APA-style references generated from folder. The PsycINFO® Database screen shot is reproduced with permission of the American Psychological Association, publisher of the PsycINFO database, all rights reserved. No further reproduction or distribution is permitted without written permission from the American Psychological Association. Screen shots also reproduced courtesy of EBSCO Information Services.

list of your paper. So instead of printing, close the print box and copy and paste the citation list into your paper.

3.23. Why Not Select "Full-Text"?

Everyone wants the full text. Of course! So why not check the full-text box when it is available? Again, let's take the case of Ebsco, although the points to be made apply to other vendors of multiple databases as well.

I indicated previously in this chapter that most of the major and well-established databases (e.g., PsycINFO, Medline, LLBA) are index/abstract databases only. They contain *no* full text. When one is using a database from a particular vendor (e.g., Ebsco) and one checks the full-text box, Ebsco restricts its results to those that contain full text, and the user will see an "HTML" or "PDF" link with the item (this is a simplified explanation). *The problem is that Ebsco can only see the full text available within databases available via Ebsco.* So, for example, at my institution we get approximately thirty databases via Ebsco. Some of those databases contain full text, and those items that meet the search criteria and have full text will appear in the results list when restricting to full text only. My institution, however, subscribes to approximately 180 databases, 150 of which are not subscribed to via Ebsco and many of which are actually publisher websites. Articles for which there is full text in the non-Ebsco databases will be excluded from the results, as Ebsco cannot "see" them. Almost all institutions subscribe to a "link-resolver," which searches all of their databases for the full text of articles. In these cases, what typically occurs is that instead of an "HTML" or "PDF" link appearing, a link indicating "Find Article" or some similar icon appears. Clicking on that link brings one to a page with a link to the full text, an indication that one should order the item through interlibrary loan, or other information on retrieving the full text of the item.

There are numerous other useful features in PsycINFO and other subscription databases available through multiple vendors. The details change among vendors, and they are too numerous to detail in this chapter. This is where my advice applies to become intimately familiar with your databases and make them your best friends!

4

Tests and Measures

INTRODUCTION

The area of tests and measures is probably one of the most problematic for beginning and experienced researchers, yet it is one of the most integral to both the science and practice of psychology. It is also the area that historically and currently strongly distinguishes psychology from the areas of medicine and social work. In addition, the acquisition of knowledge in psychology and other social sciences depends on, among other issues, the quality of the measures used to collect data. In virtually all of the materials examined for this section, the authors lament the use of poor measures used in research, due, they suspect, to the difficulty of finding substantial bodies of measures from which the researcher can then select, based on good reliabilities and validities in all of their variations.

Although the words "tests," "assessments," and "measurements" are often used interchangeably (as is done here), they actually are separate but related terms.

Psychological tests are formal instruments such as questionnaires or checklists, on which the testee's scores are norm referenced—meaning they are evaluated against scores of those with a similar age, sex, diagnosis, etc.

Psychological assessments are broader and may include interviews, norm-referenced psychological tests, behavioral observation, and other means. In any case, they usually consist of several tests and measures.

A measure is a tool that places item(s), scores(s), verbalization(s), behavior(s), and other variables on one of four types of scales (nominal, ordinal, interval, or ratio).

This section includes sources that cover all three terms. Four main types of sources in the area of tests and measures are covered in this chapter:

- Resources providing information about and evaluating tests and measures
- Resources about assessment using tests and measures
- Resources containing tests and measures
- Resources indexing tests and measures

Sometimes there is overlap among these resources. For example, a book may contain the full text of some tests but provide only information about the test and author/publisher contact information for others. Books whose primary purpose is to address the use of assessments will sometimes include information about specific instruments to illustrate the points being made. Many books that contain actual measures cover a particular topic or topics in depth and include the measures as chapter or book appendixes. *For ease of use, particularly in e-book format, items are repeated in each area for which they are appropriate, rather than using cross-references.*

Regarding *timeliness*, research in psychology often focuses on journal literature published within the previous five years. As the journal literature is extensive, research is incremental, and referencing is extensive in psychology, it is generally safe for the researcher to assume that earlier research on the topic will be referenced in the more recent literature.

In the case of tests and measures, however, this strategy is usually not effective or desirable. Before addressing why this is so, let's first review two main types of tests and measures.

COMMERCIAL AND RESEARCH TESTS

There are two major classes of tests and measures: commercial and research.

4.1. Commercial Tests

Commercial tests are *not* better than research tests. Commercial tests measure constructs that have commercial viability (i.e., the developers can earn money from them). Returning to the terminology above, they are actually *tests*; scores are norm referenced, meaning they are evaluated against the scores of those of a similar age, sex, diagnosis, etc. In order to sell a test, developers must have a high-quality product. In the case of tests and measures, this means that the products must rate highly on the factors by which they are evaluated.

Following are some examples of commercial tests are tests with which you are probably familiar:

- College and university admissions test such as the SAT, GRE, LSAT, and MCAT
- Tests used in clinical settings, such as the MMPI-, WAIS-, WISC-, and Beck Depression Inventory
- Employment screening tests

Commercial tests may be used for many purposes. In a clinical or educational setting, an issue or "symptom" may arise, and testing will be done for diagnostic purposes or to understand more precisely the nature of the problem. In workplace or educational settings, testing may be done to determine one's aptitude or "fit" for a specific position or school setting. In the settings above, as well as many others, testing may also be used to evaluate efficacy of training, teaching, therapy, and other programs and interventions.

4.2. Research Tests

Research tests often have a lot of reliability and validity data, but do not have an identified commercial viability. Following are examples of research tests:

- The Crowne-Marlowe scale of social desirability
- The Stroop test (color-word perception test)
- The ATDP (Attitudes toward Disabled Persons) scale

Research tests are typically used for in-class demonstrations, senior theses, master's theses, doctoral dissertations, and academic and research.

4.3. ETHICS IN TESTING

Ethical use of tests includes having permission to use the test. *All* tests are covered by copyright law. An author or publisher may choose to put an instrument in the public domain, making it free for anyone to use, or may permit it to be used under particular circumstances or by particular users. Unless a test clearly states that it is in the public domain or does not require permission to use it, permission is required except in situations covered by "fair use."

There are many ethical and legal issues involved in testing, some of which are specific to certain settings and others that are specific to particular populations. It is the responsibility of the user to be familiar with and adhere to legal and ethical standards. Assessments and the tests used in them are covered under chapter 9 of the American Psychological Association's (APA) Ethical Principles of Psychologists and Code of Conduct (http://www.apa.org/ethics/code/). Users of tests should also be familiar with the most recent edition of *Standards for Educational and Psychological Testing*, copublished by the American Educational Research

Association (AERA), the American Psychological Association (APA), and the National Council on Measurement in Education (NCME).

In the case of commercial tests, just because you find a test doesn't mean you can use it. Many commercial tests are "restricted" to use by those with particular credentials. An excellent overview of psychological testing is provided by the National Institutes of Health at https://www.ncbi.nlm.nih.gov/books/NBK305233/. Generally, there are three classes of restriction. Some tests require a doctorate in psychology, education, a related field, and/or licensure. Some require a master's degree in psychology, education, or a related field and some training in assessment. Others, such as some behavioral checklists, do not require advanced education or training in assessment.

Users of commercial tests must pay for the test material itself as well as all "consumables" (e.g., answer sheets, scoring sheets). It is possible that the publisher will allow a commercial test to be used at no cost or at a discounted rate for research purposes. Potential users should not be automatically discouraged by the thought of cost; some commercial tests are not at all expensive, and if the test is to be used in a dissertation, the expense may be a drop in the bucket of the total cost of the PhD!

Research tests, although free to use, are still the intellectual property of the publisher/author. Users of research tests should contact the publisher/author and advise that they will be using the test in a particular research project, unless the publisher/author has indicated otherwise in writing (on a web page, in the frontmatter of a book, etc.). It is particularly important to advise publishers/authors if you are modifying their intellectual property. I will note here that there are some who adhere to the position that use of research tests in academic research projects falls under fair use guidelines. Basic information on fair use can be found at https://www.copyright.gov/fair-use/more-info.html. Columbia University also has a useful copyright information page at https://copyright.columbia.edu/basics/fair-use/fair-use-checklist.html; the page also includes a link to an excellent "Fair Use Checklist."

Sometimes the author of a test may be deceased or otherwise inaccessible. In this case, if use of a test does not fall under fair use, the user should contact the copyright holder's institution, which may hold the copyright or be able to direct the user to the proper contact.

And users should, of course, credit the author(s)/publisher(s) in their work!

RESOURCES PROVIDING INFORMATION ABOUT AND EVALUATING TESTS AND MEASURES

Buros Products

4.4. *Mental measurements yearbook (MMY)*. Buros Center for Testing (serial, 1938–). Lincoln: University of Nebraska Press. BF431/Z5814. This serial publication, also known as "Buros" after the initial author, was published irregularly in its early years but is now published tri-annually. All tests in MMY are in English and are published, commercial tests that must be purchased. MMY entries include descriptions of the test (author, publisher, item types, administration and scoring, intended purpose and population) and two substantive and critical professional reviews, which contain reference lists. A test may be reviewed in more than one edition of MMY if it has been revised or widely used since its earlier inclusion. Each volume, however, stands on its own; later volumes do *not* supersede earlier volumes. Beginning with the fourteenth MMY in 2001, tests must also provide documentation of their technical quality in order to be reviewed. Many MMY tests are considered restricted materials and require specific credentials for purchase and use (see chapter 9 of APA's Ethical Principles of Psychologists and Code of Conduct for more information, at http://www.apa.org/ethics/code2022.html#9). The content of all volumes of MMY is also now available in electronic format by subscription via Ebsco and Ovid. As tests reviewed in MMY are commercial and sometimes restricted, this work is of most use to graduate students, researchers, and practitioners who are using these tests or in search of tests to use in research or practice.

4.5. *Pruebas publicadas en español = An index of Spanish tests in print.* Schlueter, J. E., Carlson, J. F., Geisinger, K. F., & Murphy, L. L. (2013). Lincoln: University of Nebraska Press. 450 pp. Z5814. This volume is an adaptation of *Tests in Print* (see above). It indexes and provides detailed information about 422 tests published in Spanish that are in print, as well as their appropriate use. For each entry, information is presented in both Spanish and English.

4.6. *Tests in print (TIP).* Buros Center for Testing. (serial, 1961–). Lincoln: University of Nebraska Press. BF431/LB 3051/Z5814. This serial publication provides a comprehensive index to and information about commercial tests that are currently in print in English. It also serves as a cumulative index to tests reviewed in MMY. At this time, the most recent edition is *Test in Print* IX (2016), which contains entries for 2,314 tests currently in print. For each entry, the following information is included: title; purpose; population; publication date; acronym; scores/subscores and descriptions of what they measure; administration (group or individual); forms, parts, and levels; manual; restrictions on market distribution, if any (e.g., distributed only to police departments); price date (for test, consumables, manual); foreign language availability; time needed; comments if any; author; publisher; foreign adaptations; sublistings (if levels editions or subtests of parts of a test are available individually); and cross-referencing. Cross-referencing may be to MMY, notated, for example, as 12:802 (MMY volume XII, test

number 802); an earlier edition of TIP, notated, for example, as T6:207 (TIP volume VI, test number 207); or *Personality Tests and Reviews*, notated, for example, as P:399 (Personality Tests and Reviews, test number 399). Note that if a test was included in an earlier edition of TIP, but not the current edition, the test is no longer in print. There are a number of useful indexes, covering MMY test reviewers, titles, out-of-print tests, acronyms, classified subjects, publishers directory, names index (which indicates if a name belongs to a test author or reviewer), and scores. The score index is particularly useful as it indexes subscales within a test and provides the test number, thus providing information about measurement of constructs or behaviors for which there may not be an entire test. TIP classifies tests into eighteen subject areas: achievement, behavior assessment, developmental, education, English and language, fine arts, foreign languages, intelligence and general aptitude, mathematics, miscellaneous, neuropsychological, personality, reading, science, sensory-motor, social studies, speech and hearing, and vocations. The classified subject index provides a description of what is included in each category, then lists the titles and test numbers of tests that fall within that designation. TIP does not include proprietary instruments (e.g., those used for licensure or admissions, or by highly secured markets such as some government divisions). TIP IX includes tests published in the MMY XX (2017). TIP is available with MMY in electronic format by subscription via Ebsco and Ovid at this time. As tests indexed and described in TIP are commercial and sometimes restricted, this work is of most use to graduate students, researchers, and practitioners who are using these tests or in search of tests to use for research or practice. A practitioner or researcher seeking a print version of a test to use is best off beginning the search with the latest edition of TIP, as it provides a cumulative index of tests that are in print and thus available and provides an index to the in-depth reviews and references in MMY. For other researchers, of course, the process of their search depends on what they are investigating.

In addition to MMY and TIP, Buros published a number of books on specific subsets of tests within MMY and TIP. Following is a full description of one of these books, *Personality Tests and Reviews II* (which includes coverage of TIP II). After that annotation is a list of the other Buros titles, most of which are organized in a similar fashion to *Personality Tests*. A major caveat is that unlike MMY and TIP, which are still being published, the following works were generally published from the late 1960s through the early 1970s, more than forty years ago (one was published in 1936!). In addition, they are not user friendly. Thus, as tests on these topics have continued to be developed, revised, and covered in the ongoing MMY and TIP publications, these works will be of use primarily to serious advanced researchers interested in the historical development of tests in each topic area who have the patience for a steep learning curve.

4.7. *Personality tests and reviews* and *Personality tests and reviews II (PTR)*. Buros, O. K. (Ed.). (1970, 1975). Highland Park, NJ: Gryphon Press. 2500 pp. BF698. The major purpose of the work was to make readily available information on personality tests that were included in the first six volumes of *Mental Measurements Yearbook* (MMY); information on new personality tests not included in those yearbooks; and new references on the construction, use, and validity of specific tests. The 241-page "Personality Test Index" in the first volume contains 379 entries for tests that were in print as of June 1, 1969, and 134 entries for out-of-print tests as of June 1969, but which were included in the first six volumes of MMY. Of the 379 in-print tests, 110 were new and not included in the MMY up to that time, and 58 were revised since their inclusion in MMY. The star symbol indicates titles that were not previously listed in MMY, and asterisks identify titles that were revised since their MMY entry. PTR entries include test title, description, group for whom intended, acronym, copyright/publication date, subscales, scores, whether for individual or group testing, forms, parts and levels, pages (as appropriate), reliability and validity, cost, time required, author, publisher, and cross-references. If an entry has been cited in MMY, it is cross-referenced to the MMY volume and test number; if newer references are available, they are included. If the test is a new item never included in previous MMYs, all information is in this index. If the test is out of print, that is indicated. Reviews from the first six MMYs comprise the next section of this work. Each MMY constitutes a chapter, and each MMY chapter is divided into projective and nonprojective tests. The last index in volume 1 lists all tests in the volume by category of projective or nonprojective. PTR II in essence does the same as and is organized like PTR, but it covers the *seventh* volume of MMY and also includes tests, including nonpersonality tests, indexed in *Tests in Print II* (TIP II). Before consulting these volumes, the user should be cognizant of the fact that they are dated and not particularly user friendly; they are probably best used by sophisticated researchers interested in the history of personality testing. A useful article for those using PTR is Fred Damarin's "A Special Review of Buros' *Personality Tests and Reviews*," *Educational and Psychological Measurement* 31 (1971): 21–241.

Following are the other "test and review" books published by the Institute of Mental Measurements and edited by Oscar Buros:

4.8. *Educational, psychological and personality tests of 1933, 1934, and 1935*. Buros, O. K. (Ed.). (1936). New Brunswick, NJ: School of Education, Rutgers University. 83 pp. Z5814.

4.9. *English tests and reviews: A monograph consisting of the English sections of the seven Mental Measurements Yearbooks (1938–72) and Tests in Print II (1974)*. Buros, O. K. (Ed.). (1975). Highland Park, NJ: Gryphon Press. 395 pp. PE66/Z2015.

4.10. *Foreign language tests and reviews: A monograph consisting of the foreign language sections of the seven Mental Measurements Yearbooks (1938–72) and Tests in Print II (1974)*. Buros, O. K. (Ed.). (1975). Highland Park, NJ: Gryphon Press. 312 pp. P53/Z814.

4.11. *Intelligence tests and reviews: A monography consisting of the intelligence sections of the seven Mental Measurements Yearbooks (1938–72) and Tests in Print II (1974)*. Buros, O. K. (Ed.). (1975). Highland Park, NJ: Gryphon Press. 1129 pp. BF176.

4.12. *Mathematics tests and reviews: A monograph consisting of the mathematics sections of the seven Mental Measurements Yearbooks (1938–72) and Tests in Print II (1974)*. Buros, O. K. (Ed.). (1975). Highland Park, NJ: Gryphon Press. 435 pp. QA43/Z6651.

4.13. *Reading tests and reviews, including a classified index to the Mental Measurements Yearbooks*. Buros, O. K. (Ed.). (1968). Highland Park, NJ: Gryphon Press. 520 pp. LB1050/Z5814.

4.14. *Reading tests and reviews II: A monograph consisting of the reading sections of the seventh Mental Measurements Yearbook (1972) and Tests in Print (1974)*. Buros, O. K. (1975). Highland Park, NJ: Gryphon Press. 257 pp. LB1050.

4.15. *Science tests and reviews: A monograph consisting of the science sections of the seven Mental Measurements Yearbooks (1938–1972) and Tests in Print II (1974)*. Buros, O. K. (1975). Highland Park, NJ: Gryphon Press. 182 pp. Q182/Z5814.

4.16. *Social studies tests and reviews: A monograph consisting of the social studies sections of the seven Mental Measurements Yearbooks (1938–1972) and Tests in Print II (1974)*. Buros, O. K. (1975). Highland Park, NJ: Gryphon Press. 227 pp. H62/Z5814.

4.17. *Vocational tests and reviews: A monograph consisting of the gocational sections of the seven Mental Measurements Yearbooks (1938–1972) and Tests in Print II (1974)*. Buros, O. K. (1975). Highland Park, NY: Gryphon Press. 1087 pp. HF 5381.

Non-Buros Products

4.18. *Test critiques*. Keyser, D. J., & Sweetland, R. C. (Eds.). Ten-volume set (1985–1994). Austin, TX: Pro-Ed. BF176. *Test Critiques* was developed as a companion publication to Pro-Ed's *Tests* (see above). While the information in *Tests* was intended to be, and is, easily scanned and read, for that very reason it is necessarily incomplete, not providing psychometric information or evaluation. *Test Critiques* was developed to provide that information for measures included in *Tests.* Entries are arranged alphabetically by title and generally include an introduction, general applications/uses, technical aspects, and a critique. Although not always followed exactly, this format is intended to provide the user with the instruments' developmental background and historical context; an understanding of the settings in which it is used, who are appropriate and inappropriate subjects for the measure, administration, scoring and interpretation, and reliability and validity information; and an overall critique. Beginning with volume 3, cumulative subject and test title indexes are provided, which correspond specifically with or are compatible with the categories used in *Tests.* There is an alphabetical list of tests covered in each volume on the contents page. Like *Tests,* this publication is intended to be another valuable component in the body of works describing and evaluating psychological, educational, and work measures.

4.19. *Tests: A comprehensive reference for assessments in psychology, education, and business* (irregular serial, 1983–). Austin, TX: Pro-Ed. BF431/LB 3051/Z5814. *Tests* is irregularly published; its first edition came out in 1983 and its most recent, sixth edition was published in 2008. Unlike the Buros products MMY and TIP, the purpose of *Tests* is to provide an easily scanned and readable listing of available tests (i.e., in print) with basic test, administration, availability, pricing, and publisher information; it does *not* review tests or provided psychometric data. *Tests* is organized into three main categories: psychology, education, and business. In the recent editions, each major category is subdivided into twenty to fifty subcategories, which are in alphabetical order, with individual measures listed alphabetically within the subcategory. For each measure, *Tests* provides the title, author(s), copyright date, publisher, population, purpose, description, format (if examiner is required, individual and/or group administration, time required), scoring (if computer scoring is available, hand-keyed, or examiner-evaluated), cost of materials (test, manual, consumables), and also if particular professional credentials are required for administration/scoring. In addition to providing indexes of test titles, authors, and publishers (with contact information), the later editions also provide indexes of tests and publishers not in the current edition that are no longer available or for which information was not verifiable at the time of publication (e.g., the publisher did not respond to inquiries). One weakness of this publication is that the tests are not cross-referenced across major or minor categories. As tests indexed and described in *Tests* are commercial and sometimes restricted, this work is of most use to graduate students, researchers, and practitioners who are using these tests or in search of tests to use for research or practice. The practitioner or researcher seeking a test to use is best off beginning the search with the latest edition of *Tests* for a quick scan, as it provides

an easily scanned and well-organized cumulative index of tests in print and thus available, and can provide a launching pad to other review- and reference-providing works such as those published by Buros (see above).

PsycINFO

4.20. PsycINFO. American Psychological Association (188?–). Information about development, psychometrics, use, administration and scoring, interpretation, and evaluation of tests and measures and actual tests and measures can be also be found using the PsycINFO database. I want to remind novice users that PsycINFO is an indexing/abstracting database; it contains NO full text. This was obvious when its predecessors were in print format, but is less evident in the electronic format. PsycINFO provides links to full-text articles/other items when the full text is provided by a vendor using the same platform and links out to full text in other databases via a link-resolver when the full text is available via other sources. Given that fact, sources containing information about tests and sometimes the test itself can be found using PsycINFO in several ways. (Remember that PsycINFO is not necessarily the best or most easily used source for *identifying* tests; there are many other sources earlier in this section and in other sections of this chapter better suited for that purpose.) The following illustrations are Ebscohost images because that is the vendor used at my institution. There may be some slight variations in fields among vendors, but these examples should provide guidance across vendors. Some examples include searching the test title in various fields and /or using the search term "psychometrics" to narrow the results (brackets are used in samples, not in searches). See figure 4.1.

These are some of the most basic and direct strategies, but they are in no way exhaustive. A user who does not find the information being sought can and should use a thoughtful combination of relevant search terms and the multitude of search fields and limiters available.

If the user does not have a particular title in mind, but rather wants to search on a particular topic, a different strategy is required. For details on sophisticated use of multiple search terms, truncation, and fields, the reader should consult the section on searching databases in chapter 3. Figure 4.2 shows some examples of searches for investigating information on tests when one has a *topic,* but not a *particular test* in mind.

When investigating a particular test, the title is already defined, and the population for which the test is appropriate is typically also already defined. When searching for a test on a topic, however, the indexed "subject" (as defined by the indexing organization, in this case PsycINFO) may not be known. In this case, a broader search strategy may be required both in the search terms and the fields searched. For example, to search for information on par-

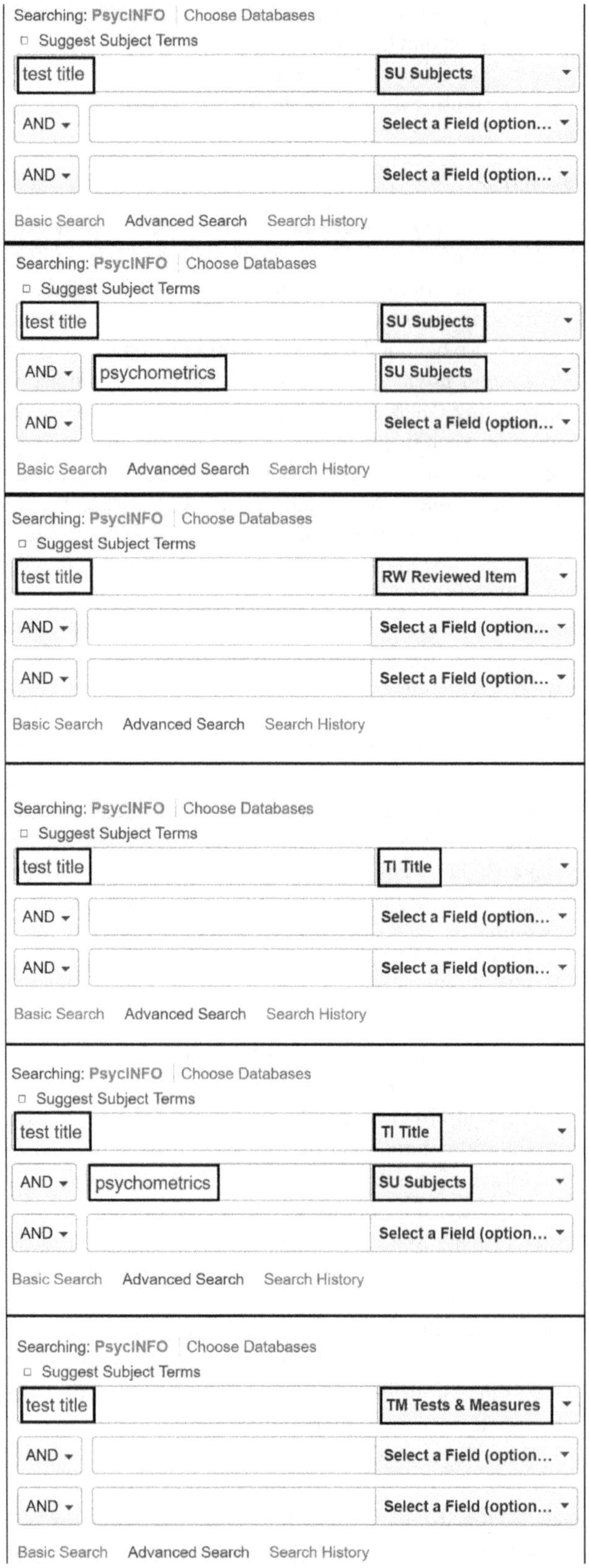

Figure 4.1. Finding information about specific tests in PsycINFO. The PsycINFO® Database screen shot is reproduced with permission of the American Psychological Association, publisher of the PsycINFO database, all rights reserved. No further reproduction or distribution is permitted without written permission from the American Psychological Association. Screen shots also reproduced courtesy of EBSCO Information Services.

ticular tests of depression, one might do a search such as that shown in figure 4.3.

This search would create a result set too large to be useful in itself, but an examination of the results would inform the user of other search terms that would help in narrowing the search (e.g., major depression, depressive symptoms, mood disorder) and subject headings (e.g., rating scales, screening tests). And of course the user would decide on other appropriate limiters such as years of publication and materials types. In addition, it is important to specify the population of interest, as most tests are appropriate to specific age groups or other populations. This may be done most specifically by using the "Age Group" limiter on the main search page (viewable in advanced search mode only). The "Tests and Measures" field lists tests and measures that were used in the study cited; it does not indicate that the full text of the test is included, although it may be. Another strategy, which is hit or miss with a likely large but unknown negative rate for finding the full text of tests in PsycINFO, is to search the test title or topic of interest as shown in the figure and to enter the term "test appended" in the "Select a Field" field.

Medical Databases

4.21. CINAHL. Ebsco Publishing (1961–). CINAHL is a nursing database, but it contains much useful information for researchers in psychology. Like PsycINFO, it is an indexing/abstracting database that links to full text available via other sources within an institution when combined with a link-resolver. Differences from PsycINFO regarding field structures are discussed fully in chapter 3. For searching on specific tests or test topics, the strategies outlined above are generally effective, but instead of the field "Tests and Measures," the field to be used in CINAHL is "Instrumentation," which will list the tests and measures used in the item cited.

4.22. Medline. National Library of Medicine (1966–). Medline is a medical database, but it contains much useful information for researchers in psychology. Like PsycINFO, it is an indexing/abstracting database with links to full text available via other sources within an institution when combined with a link-resolver. (There is a publicly available version of Medline, as well as its related products such as PubMedCentral; these are covered in chapter 3, as are differences in subject headings and search fields.) Medline does not have a field analogous to PsycINFO's "Tests and Measures" or CINAHL's "Instrumentation." Given this, when searching for a particular title or topic, it is probably most effective to use the general search strategies outlined above but search in the "Title," "Abstract," or various "subject" fields.

Searching: **PsycINFO** | Choose Databases

☐ Suggest Subject Terms

subject		SU Subjects	▼
AND ▼	psychometrics	SU Subjects	▼
AND ▼		Select a Field (option...	▼

Basic Search   Advanced Search   Search History

Searching: **PsycINFO** | Choose Databases

☐ Suggest Subject Terms

subject		TI Title	▼
AND ▼	psychometrics	SU Subjects	▼
AND ▼		Select a Field (option...	▼

Basic Search   Advanced Search   Search History

Figure 4.2. Finding information about tests on a topic in PsycINFO. The PsycINFO® Database screen shot is reproduced with permission of the American Psychological Association, publisher of the PsycINFO database, all rights reserved. No further reproduction or distribution is permitted without written permission from the American Psychological Association. Screen shots also reproduced courtesy of EBSCO Information Services.

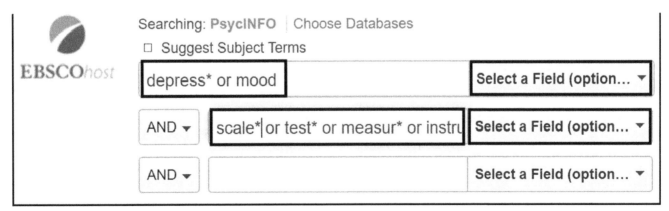

Figure 4.3. Using PsycINFO to determine subject headings for tests. The PsycINFO® Database screen shot is reproduced with permission of the American Psychological Association, publisher of the PsycINFO database, all rights reserved. No further reproduction or distribution is permitted without written permission from the American Psychological Association. Screen shots also reproduced courtesy of EBSCO Information Services.

Education Databases

4.23. Education Full-Text. H. W. Wilson Company.

ERIC (Education Resources Information Center). Institute of Education Sciences (IES) of the US Department of Education.

Professional Development Collection. Ebscohost Information Services.

These three education databases do not have fields analogous to PsycINFO's "Tests and Measures" or CINAHL's "Instrumentation." Given this, when searching for a particular title or topic, it is probably most effective to use the general search strategies outlined above but search in the "Title," "Abstract," or various "subject" fields.

RESOURCES ABOUT ASSESSMENT USING TESTS AND MEASURES

General

4.24. *APA handbook of testing and assessment in psychology.* Geisinger, K. F., & Bracken, B. A. (2013). Washington, DC: American Psychological Association. 1010 pp. BF176. Three-volume set. This set provides comprehensive coverage of issues related to psychological testing. Volume 1 consists of twenty-one chapters related to specific issues in test theory (e.g., overview and psychometric characteristics, reliability, validity, generalizability, test and item factor analyses, item response theory, bias, development strategies, measurement of change, educational and clinical standards, and ethics). These are followed by seventeen chapters on testing and assessment in industrial and organizational psychology (e.g., overview, work analysis, critical thinking, job knowledge, reasoning, leadership selection interviews, situational judgment, employment testing, performance appraisal, job satisfaction, and legal issues). Volume 2 consists of thirty-four chapters on testing in clinical and counseling psychology (e.g., assessment process, communicating results, clinical interviewing, intellectual and neuropsychological functioning, personality and psychopathology, assessment of interests, career development, needs and values, self-efficacy, identity, quality of life, marriage and family assessments, performance-based measures, self-report measures, and assessment in various settings). Volume 3 consists of twenty-eight chapters on testing in school psychology and education (e.g., preschool; intellectual functioning; academic achievement; behavioral, social, and emotional assessment of children; curricular assessment; adaptive behavior; language competence; attitudes; college, graduate, and professional school admissions testing; score reporting; and cultural and legal issues). Chapters are twenty to thirty pages long and contain useful illustrations and reference lists. This set will provide both novice and experienced researchers with a solid foundation in testing issues as well as up-to-date research on specific topics.

425..*Assessment psychology.* Vol. 10 of *Handbook of psychology* (2nd ed.). Weiner, I. B. (Ed.). (2013). Hoboken, NJ: Wiley. 715 pp. BF121. Volumes of this set can stand alone as state-of-the-discipline handbooks. The purpose of this volume is to address important issues in assessment; although it may use particular measures as examples, it is not a manual of tests. Part I ("Assessment Issues") addresses the assessment process, clinical versus mechanical prediction, psychometrics, bias, cross-cultural issues, assessment within treatment, computerized assessment, ethical issues, and education and training in psychological assessment. Part II ("Assessment Settings") covers adult and child mental health settings, schools, medical settings, industrial/organizational settings, forensic assessment and assessment in correctional settings, and geriatric settings. Part III ("Assessment Methods") covers assessment methods for intellectual and neuropsychological functioning, interests, personality, and psychopathology. Chapters are twenty-five to fifty pages long and contain extensive references. This volume will be useful to graduate students and beginning and advanced researchers interested in a wide range of assessment issues.

4.26. *Comprehensive handbook of psychological assessment.* Hersen, M. (2004). Hoboken, NJ: Wiley. 2160 pp. BF176. This four-volume set provides comprehensive coverage of assessment in four major domains. Volume 1 (*Intellectual and Neuropsychological Assessment*) provides an overview of theoretical, methodological, and validity issues; reviews specific instruments for adults and children; and covers professional issues in such assessment. Volume 2 (*Personality Assessment*) provides an overview of personality and psychopathology assessment and reviews objective and projective instruments for adults, children, and adolescents. It also reviews assessment of specific content areas and specific populations and settings. Volume 3 (*Behavioral Assessment*) provides an overview and history of the underlying concepts and methods of behavioral assessment, followed by detailed chapters on each. It covers applications of behavioral assessment in inpatient and outpatient, work, and school settings and also addresses the integration of behavioral and nonbehavioral assessment methods. Volume 4 (*Industrial and Organizational Assessment*) provides an overview of the subject, then covers use of testing in the workplace and organizations; tests of cognitive ability and basic skills; personality; integrity and interests; the use of biographical, experience, and interview information; job-specific knowledge; assessment centers; assessment of job performance; teams and teamwork; and employee reactions to the workplace. Each of these volumes is independent of the others and generally heavily focused on research. Individual volumes of this set will be highly useful to beginning and experienced researchers who want to increase their knowledge of both assessment issues and instruments commonly used in each area.

4.27. *Rand health surveys.* http://www.rand.org/health/surveys_tools.html. Free-to-use scales on aging and health, homelessness, health economics, HIV/STDs/sexual behavior, maternal/child/adolescent health, mental health, military health, quality of care, quality of life, and managed health care. A list of full-text measures at this site is located at http://libguides.hofstra.edu/TMdb/RandHealthSurveys.

4.28. *Responsible test use: Case studies for assessing human behavior* (2nd ed.). Eyde, L. D., Robertson, G. J., & Krug, S. E. (2010). Washington, DC: American Psychological Asssociation. 217 pp. BF176. The increased demand for diagnostic and treatment justification requires the appropriate and responsible use of testing. This work begins by presenting the seven competencies of testing (comprehensive assessment, proper test use, psychometric knowledge, maintaining integrity of test results, accuracy of scoring, appropriate use of norms, and interpretive feedback to clients) and the sixty-four elements of good testing, classified into five categories (professional development: training, responsibility and ethics, test selection, test administration and scoring, test interpretation: principles, norms, and psychometrics, and reporting test results to clients and administrative policy issues. The chapters are organized by the five categories of elements, presenting eighty-five cases (twenty-eight are new to this second edition, and the rest are updated and revised from the first edition). Each case presents the assessment setting, the issue, focus questions, analysis, and the competencies and elements involved. Cases are quite varied, ranging from individual testing for various issues to personnel screening, expert testimony, and appearances on television. There are appendixes that index cases by competency and by element.

4.29. *Standards for educational and psychological testing.* American Educational Research Association (AERA). (2014). Washington, DC: American Educational Research Association (AERA). 230 pp. LB3051 .A693 2014. This title is jointly developed by the American Educational Research Association (AERA), the American Psychological Association (APA), and the National Council on Measurement in Education (NCME). Part I ("Foundations") covers validity, reliability and measurement error, and fairness in testing. Part II ("Operations") covers test design and development; scores; scales; norms; score linking and cut scores; test administration; scoring, reporting, and interpretation; supporting documentation for tests; and rights and responsibilities of both test-users and test-takers. Part III ("Testing Applications") covers testing and assessment; workplace testing and credentialing; educational testing and assessment; and the use of tests for program evaluation, policy studies, and accountabil-

ity. The information covered in this book is essential for anyone involved in research or practice with tests.

4.30. *Tools for strengths-based assessment and evaluation.* Simmons, C. A., & Lehmann, P. (2013). New York: Springer. 534 pp. H62. Includes 142 full-text instruments on areas of psychological strengths, including happiness and subjective well-being; health, wellness, and health-related quality of life; acceptance, mindfulness, and situational affect; hope, optimism, and humor; resilience, coping, and post-traumatic growth; aspirations, goals, and values; self-efficacy; social support; social relationships; and emotional intelligence. It also contains tools for couples, families, and children as well as useful chapters on incorporating strengths into evaluation and selecting tools. A list of full-text measures in this book is located at http://libguides.hofstra.edu/TMdb/SimmonsLehmann2013.

Addictions

4.31. *Screening and assessing adolescents for substance abuse disorders.* Center for Substance Abuse Treatment. (2012/1998). Treatment Improvement Protocol (TIP) Series, No. 31. Rockville, MD: Substance Abuse and Mental Health Services Administration (SAMHSA). 165 pp. This document covers screening and assessment of adolescents, substance use disorders as related to adolescent development, and legal issues and juvenile justice settings for adolescents. It provides information on twenty-eight screening instruments, comprehensive assessment instruments, and general functioning instruments for use with substance-using adolescents. For each instrument, it provides title, purpose, type of assessment (e.g., interview, self-report), life areas/problems assessed, reading level if applicable, credentials required if any, commentary, pricing information if applicable, where item has been reviewed, and contact information.

Children and Adolescents

4.32. *Assessing adolescent psychopathology: MMPI-A/ MMPI-A-RF* (4th ed.). Archer, R. P. (2016). New York: Routledge. 459 pp. RJ503. The fourth edition of this work provides a strong historical foundation on the development of the MMPI-A and MMPI-A-RF. Aimed at both researchers and clinicians, it incorporates both developmental issues in assessment and the latest research on these MMPI forms. Topics covered include adolescent development and psychopathology, development of the forms, administration and scoring issues, psychometric issues, the basic clinical scale and codetype correlates for adolescents, and additional scales within each form.

4.33. *Assessing children in the urban community.* Mercer, B. L., Fong, T., & Rosenblatt, E (Eds). (2016). New York: Routledge. 245 pp. BF722. This work takes a community psychology approach to assessment, expanding traditional psychological assessment, which focuses on diagnosis and treatment, to include social and cultural contexts in the assessment process and the psychological report. Section I focuses on community psychology as it relates to managed care, policy, assessment settings, and interventions. Section II covers collaborative assessment, social justice, issues of undocumented immigrants, race and culture, cross-cultural supervision, vicarious trauma, and training. Section III presents case studies in community-based psychological assessment.

4.34. *Measuring health-related quality of life in children and adolescents: Implications for research and practice.* Drotar, D. (1998). Mahwah, NJ: Lawrence Erlbaum Associates. 372 pp. RJ380. Contains four full-text instruments and reviews of other instruments covering a broad range of topics of conceptual, ethical, and practical issues in measuring health-related quality of life in children and adolescents. Also covers assessment related to specific health-related issues such as diabetes, asthma, low birth weight, cancer, cystic fibrosis, AIDS, growth problems, and Turner syndrome. A list of full-text measures in this book is located at http://libguides.hofstra.edu/TMdb/Drotar1998.

4.35. *Mirrors for behavior III: An anthology of observation instruments.* Simon, A., & Boyer, E. G. (Eds.). (1974). Wyncote, PA: Communication Materials Center. 758 pp. LB1131. Ninety-nine full-text instruments covering school-aged children are included; most are designed to be used in some type of educational setting. Covers affective and cognitive communication, psychomotor behavior, activity, content of communication, sociological structure, and physical environment. An overview and review of specific issues in observation is followed by summaries for each of the instruments. Summaries indicate subject of observation, number of subjects to be observed, collection methods, dimensions, settings, coding units, personnel required, and uses reported. The full-text instruments follow the summary section. A list of full-text measures in this book is located at http://libguides.hofstra.edu/TMdb/SimonBoyer1974.

4.36. *Oxford handbook of child psychological assessment.* Saklofske, D. H. Reynolds, C. R., & Schwean, V. L. (Eds.). (2013). Oxford: Oxford University Press. 860 pp. BF722. This book surveys the foundations, models, special topics, and practice of assessment for clinical and educational purposes. Its thirty-six chapters begin with abstracts and keywords and are organized into four major sections. Part 1 ("Foundations") covers theory, measurement, and statistical issues; psychometric versus actuarial interpretations of intelligence and aptitude; projective techniques; group assessments; cultural variation–adapting tests for cross-language use; diagnosis; classification and screening systems; the ICF-CY; and responsible use of tests. Part 2 ("Models") covers models of intelligence, aptitude and achievement, neuropsychological

and personality assessment, behavioral assessment, and therapeutic assessments. Part 3 ("Practice") addresses history taking, clinical interviewing, the mental status exam, testing of cognitive ability, neuropsychology, memory, personality and affect, academic achievement, learning and study, creativity, and behavior. Part 4 ("Special and Emergent Topics") covers assessment alternatives, assessing mild intellectual disability, integration of models of dyslexia, testing accommodations, forensic assessment, subjective well-being, parenting style, and effective instruction. References are included; this book will be useful to graduate students and novice and experienced researchers who want to learn about or keep up to date on issues in child assessment.

4.37. *Screening and assessing adolescents for substance abuse disorders.* Center for Substance Abuse Treatment. (2012/1998). Treatment Improvement Protocol (TIP) Series, No. 31. Rockville, MD: Substance Abuse and Mental Health Services Administration (SAMHSA). 165 pp. This document covers screening and assessment of adolescents, substance use disorders as related to adolescent development, and legal issues and juvenile justice settings for adolescents. It provides information on twenty-eight screening instruments, comprehensive assessment instruments, and general functioning instruments for use with substance-using adolescents. For each instrument, it provides title, purpose, type of assessment (e.g., interview, self-report), life areas/problems assessed, reading level if applicable, credentials required if any, commentary, pricing information if applicable, where item has been reviewed, and contact information.

Clinical and Counseling

4.38. *Handbook of assessment and diagnosis of autism spectrum disorder.* Matson, J. L. (2016). New York: Springer. 477 pp. RC553. This volume addresses assessment and diagnosis of autism spectrum disorder, including developmental considerations and comorbidities with other psychiatric and medical disorders. It addresses the purposes and types of assessment for preschool, early childhood, adolescence, and adulthood. It also addresses stress, intelligence, and intellectual functions in assessment, as well as the implications of the ICD and DSM on screening, assessment, and monitoring and report writing.

4.39. *Handbook of assessment and treatment planning for psychological disorders* (2nd ed.). Antony, M. M., & Barlow, D. H. (2010). New York: Guilford Press. 706 pp. RC469. The purpose of this work is to provide detailed guidelines for assessing individuals with specific disorders, using assessment results to select effective treatments, and using standard assessment tools to measure treatment outcomes. The first section consists of four chapters covering assessment in evidence-based practice (EBP), evaluating measures, specific brief screening and outcome measures, and specific structured and semistructured diagnostic interviews. Each of the remaining thirteen chapters reviews specific measures for specific disorders. Chapters are thirty to forty pages long, including six to seven pages of references. This work will be particularly useful for graduate students, clinicians, and researchers, and faculty who teach assessment courses.

4.40. *Handbook of clinical rating scales and assessment in psychiatry and mental health.* Baer, L., & Blais, M. A. (Eds.). (2010). New York: Humana Press. 320 pp. RC473. Includes 41 full-text measures on a variety of mental health issues. In addition to the full-text instruments provided, this book covers other tests for each clinical issue and also indicates the "gold standard" test for that issue. It addresses the purpose of each scale (e.g., diagnostic, screening, treatment assessment) and provides psychometric and other information. Some tests may be copied directly without further permission; some indicate the need to contact the author/publisher for permission (if the latter, this information and contact information is usually provided immediately following the test). A list of full-text measures in this book is located at http://libguides.hofstra.edu/TMdb/BaerBlais2010.

4.41. *Handbook of psychological assessment, case conceptualization, and treatment.* Hersen, M. (2008). Hoboken, NJ: Wiley. 1509 pp. RC454. Two-volume set. In anticipation of the publication of DSM-V, this set addresses its topics in a broad manner not specifically tied to the DSM-IV. The first part of volume 1 (*Adults*) covers an overview of behavioral assessment, diagnostic issues, behavioral conceptualization, an overview of behavioral treatment, medical and pharmacological issues, and ethical issues. Part 1 of volume 2 (*Children and Adolescents*) covers the same topics as volume 1, but also covers developmental issues and the role of family. Part II of the adult volume covers assessment, conceptualization, and treatment of specific disorders, namely specific phobias, panic and agoraphobia, social anxiety, obsessive-compulsive, posttraumatic, generalized anxiety and major depressive disorders, schizophrenia, personality disorders, bulimia, organic disorders, and alcoholism. Part III of the adult volume addresses special issues such as marital distress, sexual deviation, adults with intellectual disabilities, issues related to older adults, insomnia, health anxiety, and compulsive hoarding. Part II of the children and adolescent volume also covers depressive, anxiety, and post-traumatic stress disorders as well as oppositional defiant, conduct, learning, motor, and communication disorders; attention deficit/hyperactivity disorder; early-onset schizophrenia; and substance use disorders. Part III covers special topics such as neglect and abuse, neurological impairment, habit and sleep disorders, enuresis and encopresis, and firesetting. This set has useful tables comparing measures and set-off boxes with case descriptions including assessment tools used and treatment.

Family Psychology

4.42. *Handbook of family measurement techniques.* Tsouliatos, J., Perlmutter, B. F., & Strauss, M. A. (Eds.). (2001). Thousand Oaks, CA: Sage. 1208 pp. HQ728. This three-volume set is a different item, rather than a second edition of the 1990 work with the same title and authors. Volume 1 of this set contains the contents of the entire 1990 edition. This includes an introductory chapter on family measurement principles and techniques, followed by detailed abstracts for 504 instruments measuring dimensions of marital and family interaction, intimacy and family values, parenthood, roles and power, and adjustment. Each topical chapter provides a discussion of the topic before the abstracts are presented. Detailed abstracts include availability information, variables measured, instrument type (e.g., self-report, projective), description, sample items (where permission was acquired), commentary, and references. All measures appear in their entirety in a published work (most measures), or permission was provided to deposit the entire instrument with the National Auxiliary Publication Service (NAPS 1-3). In addition to these 504 detailed abstracts, abbreviated abstracts are provided for another 472 instruments that met the same criteria (total of 976 instruments abstracted). These original abstracts from the 1990 work, now forming volume 1 of the 2001 set, are for instruments from the 1929–1986 literature, with the major focus being the 1975–1986 literature. Volume 2 of this three-volume set contains 367 additional abstracts for measures that were newly developed or substantially revised during 1987–1996. It begins with chapters on family measurement overview and developing, interpreting, and using family assessment techniques. Detailed abstracts in volume 2 cover family relations; marital relations; parent-child relations; family adjustment, health, and well-being; and family problems. Abstracts include variables measured, instrument type, samples measured, description, sample items (where permission was acquired), psychometrics, commentary, keywords, references, and availability information. Volume 3 contains the full text of 168 of the 367 instruments abstracted in volume 2. In addition to the actual instrument, scoring instructions are provided, as well as the original source of the instrument. This set will be highly valuable to clinicians, researchers, graduate students, and advanced undergraduates interested in measurement of numerous family issues. A list of full-text measures in volume 3 is located at http://libguides.hofstra.edu/TMdb/TsouliatosPerlmutterStrauss2001.

Geropsychology

4.43. *Assessing the elderly: A practical guide to measurement.* Kane, R. A., & Kane, R. L. (1981). Lexington, MA: Lexington Books. 301 pp. RC954. Covers thirty-three full-text instruments and reviews of other measures not included. This book covers the assessment of older people in long-term care, particularly physical functioning, activities of daily living, cognitive and affective functioning, general mental health, and social functioning. Chapters are thirty to sixty pages long; present a discussion of the issues; cover measures not included; and present administration, scoring, and interpretation information for full-text measures included and references. This book will be useful to researchers interested in the status and functioning of older people who are in long-term care. A list of full-text measures in this book is located at http://libguides.hofstra.edu/TMdb/KaneKane1981.

4.44. *Handbook of geriatric assessment* (4th ed.). Gallo, J. J. (2006). Sudbury, MA: Jones and Bartlett. 473 pp. RC953. Covers thirty-eight full-text instruments; also provides information on other measures not included in the book. The goal of this book is to enable multidimensional assessment by discussing the domains significant in the life of older people and providing some full-text measures of those domains. Domains covered include cognition, depression, substance use and abuse, activities of daily living, social issues (support, care, mistreatment, economic, health, environment, spiritual), physical, pain, health, home, nursing homes, hospitalization, adherence to medical regime, interdisciplinary teamwork, and disaster preparedness and response. Chapters are ten to thirty pages long and contain a discussion of the issue; description of measures not included; actual measures with administration, scoring, and interpretation information; and references. Measures are reprinted with permission. This book will be valuable to researchers interested in any of the domains covered, as well as to practitioners. A list of full-text measures in this book is located at http://libguides.hofstra.edu/TMdb/Gallo2006.

Happiness/Well-Being/Quality of Life

4.45. *Measuring health-related quality of life in children and adolescents: Implications for research and practice.* Drotar, D. (1998). Mahwah, NJ: Lawrence Erlbaum Associates. 372 pp. RJ380. Includes four full-text instruments and reviews of other instruments covering a broad range of topics of conceptual, ethical, and practical issues in measuring health-related quality of life in children and adolescents. Also covers assessment related to specific health-related issues such as diabetes, asthma, low birth weight, cancer, cystic fibrosis, AIDS, growth problems, and Turner syndrome. A list of full-text measures in this book is located at http://libguides.hofstra.edu/TMdb/Drotar1998.

4.46. *Quality of life: The assessment, analysis, and reporting of patient-reported outcomes* (3rd ed.). Fayers, P. M., & Machin, D. (2016). Chichester, England: John Wiley & Sons. 626 pp. R852. This book provides a comprehensive treatment of measuring quality of life as reported by

patients. When addressing specific domains, the focus is on quality of life as it pertains to health outcomes. In its entirety, however, it is an excellent resource for all researchers interested in quality of life. Part 1 focuses on the development and validation of instruments for assessing quality of life and patient-reported outcomes. It addresses questions such as the definition of quality of life, why it should be measured, and how to measure it; principles of measurement scales; developing questionnaires; psychometrics; item response theory; item banks; and computer-adaptive tests. Part 2 focuses on assessing, analyzing, and reporting patient-reported outcomes and quality of life. This section covers choosing and scoring questionnaires, sample sizes, cross-sectional analysis, longitudinal data, death and quality-adjusted survival, reporting bias and response shift, meta-analysis, and interpretation. Each chapter ends with a conclusion and further readings. The appendix contains samples of generic quality-of-life instruments, disease-specific instruments, and domain-specific instruments (i.e., anxiety, pain, fatigue, disability).

Health Psychology

4.47. *Assessment in health psychology.* Benyamini, Y., Johnston, M., & Karademas, E. C. (Eds.). (2016). Boston: Hogrefe. 345 pp. R726. This volume addresses key issues and reviews measures in health psychology assessment. Topics include social cognition and health behavior, self-efficacy and outcome expectancies, illness representations, health behavior, patient-physician communication and patient satisfaction, adherence to medical advice, stress and stressors, coping, social support, pain and pain behavior, functional status, self-rated health, quality of life, psychological adjustment, neuropsychological assessment, biological and physiological measures in health psychology, and assessment methods. Many useful tables listing and comparing measures are included.

4.48. *Designing and conducting health surveys: A comprehensive guide.* Aday, L. (1989). San Francisco: Jossey-Bass. 535 pp. RA408. Includes four full-text instruments (sections A–D at the end of the book) and lists other measures. Provides information on designing and conducting health surveys, including selecting topics; matching survey design to survey objectives; defining variables; selecting data collection methods; sample selection and size; formulation of questions about health, behavior, demographics, knowledge, and attitudes; data analysis; and research reporting. A list of full-text measures in this book is located at http://libguides.hofstra.edu/TMdb/Aday1989.

4.49. *Quality of life: The assessment, analysis, and reporting of patient-reported outcomes* (3rd ed.). Fayers, P. M., & Machin, D. (2016). Chichester, England: John Wiley & Sons. 626 pp. R852. This book provides a comprehensive treatment of measuring quality of life as reported by patients. When addressing specific domains, the focus is on quality of life as it pertains to health outcomes. In its entirety, however, it is an excellent resource for all researchers interested in quality of life. Part 1 focuses on the development and validation of instruments for assessing quality of life and patient-reported outcomes. It addresses questions such as the definition of quality of life, why it should be measured, and how to measure it; principles of measurement scales; developing questionnaires; psychometrics; item response theory; item banks; and computer-adaptive tests. Part 2 focuses on assessing, analyzing, and reporting of patient-reported outcomes and quality of life. This section covers choosing and scoring questionnaires, sample sizes, cross-sectional analysis, longitudinal data, death and quality-adjusted survival, reporting bias and response shift, meta-analysis, and interpretation. Each chapter ends with a conclusion and further readings. The appendix contains samples of generic quality-of-life instruments, disease-specific instruments, and domain-specific instruments (i.e., anxiety, pain, fatigue, disability).

4.50. Rand health surveys. http://www.rand.org/health/surveys_tools.html. Free-to-use scales on aging and health, homelessness, health economics, HIV/STDs/sexual behavior, maternal/child/adolescent health, mental health, military health, quality of care, quality of life, and managed health care. A list of full-text measures at this site is located at http://libguides.hofstra.edu/TMdb/RandHealthSurveys.

Industrial and Organizational

4.51. *Oxford handbook of personnel assessment and selection.* Schmitt, N. (Ed.). (2012). New York: Oxford University Press. 973 pp. BF431. This volume provides a comprehensive treatment of issues in and measurement in personnel assessment and selection. Part 1 provides an overview of the main topic, followed by the history and social context of personnel selection in part 2. Part 3 addresses research strategies, including concept and process of validation, job analysis, predictor measures, performance outcomes, organizational strategy and staffing, and meta-analysis. Part 4 focuses on constructs of individual differences, including cognitive abilities, personality, person-environment fit, physical capabilities, and use of composite predictors in selection. Part 5 covers predictor constructions, including selection interview, background data, simulations, individual psychological assessment, self-reports, predictive bias, and web-based assessments. Part 6 focuses on performance and outcomes assessment, including supervisor ratings, objective measures, organizational citizenship, voluntary turnover, trainability, and occupational safety. Part 7 covers societal and organizational issues such as applicant reaction to testing, legal constraints, time, diversity, team selection, globalization, "retooling," layoff selection, and contingent workers.

Parts 8 and 9 cover implementation and sustainability of selection systems, conclusions, and future directions. Each chapter begins with an abstract and keyword box.

4.52. *Pfeiffer's classic inventories, questionnaires, and surveys for training and development.* Gordon, J. (2004). San Francisco, CA: Pfeiffer. 549 pp. HF5549. Includes thirty-seven full-text instruments. This work covers beliefs about working people and the management role; views of manager" current behavior, both self-rated and other-rated; and climate factors that shape organizations" practices and will help or hinder desired changes in management behavior. It includes measures of supervision, motivation, work values, locus of control, barriers to creativity and innovation, time management, mentoring, collaboration, leadership, communication, cross-cultural issues, trust, leadership, conflict management, and organizational type. Each measure is contained within its own chapter, each of which is fifteen to twenty pages long and typically includes a summary and discussion of the topic to be measured; the theory underlying the measure; existing research findings, with the questionnaire, administration, scoring, and interpretation information; and references. Measures have been reproduced with permission. This work will be useful to industrial/organizational psychologists and others conducting research in the workplace as well as for practitioners engaging in organizational and personnel assessment and development. A list of full-text measures in this book is located at http://libguides.hofstra.edu/TMdb/Gordon2004.

Mood and Mood Disorders

4.53. *Assessment of depression.* Sartorius, N., & Ban, T. A. (Eds.). (1986). Berlin: Springer-Verlag. 376 pp. RC537. Covers thirteen full-text instruments. Reviews self-report and clinical interview assessments of depression used around the world. A list of full-text measures in this book is located at http://libguides.hofstra.edu/TMdb/SartoriusBan1986.

4.54. *Measurement of affect, mood, and emotion: A guide for health-behavioral research.* Ekkekakis, P. (2013). Cambridge, England: Cambridge University Press. 206 pp. BF511. This volume addresses issues researchers deal with (or worse, don't deal with) when selecting measures of affect, mood, and emotion. It begins by documenting the problems and distinguishing among the three concepts. The author then outlines a three-step process: deciding which construct to study, deciding which theoretical model one is using, and deciding which measure one might use among those available and which fits the theoretical model being used. The book then reviews a number of measures of distinct states, dimensional measures, and domain-specific measurement and addresses issues related to each. The nine chapters are twenty to thirty pages long and contain illustrations that are useful in understanding the points being made. This book will be most useful to graduate students and new and experienced researchers interested in the measurement of affect, mood, and emotion; problems with such measurement; and how best to measure these constructs.

Multicultural Assessment

4.55. *Handbook of tests and measurements for black populations.* Jones, R. L. (Ed.). (1996). Hampton, VA: Cobb & Henry. 1205 pp. BF176. Two-volume set. Covers eighty-two full-text measures. Other measures for which full text is not in this set are also covered. Measures in this set were developed in response to concerns about measures developed and validated on white populations being administered to black populations. Underlying the work is the view that tests and measures should be based on African American history, characteristics, experiences, behaviors, and needs. Many of the constructs have applicability to other populations, but some are specific to African Americans or other racial/ethnic minorities (e.g., coping with racism, African American identity development, African self-consciousness). Rationale, development, and psychometrics are provided for all measures; some of the measures are from theses and dissertations, and they may have more and newer documentation since publication of this volume. With the exception of the introductory chapter, each chapter begins with an abstract, discusses its topic, presents full-text assessment tools and/or reviews them, and ends with a "for further information, contact" box. Volume 1 covers measures for infants, cognitive approaches and measures for children, self-esteem measures for children, race-related measures for children, a variety of measures for adolescents and young adults, language assessment and attitude measures, parental attitudes and values measures, and measures of family structure and dynamics. Volume 2 contains worldview measures; physiological measures and neuropsychological assessment; measures of spirituality, acculturation, life experiences, and values; race identity attitude measures; stress, racism and coping measures; mental health delivery measures; fair employment testing concepts and work environment and organizational assessment measures; research program–based measures; and a variety of other measures. In addition to the eighty-two full-text measures, chapters contain many useful tables and diagrams. A list of full-text measures in this book is located at http://libguides.hofstra.edu/TMdb/Jones1996.

4.56. *Psychological testing of Hispanics: Clinical, cultural, and intellectual Issues* (2nd ed.). Geisinger, K. F. (2015). Washington, DC: American Psychological Association. 336 pp. E184. The second edition of this work incorporates new assessment research as well as changes within the Hispanic communities of the United States. The first chapter addresses the existence and use of *Pruebas Pub-*

licadas en Espanol for expanded test selection. It also addresses differences among various Hispanic and Latino/a populations. Other topics covered are issues pertaining to intelligence testing and learning disabilities evaluation with Spanish speakers; neuropsychological testing; clinical interviews; personality assessment; assessment of ADHD; anxiety, depression, and cultural issues related to stress assessment; sexual orientation; and gender identity.

Neuropsychology

4.57. *Compendium of neuropsychological tests: Administration, norms, and commentary* (3rd ed.). Strauss, E., Sherman, E. M. S., & Spreen, O. (2006). New York: Oxford University Press. 1216 pp. RC386. Covers sixteen full-text instruments. Although this work does contain some full-text measures, it has two other main purposes. It was designed to provide an overview of basic and advanced issues critical to neuropsychological assessment, develop a strong working knowledge of the strengths and weaknesses of instruments, and present information necessary to empirically based assessment. This is covered in chapters on psychometrics, norms selection, history taking, preparation of the patient, report writing and feedback, and assessment of premorbid functioning. The second purpose, which forms most of the volume, is to provide an easy-to-use tool in which the user would find the major highlights of commonly used neuropsychological tests. The authors' mantra is "Know Your Tools." Instruments included in earlier editions but no longer commonly used have been removed, and many newer instruments have been added. Test reviews follow a fixed format, with purpose, source, age range, description, administration, administration time, scoring, demographic effects, normative data, reliability, validity, and commentary. Major domains covered are achievement, executive functions, attention, memory, language, visual perception, somatosensory function, olfactory function, body orientation, motor function, mood, personality and adaptive functions, and response bias and suboptimal performance. In the introduction to each domain, there is a table that summarizes important features such as age range, tasks, administration time, key processes, test-retest reliability, and other features. Following the standard information and commentary for each test there is a reference list of major articles and books on the test. This work is aimed at clinicians and researchers using neuropsychological measures. A list of full-text measures in this book is located at http://libguides.hofstra.edu/TMdb/StraussShermanSpreen2006.

4.58. *Measurement in neurological rehabilitation.* Wade, D. T. (1992). Oxford: Oxford University Press. 388 pp. RC386. Covers 141 full-text instruments. This volume begins by presenting a useful model of thinking about pathology, impairment, disability, and handicap, followed by classifications; suggestions on how to choose the most appropriate measure(s); and discussion of measuring motor and sensory impairments, cognitive and emotional impairments, physical disability, social interaction, quality of life, specific diseases, specific circumstances, and miscellaneous. It then presents actual measures of cognitive impairment; motor impairment; focal disabilities; activities of daily living (ADL); global measures of disability; handicap and quality of life; emotions and social interactions; and specific measures for multiple sclerosis, stroke, head injury, Parkinson's disease, and other movement disorders. Instructions, comments, psychometrics, and references are provided. This work will be most useful to those conducting research in clinical settings. A list of full-text measures in this book is located at http://libguides.hofstra.edu/TMdb/Wade1992.

4.59. *Neuropsychological assessment* (5th ed.). Lezak, M. D. (Ed.). (2012). Oxford: Oxford University Press. 1161 pp. RC386. The fifth edition of this now-classic work provides a comprehensive review of major neurobehavioral disorders and a detailed treatment of assessment practices and issues. There are two main divisions. Part I ("Theory and Practice of Neuropsychological Assessment") covers basic concepts, behavioral geography of the brain, rationale of deficit measurement, procedures and interpretation of the neuropsychological exam, etiology of symptoms, and diagnostic issues. Part II ("A Compendium of Tests and Assessment Techniques") covers assessments of orientation, attention, perception, memory, language, motor performance, concept formation and reasoning, executive functions, emotional functioning, and effort, as well as assessment batteries, observational methods, rating scales, and inventories. Publisher or citation, test characteristics, and neurological findings are provided for each test. Appendix A is a neuroimaging primer providing images and explanations; appendix B contains publisher information. The twenty chapters are each twenty-five to fifty pages long and contain test images, samples, and references.

Personality

4.60. *Wiley handbook of personality assessment.* Kumar, U. (Ed.). (2016). Chichester, England: John Wiley & Sons. 437 pp. BF698. This handbook presents current trends in personality assessment, both conceptual and methodological. The first section focuses on emerging conceptual trends; it begins with a presentation of its agenda, which is to integrate trait and process approaches to personality and theories of personality assessment. It addresses situational perception, temperament in personality development, integrity tests, network analysis, emotional intelligence, assessing the darker side of personality, advances in use and interpretation of the MMPI-2, diversity in assessment, and an African perspective on future directions for personality research. The second section focuses

on emerging assessment perspectives and methodological issues; it begins with the international adaptability of the MMPI-2. It then addresses a combination of issues and use of particular measures, covering precision assessment using temporally dynamic data, situational judgment tests versus traditional personality tests, self-report versus conditional reasoning problems, therapeutic assessment in counseling and clinical practice, assessment via virtual reality, correlates of military suicide, assessment of sexual and gender minorities, user reactions to assessment, applicant faking behavior, ethical issues, and issues and challenges in assessment paradigms.

Sexuality and Gender

4.61. *Handbook of gender and sexuality in psychological assessment.* Brabender, V., & Mihura, J. L. (Eds.). (2016). New York: Routledge. 704 pp. BF176. This volume addresses six areas pertaining to gender and sexual identity. Part I addresses terminology, construction of identity, issues needing theoretical and empirical attention, competent respectful practice, and how gender and sexual identities intersect with other identities of the individual. Part II addresses how to broach the topic of gender and sexuality; how gender and sexuality variables influence performance on psychological tests; and the implications of the latter, particularly regarding the MMPI-2, MCMI-III, PAI, the Rorschach, narrative, and drawing assessment. Part III addresses gender and sexual identity in terms of assessing attachment, personality, psychosis, affective and anxiety disorders, feeding and eating disorders, and suicide assessment. Part IV provides case illustrations of assessments. Part V addresses lifespan developmental issues, and part VI addresses practitioner training and ethical conundrums regarding assessment and gender and sexual identity. This book is aimed at and will be most useful to graduate students; researchers; and practitioners of clinical, counseling, and school psychology.

Social Psychology

4.62. *Scales for the measurement of attitudes.* Shaw, M. E., & Wright, J. M. (1967). New York: McGraw-Hill Books. 604 pp. BF378. Includes 186 full-text instruments. This work begins with a discussion of the nature, conceptualizations, and definitions of attitudes and methods of scaling and measurement. Each chapter begins with a brief discussion of the topic, then discusses why some measures are and others are not included, followed by measures in that area. Topics for which measures are provided include social practices and social issues and problems (family, education, religious, health, economics), international issues (political relations, conflict, economics), abstract concepts (education, law), political and religious issues, ethnic and national groups, significant others, and social institutions. For each measure, the title, source, and description are provided, as well as administration and scoring information, psychometrics, and comments. Items, directions for use, and scale values and/or response alternatives are provided. A list of measures included is in the frontmatter. This work will be valuable to undergraduates, graduate students, and beginning and experienced researchers. A list of full-text measures in this book is located at http://libguides.hofstra.edu/TMdb/ShawWright1967.

Stress and Trauma

4.63. *Assessing psychological trauma and PTSD* (2nd ed.). Wilson, J. P., & Keane, T. M. (2004). New York: Guilford Press. 668 pp. RC552. This volume provides both an in-depth discussion of issues in assessing psychological trauma and PTSD and information on various measures that have been developed for assessing these issues. It contains twenty-one chapters in six major sections. Part I ("Understanding and Assessing Trauma and PTSD") provides an overview of symptoms, syndromes, diagnoses, and the assessment of acute stress. Part II ("Assessment Methods") covers standardized self-report measures of civilian trauma and PTSD, structured clinical interview techniques, a questionnaire on dissociative experiences, impact of event, projective techniques, epidemiological measurement, and measurement of military-related PTSD. Part III ("Psychobiology") covers psychophysiological assessment, neuropsychological symptoms, and neuroimaging studies. Part IV ("Physical Health, Substance Use Disorder, and Bereavement") covers assessment instruments for those areas. Part V ("Psychosocial Development and Gender Issues") covers assessment of trauma and PTSD in children and adolescents, assessment of childhood trauma sequelae in adulthood, and gender issues in the assessment of PTSD. Part IV ("Assessing Traumatic Injury in Litigation") covers forensic as well as clinical assessment and also contains a wealth of information on assessment of malingering. Each section reviews multiple instruments for the specific topic, covering development, overview, purpose, population, reliability and validity, and how the instrument complements other instruments. This volume will be of particular value to graduate students, researchers, and clinicians.

Violence and Aggression

4.64. *Assessment of partner violence: A handbook for researchers and practitioners.* Rathus, J. H., & Feindler, E. L. (2004). Washington, DC: American Psychological Association. 392 pp. RC560. This volume addresses various issues in the assessment of partner violence, such as assessment modalities, assessment in clinical practice, research considerations in scale development, psycho-

metrics, measuring treatment outcomes, and research issues and challenges particular to the assessment of partner violence. It covers interview measures and self-report measures specific to partner violence, as well as measures of general relationship functioning, anger and hostility, and other correlates of partner violence. For each measure it provides a description and the development of the method, target population, format, administration and scoring, psychometrics, advantages and limitations, primary reference to the scale, scale availability information, and related references. There is a list of measures reviewed in the beginning of the book, organized according to chapter.

4.65. *MMPI-2: A practitioner's guide.* Butcher, J. N. (2006). Washington, DC: American Psychological Association. 632 pp. RC473. This work is organized into four major sections. Section I ("Perspectives on MMPI-2 Interpretation") provides a guide to test usage in various settings and an evaluation of MMPI-2 research, and also covers underreporting and overreporting response styles. Section II ("Applications for the MMPI-2 in Assessment and Therapy") covers the Personality Psychopathology Five (PSY-5) scales, diagnosis of personality disorders, posttraumatic stress disorders, and therapeutic assessment and treatment planning based on the MMPI-2. Section III ("Applications of the MMPI-2 Across Diverse Populations") covers use in inpatient and outpatient mental health settings, medical settings, neuropsychological evaluations, correctional settings, personnel screening, working with alcohol and drug abusers, and disability and personal injury evaluations. Section IV ("Special Considerations in MMPI-2 Interpretation") covers computer-based assessment, Latino/a populations, and other cross-cultural applications.

Other

4.66. *Handbook of cognition and assessment: Frameworks, methodologies, and applications.* Rupp, A. A., & Leighton, J. P. (2017). Chichester, England: John Wiley and Sons. 623 pp. LB1062. In a period when education, learning, and educational assessment are under serious scrutiny, this handbook seems to present some of the best current practices while also considering further ways of enhancing and keeping those practices at the cutting edge of educational assessment, incorporating psychometrics and cognition. Section I ("Frameworks") focuses on how various models of cognition inform assessment design, delivery, scoring, and validation. It covers learning and cognitive theories as they apply to assessment design, development, implementation, validation, automatic item generation, social models and socio-emotional and self-management variables in learning and assessment, understanding and improving accessibility for special populations, and relationship of automatic scoring with validity.

Section II ("Methodologies") covers item response, longitudinal, and diagnostic classification models; Bayesian networks; rule space and attribute hierarchy methods; and educational data mining and learning analytics. Section III ("Applications") focuses on large-scale standards-based assessments of educational achievement, educational survey assessments, professional certification and licensure examinations, in-task assessment framework for behavioral data, digital assessment environments for scientific inquiry practices, assessing constructs in video games, and conversation-based assessment, followed by a concluding chapter. This is an advanced work that will chiefly be of interest to psychometricians, educational measurement researchers, cognitive psychologists interested in assessment, assessment developers, and graduate students who want to learn more about the issues in assessment design.

RESOURCES CONTAINING FULL-TEXT TESTS AND MEASURES

Remember!!! All tests are covered by copyright law.

Books are sometimes reprinted; in such cases, you may see a later date of publication, but you will NOT see an "edition" statement (e.g., "second edition"). In the case of reprints, it does not matter which version is used. In the case of later editions of books containing tests, typically a greater number of tests are included.

It is important that the user read the introductory chapters of these resources, which will advise them about

- what types of measures are included and excluded;
- permissions to use, copy, and so forth; and
- useful information such as quick comparison charts in appendixes and guidance on selecting measures.

General

4.67. *ETS test collection catalog.* https://www.ets.org/test_link/about/. Princeton, NJ: Educational Testing Service. In addition to standardized tests published by ETS (e.g., SAT, GRE), ETS provides scope, target audience, and availability on approximately 25,000 standardized, commercially available tests and research instruments created outside of ETS. Users can search for these tests at https://www.ets.org/test_link/find_tests/. Many tests are downloadable, and as all are commercial, there is a fee for the tests, any manuals, and consumables. Some *ETS Test Collection* tests are restricted, requiring documentation of training or academic credentials.

4.68. *Tests in microfiche (TIM).* Princeton, NJ: Educational Testing Service. In addition to commercial tests available through ETS, ETS also indexes research tests that are available without charge. Instructions for searching the TIM collection are available at https://www.ets.org/test_link/find_tests/ (scroll down page). More than 1,200 tests are indexed in TIM. The actual tests, with accompanying information, are available on the TIM microfiche cards. Each TIM test has an identification number that corresponds to the microfiche card(s) with the test and information. Permission is not required for use of TIM tests unless one is making changes to the test.

Addictions

4.69. *Assessing alcohol problems: A guide for clinicians and researchers* (2nd ed.). Allen, J. P., & Wilson, V. B. (2003). Washington, DC: US Department of Health and Human Services, Public Health Service, National Institutes of Health, National Institute on Alcohol Abuse and Alcoholism. 571 pp. HV5279. Covers seventy-five full-text instruments related to diagnosis, treatment planning, and outcome evaluation. Pages 1–234 contain an overview, a discussion of how to select instruments, quick-reference tables comparing instruments, and other information. The instruments and their individual information and permissions information start on page 235. An index to the full-text instruments included starts on page 667. This document is available at and can be downloaded from http://pubs.niaaa.nih.gov/publications/AssessingAlcohol/index.pdf. A list of full-text measures in this book is located at http://libguides.hofstra.edu/TMdb/AllenWilson2003.

4.70. *Can we measure recovery? A compendium of recovery and recovery-related instruments.* Vol. 1 of *A compendium of recovery measures.* Ralph, R. O., Kidder, K., & Phillips, D. (2000). Washington, DC: US Department of Health and Human Services/Evaluation Center @ HRSI. 227 pp. Includes twenty full-text instruments covering conceptualization and measurement of recovery. Concise charts of recovery measures are on pages 13–15 and recovery-related measures are on pages 24–28. Charts contain title, author/date, development, number of items and type of scaling, domains measured, reliability and validity data, and populations. Full-text instruments are in appendix B. Information and permissions contact information is provided for each measure. This document can be downloaded from http://www.hsri.org/publication/Can_We_Measure_Recovery_A_Compendium_of_Recovery_and_Recovery-Related_. A list of full-text measures in this book is located at http://libguides.hofstra.edu/TMdb/RalphKidderPhillips2000.

4.71. *Integrated treatment for dual disorders: A guide to effective practice.* Mueser, K. T. (2003). New York: Guilford Press. 470 pp. RC564. Twenty full-text instruments and sixteen educational handouts are included. Handouts are in appendix B and instruments are in appendix C. Instruments cover substance use, functioning, treatment, relapse prevention, activities and lifestyle, and family awareness/involvement. See "limited photocopy license" on verso for information on permissions. A list of full-text measures in this book is located at http://libguides.hofstra.edu/TMdb/Mueser2003.

4.72. *Measuring the promise: A compendium of recovery measures.* Vol. 2 of *A compendium of recovery measures.* Orde, T. C., Chamberlin, J., Carpenter, J., & Leff, H. S. (2005). Washington, DC: US Department of Health and Human Services/Evaluation Center @ HRSI. Covers fourteen full-text instruments. Includes measures of individual recovery and of recovery-promoting environments. Information about scales is on pages 24–91; scales are on pages 111–244. Scale summaries provide an introduction, development, stakeholders in development, alternate forms, item and domain information, populations, administration and scoring, psychometrics, utility, permission information, and references. Permission statements indicate if the measure is free to use without further permissions or provide publisher information. This document can be downloaded from http://www.hsri.org/publication/measuring-the-promise-a-compendium-of-recovery-measures-volume-ii/. A list of full-text measures in this book is located at http://libguides.hofstra.edu/TMdb/OrdeChamberlinCarpenterLeff2005.

4.73. *Measuring violence-related attitudes, behaviors and influences among youth: A compendium of assessment tools.* Dahlberg, L. L., Toal, S. B., Swahn, M., & Behrens, C. B. (2005). Atlanta, GA: Centers for Disease Control and Prevention, National Center for Injury Prevention and Control. 373 pp. Includes 167 actual instruments on many components of issues related to violence. Broad categories include attitude and belief assessments (aggression/delinquency, couple violence, education and school, employment, gangs, gender roles, guns, and television), psychosocial and cognitive assessments (aggressive fantasies, attachment to role models, attributional bias, psychological distress, ethnic identity, fatalism, future aspirations, hopelessness, hostility, moral reasoning, self-perception, personal safety, citizenship, self-efficacy, impulse control, coping, self-esteem, sense of caring and support, and social consciousness), behavioral assessments (aggressive and violent behavior, concentration, conflict resolution skills, dating violence, delinquent and disciplinary behavior, drug and alcohol use, exposure to gangs, handgun access, impulsivity, leisure activity, parental control, safety and threats, social competence, social problem-solving skills, victimization, and weapon carrying), and environmental assessments as they relate to violence (disciplinary practices, family communication, family conflict and hostility, parent/child relationships, parental attitudes, involvement, and supervision, quality of life, collective efficacy, community resources, exposure to violence, fear of crime, and neighborhood characteristics). Each of the four sections begins with a chart of the measures to follow, indicating the construct being measured, number of items, target groups, psychometric data if available, and citation to the original source (reference list follows each section). Document is available at http://www.cdc.gov/violenceprevention/pdf/yv_compendium.pdf. A list of full-text measures in this book is located at http://libguides.hofstra.edu/TMdb/DahlbergToalSwahnBehrens2005.

4.74. *Treating alcoholism: Helping your clients find the road to recovery.* Perkinson, R. R. (2004). Hoboken, NJ: Wiley. 326 pp. RC565. Includes thirty-three full-text instruments measuring alcohol-related issues as well as fetal alcohol syndrome, gambling, sex addiction, obsessive-compulsive behavior, and social anxiety. As this book is also a treatment manual, it addresses concepts of alcoholism, treatment planning, dual diagnosis, adolescent treatment, relapse prevention, and the recovery community. A list of full-text measures in this book is located at http://libguides.hofstra.edu/TMdb/Perkinson2004.

Anxiety and Anxiety Disorders

4.75 *Assessment scales in depression, mania, and anxiety.* Lam, R. W., Michalak, E. E., & Swinson, R. P. (2005). London: Taylor & Francis. 198 pp. RC537. Includes sixty-four full-text instruments; there are additional instruments for which full text is not included, but sample items may be included. This book also includes a section on how to select an assessment scale. Instruments cover depression, mania, anxiety, related symptoms, side effects, functioning, quality of life, and special populations. For all instruments, there are commentary on the instrument, scoring information, alternate forms, references, and author/publisher contact information. A list of full-text measures in this book is located at http://libguides.hofstra.edu/TMdb/LamMichalakSwinson2005.

4.76 *Practitioner's guide to empirically based measures of anxiety.* Antony, M. M., Orsillo, S. M., & Roemer, L. (Eds.). (2001). New York: Kluwer Academic/Plenum. 512 pp. RC531. Includes 77 full-text instruments and reviews of more than 200 instruments. This book, published under the auspices of the Association for Advancement of Behavior Therapy (AABT), covers general issues in the assessment of anxiety disorders and assessment strategies for assessing panic disorder and agoraphobia, generalized anxiety disorder, social phobia, acute stress disorder, post-traumatic stress disorder, specific phobias, and obsessive-compulsive disorder. Scale summaries include original citation, purpose, description, administration and scoring, psychometrics, alternative forms, and author/publisher information. Instruments are in appendix B. Each instrument is followed by a "permission" statement. A list of full-text measures in this book is located at http://libguides.hofstra.edu/TMdb/AntonyOrsilloRoemer2001.

Body Image and Appearance

4.77. *Exacting beauty: Theory, assessment, and treatment of body image disturbance.* Thompson, J. K. (Ed.). (1999).

Washington, DC: American Psychological Association. 396 pp. RC569. Includes thirty-six full-text instruments. Covers virtually all areas of body image disturbance, with accompanying instruments. Instruments are in appendixes numbered according to corresponding chapter. A list of full-text measures in this book is located at http://libguides.hofstra.edu/TMdb/Thompson1999.

Children and Adolescents

4.78. *Assessing children's well-being: A handbook of measures.* Naar-King, S., Ellis, D. A., & Frey, M. A. (Eds.). (2004). Mahwah, NJ: Lawrence Erlbaum. 307 pp. RJ50. Contains twenty full-text instruments; an additional forty-four instruments are reviewed. Topics covered are health status and quality of life, adherence, pain management, child behavior, child development, child coping, cognition, attributions, attitudes, environment, and consumer satisfaction. Full-text measures are in the appendixes. A list of full-text measures in this book is located at http://libguides.hofstra.edu/TMdb/Naar-KingEllisFrey2004.

4.79. *Assessment scales in child and adolescent psychiatry.* Verhulst, F. C., & Van Der Ende, J. (2006). Abingdon, England: Taylor and Francis. 220 pp. RJ503. Includes forty-six full-text measures used with children and adolescents; also contains reviews and sample items from other measures. Contains general rating scales of behavior and symptoms, strengths, and difficulties. Also includes scales for specific problems, including anxiety, obsessive-compulsive disorder, depression, suicide, eating disorders, tics, ADHD, conduct disorders, substance abuse, and global impairment. For each scale there are commentary, information on alternate forms, properties of the scale and subscales, psychometric information, information on use, key references, and author/publisher contact information. Some scales are in the public domain, others are reproduced with permission, and some are commercial. An alphabetical list of measures is on pages 219–220. This work will be valuable to researchers at all levels, although some commercial tests may be restricted to those with professional credentials. A list of full-text measures in this book is located at http://libguides.hofstra.edu/TMdb/VerhulstVanDerEnde2006.

4.80. *KIDSCREEN questionnaires: Quality of life questionnaires for children and adolescents.* KIDSCREEN Group Europe. (2006). Berlin: Pabst Science. 231 pp. BF722. Includes six full-text instruments. The Health-Related Quality of Life (HRQoL) questionnaire is available in fifty-two-, twenty-seven-, and ten-item format; one set (three) is for the child/adolescent and one set (three) is for the proxy (parent/caregiver). The fifty-two-item questionnaire was designed for research purposes and measures physical well-being, psychological well-being, moods and emotions, self-perception, autonomy, parent relation and home life, financial resources, social

support and peers, school environment, and social acceptance (bullying). The twenty-seven-item version is designed for epidemiological studies and screening and measures a subset of the constructs measured by the longer version. The ten-item version results in one global health-related quality of life score and is recommended for use in large epidemiological studies. This volume covers theoretical background and development of the instruments; psychometrics; administration and scoring; and norms for children, adolescents, and parents. The measures are presented in the book in English; the accompanying CD contains the measures in Czech, Dutch, French, German, Greek, Hungarian, Polish, Spanish, and Swedish. A list of full-text measures in this book is located at http://libguides.hofstra.edu/TMdb/KIDSCREENEuropeGroup2006.

4.81. *Measuring health-related quality of life in children and adolescents: Implications for research and practice.* Drotar, D. (1998). Mahwah, NJ: Lawrence Erlbaum Associates. 372 pp. RJ380. Includes four full-text instruments, as well as reviews of other instruments covering a broad range of topics of conceptual, ethical, and practical issues in measuring health-related quality of life in children and adolescents. Also covers assessment related to specific health-related issues such as diabetes, asthma, low birth weight, cancer, cystic fibrosis, AIDS, growth problems, and Turner syndrome. A list of full-text measures in this book is located at http://libguides.hofstra.edu/TMdb/Drotar1998.

4.82. *Pain in children: Nature, assessment, and treatment.* McGrath, P. A. (1990). New York: Guilford Press. 466 pp. RJ365. Contains twenty full-text instruments. This volume covers nature of children's pain experiences, assessment of pain, complexity of the nociceptive system, pharmacological interventions, nonpharmacological interventions, integrated pain management, acute pain, recurrent pain, and chronic pain. Instruments are in the appendix. A list of full-text measures in this book is located at http://libguides.hofstra.edu/TMdb/McGrath1990.

Clinical and Counseling

4.83. *Acceptance and commitment therapy measures package: Process measures of potential relevance to ACT.* http://integrativehealthpartners.org/downloads/ACT-measures.pdf. Ciarrochi, J., & Bilich, L. (Comps.). (2006). 159 pp. RC489. Contains thirty-nine instruments measuring various processes believed by the authors to be potentially relevant to acceptance and commitment therapy (ACT). Measures are organized into six areas: avoidance/acceptance, fusion/dysfunctional thinking, mindfulness/awareness of feelings, value clarification/goal striving/action orientation, measures for specific populations, and general ACT measures. The author, contact information, scoring, reliability and validity, references about development and use of the measure, and permission information are provided. A list of full-text measures in this book is located at http://libguides .hofstra.edu/TMdb/CiarrochiBilich2006.

4.84. *Assessment scales in child and adolescent psychiatry.* Verhulst, F. C., & Van Der Ende, J. (2006). Abingdon, England: Taylor and Francis. 220 pp. RJ503. Includes forty-six full-text measures used with children and adolescents, as well as reviews and sample items from other measures. Contains general rating scales of behavior and symptoms, strengths, and difficulties. Also includes scales for specific problems, including anxiety, obsessive-compulsive disorder, depression, suicide, eating disorders, tics, ADHD, conduct disorders, substance abuse, and global impairment. For each scale, there is a commentary, information on alternate forms, properties of the scale and subscales, psychometric information, information on use, key references, and author/publisher contact information. Some scales are in the public domain, others are reproduced with permission, and some are commercial. An alphabetical list of measures is on pages 219–220. This work will be valuable to researchers at all levels, although some commercial tests may be restricted to those with professional credentials. A list of full-text measures in this book is located at http://libguides.hofstra.edu/TMdb/ VerhulstVanDerEnde2006.

4.85. *Handbook of clinical rating scales and assessment in psychiatry and mental health.* Baer, L., & Blais, M. A. (Eds.). (2010). New York: Humana Press. 320 pp. RC473. Includes forty-one full-text measures on a variety of mental health issues. In addition to the full-text instruments provided, this book covers other tests for each clinical issue and also indicates the "gold standard" test for that issue. It also addresses the purpose of each scale (e.g., diagnostic, screening, treatment assessment) and provides psychometric and other information. Some tests may be copied directly without further permission; some indicate the need to contact author/publisher for permission (if the latter, this information and contact information are usually provided immediately following the test). A list of full-text measures in this book is located at http://lib guides.hofstra.edu/TMdb/BaerBlais2010.

4.86. *Handbook of psychiatric measures* (2nd ed.). Rush, A. J., First, M. B., & Blacker, D. (Eds.). (2008). Washington, DC: American Psychiatric Association. 828 pp. RC473. Contains 136 full-text instruments on the accompanying CD. An alphabetical list of the full-text instruments is on pages 755–757. A list by chapter (topic) is on pages 757–761. Covers general psychiatric symptoms, mental health status, functioning, and disability; general health status, functioning, and disability; quality of life; adverse effects; patient perceptions of care; stress and life events; family risk factors; suicide risk; child and adolescent measures; symptom-specific measures for infancy, childhood, and adolescence; child and adolescent functional

status; delirium and cognition; neuropsychiatric symptoms; substance use disorders; psychotic disorders; mood disorders; anxiety disorders; somatoform and factitious disorders and malingering; sexual dysfunction; eating disorders; sleep disorders; impulse control; personality traits and disorders; defense mechanisms; and aggression. Also covered are another 139 instruments for which full text is not included. The book provides a "practical issues" section for each instrument, including permission information and cost if any. A list of full-text measures in this book is located at http://libguides.hofstra.edu/TMdb/ RushFirstBlacker2008.

4.87. *Integrated treatment for dual disorders: A guide to effective practice.* Mueser, K. T. (2003). New York: Guilford Press. 470 pp. RC564. Contains twenty full-text instruments and sixteen educational handouts. Handouts are in appendix B and instruments are in appendix C. Instruments cover substance use, functioning, treatment, relapse prevention, activities and lifestyle, and family awareness/involvement. See "limited photocopy license" on verso for information on permissions. A list of full-text measures in this book is located at http://libguides. hofstra.edu/TMdb/Mueser2003.

4.88. *Measures for clinical practice and research: A sourcebook* (5th ed.). Corcoran, K., & Fischer, J. (2013). Oxford: Oxford University Press. 1628 pp. BF176. Two-volume set. Covers 500 full-text instruments for adults, children, couples, and families. Volume 1 contains measures for couples, family, and children. Volume 2 contains measures for adults. Frontmatter includes an alphabetical list and a topical list as well as guidance in test selection. Topics covered are abuse, acculturation, addiction, anger, hostility, assertiveness, beliefs, child behaviors/problems, client motivation, depression and grief, eating problems, ethnic identity, family functioning, geriatrics, guilt, general health, mental health, identity, impulsivity, interpersonal behavior, locus of control, loneliness, love, couple/ marital relationships, obsessive-compulsive behavior, pain, family relations, perfectionism, phobias, post-traumatic stress, problem-solving, procrastination, rape, life satisfaction, schizotypal symptoms, self-concept, self-control, self- efficacy, sexuality, social functioning, social support, stress, suicide, substance abuse, and treatment issues. Psychometric and other necessary information is provided for each instrument, and at the end of each instrument's information profile, "availability" is indicated. Most instruments indicate "may be copied from book," some indicate "journal article" and indicate the primary reference citation, and some indicate the author/publisher's contact information. A list of full-text measures in this book is located at http://libguides.hofstra.edu/TMdb/ CorcoranFischer2013.

4.89. *Rating scales in mental health* (3rd ed.). Sajatovic, M., & Ramirez, L. F. (2012). Baltimore, MD: Johns Hopkins University Press. 502 pp. RC473. Includes 119 full-text tests. Copyright information is provided for each test; some will indicate "N/A" or "public domain" and do not need further permission. In other cases, contact information is provided. Some tests are very long, so representative sample items are provided. Chapters are organized by condition and cover anxiety, mood disorders, psychosis, social functioning, general health, insight, involuntary movement, satisfaction with health care, quality of life, substance abuse, suicide risk, impulsivity, aggression, eating disorders, premenstrual dysphoria, sleep disorders, sexual disorders, and geriatric and childhood disorders. Scale summaries include overview, applications, psychometrics, copyright holder, administration, completion time, representative study, references, and the scale itself. A list of full-text measures in this book is located at http://libguides.hofstra.edu/TMdb/SajatovicRamirez2012.

4.90. *Sourcebook of adult assessment strategies.* Schutte, N. S., & Malouff, J. M. (2014/1995). New York: Plenum Press. 471 pp. RC473. Includes seventy-five full-text instruments organized around broad categories of psychopathology in DSM-IV. Scale summaries include purpose and development, administration and scoring, sample and cutoff scores, psychometrics, subscales, alternate forms and the scale itself. Scales cover disorders of delirium and dementia, substance use, schizophrenia and related psychosis, mood, anxiety, somatoform, pain and related phenomena, dissociation, sexual function, eating, sleep, impulse control, relationships, and other areas of clinical interest and global functioning. Instruments are reprinted with permission from the author/publisher and require author/publisher permission for use. A list of full-text measures in this book is located at http://libguides.hofstra.edu/TMdb/SchutteMalouff2014.

Eating Disorders and Obesity

4.91 *Handbook of assessment methods for eating behaviors and weight-related problems: Measures, theory, and research* (2nd ed.). Allison, D. B., & Baskin, M. L. (2009). Los Angeles, CA: Sage. 701 pp. RC552. Contains forty-five full-text instruments. Covers quality of life in obesity and eating disorders; attitudes toward obese people; body image; restrained eating; physical activity; food intake; hunger and satiety; binge-eating and purging; eating-disordered thoughts, feelings, and behaviors; and eating and weight-related problems in children. Instruments are in appendixes organized by chapter. Psychometric and administration/scoring information is provided, as well as author/publisher contact information. A list of full-text measures in this book is located at http://libguides.hofstra.edu/TMdb/AllisonBaskin2009.

4.92 *Obesity assessment: Tools, methods, interpretations (a reference case: The RENO Diet-Heart Study).* St. Jeor, S. (Ed.). (1997). New York: Chapman & Hall. 932 pp. RC628. Includes forty-four full-text instruments. Based on the RENO Diet-Heart Study, this book examines diagnosis and treatment of obesity. Instruments can be used in normal weight and obese adults and cover physical activity, dietary intake, attitudes, eating and dieting behaviors, personality and psychological factors, emotions and stress, genetics, and lifestyle. A list of full-text measures in this book is located at http://libguides.hofstra.edu/TMdb/StJeor1997.

Educational and School Psychology

4.93. *Handbook of tests and measurement in education and the social sciences* (3rd ed.). Lester, P. E., Inman, D., & Bishop, L. K. (2014). Lanham, MD: Rowman & Littlefield. 343 pp. LB3051. Includes 126 full-text instruments covering forty domains in education and social sciences, particularly industrial and organizational psychology. Most are from published (but noncommercial) sources; several are from dissertations. Test summaries include comments, test construction, sample(s), psychometrics, references, and the measure itself. There is also a chapter with information on related commercial instruments. A list of full-text measures in this book is located at http://libguides.hofstra.edu/TMdb/LesterInmanBishop2014.

4.94. *Mirrors for behavior III: An anthology of observation instruments.* Simon, A., & Boyer, E. G. (Eds.). (1974). Wyncote, PA: Communication Materials Center. 758 pp. LB1131. Contains ninety-nine full-text instruments covering school-aged children; most of the instruments are designed to be used in some type of educational setting. Covers affective and cognitive communication, psychomotor behavior, activity, content of communication, sociological structure, and physical environment. An overview and review of specific issues in observation is followed by summaries for each of the instruments. Summaries indicate subject of observation, number of subjects to be observed, collection methods, dimensions, settings, coding units, personnel required, and uses reported. The full-text instruments follow the summary section. A list of full-text measures in this book is located at http://libguides.hofstra.edu/TMdb/SimonBoyer1974.

Family and Marriage

4.95. *Handbook of family measurement techniques.* Tsouliatos, J., Perlmutter, B. F., & Strauss, M. A. (Eds.). (2001). Thousand Oaks, CA: Sage. 1208 pp. HQ728. This three-volume set is a different item, rather than a second edition of the 1990 work with the same title and authors. Volume 1 of this set contains the contents of the entire 1990 edition. This includes an introductory chapter on family measurement principles and techniques, followed by detailed abstracts for 504 instruments measuring dimensions of marital and family interaction, intimacy and family values, parenthood, roles and power, and adjustment.

Each topical chapter provides a discussion of the topic before the abstracts are presented. Detailed abstracts include availability information, variables measured, instrument type (e.g., self-report, projective), description, sample items (where permission was acquired), commentary, and references. All measures appear in their entirety in a published work (most measures), or permission was provided to deposit the entire instrument with the National Auxiliary Publication Service (NAPS 1-3). In addition to these 504 detailed abstracts, abbreviated abstracts are provided for another 472 instruments that met the same criteria (total of 976 instruments abstracted). These original abstracts from the 1990 work, now forming volume 1 of the 2001 set, are for instruments from the 1929–1986 literature, with the major focus being the 1975–1986 literature. Volume 2 of this three-volume set contains 367 additional abstracts for measures that were newly developed or substantially revised during 1987–1996. It begins with chapters on family measurement overview and developing, interpreting, and using family assessment techniques. Detailed abstracts in volume 2 cover family relations; marital relations; parent-child relations; family adjustment, health, and well-being; and family problems. Abstracts include variables measured, instrument type, samples measured, description, sample items (where permission was acquired), psychometrics, commentary, keywords, references, and availability information. Volume 3 contains the full text of 168 of the 367 instruments abstracted in volume 2. In addition to the actual instrument, scoring instructions are provided, as well as the original source of the instrument. This set will be highly valuable to clinicians, researchers, graduate students, and advanced undergraduates interested in measurement of numerous family issues. A list of full-text measures in volume 3 is located at http://libguides.hofstra.edu/TMdb/TsouliatosPerlmutterStrauss2001.

4.96. *Handbook of measurements for marriage and family therapy.* Fredman, N., & Sherman, R. (1987). New York: Brunner/Mazel. 218 pp. RC488. Contains twenty-four full-text measures; also includes reviews of other measures. The full-text measures in this volume cover marital satisfaction, adjustment, agendas, trust, jealousy, conflict, and instability. Also included are measures of attitudes toward feminism and working women. Family-oriented measures include tests of family feeling, cohesion, strength, and adaptability. There are also quality-of-life scales for parents and adolescents and a family therapist rating scale. Entries for full-text measures typically contain an introduction, description, subscale descriptions, psychometrics, administration and scoring information, and a brief discussion. Some measures are longer than suitable for a book; for these items, samples are included and the location of the entire measure is identified. A list of full-text measures in this book is located at http://libguides.hofstra.edu/TMdb/FredmanSherman1987.

4.97. *Marriage and family assessment: A sourcebook for family therapy.* Filsinger, E. E. (Ed.). (1983). Beverly Hills, CA: Sage. 338 pp. HV697. Includes six full-text instruments. Also reviews other instruments. Full-text instruments include measures for marital adjustment, communication, agendas, and conflict, as well as family events and change, adaptability, and cohesion. There is also an entire section on observation in marriages, as well as discussion and review of other marriage and family measures. A list of full-text measures in this book is located at http://libguides.hofstra.edu/TMdb/Filsinger1983.

Geropsychology

4.98. *Assessing older persons: Measures, meaning and practical applications.* Kane, R. L., & Kane, R. A. (Eds.). (2000/2004). Oxford: Oxford University Press. 542 pp. HQ1061. Includes one hundred full-text instruments, as well as information on other instruments for which the full text is not included. This volume is a sequel to, rather than a second edition of, Kane and Kane's 1981 book *Assessing the Elderly: A Practical Guide to Measurement* (see below). It addresses the areas of assessment in the 1981 volume (function, health, emotion, cognition, and social well-being) and also addresses new areas such as assessment of family caregivers, physical environments, values and preferences, spirituality, and satisfaction. In addition to the full-text measures, this book provides information on selecting and using instruments, psychometric information, and caveats about their use. The section on applications of assessment covers comprehensive assessment and management, care planning for those in health-care settings, long-term case management, mandated assessments, and assessment of older adults who cannot communicate. A list of full-text measures in this book is located at http://libguides.hofstra.edu/TMdb/KaneKane2000.

4.99. *Assessing the elderly: A practical guide to measurement.* Kane, R. A., & Kane, R. L. (1981). Lexington, MA: Lexington Books. 301 pp. RC954. Contains thirty-three full-text instruments and reviews of other measures not included. This book covers the assessment of older people in long-term care, particularly physical functioning, activities of daily living, cognitive and affective functioning, general mental health, and social functioning. Chapters are thirty to sixty pages long; present a discussion of the issues; cover measures not included; present administration, scoring, and interpretation information for the included full-text measures, and have references. This book will be useful to researchers interested in the status and functioning of older people who are in long-term care. A list of full-text measures in this book is located at http://libguides.hofstra.edu/TMdb/KaneKane1981.

4.100. *Assessment scales in old age psychiatry* (2nd ed.). Burns, A., Lawlor, B., & Craig, S. (2009). New York, NY:

Informa Healthcare. 383 pp. RC473. Contains 163 full-text instruments, as well as information on other instruments for which full text is not provided. Includes scales of depression, dementia, cognition, neuropsychological functioning, neuropsychiatry, activities of daily living, global assessments, quality of life, global mental health assessments, physical assessments, delirium, caregiving, and memory, as well as an assortment of scales on miscellaneous topics of use with older populations. Each section begins with a brief introduction of the topic, followed by full-text tests and information about tests not included. Information includes time required, main indications, description and purpose, additional references, foreign-language availability if any, and address for correspondence. A list of full-text measures in this book is located at http://libguides.hofstra.edu/TMdb/BurnsLawlorCraig2009.

4.101. *Handbook of geriatric assessment* (4th ed.). Gallo, J. J. (2006). Sudbury, MA: Jones and Bartlett. 473 pp. RC953. Includes thirty-eight full-text instruments; also provides information on other measures not included in the book. It also includes scoring criteria for measures that are client-produced (e.g., House-Tree-Person test). The goal of this book is to enable multidimensional assessment by discussing the domains that are significant in the lives of older people and providing some full-text measures of those domains. Domains covered include cognition, depression, substance use and abuse, activities of daily living, social issues (support, care, mistreatment, economic, health, environment, spiritual), physical, pain, health, home, nursing homes, hospitalization, adherence to medical regime, interdisciplinary teamwork, and disaster preparedness and response. Chapters are ten to thirty pages long and contain a discussion of the issue; description of measures not included; actual measures with administration, scoring, and interpretation information; and references. Measures are reprinted with permission. This book will be valuable to researchers interested in any of the domains covered, as well as to practitioners. A list of full-text measures in this book is located at http://libguides.hofstra.edu/TMdb/Gallo2006.

4.102. *Research instruments in social gerontology*. Mangen, D. J., & Peterson, W. A. (1982–1984). Minneapolis: University of Minnesota Press. 1664 pp. HQ1061. Three-volume set. Contains 298 full-test instruments. Also reviews other instruments for which full text is not included. Volume 1 (*Clinical and Social Psychology*) covers intellectual functioning, personality, adaptation, morale and life satisfaction, self-concept and self-esteem, death and dying, environments, ethnic group identification, subjective age identification, life phase analysis, and perceptions of old people. Volume 2 (*Social Roles and Social Participation*) covers social participation roles, dyadic relations, parent-child relations, kinship relations, work and retirement, socioeconomic status and poverty, religiosity, friends, neighbors and confidants, voluntary associations, and leisure activities. Volume 3 (*Health, Program Evaluation, and Demography*) covers functional capacity, health, utilization of health services, individual needs and community resources, social program tracking and evaluation, effectiveness of long-term care, evaluating of cost of services, organizational properties, indexes for the aging of populations, demographic characteristics, and geographic mobility. A list of full-text measures in this book is located at http://libguides.hofstra.edu/TMdb/MangenPeterson1984.

Happiness/Well-Being/Quality of Life

4.103. *Assessing children's well-being: A handbook of measures*. Naar-King, S., Ellis, D. A., & Frey, M. A. (Eds.). (2004). Mahwah, NJ: Lawrence Erlbaum. 307 pp. RJ50. Includes twenty full-text instruments; an additional forty-four instruments are reviewed. Topics covered are health status and quality of life, adherence, pain management, child behavior, child development, child coping, cognition, attributions, attitudes, environment, and consumer satisfaction. Full-text measures are in the appendixes. A list of full-text measures in this book is located at http://libguides.hofstra.edu/TMdb/Naar-KingEllisFrey2004.

4.104. *KIDSCREEN questionnaires: Quality of life questionnaires for children and adolescents*. KIDSCREEN Group Europe. (2006). Berlin: Pabst Science. 231 pp. BF722. Includes six full-text instruments. The Health-Related Quality of Life (HRQoL) questionnaire is available in fifty-two-, twenty-seven-, and ten-item formats; one set (three) is for the child/adolescent and one set (three) is for the proxy (parent/caregiver). The fifty-two-item questionnaire was designed for research purposes and measures physical well-being, psychological well-being, moods and emotions, self-perception, autonomy, parent relation and home life, financial resources, social support and peers, school environment, and social acceptance (bullying). The twenty-seven-item version is designed for epidemiological studies and screening and measures a subset of the constructs measured by the fifty-two-item version. The ten-item version results in one global health-related quality of life score and is recommended for use in large epidemiological studies. This volume covers theoretical background and development of the instruments; psychometrics; administration and scoring; and norms for children, adolescents, and parents. The measures are presented in the book in English; the accompanying CD contains the measures in Czech, Dutch, French, German, Greek, Hungarian, Polish, Spanish, and Swedish. A list of full-text measures in this book is located at http://libguides.hofstra.edu/TMdb/KIDSCREENEuropeGroup2006.

4.105. *Measuring health: A review of quality of life measurement scales* (3rd ed.). Bowling, A. (2005). Maidenhead/Berkshire, England: Open University Press. 221 pp.

RA407. Contains three full-text instruments. Reviews concepts of functioning, health, well-being, and quality of life and methodologies of measurement, including for psychological well-being, social networks and social support, subjective well-being, and broad quality of life. A list of full-text measures in this book is located at http://libguides.hofstra.edu/TMdb/Bowling2005.

4.106. *Measuring health-related quality of life in children and adolescents: Implications for research and practice.* Drotar, D. (1998). Mahwah, NJ: Lawrence Erlbaum Associates. 372 pp. RJ380. Contains four full-text instruments; also includes reviews of other instruments covering a broad range of topics of conceptual, ethical, and practical issues in measuring health-related quality of life in children and adolescents. Also covers assessment related to specific health-related issues such as diabetes, asthma, low birth weight, cancer, cystic fibrosis, AIDS, growth problems, and Turner syndrome. A list of full-text measures in this book is located at http://libguides.hofstra.edu/TMdb/Drotar1998.

Health Psychology

4.107. *Designing and conducting health surveys: A comprehensive guide* (2nd ed.). Aday, L. (1989). San Francisco: Jossey-Bass. 535 pp. RA408. Contains four full-text instruments (sections A–D at end of book) and lists other measures. Provides information on designing and conducting health surveys, including selecting topics; matching survey design to survey objectives; defining variables; selecting data collection methods; sample selection and size; formulation of questions about health, behavior, demographics, knowledge, and attitudes; data analysis; and research reporting. A list of full-text measures in this book is located at http://libguides.hofstra.edu/TMdb/Aday1989.

4.108. *Measuring health: A review of quality of life measurement scales* (3rd ed.). Bowling, A. (2005). Maidenhead/Berkshire, England: Open University Press. 221 pp. RA407. Contains three full-text instruments. Reviews concepts of functioning, health, well-being, and quality of life and methodologies of measurement, including for psychological well-being, social networks and social support, subjective well-being, and broad quality of life. A list of full-text measures in this book is located at http://libguides.hofstra.edu/TMdb/Bowling2005.

Industrial and Organizational

4.109. *Handbook of marketing scales: Multi-item measures for marketing and consumer behavior research* (3rd ed.). Bearden, W. O., Netemeyer, R. G., & Haws, K. L. (Eds.). (2011). Los Angeles, CA: Sage. 601 pp. HF5415. Contains 183 full-text instruments. This work includes scales related to traits and individual differences in interpersonal orientation, needs/preferences, self-concept, compulsive-

ness and impulsiveness, country image and affiliation, consumer opinion leadership and opinion seeking, innovativeness, and consumer social influence. Also includes scales of values and goals, including general values, environmentalism, socially responsible consumption, materialism and possession-orientation, goal-orientation, and planning. Scales on involvement, information, and affect include involvement with product classes, purchasing involvement, optimal stimulation, processing style, and affect. Includes scales related to marketing, such as ad content and emotions, brand/product responses, and shopping style and pricing response. Scales on attitudes about performance of business firms, satisfaction, postpurchase behavior, social agencies, and the marketplace are included. Scales on sales management, organizational behavior, and internal-external issues cover job satisfaction, role perception and role conflict, job burnout and tension, performance measures, control and leadership, organizational commitment, sales/marketing approaches, and intra- and interfirm influence and power. A list of full-text measures in this book is located at http://libguides.hofstra.edu/TMdb/BeardenNetemeyerHaws2011.

4.110. *Handbook of tests and measurement in education and the social sciences* (3rd ed.). Lester, P. E., Inman, D., & Bishop, L. K. (2014). Lanham, MD: Rowman & Littlefield. 343 pp. LB3051. Includes 126 full-text instruments covering forty domains in education and social sciences, particularly industrial and organizational psychology. Most are from published (but noncommercial) sources; several are from dissertations. Test summaries include comments, test construction, sample(s), psychometrics, references, and the measure itself. There is also a chapter with information on related commercial instruments. A list of full-text measures in this book is located at http://libguides.hofstra.edu/TMdb/LesterInmanBishop2014.

4.111. *Pfeiffer's classic inventories, questionnaires, and surveys for training and development.* Gordon, J. (2004). San Francisco, CA: Pfeiffer. 549 pp. HF5549. Contains thirty-seven full-text instruments. This work covers beliefs about working people and the management role; views of managers' current behavior, both self-rated and other-rated; and climate factors that shape organizations' practices and will help or hinder desired changes in management behavior. It includes measures of supervision, motivation, work values, locus of control, barriers to creativity and innovation, time management, mentoring, collaboration, leadership, communication, cross-cultural issues, trust, leadership, conflict management, and organizational type. Each measure is contained within its own chapter, which are fifteen to twenty pages long and typically include a summary and discussion of the topic to be measured; the theory underlying the measure; existing research findings, with the questionnaire, administration, scoring, and interpretation information; and references. Measures have been reproduced with permission. This work will be useful to industrial/organizational psychologists and others conducting research in the workplace as well as for practitioners engaging in organizational and personnel assessment and development. A list of full-text measures in this book is located at http://libguides.hofstra.edu/TMdb/Gordon2004.

4.112. *Taking the measure of work: A guide to validated scales for organizational research and diagnosis.* Fields, D. L. (2013). Charlotte, NC: Information Age Publishing. 326 pp. HM786. Includes 137 full-text measures. Measures in this work cover job satisfaction, organizational commitment, job characteristics, job stress, job roles, organizational justice, work-family conflict, person-organization fit, work behaviors, and work values. With few exceptions, measures are those asking employees to choose one or more preselected responses (i.e., close-ended questions). Each chapter begins with a brief discussion of the construct addressed within, followed by the relevant measures. For each measure, the following information is provided: title, description, reliability, validity, source/availability, items, and scoring. A list of full-text measures in this book is located at http://libguides.hofstra.edu/TMdb/Fields2013.

Mood and Mood Disorders

4.113. *Assessment of depression.* Sartorius, N. & Ban, T. A. (Eds.). (1986). Berlin: Springer-Verlag. 376 pp. RC537. Contains thirteen full-text instruments. Reviews self-report and clinical interview assessments of depression used around the world. A list of full-text measures in this book is located at http://libguides.hofstra.edu/TMdb/SartoriusBan1986.

4.114. *Assessment scales in depression, mania, and anxiety.* Lam, R. W., Michalak, E. E., & Swinson, R. P. (2005). London: Taylor & Francis. 198 pp. RC537. Includes sixty-four full-text instruments; there are additional instruments for which full text is not included, but sample items may be provided. This book also contains a section on how to select an assessment scale. Instruments cover depression, mania, anxiety, related symptoms, side effects, functioning, quality of life, and special populations. For all instruments, there are commentary on the instrument, scoring information, alternate forms, references, and author/publisher contact information. A list of full-text measures in this book is located at http://libguides.hofstra.edu/TMdb/LamMichalakSwinson2005.

4.115. *Practitioner's guide to empirically based measures of depression.* Nezu, A. M. (Ed.). (2000). New York: Kluwer Academic/Plenum. 353 pp. RC537. Contains twenty-four full-text instruments; ninety measures of depression are reviewed. Full-text measures are in appendix B. Scale summaries include original citation, purpose, description, administration and scoring, psychometrics, alternative forms, and author/publisher information. Appendix A

contains "Quick-View Guide' to instruments, which allows quick comparison of measures on target population, type of measure, measurement focus, time to complete, norm(s) availability, whether a fee is required, and availability of alternate forms. Each instrument is followed by a permission statement. Unless the statement indicates that the instrument may be copied freely, permission from the author/publisher is required. A list of full-text measures in this book is located at http://libguides.hofstra.edu/TMdb/Nezu2000.

Multicultural Assessment

4.116. *Handbook of tests and measurements for black populations.* Jones, R. L. (Ed.). (1996). Hampton, VA: Cobb & Henry. 1205 pp. BF176. Two-volume set. Includes eighty-two full-text measures. Other measures for which full text is not provided in this set are also covered. Measures in this set were developed in response to concerns about measures developed and validated on white populations being administered to black populations. Underlying the work is the view that tests and measures should be based on African American history, characteristics, experiences, behaviors, and needs. Many of the constructs have applicability to other populations, but some are specific to African Americans or other racial/ethnic minorities (e.g., coping with racism, African American identity development, African self-consciousness). Rationale, development, and psychometrics are provided for all measures. Some of the measures are from theses and dissertations; they may have more and newer documentation since publication of this volume. With the exception of the introductory chapter, each chapter begins with an abstract, discusses its topic, presents full-text assessment tools and/or reviews them, and ends with a "for further information, contact" box. Volume 1 covers measures for infants, cognitive approaches and measures for children, self-esteem measures for children, race-related measures for children, a variety of measures for adolescents and young adults, language assessment and attitude measures, parental attitudes and values measures, and measures of family structure and dynamics. Volume 2 contains worldview measures, physiological measures, and neuropsychological assessment; measures of spirituality, acculturation, life experiences, and values; race identity attitude measures; stress, racism and coping measures; mental health delivery measures; fair employment testing concepts and work environment and organizational assessment measures; research program–based measures; and a variety of other measures. In addition to the eighty-two full-text measures, chapters contain many useful tables and diagrams. A list of full-text measures in this book is located at http://libguides.hofstra.edu/TMdb/Jones1996.

4.117. *Measuring race and ethnicity.* Davis L. E., & Engel, R. J. (2011). New York: Springer. 198 pp. HT1523. Contains

sixty-one full-text instruments. Scales measure how individuals from various racial/ethnic groups think about
themselves and about members of other racial/ethnic
groups. Measures identity and acculturation for Asian and
Pacific Islanders, Hispanic Americans, African Americans,
Caucasian Americans, and Native Americans. Some scales
are for administration to members of specific groups, while
others are designed to be used with members of all groups.
A list of full-text measures in this book is located at http://
libguides.hofstra.edu/TMdb/DavisEngel2011.

Neuropsychology

4.118. *Compendium of neuropsychological tests: Administration, norms, and commentary* (3rd ed.). Strauss, E.,
Sherman, E. M. S., & Spreen, O. (2006). New York:
Oxford University Press. 1216 pp. RC386. Includes
sixteen full-text instruments. Although this work does
contain some full-text measures, it has two other main
purposes. It was designed to provide an overview of
basic and advanced issues critical to neuropsychological
assessment, develop a strong working knowledge of the
strengths and weaknesses of instruments, and present
information necessary to empirically based assessment.
This is covered in chapters on psychometrics, norms
selection, history taking, preparation of the patient, report writing and feedback, and assessment of premorbid
functioning. The second purpose, which forms most of
the volume, is to provide an easy-to-use tool in which the
user would find the major highlights of commonly used
neuropsychological tests. The authors' mantra is "Know
Your Tools." Instruments included in earlier editions but
no longer commonly used have been removed, and many
newer instruments have been added. Test reviews follow a
fixed format with purpose, source, age range, description,
administration, administration time, scoring, demographic
effects, normative data, reliability, validity, and commentary. Major domains covered are achievement, executive
functions, attention, memory, language, visual perception,
somato-sensory function, olfactory function, body orientation, motor function, mood, personality and adaptive functions, and response bias and suboptimal performance. In
the introduction to each domain, there is a table that summarizes important features such as age range, tasks, administration time, key processes, test-retest reliability, and
other features. Following the standard information and
commentary for each test, there is a reference list of major
articles and books on the test. This work is aimed at clinicians and researchers using neuropsychological measures.
A list of full-text measures in this book is located at http://
libguides.hofstra.edu/TMdb/StraussShermanSpreen2006.

4.119. *Compendium of tests, scales and questionnaires:
The practitioner's guide to measuring outcomes after ac-
quired brain impairment.* Tate, R. L. (Ed.). (2010). Hove:
Psychology Press. 746 pp. RC386. Includes 107 full-text

instruments. Scales of consciousness and orientation;
general and specific cognitive functions; regulation of
behavior, thought, and emotion; sensory, ingestion, and
motor functions; activities of daily living (ADLs); participation and social role; environmental factors; and
quality of life. Information on each measure includes the
source, purpose, scale development, administration and
scoring, psychometrics, commentary, references, and the
scale itself. Permission information is generally located
immediately following the instrument. This work will
be of greatest use to researchers and clinicians interested
in measuring outcomes of rehabilitation from traumatic
brain injury. A list of full-text measures in this book is
located at http://libguides.hofstra.edu/TMdb/Tate2010.

4.120. *Handbook of neurologic rating scales* (2nd ed.).
Herndon, R. M. (Ed.). (2006). New York: Demos Medical. 441 pp. RC348. Contains 130 full-text measures; also
includes reviews of other measures. This handbook covers neurological rating scales frequently used in clinical
trials and practice. Entries include a description, original
purpose and current use, psychometrics, administration
and scoring, advantages and disadvantages of particular
measures, key references, and in most cases the measure
itself. There are also a link and password at the end of
the table of contents that enables one to access PDFs of
the scales in the book. Although one can access the measures online as well as in the book itself, the true value
of this volume is in the discussion and assessment of the
measures. Measures cover general neuropsychological
symptoms, pediatric development, pediatric neurologic
and rehabilitation, amyotrophic lateral sclerosis (ALS),
movement disorders, multiple sclerosis and other demyelinating diseases, dementia, stroke, peripheral neuropathy,
pain, headache, ataxia, traumatic brain injury, epilepsy,
HIV-related cognitive impairment, rehabilitation outcome, and quality of life. This volume will be very useful
to researchers involved in clinical trials or outcome studies measuring neuropsychological symptoms and outcomes. A list of full-text measures in this book is located
at http://libguides.hofstra.edu/TMdb/Herndon2006.

4.121. *Measurement in neurological rehabilitation.* Wade,
D. T. (1992). Oxford: Oxford University Press. 388 pp.
RC386. Contains 141 full-text instruments. This volume
begins by presenting a useful model of thinking about
pathology, impairment, disability, and handicap, followed
by classifications; suggestions on how to choose the most
appropriate measure(s); and discussion of measuring motor and sensory impairments, cognitive and emotional
impairments, physical disability, social interaction, quality of life, specific diseases, specific circumstances, and
miscellaneous. It then presents actual measures of cognitive impairment; motor impairment; focal disabilities;
activities of daily living (ADLs); global measures of disability; handicap and quality of life; emotions and social
interactions; and specific measures for multiple sclerosis,

stroke, head injury, Parkinson's disease, and other movement disorders. Instructions, comments, psychometrics, and references are provided. This work will be most useful to those conducting research in clinical settings. A list of full-text measures in this book is located at http://libguides.hofstra.edu/TMdb/Wade1992.

Personality

4.122. *Measures of personality and social psychological constructs.* Boyle, G. J. (Ed.). (2015). Amsterdam: Academic Press. 776 pp. BF698. Includes 123 full-text measures; many more are reviewed, and sample items are provided. The focus is on frequently used and cited measures, particularly those developed in recent years to assess constructs of current interest. Five major areas of personality and social-psychological assessment are covered. Part I covers core issues in assessment, including response bias, malingering, and impression management. Part II ("Emotional Dispositions") covers hope, optimism, anger, hostility, life satisfaction, self-esteem, confidence, and affect. Part III ("Emotion Regulation") covers alexithymia, empathy, resiliency, well-being, sensation seeking, ability, and emotional intelligence. Part IV ("Interpersonal Styles") covers adult attachment, public image, social evaluation, and forgiveness. Part V ("Vices and Virtues") covers values, morality, religiosity, dark personality, and perfectionism. Part VI ("Sociocultural Interaction and Conflict") covers cross-cultural values and beliefs, intergroup contact, stereotyping and prejudice, and sexual orientation. For each measure, it provides a description, the sample populations, psychometrics, location of scale, original study or publisher, and results and comments. A list of full-text measures in this book is located at http://libguides.hofstra.edu/TMdb/Boyle2015.

Sexuality and Gender

4.123. *Handbook of sexuality-related measures* (3rd ed.). Fisher, T. D. (2011). New York: Routledge. 656 pp. HQ60. Contains 209 full-text instruments covering topics including, but not limited to, abuse, aging, anxiety, arousal, assault attitudes, attraction, behavior, beliefs, body image, coercion, communication, compulsion, contraception, consent, double-standard, dysfunction, education, fantasy, functioning, harassment, homophobia, GLBTQI, knowledge, masturbation, orgasm, motivation, risk, STDs, and more. A description, reliability and validity data, and author/publisher contact information are provided for each instrument. A list of full-text measures in this book is located at http://libguides.hofstra.edu/TMdb/Fisher2011.

Social Psychology

4.124. *Measurement of attitudes toward people with disabilities: Methods, psychometrics and scales.* Antonak, R. F., & Livneh, H. (1988). Springfield, IL: Charles C. Thomas. 306 pp. HV1553. Includes twenty-four full-text measures; discussions and sample items from other measures are also provided. This volume addresses direct and indirect methods of attitude measurement; multidimensional scaling; psychometric guidelines for attitude scales; and twenty-four full-text measures of general attitudes toward people with disabilities, attitudes toward physical disabilities, psychiatric disabilities, the mentally retarded, and societal responsibilities toward people with disabilities. Tables and charts enhance the text; this volume will provide valuable information in addition to the measures for any researcher interested in the measurement of attitudes toward disabled persons. A list of full-text measures in this book is located at http://libguides.hofstra.edu/TMdb/AntonakLivneh1988.

4.125. *Measures of personality and social psychological constructs.* Boyle, G. J. (Ed.). (2015). Amsterdam: Academic Press. 776 pp. BF698. Includes 123 full-text measures; many more are reviewed, and sample items are provided. The focus is on frequently used and cited measures, particularly those developed in recent years to assess constructs of current interest. Five major areas of personality and social-psychological assessment are covered. Part I covers core issues in assessment, including response bias, malingering, and impression management. Part II ("Emotional Dispositions") covers hope, optimism, anger, hostility, life satisfaction, self-esteem, confidence, and affect. Part III ("Emotion Regulation") covers alexithymia, empathy, resiliency, well-being, sensation seeking, ability, and emotional intelligence. Part IV ("Interpersonal Styles") covers adult attachment, public image, social evaluation, and forgiveness. Part V ("Vices and Virtues") covers values, morality, religiosity, dark personality, and perfectionism. Part VI ("Sociocultural Interaction and Conflict") covers cross-cultural values and beliefs, intergroup contact, stereotyping and prejudice, and sexual orientation. For each measure, it provides a description, the sample populations, psychometrics, location of scale, original study or publisher, and results and comments. A list of full-text measures in this book is located at http://libguides.hofstra.edu/TMdb/Boyle2015.

4.126. *Measures of social psychological attitudes.* Robinson, J. P., Shaver, P. R., & Wrightsman, L. S. (1969). Ann Arbor, MI: Survey Research Center, Institute for Social Research. 662 pp. JA74 or HM. Includes 149 full-text measures of life satisfaction/happiness; self-esteem and related constructs; alienation and anomie; authoritarianism, dogmatism, and related constructs; other sociopolitical attitudes; values; general attitudes toward people; religious attitudes; and methodologies. NOTE: This individual volume is appendix B of Robinson et al., *Measures of Political Attitudes*; volumes may be located together in JA or separated by topic to JA and HM. A list of full-text measures in this book is located at http://libguides.hofstra.edu/TMdb/RobinsonShaverWrightsman1969.

4.127. *Measuring race and ethnicity.* Davis L. E., & Engel, R. J. (2011). New York: Springer. 198 pp. HT1523. Contains sixty-one full-text instruments. Scales measure how individuals from various racial/ethnic groups think about themselves and about members of other racial/ethnic groups. Measures identity and acculturation for Asian and Pacific Islanders, Hispanic Americans, African Americans, Caucasian Americans, and Native Americans. Some scales are for administration to members of specific groups, while others are designed to be used with members of all groups. A list of full-text measures in this book is located at http://libguides.hofstra.edu/TMdb/DavisEngel2011.

4.128. *Scales for the measurement of attitudes.* Shaw, M. E., & Wright, J. M. (1967). New York: McGraw-Hill Books. 604 pp. BF378. Includes 186 full-text instruments. This work begins with a discussion on the nature, conceptualizations, and definitions of attitudes and methods of scaling and measurement. Each chapter begins with a brief discussion of the topic and why some measures are included and others are not, followed by measures in that area. Topics for which measures are provided include social practices and social issues and problems (family, education, religious, health, economics), international issues (political relations, conflict, economics), abstract concepts (education, law), political and religious issues, ethnic and national groups, significant others, and social institutions. For each measure, the title, source, and description are provided, as well as administration and scoring information, psychometrics, and comments. Items, directions for use, and scale values and/or response alternatives are provided. A list of measures included is in the frontmatter. This work will be valuable to undergraduates, graduate students, and beginning and experienced researchers. A list of full-text measures in this book is located at http://libguides.hofstra.edu/TMdb/ShawWright1967.

Violence and Aggression

4.129. *Measuring bullying victimization, perpetration, and bystander experiences: A compendium of assessment tools.* Hamberger, M. E., Basile, K. C., Vivolo, A. M. (Comps. and Eds.). (2011). Atlanta, GA: Centers for Disease Control and Prevention (CDC), National Center for Injury Prevention and Control. 119 pp. SUDOC HE 20. Includes thirty-three full-text instruments. There are four sections, containing "bully only" scale, "victim only" scales, "bully and victim" scales, and "bystander, fully, and/or victim" scales. Most, though not all, scales are Likert-type scales. They are available online at http://www.cdc.gov/violenceprevention/pub/measuring_bullying.html. A list of full-text measures in this book is located at http://libguides.hofstra.edu/TMdb/HambergerBasileVivolo2011.

4.130. *Measuring intimate partner violence, victimization and perpetration: A compendium of assessment tools.*

Thompson, M. P., Basile, K. C., Hertz, M. F., & Sitterle D. (2006). Atlanta, GA: Centers for Disease Control and Prevention, National Center for Injury Prevention and Control. 163 pp. HV6626. Contains forty-two full-text instruments. Scales measure physical victimization, sexual victimization, psychological/emotional victimization, stalking victimization, physical perpetration, sexual perpetration, psychological/emotional perpetration, and stalking perpetration. Available online at https://stacks.cdc.gov/view/cdc/11402. A list of full-text measures in this book is located at http://libguides.hofstra.edu/TMdb/ThompsonBasileHertzeSitterle2006.

Other

4.131. *Handbook of research design & social measurement* (6th ed.). Miller, D. C., & Salkind, N. J. (2002). Thousand Oaks, CA: Sage. 786 pp. H62. Includes thirty-three full-text instruments covering social status, group structure and dynamics, social indicators, organizational structure, community, social participation, leadership, morale and job satisfaction, attitudes, values, norms, family, and marriage. Also provides extensive references to instruments for which full text is not included in this book. A list of full-text measures in this book is located at http://libguides.hofstra.edu/TMdb/MillerSalkind2002.

4.132. *Positive psychological assessment: A handbook of models and measures.* Lopes, S. J., & Snyder, C. R. (Eds.). (2003). Washington, DC: American Psychological Association. 495 pp. BF176. Contains nineteen full-text instruments; many others are reviewed in chapters covering positive psychological assessment through measures of optimism, hope, locus of control, creativity, positive emotions, self-esteem, forgiveness, gratitude, positive coping, and quality of life, among other constructs. A list of full-text measures in this book is located at http://libguides.hofstra.edu/TMdb/LopesSnyder2003.

4.133. *Practitioner's guide to empirically based measures of social skills.* Nangle, D. W., Hansen, D. J., Erdley, C. A., & Norton, P. J. (Eds.). (2010). New York: Springer. 538 pp. HM691. Includes twenty full-text measures; one hundred instruments are reviewed. Part of the Association for Behavioral and Cognitive Therapies (ABCT) Clinical Assessment Series, this volume covers a wide range of issues in the measurement of social skills in adults, children, and adolescents. It begins by addressing definitions and target skills, social-cognitive models, and learning theory. It then goes on to practical issues in assessment and interventions, as well as special factors in measuring social skills such as diversity, anger and aggression, social anxiety and withdrawal, intellectual disability, autism spectrum disorders, schizophrenia, and substance use. For measures discussed and included, the original citation is provided, as are the purpose, population, description, administration and scoring information, psychometrics, source, cost (if any), and alternative forms (if any). There is a "Quick-View Guide" appendix that facilitates identification and comparison by age level. Full-text measures are located in the reprints appendix. A list of full-text measures in this book is located at http://libguides.hofstra.edu/TMdb/NangleHansenErdleyNorton2010.

4.134. *Sourcebook of nonverbal measures: Going beyond words.* Manusov, V. (2009/2005). New York: Routledge. 540 pp. P99. Includes twenty-seven full-text instruments. Covers social skills, affectionate communication, touch avoidance, perception, emotional expressiveness, visual affect, interactional synchrony, conversational equality, speech rate, expression of rapport, and other variables for individuals and dyads. Contains participant-completed measures, passive observation coding systems, and observational measures and methods for dynamic interactive behaviors. A list of full-text measures in this book is located at http://libguides.hofstra.edu/TMdb/Manusov2009.

4.135. *Tools for strengths-based assessment and evaluation.* Simmons, C. A., & Lehmann, P. (2013). New York: Springer. 534 pp. H62. Includes 142 full-text instruments on areas of psychological strengths, including happiness and subjective well-being, health, wellness, and health-related quality of life; acceptance, mindfulness, and situational affect; hope, optimism, and humor; resilience, coping, and post-traumatic growth; aspirations, goals, and values; self-efficacy; social support; social relationships; and emotional intelligence. It also contains tools for couples, families, and children as well as useful chapters on incorporating strengths into evaluation and selecting tools. A list of full-text measures in this book is located at http://libguides.hofstra.edu/TMdb/SimmonsLehmann2013.

RESOURCES INDEXING/ABSTRACTING TESTS AND MEASURES

The resources in this section contain information about specific tests but generally do not provide actual measures. Information in these resources typically includes development of the test; test description; purpose; citations to studies in which the test was used; reliability and validity data; administration, scoring, and norms information; and author/publisher contact information.

Resources that contain actual measures are described in the previous sections. If they also provide information about measures for which they do not contain the full text, they are also included in the following sections.

General

Databases

4.136. Health and Psychosocial Instruments (HaPI). Pittsburgh, PA: Behavioral Measurement Database Services.

This subscription database includes more than 180,000 citation/abstract records from journals covering a variety of behavioral measurement tools, including checklists, coding schemes, indexes, interview schedules, projective techniques, questionnaires, rating scales, surveys, tasks, tests, and vignettes/scenarios instruments. Available via Ebsco and Ovid.

4.137. PsycTESTS. Washington, DC: American Psychological Association. This subscription database contains more than 47,000 records (in 2017), 76 percent of which include full text of measures or sample items. Sources include authors, peer-reviewed journals, books, dissertations, websites, Archives of the History of American Psychology Test Collection, and commercial test publishers.

Print Sources

4.138. *Directory of unpublished experimental mental measures.* American Psychological Association. (1974–). Washington, DC: American Psychological Association. BF176. This is an open-ended set; the last published volume is volume 9 (2008). Each volume covers tests described in American Psychological Association (APA) journals during a particular time period, generally in the areas of psychology, education, personnel, and sociology. It does not evaluate the measures, but provides the test title, purpose, description, format, reliability and validity statistics as available, source (citation information), and related information as available (may include original source of test, use with various populations, etc.). The format covers the type of scaling (e.g., Likert, true/false, checklist, semantic differential). Not included are commercial tests, task-type tests, and achievement tests for a single area of study. Test information is organized by topic category, which varies among the existing volumes published between 1974 and 2008. There is a separate title index; volumes 1–7 were published in 2001. Indexes in volumes after 7 are cumulative back to volume 1. This set is valuable to undergraduate and graduate students who are seeking noncommercial measures, as well as advanced researchers and graduate students seeking measures on interesting but not commercially viable topics.

4.139. *Measures for psychological assessment: A guide to 3000 original sources and their applications.* Chun, K., Cobb, S., & French, J. R. P. (1978). Ann Arbor: University of Michigan Survey Research Center, Institute for Social Research. 664 pp. BF698. This volume contains references to studies in which particular tests were used cited in selected psychology journals between 1960 and 1970. The references include articles using both commercial and research tests. Author, descriptor, and "supplement to the descriptor" indexes are in the front of the book (pp. 1–56). The articles referenced may, but do not necessarily, contain the actual tests; for research tests, they will help the researcher identify the author or publisher. Tests cover virtually all areas of psychology that were extant at the time of publication. This work is more difficult to use than some others and thus will be most useful to researchers looking for measures of less frequently researched phenomena, interested in what was being measured in psychology during the 1960s, or looking for articles measuring particular topics during that time.

Addictions

4.140. *Screening and assessing adolescents for substance abuse disorders*. Center for Substance Abuse Treatment. (2012/1998). Treatment Improvement Protocol (TIP) Series, No. 31. Rockville, MD: Substance Abuse and Mental Health Services Administration (SAMHSA). 165 pp. This document covers screening and assessment of adolescents, substance use disorders related to adolescent development, and legal issues and juvenile justice settings for adolescents. It provides information on twenty-eight screening instruments, comprehensive assessment instruments, and general functioning instruments for use with substance-using adolescents. For each instrument, it provides title, purpose, type of assessment (e.g., interview, self-report), life areas/problems assessed, reading level if applicable, credentials required if any, commentary, pricing information if applicable, where item has been reviewed, and contact information.

Anxiety and Anxiety Disorders

4.141. *Practitioner's guide to empirically based measures of anxiety*. Antony, M. M., Orsillo, S. M., & Roemer, L. (Eds.). (2001). New York: Kluwer Academic/Plenum. 512 pp. RC531. Contains seventy-seven full-text instruments and reviews more than 200 instruments. This book, published under the auspices of the Association for Advancement of Behavior Therapy (AABT), covers general issues in the assessment of anxiety disorders and assessment strategies for assessing panic disorder and agoraphobia, generalized anxiety disorder, social phobia, acute stress disorder, post-traumatic stress disorder, specific phobias, and obsessive-compulsive disorder. Scale summaries include original citation, purpose, description, administration and scoring, psychometrics, alternative forms, and author/publisher information. Instruments are in appendix B. Each instrument is followed by a "permission" statement. A list of full-text measures in this book is located at http://libguides.hofstra.edu/TMdb/AntonyOrsilloRoemer2001.

Children and Adolescents

4.142. *Assessing children's well-being: A handbook of measures*. Naar-King, S., Ellis, D. A., & Frey, M. A. (Eds.). (2004). Mahwah, NJ: Lawrence Erlbaum. 307 pp. RJ50. Includes twenty full-text instruments; an additional forty-four instruments are reviewed. Topics covered are health status and quality of life, adherence, pain management, child behavior, child development, child coping, cognition, attributions, attitudes, environment, and consumer satisfaction. Full-text measures are in the appendixes. A list of full-text measures in this book is located at http://libguides.hofstra.edu/TMdb/Naar-KingEllisFrey2004.

4.143. *Assessment scales in child and adolescent psychiatry*. Verhulst, F. C., & Van Der Ende, J. (2006). Abingdon, England: Taylor and Francis. 220 pp. RJ503. Includes forty-six full-text measures used with children and adolescents; also contains reviews and sample items from other measures. Provides general rating scales of behavior and symptoms, strengths, and difficulties. Also includes scales for specific problems, including anxiety, obsessive-compulsive disorder, depression, suicide, eating disorders, tics, ADHD, conduct disorders, substance abuse, and global impairment. For each scale, there are commentary, information on alternate forms, properties of the scale and subscales, psychometric information, information on use, key references, and author/publisher contact information. Some scales are in the public domain, others are reproduced with permission, and some are commercial. An alphabetical list of measures is on pages 219–220. This work will be valuable to researchers at all levels, although some commercial tests may be restricted to those with professional credentials. A list of full-text measures in this book is located at http://libguides.hofstra.edu/TMdb/VerhulstVanDerEnde2006.

4.144. *Measures for children with developmental disabilities: An ICF-CY approach*. Majnemer, A. (Ed.). (2012). London: Mac Keith Press. 538 pp. RM930. This volume contains information on assessment tools and outcome measures based on the International Classification of Functioning, Disability and Health—Children and Youth (ICF-CY) framework. It is not exhaustive, but covers what experts in each area consider to be the best measures available. It covers a wide range of measurement, including body functions, intellectual and interpersonal functioning, behavior, learning, communication, self-care, environmental, health, quality of life, and global development. Chapters contain a description of the construct; information on measurement within the particular domain; and a description of the best measures, including an outline of their purpose, content, and psychometric properties. There is also a table providing a capsule summary for each instrument, information on how to acquire it, and key references. Chapters are ten to twenty pages long, with reference lists.

4.145. *Tests and measurements in child development: Handbook I*. Johnson, O. G., & Bommarito, J. W. (1976). San Francisco, CA: Jossey-Bass. 524 pp. BF722. This work covers tests for children aged birth to twelve years. It provides information on approximately 300 measures of cognition, personality and emotional characteristics, perceptions of environment (nonfamily), self-concept, environment (family), motor skills, brain injury, sensory perception, physical attributes, miscellaneous attitudes and interests, social behavior, and other variables. For each measure, it provides title, author, population for use, variable measured, type of measure, source from which measure may be obtained (frequently an item in the bibliography), description of the measure, reliability and validity information, and a bibliography referencing works on the measure. It also contains a useful test title index as well as other indexes. **NOTE:** See *Tests and Measurements in Child Development: Handbook II* for tests for children twelve to eighteen years old.

4.146. *Tests and measurements in child development: Handbook II.* Johnson, O. G. (1976). San Francisco, CA: Jossey Bass. 1327 pp. BF 722. Two-volume set. This work covers tests for children twelve to eighteen years old. It provides information on approximately 900 measures of cognition, personality and emotional characteristics, perceptions of environment (nonfamily), self-concept, environment (family), motor skills, brain injury, sensory perception, physical attributes, miscellaneous attitudes and interests, social behavior, vocational interests, and other variables. For each measure, it provides title, author, population for use, variable measured, type of measure, source from which measure may be obtained (frequently an item in the bibliography), description of the measure, reliability and validity information, and a bibliography referencing works on the measure. It also contains a useful test title index as well as other indexes. **NOTE:** See *Tests and Measurements in Child Development: Handbook I* for tests for children aged birth to twelve years.

Clinical and Counseling

4.147. *Compendium of psychosocial measures: Assessment of people with serious mental illnesses in the community.* Johnson, D. L. (2010). New York: Springer. 545 pp. RC473. This volume provides information about 372 measures intended to be used in research with severely mentally ill individuals. The measures are divided into twenty-nine areas: general background information; functional assessment; community living; social functioning; global assessment; level of psychopathology; insight and judgment; stress; social problem solving and coping; social support; quality of life; consumer satisfaction; continuity of care; treatment adherence; substance abuse; environmental measures and group processes; housing; cultural issues; special purpose methods; agency performance evaluation; work behavior; family measures; premorbid adjustment; psychotic symptoms; depression; mania; anxiety; screening; and empowerment, recovery, and stigma. For each measure, the title, primary source(s), purpose, description, reliability, validity, measure source, and comments are provided. Because these measures are

all intended for use with severe mental illness, it will be most useful to advanced graduate students and researchers working with that population.

4.148. *Handbook of psychiatric measures* (2nd ed.). Rush, A. J., First, M. B., & Blacker, D. (Eds.). (2008). Washington, DC: American Psychiatric Association. 828 pp. RC473. Includes 136 full-text instruments on the accompanying CD. An alphabetical list of the full-text instruments is on pages 755–757. A list by chapter (topic) is on pages 757–761. Covers general psychiatric symptoms; mental health status, functioning, and disability; general health status, functioning, and disability; quality of life; adverse effects; patient perceptions of care; stress and life events; family risk factors; suicide risk; child and adolescent measures; symptom-specific measures for infancy, childhood, and adolescence; child and adolescent functional status; delirium and cognition; neuropsychiatric symptoms; substance use disorders; psychotic disorders; mood disorders; anxiety disorders; somatoform and factitious disorders and malingering; sexual dysfunction; eating disorders; sleep disorders; impulse control; personality traits and disorders; defense mechanisms; and aggression. Also covered are another 139 instruments for which full text is not included. The book provides a "practical issues" section for each instrument, including permission information and cost if any. A list of full-text measures in this book is located at http://libguides.hofstra.edu/TMdb/RushFirstBlacker2008.

Eating Disorders and Obesity

4.149. *Handbook of assessment methods for eating behaviors and weight-related problems: Measures, theory, and research* (2nd ed.). Allison, D. B., & Baskin, M. L. (2009). Los Angeles, CA: Sage. 701 pp. RC552. Contains forty-five full-text instruments. Covers quality of life in obesity and eating disorders; attitudes toward obese people; body image; restrained eating; physical activity; food intake; hunger and satiety; binge-eating and purging; eating-disordered thoughts, feelings, and behaviors; and eating and weight-related problems in children. Instruments are in appendixes organized by chapter. Psychometric and administration/scoring information is provided, as well as author/publisher contact information. A list of full-text measures in this book is located at http://libguides.hofstra.edu/TMdb/AllisonBaskin2009.

Educational and School Psychology

4.150. *Handbook of psychoeducational assessment: Ability, achievement, and behavior in children.* Andrews, J., Janzen, H. L., & Saklofske, D. H. (Eds.). (2001). San Diego, CA: Academic Press. 512 pp. LB3051. This handbook provides a brief summary of some of the major tests for assessing ability, achievement, and behavior in children and adolescents. Data from other review publications are included, as well as reliability and validity findings. The case studies and references will be particularly useful to graduate students, faculty, and practitioners in school psychology.

4.151. *Practitioner's guide to empirically based measures of school behavior*. Kelley, M. L., & Noell, G. (Eds.). New York: Kluwer Academic/Plenum. 231 pp. RJ503. This volume reviews approximately one hundred tests used to measure child and adolescent behaviors in the school setting, focusing particularly on functional behavior assessment (FBA) and curriculum-based assessment (CBA). Topics covered include ADHD, oppositional defiant disorder, conduct disorder, adjustment, interpersonal relations, attention, personality, home situations, school situations, self-concept, social behavior, and social skills, among others. For each test, the guide includes the purpose, population, description, administration and scoring, psychometrics, clinical utility, strengths and limitations, and author/publisher information. Most, but not all, of the measures reviewed are commercial and require a fee, and some may also require professional credentials for purchase. This volume will be of use to advanced graduate students and beginning and advanced researchers in school psychology.

4.152. *Special educator's comprehensive guide to 301 diagnostic tests* (rev. ed.). Pierangelo, R., & Giuliani, G. (2006). San Francisco, CA: Jossey-Bass. 484 pp. LC 4019. This volume provides an overview of assessment in special education, including how a child is recommended for assessment, the role of the family, the role of the evaluator, understanding the student's behavior during testing, and reporting test results. It provides one to two pages of information for each of 301 tests in twenty-five domains. The chapter for each domain begins with a brief introduction to issues in that domain, followed by information for each test, which includes author/publisher contact information, administration time, type of administration (group, individual), age/grade level, purpose of the test, subtest information, and strengths of the test. Virtually all of the tests are commercial tests that have undergone extensive psychometric evaluation. Tests cover academic achievement; anxiety and depression; aptitude; attention-deficit/hyperactivity; auditory processing; autism spectrum; behavioral disorders; deafness and hearing impairments; emotional disturbance; English as a second language and bilingual education; gifted and talented; infants, toddlers, and preschoolers; intelligence; learning disabilities; mathematics; mental retardation; neuropsychology; occupational therapy; personality; other psychological issues; reading; speech and language; visual processing; and written language. There is also an appendix containing referral forms commonly used in the special education process. **NOTE:** This is the revised edition of the 1998 *Special Educator's Complete Guide to 109 Diagnostic Tests*.

Family

4.153. *Handbook of family measurement techniques*. Tsouliatos, J., Perlmutter, B. F., & Strauss, M. A. (Eds.). (2001). Thousand Oaks, CA: Sage. 1208 pp. HQ728. This three-volume set is a different item, rather than a second edition of the 1990 work with the same title and authors. Volume 1 of this set contains the contents of the entire 1990 edition. This includes an introductory chapter on family measurement principles and techniques, followed by detailed abstracts for 504 instruments measuring dimensions of marital and family interaction, intimacy and family values, parenthood, roles and power, and adjustment. Each topical chapter provides a discussion of the topic before the abstracts are presented. Detailed abstracts include availability information, variables measured, instrument type (e.g., self-report, projective), description, sample items (where permission was acquired), commentary, and references. All measures appear in their entirety in a published work (most measures), or permission was provided to deposit the entire instrument with the National Auxiliary Publication Service (NAPS 1-3). In addition to these 504 detailed abstracts, abbreviated abstracts are provided for another 472 instruments that met the same criteria (total of 976 instruments abstracted). These original abstracts from the 1990 work, now forming volume 1 of the 2001 set, are for instruments from the 1929–1986 literature, with the major focus being the 1975–1986 literature. Volume 2 of this three-volume set contains 367 additional abstracts for measures that were newly developed or substantially revised during 1987–1996. It begins with chapters on family measurement overview and developing, interpreting, and using family assessment techniques. Detailed abstracts in volume 2 cover family relations; marital relations; parent-child relations; family adjustment, health, and well-being; and family problems. Abstracts include variables measured, instrument type, samples measured, description, sample items (where permission was acquired), psychometrics, commentary, keywords, references, and availability information. Volume 3 contains the full text of 168 of the 367 instruments abstracted in volume 2. In addition to the actual instrument, scoring instructions are provided, as well as the original source of the instrument. This set will be highly valuable to clinicians, researchers, graduate students, and advanced undergraduates interested in measurement of numerous family issues. A list of full-text measures in volume 3 is located at http://libguides.hofstra.edu/TMdb/TsouliatosPerlmutterStrauss2001.

Geropsychology

4.154. *Assessing older persons: Measures, meaning and practical applications*. Kane, R. L., & Kane, R. A. (Eds.). (2000/2004). Oxford: Oxford University Press. 542 pp. HQ1061. Includes one hundred full-text instruments, as well as information on other instruments for which the full text is not included. This volume is a sequel to, rather than a second edition of, Kane and Kane's 1981 book *Assessing the Elderly: A Practical Guide to Measurement* (see below). It addresses the areas of assessment in the 1981 volume (function, health, emotion, cognition, and social well-being) and also addresses new areas such as assessment of family caregivers, physical environments, values and preferences, spirituality, and satisfaction. In addition to the full-text measures, this book provides information on selecting and using instruments, psychometric information, and caveats about their use. The section on applications of assessment covers comprehensive assessment and management, care planning for those in health-care settings, long-term case management, mandated assessments, and assessment of older adults who cannot communicate. A list of full-text measures in this book is located at http://libguides.hofstra.edu/TMdb/KaneKane2000.

4.155. *Assessing the elderly: A practical guide to measurement.* Kane, R. A., & Kane, R. L. (1981). Lexington, MA: Lexington Books. 301 pp. RC954. Contains thirty-three full-text instruments and reviews of other measures not included. This book covers the assessment of older people in long-term care, particularly physical functioning, activities of daily living, cognitive and affective functioning, general mental health, and social functioning. Chapters are thirty to sixty pages long; present a discussion of the issues; cover measures not included; present administration, scoring, and interpretation information for the included full-text measures, and have references. This book will be useful to researchers interested in the status and functioning of older people who are in long-term care. A list of full-text measures in this book is located at http://libguides.hofstra.edu/TMdb/KaneKane1981.

4.156. *Handbook of geriatric assessment* (4th ed.). Gallo, J. J. (2006). Sudbury, MA: Jones and Bartlett. 473 pp. RC953. Contains thirty-eight full-text instruments; also provides information on other measures not included in the book. The goal of this book is to enable multidimensional assessment by discussing the domains that are significant in the lives of older people and providing some full-text measures of those domains. Domains covered include cognition, depression, substance use and abuse, activities of daily living, social issues (support, care, mistreatment, economic, health, environment, spiritual), physical, pain, health, home, nursing homes, hospitalization, adherence to medical regime, interdisciplinary teamwork, and disaster preparedness and response. Chapters are ten to thirty pages long and contain a discussion of the issue; description of measures not included; actual measures with administration, scoring, and interpretation information; and references. Measures are reprinted with permission. This book will be valuable to researchers interested in any of the domains covered, as well as to

practitioners. A list of full-text measures in this book is located at http://libguides.hofstra.edu/TMdb/Gallo2006.

Happiness/Well-Being/Quality of Life

4.157. *Assessing children's well-being: A handbook of measures.* Naar-King, S., Ellis, D. A., & Frey, M. A. (Eds.). (2004). Mahwah, NJ: Lawrence Erlbaum. 307 pp. RJ50. Includes twenty full-text instruments; an additional forty-four instruments are reviewed. Topics covered are health status and quality of life, adherence, pain management, child behavior, child development, child coping, cognition, attributions, attitudes, environment, and consumer satisfaction. Full-text measures are in the appendixes. A list of full-text measures in this book is located at http://libguides.hofstra.edu/TMdb/Naar-KingEllisFrey2004.

Industrial and Organizational

4.158. *Directory of human resource development instrumentation.* University Associates. (1985). San Diego, CA: University Associates. This volume provides information on several hundred commercial scales related to the workplace. Scales cover career assessment, change, coaching, communication style, conflict, creativity, discipline, facilitator development, general abilities, grammar, grievances, health and wellness, human relations, influence, instructional design, interpersonal communications, interpersonal relationships, interviewing, job aptitude, job evaluation, job instruction training, labor relations, leadership style, learning style, listening, management practices, management style, motivation, needs assessment, nonverbal communication, organizational climate, organizational communications, performance appraisal, personality, planning, power, productivity, relationships, retirement planning, safety, sales, situational leadership, social style, style assessment, supervisory style, team building, time management, union relations, and values. For each instrument, information provided includes publisher, description, purpose, design, whether facilitator training is required, data source (self, other, etc.), theoretical base reference, intended audience, time to complete, number of items and subscales, scoring, interpretation source, psychometrics if available, and typical uses.

Mood and Mood Disorders

4.159. *Assessment of depression.* Sartorius, N., & Ban, T. A. (Eds.). (1986). Berlin: Springer-Verlag. 376 pp. RC537. Contains thirteen full-text instruments. Reviews self-report and clinical interview assessments of depression used around the world. A list of full-text measures in this book is located at http://libguides.hofstra.edu/TMdb/SartoriusBan1986.

4.160. *Practitioner's guide to empirically based measures of depression.* Nezu, A. M. (Ed.). (2000). New York: Kluwer Academic/Plenum. 353 pp. RC537. Contains twenty-four full-text instruments; ninety measures of depression are reviewed. Full-text measures are in appendix B. Scale summaries include original citation, purpose, description, administration and scoring, psychometrics, alternative forms, and author/publisher information. Appendix A contains "Quick-View Guide" to instruments, which allows quick comparison of measures on target population, type of measure, measurement focus, time to complete, norm(s) availability, whether a fee is required, and availability of alternate forms. Each instrument is followed by a permission statement. Unless the statement indicates that the instrument may be copied freely, permission from the author/publisher is required. A list of full-text measures in this book is located at http://libguides.hofstra.edu/TMdb/Nezu2000.

Neuropsychology

4.161. *Compendium of neuropsychological tests: Administration, norms, and commentary* (3rd ed.). Strauss, E., Sherman, E. M. S., & Spreen, O. (2006). New York: Oxford University Press. 1216 pp. RC386. Includes sixteen full-text instruments. Although this work does contain some full-text measures, it has two other main purposes. It was designed to provide an overview of basic and advanced issues critical to neuropsychological assessment, develop a strong working knowledge of the strengths and weaknesses of instruments, and present information necessary to empirically based assessment. This is covered in chapters on psychometrics, norms selection, history taking, preparation of the patient, report writing and feedback, and assessment of premorbid functioning. The second purpose, which forms most of the volume, is to provide an easy-to-use tool in which the user would find the major highlights of commonly used neuropsychological tests. The authors' mantra is "Know Your Tools." Instruments included in earlier editions but no longer commonly used have been removed, and many newer instruments have been added. Test reviews follow a fixed format with purpose, source, age range, description, administration, administration time, scoring, demographic effects, normative data, reliability, validity, and commentary. Major domains covered are achievement, executive functions, attention, memory, language, visual perception, somato-sensory function, olfactory function, body orientation, motor function, mood, personality and adaptive functions, and response bias and suboptimal performance. In the introduction to each domain, there is a table that summarizes important features such as age range, tasks, administration time, key processes, test-retest reliability, and other features. Following the standard information and commentary for each test, there is a reference list of major articles and books on the test. This work is aimed at clinicians and researchers using neuropsychological measures. A list of full-text measures in this book is located at http://libguides.hofstra.edu/TMdb/StraussShermanSpreen2006.

Personality

4.162. *Measures of personality and social psychological constructs.* Boyle, G. J. (Ed.). (2015). Amsterdam: Academic Press. 776 pp. BF698. Includes 123 full-text measures; many more are reviewed, and sample items are provided. The focus is on frequently used and cited measures, particularly those developed in recent years to assess constructs of current interest. Five major areas of personality and social-psychological assessment are covered. Part I covers core issues in assessment, including response bias, malingering, and impression management. Part II ("Emotional Dispositions") covers hope, optimism, anger, hostility, life satisfaction, self-esteem, confidence, and affect. Part III ("Emotion Regulation") covers alexithymia, empathy, resiliency, well-being, sensation seeking, ability, and emotional intelligence. Part IV ("Interpersonal Styles") covers adult attachment, public image, social evaluation, and forgiveness. Part V ("Vices and Virtues") covers values, morality, religiosity, dark personality, and perfectionism. Part VI ("Sociocultural Interaction and Conflict") covers cross-cultural values and beliefs, intergroup contact, stereotyping and prejudice, and sexual orientation. For each measure, it provides a description, the sample populations, psychometrics, location of scale, original study or publisher, and results and comments. A list of full-text measures in this book is located at http://libguides.hofstra.edu/TMdb/Boyle2015.

Sexuality and Gender

4.163. *Gender roles: A handbook of tests and measures.* Beere, C. A. (1990). Westport, CT: Greenwood Press. 575 pp. HM253. Covers scales of gender roles, children and gender, gender stereotypes, marital and parental roles, employee roles, multiple roles, and attitudes toward gender roles. Provides test title, authors, publication date, variables measured, description, psychometrics, extensive notes and comments, author/publisher contact information, and a reference list of works in which the scale was used. A very useful feature is the "Index of Variables Measured by Scales."

4.164. *Sex and gender issues: A handbook of tests and measures.* Beere, C. A. (1990). New York: Greenwood Press. 605 pp. BF692. This handbook provides information and citations on availability of 197 scales on heterosexual relations, sexuality, contraception and abortion, pregnancy and childbirth, somatic issues, homosexuality, rape and sexual coercion, family violence, body image and appearance, and eating disorders. For each test, the following information is provided: author(s), earliest date in a publication, variables examined, format (e.g., true/false, multiple-choice, forced choice, observational, semantic differentials, physiological), description, sample items, development of measure, previous subjects who have completed the measure, "appropriate for," administration (most are self-administered), scoring information, reliability and validity information, "available from," and "used in" (reference list of studies in which each measure was used). "Notes and Comments" are also provided as appropriate for the particular measure. Most of the measures are available in journal articles; some are available in ETS *Tests in Microfiche* (TIM), books, dissertations, dissertations, and National Auxiliary Publication Service (NAPS); and others may be commercial tests for which publisher information is provided.

4.165. *Women and women's issues: A handbook of tests and measures.* Beere, C. A. (1979). San Francisco, CA: Jossey-Bass. 550 pp. HQ1180. This volume reviews 235 instruments on a broad spectrum of issues pertaining to women. Measures cover sex roles, sex stereotypes, sex-role prescriptions, children's sex roles, gender knowledge, marital and parental roles, employee roles, multiple roles, attitudes toward women's issues, somatic and sexual issues, and some miscellaneous women-related topics. Descriptions of measures follow a standard format, which includes the title and author, year it first appeared in the literature, characteristics of respondents who have competed the measure, respondents for which the instrument is appropriate, a description of the instrument, psychometric information, information about alternate forms, availability and acquisition information, and references to studies in which the measure has been used. This book will be valuable to undergraduates, graduate students, and beginning and experienced researchers interested in the measurement of issues related to women.

Social Psychology

4.166. *Measures of personality and social psychological constructs.* Boyle, G. J. (Ed.). (2015). Amsterdam: Academic Press. 776 pp. BF698. Includes 123 full-text measures; many more are reviewed, and sample items are provided. The focus is on frequently used and cited measures, particularly those developed in recent years to assess constructs of current interest. Five major areas of personality and social-psychological assessment are covered. Part I covers core issues in assessment, including response bias, malingering, and impression management. Part II ("Emotional Dispositions") covers hope, optimism, anger, hostility, life satisfaction, self-esteem, confidence, and affect. Part III ("Emotion Regulation") covers alexithymia, empathy, resiliency, well-being, sensation seeking, ability, and emotional intelligence. Part IV ("Interpersonal Styles") covers adult attachment, public

image, social evaluation, and forgiveness. Part V ("Vices and Virtues") covers values, morality, religiosity, dark personality, and perfectionism. Part VI ("Sociocultural Interaction and Conflict") covers cross-cultural values and beliefs, intergroup contact, stereotyping and prejudice, and sexual orientation. For each measure, it provides a description, the sample populations, psychometrics, location of scale, original study or publisher, and results and comments. A list of full-text measures in this book is located at http://libguides.hofstra.edu/TMdb/Boyle2015.

Violence and Aggression

4.167. *Assessment of partner violence: A handbook for researchers and practitioners.* Rathus, J. H., & Feindler, E. L. (2004). Washington, DC: American Psychological Association. 392 pp. RC560. This volume addresses various issues in the assessment of partner violence, such as assessment modalities, assessment in clinical practice, research considerations in scale development, psychometrics, measuring treatment outcomes, and research issues and challenges particular to the assessment of partner violence. It covers interview measures and self-report measures specific to partner violence, as well as measures of general relationship functioning, anger and hostility, and other correlates of partner violence. For each measure it provides a description and the development of the method, target population, format, administration and scoring, psychometrics, advantages and limitations, the primary reference to the scale, scale availability information, and related references. There is a list of measures reviewed in the beginning of the book, organized according to chapter.

Other

4.168. *Positive psychological assessment: A handbook of models and measures.* Lopes, S. J., & Snyder, C. R. (Eds.). (2003). Washington, DC: American Psychological Association. 495 pp. BF176. Contains nineteen full-text instruments; many others are reviewed in chapters covering positive psychological assessment through measures of optimism, hope, locus of control, creativity, positive emotions, self-esteem, forgiveness, gratitude, positive coping, and quality of life, among other constructs. A list of full-text measures in this book is located at http://libguides.hofstra.edu/TMdb/LopesSnyder2003.

4.169. *Practitioner's guide to empirically based measures of social skills.* Nangle, D. W., Hansen, D. J., Erdley, C. A., & Norton, P. J. (Eds.). (2010). New York: Springer. 538 pp. HM691. Includes twenty full-text measures; one hundred instruments are reviewed. Part of the Association for Behavioral and Cognitive Therapies (ABCT) Clinical Assessment Series, this volume covers a wide range of issues in the measurement of social skills in adults, children, and adolescents. It begins by addressing definitions and target skills, social-cognitive models, and learning theory. It then goes on to practical issues in assessment and interventions, as well as special factors in measuring social skills such as diversity, anger and aggression, social anxiety and withdrawal, intellectual disability, autism spectrum disorders, schizophrenia, and substance use. For measures discussed and included, the original citation is provided, as are the purpose, population, description, administration and scoring information, psychometrics, source, cost (if any), and alternative forms (if any). There is a "Quick-View Guide" appendix that facilitates identification and comparison by age level. Full-text measures are located in the reprints appendix. A list of full-text measures in this book is located at http://libguides.hofs tra.edu/TMdb/NangleHansenErdleyNorton2010.

5
Theses and Dissertations

INTRODUCTION

What are theses and dissertations, and what is their purpose? The primary purpose of a thesis or dissertation is for the student to engage in the processes of scholarly research and writing under the direction of experienced faculty members and thus become part of the productive community of scholars. After the student has graduated and the work is published, it serves as a contribution to human knowledge, useful to other scholars and perhaps even to a more general audience.

Theses and dissertations are the intellectual capital of both the author and the institution at which they were created and are typically an original piece of research or creative work. In the United States and Canada, the term "thesis" is used for the culminating requirement for the master's degree (although not all master's programs require a thesis), and the term "dissertation" is used for the culminating requirement for the doctoral degree. In Great Britain, however, the term "thesis" is preceded by the term that identifies the degree associated with it ("master's thesis" or "doctoral thesis"), and other countries have their own variations of terms. The US and Canadian usage of "thesis" for master's level works and "dissertation" for doctoral level works is applied in this chapter.

5.1. BENEFITS OF THESES AND DISSERTATIONS IN CURRENT RESEARCH

Theses and dissertations are often overlooked in the research process. They are typically lengthy and often need to be acquired via interlibrary loan (sometimes on microfiche) or purchased in print or electronic format. There are, however, benefits of dissertations and theses for the serious researcher. Recent works can provide an early look at upcoming areas of research and extensive, if not exhaustive, reference lists. Earlier works can provide insight into the early thinking and research of prominent researchers and provide historical background on the development of a particular area of research.

5.2 IDENTIFICATION AND ACQUISITION OF THESES AND DISSERTATIONS

As theses and dissertations are considered part of the intellectual capital of the institutions, electronic and/or microform and/or print copies are held by the home institution. Non-home institutions may also purchase selected theses and dissertations for their collections. Such purchases are typically not part of the normal selection process, however, and are usually made based on a specific need or as part of a special collection.

Lending policies regarding theses and dissertations vary among institutions, among departments within an institution, and among authors, and may be different from general lending policies. This occurs for several reasons: the location of the holding (e.g., archives, which do not circulate in or out of the institution, vs. stacks or microform, which typically will circulate in and out of the institution) and departmental and individual author embargoes.

There are two contradictory trends occurring in the availability of theses and dissertations. One recent trend is to make theses and dissertations open access. The other recent trend is for authors and/or institutions to place a time limit on thesis and dissertation availability in order to protect the intellectual property rights of the individual and/or institution. Many institutions now require that authors complete a form indicating whether they want their theses/dissertations to be fully open access (i.e., full-text available at no charge via an open-access portal), institution available only for a specified period (typically two years), or fully embargoed for a specified period. The last option is usually applied to cases in which patents and/or proprietary rights are involved.

There are various tools available to identify and acquire theses and dissertations. Some of these are country, hemisphere, or discipline specific, while others are global. They also vary in terms of comprehensiveness, time period covered, the inclusion of dissertations only or both dissertations and theses, access to full text, and paid subscription access versus free open access.

Coverage in this chapter is selective, not exhaustive. As this book is aimed at those interested in psychology, the goal is to cover as many countries and time periods as possible in a manner most useful to these particular users. It does not attempt to be an exhaustive source of all bibliographies for all countries for all time periods.

Most master's- and doctoral degree-granting institutions now have a searchable database of their own theses or dissertations, or their works can be identified in their general catalogs by including "thesis" or "dissertation" as a keyword or the institution as a publisher. As the contents of such depositories are limited by definition and they are easily found, they are not covered in this chapter. In addition, theses and dissertations can almost always be found in the national library of each country. In this case, unless there is a separate database of theses and dissertations, the national libraries and/or national print bibliographies are not listed, as they are numerous and easily found via Google and WorldCat. In the case of older print bibliographies of theses and dissertations, they often cover very brief periods; in such cases, an attempt has been made to cover time periods as comprehensively as possible with bibliographies that span longer periods.

INSTITUTIONAL PRODUCTS

5.3. Proquest products. US and Canadian dissertations completed from 1861 through and including the present have been held by and published by UMI (University Microfilms International)[1] since 1938, which was recognized by the US Library of Congress as the offsite repository of its Digital Dissertations Library in 1998. Selected theses have been included since 1962, and dissertations from more than fifty British universities have been included since 1988. Proquest Dissertations and Theses (PQDT) is the online access point to UMI holdings. At this time it indexes and abstracts, and has digitized, over 2.3 million works. UMI has digitized all of its holdings back to 1997 (approximately 1.9 million works). Subscribing institutions have access to the full text of their own works via the Dissertations and Theses @ product. PQDT subscribing institutions can also have their pre-1997 works digitized for a fee. Proquest Dissertations and Theses Global (PQDT Global) contains over 3.8 million works from more than 3,000 universities in eighty-five countries. Both PQDT and PQDT Global are subscription databases. Proquest Dissertations and Theses Open (PQDT Open) (http://pqdtopen.proquest.com) provides free public indexing, abstracting, and full text of US and Canadian works for which the author has granted open access. Pro-

quest also has a free Dissertation Alert product (http://www.proquest.com/products-services/dissertations/dissertation-alerts.html). Aimed at users without access to subscription products and using keywords the user specifies, Proquest will review its entire database and retrieve up to 500 titles per search. The user receives a printout of the citations and ordering information.

5.4. Center for Research Libraries (CRL). https://www.crl.edu. An international consortium of university, college, and independent research libraries that supports original research and inspired teaching in the humanities, sciences, and social sciences by preserving and making available to scholars rare and uncommon primary source materials from around the world. CRL holds more than 800,000 doctoral dissertations from universities outside of the United States and Canada. The dissertation dates range from 1800, but most dissertations are from the late nineteenth and early twentieth centuries. Most are from Western Europe countries, such as Germany, the Netherlands, France, Switzerland, Denmark, Norway, Sweden, and the United Kingdom, although a sizable number are from other countries in Europe as well as Latin America, South America, and Africa. More than eighty languages are represented in the collection with 66 percent in German, 16 percent in French, 6 percent in English, 2 percent in Dutch, 1 percent in Latin and Swedish, and less than 1 percent in the remaining languages. Dissertations are most easily searched in the CRL catalog (http://catalog.crl.edu/; use advanced search and include "dissertation" as a keyword). CRL acquires approximately 5,000 non-US, non-Canadian doctoral dissertations each year; acquisitions are primarily through the demand purchase program available to scholars at member universities.

INDEXES/ABSTRACTS OF DISSERTATIONS

5.5. WorldCat. https://www.worldcat.org/. The world's largest catalog, with international coverage. WorldCat is freely available on the Internet and also as a subscription product to participating libraries. Institutions submit their holdings to WorldCat on a regular basis. To identify theses and dissertations, click on "content," select "thesis and dissertations," and enter at least one search term in another field (one must be in "advanced search" mode to see the "content" field). One can determine if an institution is represented in WorldCat by visiting https://www.worldcat.org/registry/institutions and entering the institution name.

5.6. National Technical Information Service (NTIS). http://www.ntis.gov/. Freely available US government website provides access point to the Public Access National Technical Reports Library (NTRL). Indexes and provides abstracts to theses and dissertations completed by students who are in the military or who have conducted federally funded research. Works are submitted to or collected by NTIS directly from federal agencies for permanent access by businesses, academia, and the public. NTIS also provides premium subscriptions to individuals, corporations, and educational institutions in and outside of the United States for a fee. Items may be purchased from NTIS directly, but the site advises that users should check for free access from any of the following before direct purchase: the issuing organization's website; the US Government Publishing Office Federal Digital System website (https://www.gpo.gov/fdsys/); the federal government Internet portal (https://www.usa.gov/); or a public search engine such as Google.

DISCIPLINE-SPECIFIC THESIS AND DISSERTATION DATABASES

In this section, only discipline-specific sources that are related to psychology or have a subset of works related to psychology are included.

5.7. PsycINFO. Commercial database available via numerous vendors. Indexes/abstracts approximately 425,000 dissertations from the 1930s to the present.

5.8. Education Resources Information Center (ERIC). https://eric.ed.gov. Contains approximately 30,000 theses and dissertations related to education, dated 1997 to the present. Some are available as open-access full text.

5.9. NASA Technical Reports Server (NTRS). https://ntrs.nasa.gov. NASA Technical Reports Server (NTRS) provides access to more than 10,000 dissertations, many of which are full text and some of which are in areas of importance to psychology, such as personality and behavioral variables, performance, stress, privacy needs, human factors, and risk of psychiatric disturbance.

5.10. Ethnolinguistica. http://www.etnolinguistica.org/teses. Approximately 350 dissertations on indigenous languages of South America, many of which are available full text via the site.

OPEN-ACCESS THESIS AND DISSERTATION PORTALS

5.11. DART-Europe. http://www.dart-europe.eu. Provides full-text open access to more than 700,000 research theses from 597 universities in 28 European countries.

5.12. EThOS. http://ethos.bl.uk. The United Kingdom's national doctoral thesis database. See the discussion of EThOS below for more information.

5.13. Networked Digital Library of Theses and Dissertations (NDLTD). http://www.ndltd.org/. Indexes, abstracts, and provides full-text access to theses and dissertations around the world. At this time, over 4.5 million thesis

and dissertation citations and abstracts are contained in NDLTD, dating from the early 1900s to the present. In addition to providing access to theses and dissertations, NDLTD promotes open access and provides guidance to institutions on how to include their open-access works included in NDLTD and/or become participating members. NDLTD is a free, open-access database; institutions do not need to become members to have their works included in it. NDLTD can be searched at http://search.ndltd.org/, and a list of contributing institutions and the number of works included from those institutions can be found at http://union.ndltd.org/portal/.

5.14. Open Access Theses and Dissertations. http://oatd.org. Indexes and abstracts of open-access dissertations and theses from more than 1,100 institutions worldwide, with links to the full-text works. At this time, it includes more than 3.4 million theses and dissertations.

5.15 Proquest Dissertations and Theses Open (PQDT Open). http://pqdtopen.proquest.com. Provides free public indexing, abstracting, and full text of US and Canadian works for which the author has granted open access. See the previous discussion under "Proquest products" for more information.

NATIONAL AND INTERNATIONAL THESIS AND DISSERTATION SOURCES

International Sources

5.16. DATAD (Database of African Theses and Dissertations). http://datad.aau.org/ (currently also known as DATAD-R (Database of African Theses and Dissertations—including Research Articles). Although it originated as a depository for abstracts of theses and dissertations from universities throughout Africa, as of August 2017, this database contained records only from the University of Pretoria in South Africa. At that time, there were 11,491 records, 475 of which were theses and dissertations.

5.17. *Guide to theses and dissertations: An international bibliography of bibliographies*. Reynolds, M. M. (1985). Phoenix, AZ: Oryx Press. 263 pp. Z5053.A1 R49 1985.

5.18. NORDICOM (Nordic Information Centre for Media and Communication Research)—Doctoral Dissertations. http://www.nordicom.gu.se/en/media-research/doctoral-dissertations. Contains approximately 1,000 open-access full-text dissertations completed at universities in Denmark, Finland, Norway, and Sweden dating from 2007 to the present.

Country Resources

Australia/Australasia

5.19. National Library of Australia's TROVE service. http://www.bac-lac.gc.ca. The Australasian Digital Theses Program database was closed in 2011; the content within that database is now searchable via the National Library of Australia's TROVE service. TROVE contains many other items, including theses from other countries that are held in Australian libraries. In the advanced search screen, there is an option to limit to Australian works and theses. TROVE contains a total of more than 500,000,000 items; some of the theses are available full text, others are not.

5.20. *Union list of higher degree theses in Australian university libraries: Cumulative edition to 1965.* Wylie, E. (Ed.). (1967). Hobart, Tasmania: University of Tasmania Library. 563 pp. Z5055. A79 U5. [Supplements continue coverage].

Austria

5.21. Austrian dissertations database. https://www.obvsg.at/services/dissertationsdatenbank. Dissertations from 1990 to the present.

Belgium

5.22. *Répertoire commun des thèses électroniques des universités de la Communauté Française de Belgique.* http://www.bictel.be. French-language dissertations from Belgian universities.

Canada

5.23. Theses Canada portal. http://www.bac-lac.gc.ca. Started in 1965, this site holds all Canadian theses and dissertations from seventy accredited Canadian universities. More recent works have been digitized, and open-access full text is available. Older nondigitized works can be ordered.

China

5.24. China doctoral dissertations full-text database (CDFD). http://oversea.cnki.net/kns55/brief/result.aspx?dbPrefix=CDFD. Open-access full-text coverage of more than 300,000 doctoral dissertations from more than 400 Chinese institutions from 1894 to the present.

France

5.25. *Catalogue des thèses de doctorat soutenues devant les universités françaises.* Ministère de l'éducation nationale, Direction des bibliothèques de France (annual, 1960–1985). Paris, France: Cercle de la librairie. Z5055. F78. Various volumes cover from 1874 to 1985.

5.26. *Répertoire alphabétique des thèses de doctorat ès lettres des universités françaises, 1810–1900.* Maire, A. (1903). Paris, France: A Picard et fils. 226 pp. Z5055.

F79 M22 1903. Bibliography of doctoral dissertations completed at French universities between 1810 and 1900.

5.27. Theses.FR. http://www.theses.fr/en. Abstracts and some full text for all theses and dissertations completed in French universities since 1985. Some works are in English, others in French.

Iceland

5.28. Skemman. http://skemman.is/en. Online institutional repository for seven universities in Iceland. Includes digital theses and dissertations, articles, and other research material.

India

5.29. Shodhganga. http://shodhganga.inflibnet.ac.in. Platform for students at universities in India to deposit their doctoral dissertations. At this time, Shodhganga has approximately 113,000 full-text dissertations and 3,500 dissertation abstracts from approximately 300 Indian universities. Approximately 4,000 full-text dissertations are on the subject of psychology, and half of these were written from 2010 to 2016.

Japan

5.30. JAIRO (Japanese Institutional Repositories Online). http://jairo.nii.ac.jp/en. Contains materials from 585 Japanese organizations, not all of which are universities. Contains approximately 2,400,000 records, about half of which are open-access full text. Theses and dissertations comprise approximately 5 percent of items in JAIRO.

Netherlands

5.31 *Catalogus van academische geschriften in Nederland en Nederlandsch-Indië verschenen* (annual, 1925–). Utrecht, Netherlands: Nederlandse Vereniging van Bibliothecarissen en Bibliotheek-Ambtenaren (UTRECHT). Catalog of theses and dissertations at universities in the Netherlands.

5.32. NARCIS. http://www.narcis.nl. Gateway to scholarly research in the Netherlands. Includes theses and dissertations from all Dutch universities, other publications, and data sets from approximately 2,900 organizations dating from 2000 to the present. About half of the materials are full text, including approximately 30,000 open-access theses and dissertations.

Russia and the Former Soviet Union

5.33. Digital dissertations. http://diss.rsl.ru. Approximately one million full-text theses and dissertations completed in

Russia and former Soviet Union states dating from 1985 to the present.

South Africa

5.34. *Gesamentlike katalogus van proefskrifte en verhandelinge van die Suid-Afrikaanse universiteite, 1918–1989 (Union catalogue of theses and dissertations of South African universities, 1918–1989)*. Ferdinand Postma Library (1990). Potchefstroom, South Africa: Ferdinand Postma-Biblioteek, Potchefstroomse Universiteit vir Christelike Hoër Onderwys. In Africaans and English. Various versions of this title have been published for subsequent years.

Spain

5.35. Dialnet. https://dialnet.unirioja.es/tesis. Open-access theses and dissertations completed at universities in Spain. Date coverage varies by university, but some coverage extends from the 1940s to the present.

Sweden

5.36. Swedish universities dissertations. http://www.dissertations.se. Contains approximately 55,000 theses and dissertations completed at Swedish universities but written in English. Approximately half are available as open-access full text.

Switzerland

5.37. *Jahresverzeichnis der schweizerischen Hochschulschriften = Catalogue des Écrits académiques suisses*. Universitätsbibliothek Basel. (various dates). Basel, Switzerland: Verlag der Universitätsbibliothek. Published in various years, coverage extends from 1897 to 1991. Available in Hathitrust.

Turkey

5.38. The National Thesis Center of the Turkish Council of High Education. https://tez.yok.gov.tr/UlusalTezMerkezi. Contains theses and dissertations completed at universities in Turkey dating 2006 to the present, with sporadic coverage before 2006. Some open-access full text.

United Kingdom

5.39. EThOS. http://ethos.bl.uk. The United Kingdom's national doctoral thesis database; its goal is to maximize the visibility and availability of UK doctoral research theses. The United Kingdom's open access policy is that publicly funded research should be available to all researchers. At this time, it holds approximately 440,000 doctoral thesis records from more than 120 UK institutions. Approximately 160,000 of these are full text, available via download from the EThOS database or via links to the institution's own repository. Of the remaining 240,000 records dating back to 1800, approximately 75 percent are available through the EThOS digitization-on-demand facility. While EthOS policy is that records are held for all UK institutions awarding PhDs, the holdings are not complete; each month approximately 3,000 new records are added, and 2,000 full-text doctoral theses become available.

6
Annotated and Unannotated Bibliographies

INTRODUCTION

Until the development of the Internet, and particularly the graphic user interface (GUI), book-type bibliographies and annotated bibliographies were a core resource for the serious researcher. Prior to databases such as PsycINFO (then PsycLIT) becoming available on the Internet (with keyword searching), the researcher had to search individual annual volumes of *Psychological Abstracts* and other indexes/abstracts to identify relevant research materials. So bibliographies—which typically included materials gathered from identified sources (such as *Psychological Abstracts*) published during a particular time period on a specific topic, organized in a meaningful way—were invaluable resources and time-savers for researchers.

Currently, databases such as PsycINFO, Medline, PubMed, CINAHL, Health Source Nursing Academic, ERIC, Education Full-Text, and Professional Development Collection serve as bibliographies, particularly as they have begun to index/abstract books and book chapters. WorldCat serves as a bibliography for books and other materials and formats. Research guides, such as this volume and earlier works, also serve as bibliographies.

6.1. Why Are Bibliographies Still Important?

The advantage of using works published as bibliographies qua bibliographies is that they are expressly written to cover a particular topic and will often cross disciplinary boundaries as well as publication format boundaries, including items such as organizational and government agency reports, which are not included in databases such as those just listed (with the exception of ERIC). The disadvantage of using bibliographies is that they are time limited (i.e., they cover a specific time period typically ending right before the date of their own publication).

When I started working on this chapter, I expected to find few recent bibliographies. I was wrong. The expansion of the World Wide Web into everyday life, and particularly

academic life, enables one to identify *thousands* of bibliographies created each year. Many of these are by undergraduate and graduate students or are otherwise not "published" by a recognized publisher; as such, they do not necessarily define the parameters of what is included or excluded, and they are often developed to serve a particular but typically unidentified purpose. So how did I identify "published" bibliographies for this chapter?

Based on my experience in developing this chapter, two sections follow. The first section discusses my successful and unsuccessful search methods, which hopefully will be of service to users in their own searches. The second section lists *selected* bibliographies (annotated and unannotated) published within the last twenty years (1998–2017) and identified from PsycINFO, and selected bibliographies identified via Google Scholar published within the past five years. Bibliographies of individuals' works have been included only for major figures in psychology.

It is interesting to note that the number of bibliographies identified in PsycINFO dropped off precipitously after 1998. Many of the recent bibliographies identified via Google Scholar are web-based PDF documents published by organizations rather than in journals. These were identified by using Google Scholar's "advanced search" and, similar to the strategy used in the databases, entering "annotated bibliography" in the title field. I searched by reverse year, starting with 2017. There were 150–250 results for each year, in all disciplines; I waded through them to select items with appropriate authorship and topics relevant to psychology.

6.2. Successful and Unsuccessful Search Strategies

Under "Document Type," PsycINFO has a field labeled "bibliography." Using this limiter, however, did not limit results to materials of interest (bibliographies). Book chapters that contain a bibliography in a nonbibliographical book were in the result lists as well as empirical studies with reference lists. This search, at the time this was written, resulted in 1,643 hits for the period between 1884 and

2015. Adding the search term "bibliography" in the "title" field narrowed the results to 790 for the period between 1930 and 2012. This strategy was overly restrictive, as I knew of at least one annotated bibliography indexed in PsycINFO in 2017. For reasons unknown to me, [document type = bibliography] is not attached to some records that clearly are bibliographies. Removing the [document type = bibliography] limiter and searching solely for "bibliography" in the title field resulted in 1,690 hits for the period between 1895 and 2017 and captured the materials being sought. Medline also has a [publication type = bibliography] limiter; my experiences with using the limiter compared to solely searching for "bibliography" in the title field were similar to those with PsycINFO. Looking through the 200 most recent Medline results, most were on medical topics not related to psychology; those that were had already been identified via PsycINFO. Incremental gains from searching Medline in addition to PsycINFO are virtually zero, so this is not a useful search strategy. The same pattern emerged when I searched education-related databases such as Education Full-Text, ERIC, and Ebsco Professional Development Collection.

Psychology is a broad discipline, so I also searched Google Scholar. As anyone who has searched Google Scholar knows, the results can be overwhelming. This was particularly true because I wasn't searching on a specific topic, but rather for bibliographies on any topics related to psychology. The "advanced search" function in Google Scholar does not have the flexibility of subscription databases; to make the results manageable, I had to put "annotated bibliography" in the title field and limited results to one year at a time, working in reverse chronological order from 2017 to earlier years. Each of these searches yielded 150–250 results in all disciplines. I reviewed the results for each year from 2012 to 2017 and have included annotated bibliographies related to psychology from those years. Bibliographies identified via PsycINFO and other sources are also selectively included here.

Also included are older general bibliographies of psychology that are considered of major importance in the field despite their age.

Several topic-specific journals publish bibliographies each year covering works on that topic published in other journals. These are noted, and only the most recent bibliography for each is presented. As in other sections, there is uneven coverage of areas in this chapter, as there is in the literature itself.

There are two resources that include bibliographies, but which I did *not* include in this chapter. Oxford University Press publishes *Oxford Bibliographies* (http://www.oxfordbibliographies.com/); this is an ongoing bibliography product that covers a variety of subjects. Currently, there are 190 bibliographies under the "Psychology" subject heading. *Oxford Bibliographies*, however, is available only by institutional subscription. The second source of unannotated bibliographies is theses and dissertations. Doctoral dissertations in particular are expected to provide an exhaustive review of the research subject and so typically include lengthy and up-to-date bibliographies as of the time they were submitted. For information on accessing theses and dissertations, see chapter 5.

BIBLIOGRAPHIES

General

6.3. *Bibliographic guide to psychology*. New York Public Library, Research Libraries. (annual serial, 1975–2003). Boston: C. K. Hall. Z2703. This serial was entitled "*The G. K. Hall Bibliographic Guide to Psychology*" for 1999–2003 and "*Psychology Book Guide*" for 1974–1998. This work is an annual index of books cataloged by the Library of Congress with BF call numbers and those cataloged by New York Public Library Research Libraries that contain at least two subject headings from the Library of Congress records even if they do not have BF call numbers. Books are in the annual bibliography based on the year they were cataloged, not the year they were published.

6.4. *Eminent contributors to psychology*. Watson, R. I. (Ed.). (1974–1976). New York: Springer. BF38. Two-volume set. Volume 1, "A *Bibliography of Primary References*," lists the works of approximately 500 individuals who lived from 1600 to 1967 and made significant contributions to psychology. Volume 2, "*A Bibliography of Secondary References*," contains more than 50,000 references to the individuals addressed in volume 1.

6.5. *Guide to reference works* (11th ed.). Balay, R. (Ed.). (1996). Chicago: American Library Association. 2020 pp. Z1035. This is the last print edition of this work. Originally published as a pamphlet by Alice Kroeger (Drexel University) in 1902, it became a major print reference work. The primary editor of earlier editions was Eugene Sheehy, and the work is popularly known as "Sheehy's." An electronic version was published by the American Library Association (ALA) in 2008; this electronic version was discontinued in 2016.

6.6. *Harvard list of books in psychology* (4th ed.). Compiled and annotated by the psychologists in Harvard University. (1971). Cambridge, MA: Harvard University Press. 108 pp. Z7201. Briefly annotated bibliography of 740 selected books of significance to psychology, published in English and arranged by area of the discipline.

6.7. *New Walford: Guide to reference resources*. Volume 2, *Social sciences*. (2008). London: Facet. 699 pp. Z7161. 02.

6.8. *Psychology: An introductory bibliography*. Beers, S. E. (Ed.). (1996). Lanham, MD: Scarecrow Press. 431 pp. Z7201 or BF121. Annotated bibliography of many areas of psychology, including history, definitions, careers, methodologies, biological bases, sensation and perception, emotion, motivation, learning, cognition, consciousness, memory, language, developmental psychology, social psychology, assessment, personality, stress, psychopathology, and psychotherapy.

6.9. *Research guide for psychology*. McInnis, R. G. (1982). Westport, CT: Greenwood Press. 604 pp. Z7201 or BF76. This volume was the last major research guide dedicated specifically to psychology. It presents detailed descriptions of works in bibliographies, biography, book reviews, encyclopedias, dictionaries, literature reviews, handbooks, directories of associations, research methodologies and statistics, experimental psychology (human and animal), physiological psychology, physiological interventions, communications, developmental psychology, social processes and issues, social psychology, personality, physical and psychological disorders, treatment and prevention, educational psychology, applied psychology, parapsychology, professional personnel and professional issues, and multicultural psychology. Some, but not all, of the serial-type indexes and abstracts in this work were later incorporated into other products. For the scholar interested in identifying major works and finding tools in use before the advent of the graphic user interface (GUI) functionality of the Internet led to their *seeming* obsolescence, this is an invaluable resource.

Addictions

6.10. Alcohol and drug prevention, intervention, and treatment literature: A bibliography for best practices. Nissen, L. B. (2014). *Best Practices in Mental Health: An International Journal*, 10(1), 59–97. Comprehensive bibliography on best practices drawn from a variety of sources, perspectives, and ideologies.

6.11. *Annotated bibliography of behavior analytic scholarship outside of "Analysis of Gambling Behavior," 2013–2015*. Costello, M. S., Whiting, S. W., Hirsh, J. L., Deochand, N., & Spencer, T. (2016). Vol. 10(1). Annotated bibliography of scholarly literature outside of this journal dedicated to gambling behavior. This open-access article is available at http://repository.stcloudstate.edu/agb/vol10/iss1/1.

6.12. Bibliography of literature reviews on drug abuse treatment. Prendergast, M., Podus, D., & McCormack, K. (1998). *Journal of Substance Abuse Treatment*, 15(3), 267–270. Bibliography of literature reviews on drug abuse treatment efficacy found in articles and books. Covers categories of drug abuse treatment (general), opiate treatment, cocaine treatment, therapeutic communities, adolescent treatment, behavioral and cognitive treatment, family therapy, Minnesota model, relapse prevention, acupuncture, transcendental meditation, 12–step programs, and natural recovery.

6.13. Cultural identification and substance use in North America: An annotated bibliography. Beauvais, F. (1998). *Substance Use & Misuse*, 33(6), 1315–1336. Annotated bibliography on issues related to cultural identification and substance abuse. Includes items on ethnic identification in general, specific ethnic identities, and measurement issues. Reference list includes citations to related readings not annotated.

6.14. Primary prevention of alcohol misuse: Overview and annotated bibliography. Hittner, J. B., Levasseur, P. W., & Galante, V. (1998). *Substance Use & Misuse*, 33(10), 2131–2178. Comprehensive, annotated bibliography on alcohol misuse primary prevention literature, including a review of conceptual and methodological issues.

6.15. A select annotated bibliography: Illegal drug research in rural and suburban areas. Hunt, K., & Furst, R. T. (2006). *Journal of Psychoactive Drugs*, 38(2), 173–188. Annotated bibliography covering drug consumption, drug distribution, drug prices, and ethnography.

6.16. A tribute to Bunky at 125: A comprehensive bibliography of E. M. Jellinek's publications. Ward, J. H., & Bejarano, W. (2016). *Journal of Studies on Alcohol and Drugs*, 77(3), 371–374. This comprehensive bibliography of Jellinek, considered the father of alcoholism studies, includes 165 original works published between 1912 and 1982. Many of his works were reprinted; in these entries the original publication information is included followed by the reprint information. Jellinek also published in other areas, and these works are included as well.

Affect/Mood/Emotion

6.17. *Emotion and religion: A critical assessment and annotated bibliography*. Corrigan, J., Crump, E., & Kloos, J. (2000). Westport, CT: Greenwood Press. 242 pp. Annotated bibliography containing more than 1,200 entries from the scholarly literature in psychology, sociology, anthropology, history, theology, and philosophy. Contains an extensive introductory essay and covers various disciplinary methods.

Altruism/Prosocial Behavior

6.18. *Annotated bibliography: Altruism, empathy, and prosocial behavior (1998–2013)*. Yahner, E. (2014). Washington, DC: Humane Society of the United States Institute for Science and Policy. Annotated bibliography of books, chapters, and articles on the relationship of human/animal interaction and the development of altruism, empathy, and prosocial behavior in children. Downloadable from http://animalstudiesrepository.org/hum_ed_bibs/9/.

6.19. *Research on altruism and love: An annotated bibliography of major studies in psychology, sociology, evolutionary biology and theology*. Post, S. G. (Ed.). (2007/2003). Philadelphia, PA: Templeton Foundation Press. 292 pp. BJ474. This volume is organized into five bibliographic chapters covering altruism and helping behavior works from the disciplines of psychology, sociology, evolution, and biology, as well as the religious love interface with science. It also contains a nonbibliographic biographical chapter on major figures such as Gandhi, Martin Luther King Jr., and the Dalai Lama.

Behaviorism

6.20. Bibliographic processes and products, and a bibliography of the published primary-source works of B. F. Skinner. Morris, E. K., & Smith, N. G. (2003). *The Behavior Analyst*, 26(1), 41–67. Article reviews extant B. F. Skinner bibliographies created from 1958 to 2001. It then describes the methods used in constructing this new, comprehensive, and corrected bibliography of Skinner's primary-source published works, which includes 291 items from books, articles, chapters, monographs, book reviews, manuals, encyclopedia entries, letters to the editor, and so forth, from 1930 to 1999.

6.21. Continued trends in the conditioned place preference literature from 1992 to 1996, inclusive, with a cross-indexed bibliography. Schechter, M. D., & Calcagnetti, D. J. (1998). *Neuroscience and Biobehavioral Reviews*, 22(6), 827–846. Bibliography of empirical research in this behavioral paradigm from 1992 to 1996. This is a follow-up to an earlier work that had covered the thirty-five years before 1992.

Bereavement and Grief

6.22. *Death and dying: A bibliographical survey.* Southard, S. (1991). New York: Greenwood Press. 514 pp. Z5725 or HQ1073 This work is an annotated bibliography containing citations and abstracts for more than 2,200 books, book chapters, articles, and reports. Covers ancient and modern thinking, philosophical theology, counseling the terminally ill, grief, caretaking professions, and education for death. Although it covers many areas, the major focus is on counseling the terminally ill and the grieving.

6.23. *Death and dying: An annotated bibliography of the thanatological literature.* Szabo, J. F. (2009). Lanham, MD: Scarecrow Press. 382 pp. Z5725. More than 2,200 citations to monographs on the science and study of death and dying. Covers psychology, philosophy, and attitude issues, coping and dealing with caregiving and working in the helping professions, cultural differences in bereavement rituals and grief and mourning, childhood bereavement, mental health issues, and legal issues. Also covers death themes in literature, ethical and policy issues, and popular literature on death and dying. Only selected items are annotated.

Clinical and Counseling

6.24. Bibliography. (no authorship indicated). (2004). *Psychoanalytic Psychotherapy*, 18(1), 139. List of references on therapist pregnancy.

6.25. A bibliography of articles relevant to the application of virtual reality in the mental health field. Rizzo, A. A., Wiederhold, B., Riva, G., & Van Der Zaag, C. (1998). *CyberPsychology & Behavior*, 1(4), 411–425. Bibliography containing more than 200 items on virtual reality and mental health. Items are classified into twelve categories: general theory, spatial skills and navigation, memory, attention, neglect, traumatic brain injury, developmental and learning disabilities, neurological diseases, transfer of training, auditory virtual reality, brain imaging, human factors, and clinical psychology.

6.26. Bibliography of literature reviews on drug abuse treatment. Prendergast, M., Podus, D., & McCormack, K. (1998). *Journal of Substance Abuse Treatment*, 15(3), 267–270. Bibliography of literature reviews on drug abuse treatment efficacy from articles and books. Covers categories of drug abuse treatment (general), opiate treatment, cocaine treatment, therapeutic communities, adolescent treatment, behavioral and cognitive treatment, family therapy, Minnesota model, relapse prevention, acupuncture, transcendental meditation, 12-step programs, and natural recovery.

6.27. A bibliography of mental patients' autobiographies: An update and classification system. Sommer, R., Clifford, J. S., & Norcross, J. C. (1998). *An American Journal of Psychiatry*, 155(9), 1261–1264. Seven anthologies and forty-eight autobiographies of former psychiatric patients published between 1980 and 1998.

6.28. Bibliography of Michael Balint's related works. Hudon, M., & Haynal, A. (2003). *The American Journal of Psychoanalysis*, 63(3), 275–279. Bibliography of Michael Balint's related works, incorporating references from various sources, including the Balint Archives and the Balint Society website.

6.29. Carl Rogers bibliography of English and German sources. Schmid, P. F. (2005). *Person-Centered and Experiential Psychotherapies*, 4(3–4), 153–160. This bibliography lists all original publications of Carl Rogers from 1922 onward, including German translations. Following English-, German-, and Spanish-language introductory remarks, the chronological part lists unpublished papers and interviews, and, separately, films. The alphabetical part consists of both name and title indexes. The bibliography is also available online at http://www.pfs-online.at/1/indexbibliocrr0.htm, where it is updated.

6.30. *Cognitive-behavioral therapy.* https://nicic.gov/library/package/cbt. National Institute of Corrections (NIC). Links to reports on and evaluations of cognitive-behavioral therapy (CBT) and evidence-based practice (EBP), CBT and female offenders, CBT and mentally ill offenders, CBT and probation, CBT and sex offenders, CBT program evaluations, CBT effectiveness with youth, moral reconciliation therapy (MRT), "Thinking for a Change" CBT programs, and general CBT effectiveness reports.

6.31 *Jacques Lacan: An annotated bibliography.* Clark, M. (2014/1988). New York: Routledge. 893 pp. Z8469 or BF109. 2 vols. Covers primary and secondary works by and about Lacan, including books, essays, seminars, interviews, and dissertations. Incorporates (and corrects where appropriate) information from all earlier published bibliographies of Lacan's work, including Joel Dor's *Bibliographie des travaux de Jacques Lacan*. Also includes all information about Lacan's published work on record in the Bibliotheque de I'Ecole de la Cause Freudienne Includes items in English, French, Japanese, Russian, and five other languages.

6.32 Karen Horney: A bibliography of her writings. Paris, B. J. (2001). *American Journal of Psychoanalysis*, 60(2), 165–172. Bibliography of Karen Horney's books, articles, essays, lectures and talks, and other writings.

6.33 Managed behavioral health services: A bibliography of empirical studies, articles of interest, and books. Feldman, S., Cuffel, B., & Hausman, J. (1999). *Administration and Policy in Mental Health*, 27(1–2), 5–88. Selective bibliography on managed behavioral health services. Part I is annotated and focuses on benefit design and insurance arrangements, managed mental health's effects on cost and utilization, and managed care in the public sector. Parts II and III are not annotated; they focus on theory, policy, and analysis.

6.34 Mental health parity: A review of research and a bibliography. Feldman, S., Bachman, J., & Bayer, J. (2002). *Administration and Policy in Mental Health*, 29(3), 215–228. Summarizes the content of a 2001 meeting held to review existing research on the effects of mental health parity, identify what knowledge can be gleaned from research in progress, and identify knowledge gaps. Includes bibliography of materials on parity published from 1996 to 2001.

6.35. *Mental health services in criminal justice system settings: A selectively annotated bibliography, 1970–1997.* Van Whitlock, R., & Lubin, B. (1999). Westport, CT: Greenwood Press. 190 pp. Contains 1,264 citations to books and scholarly articles, about half of which are annotated. Most empirically based works are annotated; theoretical and practical works are annotated only if they are of major value. Items are from psychology, psychiatry, nursing, education, social work, and other related areas and are related to service provision to mentally ill and substance-abusing offenders in criminal justice settings.

6.36. MMPI-2 and MMPI-A research with U.S. Latinos: A bibliography. Corrales, M. L., Cabiya, J. J., Gomez, F., Ayala, G. X., Mendoza, S., & Velasquez, R. J. (1998). *Psychological Reports*, 83(3, pt. 1), 1027–1033. Comprehensive listing of research conducted on US Latinos, including Puerto Ricans, with the MMPI-2 and MMPI-A from 1989 through 1998.

6.37. Multilingual bibliography of the works of Michael Balint. Haynal, A., & Hudon, M. (2003). *The American Journal of Psychoanalysis*, 63(3), 257–273. Multilingual and chronologically arranged bibliography of the works of Michael Balint.

6.38. Principles of multicultural counseling and therapy: A selective bibliography. Gielen, U. P., Draguns, J. G., & Fish, J. M. (2008). In *Principles of multicultural counseling and therapy* (pp. 419–432). New York: Routledge. Selective bibliography includes books, book chapters, and journal articles classified under nineteen categories, covering multicultural therapy and counseling, special populations and issues, therapy with children and adolescents, family therapy, care of refugees and immigrants, history of psychological healing in the West, psychopathology and mental health across cultures, transcultural psychiatry, culture and assessment, shamanism, altered states of consciousness, indigenous North American healing traditions, indigenous healing traditions in Latin America and the Caribbean, Asian and Oceanic healing traditions, Western psychology and Asian traditions, and African and Islamic healing traditions.

6.39. *Psychiatry in Nigeria: A partly annotated bibliography.* Boroffka, A. (2006). Kiel, Germany: Brunswiker Universitätsbuchhandlung–Medizin. 560 pp. Bibliography of almost 2,500 papers, rare documents, articles, and books related to psychiatry and neighboring disciplines, written in and about Nigeria and other parts of Africa, including early history of psychiatry and related research, and covering most of the twentieth century. Approximately half of the items are annotated.

6.40. Seventy-five years of Kleinian writing 1920–1995: A bibliography. Hinshelwood, R. D. (2000). *Kleinian Studies E-journal*. Bibliography of Kleinian writings by Melanie Klein and other authors from 1920 to 1995. Available online at http://ww.psychoanalysis-and-therapy.com/human_nature/ksej/hinbib.html.

6.41 Sixty years of client-centered/experiential psychotherapy and counseling: Bibliographical survey of books 1940–2000. Lietaer, G. (2002). *Journal of Humanistic Psychology*, 42(2), 97–131. Bibliographical, three-part survey of books published from 1940 to 2000. Part one focuses on books about client-centered/experiential psychotherapy (1939–1989) in their original language. Part two contains books about client-centered/experiential psychotherapy (1990–2000); items pre-1989 that were revised after 1989; and subsections on publications in English, German, French, and Dutch. Part three focuses on books about related approaches published in 1990–2000. Includes existential, interpersonal, Gestalt, narrative-constructivist, feminist, and integrative/eclectic approaches.

6.42 The treatment of attention-deficit hyperactivity disorder: An annotated bibliography and critical appraisal of published systematic reviews and meta-analyses. Jadad, A. R., Booker, L., Gauld, M., Kakuma, R., Boyle, M., Cunningham, C. E., Kim, M., & Schachar, R. (1999). *Canadian Journal of Psychiatry (La Revue Canadienne de*

Psychiatrie), 44(10), 1025–1035. Annotated bibliography of meta-analyses and systematic reviews on the treatment of attention deficit hyperactivity disorder (ADHD). Items cover various aspects of treatment, including nonpharmacological, pharmacological, and combination treatments for children and adults.

6.43 Work with older people: A bibliography. Kegerreis, P. (2012). *British Journal of Psychotherapy*, 28(1), 117–124. References to books and articles on psychodynamically oriented treatment covering general issues; individual, couples; and family, group, and creative therapies.

Cognition and Cognitive Disorders

6.44. Cognitive rehabilitation: An annotated bibliography. Martin, S., & Pauly, F. (2000). *Journal of Cognitive Rehabilitation*, 18(2), 6–13. Annotated bibliography of literature on cognitive rehabilitation after traumatic brain injury published between 1986 and 2000. Citations include both theoretical and empirical works, covering concepts, procedures, theories, applications, and the effects of cognitive rehabilitation on recovery from traumatic brain injury.

6.45. Viaggio attraverso la bibliografia di Jerome Bruner: Dagli anni della formazione alla psicologia culturale (Journey through the bibliography of Jerome Bruner: Toward the development of cultural psychology). Ornaghi, V., & Groppo, M. (1998). *Archivio di Psicologia, Neurologia e Psichiatria*, 59(2), 199–244. Includes an extensive bibliography, organized by date, and discusses J. Bruner's bibliography relative to the central themes of his works and outside influences. The works are analyzed by the period of formation: World War II (1939–1945), the influence of European Gestalt and the New Look movement (1946–1950), the influence of Piaget and Vygotsky (1956–1966), research on infancy and initial language studies (1967–1971), studies on the development of communicative and linguistic competence (1972–1979), interactionism and cultural roles (1980–1984), and autobiographical narrative and the construction of self (1991–1998).

Community Psychology

6.46. Families and communities: An annotated bibliography. Brossoie, N., Graham, B., & Lee, S. (2005). *Family Relations: An Interdisciplinary Journal of Applied Family Studies*, 54(5), 666–675. Resources for family social scientists focusing on the nexus of families and communities by highlighting recent theoretical, methodological, and empirical contributions.

6.47. La ricerca-azione in Italia: Spunti per una bibliografia (Action research in Italy: A bibliography). Galuppo, L., & Risorsa, U. (2006). *Rivista di Psicologia del Lavoro e dell' Organizzazione*, 12(2–3), 261–268. Brief Italian bibliography on action research published from the 1970s

through 2006. Items are organized into methodological and epistemological studies, community psychology, educational psychology, and organizational studies.

Creativity

6.48. Bibliography of recently published books on creativity and problem solving. Dutcher, A. J. (2004). *Journal of Creative Behavior*, 38(4), 282–284. Bibliography of published books on creativity and problem solving.

Developmental

6.49 *Annotated bibliography: The impact of deployment on children; A review of the quantitative and qualitative literature.* Borden, L. M., et al. (2011?). Tucson: Arizona Center for Research and Outreach (AZ REACH). 101 pp. Detailed, annotated bibliography on the impact of parental deployment on child and family functioning during Operation Enduring Freedom (OEF) and Operation Iraqi Freedom (OIF). Annotations cover works on internalizing behavior problems, externalizing behavior problems, academic adjustment, family problems (family violence and other family problems), peer problems and physical health. This document is available online at https:// reachmilitaryfamilies.umn.edu/sites/default/files/upload_ material/Compiled Annotated Bibliography_Impact of Deployment on Children_AZ REACH.pdf.

6.50 *An annotated bibliography on children's development of social inclusion and respect for diversity.* Romero, M. (2010). New York: Columbia University–National Center for Children in Poverty. 8 pp. Annotated bibliography of books, articles, reports, and other resources on how children aged birth to ten years develop concepts related to social inclusion and respect for diversity. Available at https://academiccommons.columbia.edu/catalog/ ac:135666.

6.51. Annotated bibliography supporting high-risk foster youth in transition: Research findings. Martinez, N. I. (2010). *Illinois Child Welfare*, 5(1), 169–183. Annotated bibliography of articles addressing the following in high-risk foster youth: mental health outcomes, such as symptoms of depression or post-traumatic stress disorder; educational outcomes (e.g., short term such as attendance and long term such as graduation); placement stability (reunification, adoption, or preventing premature placement disruption); independent living or independence upon aging out of foster care; and reduction in risk of violence or delinquency.

6.52. Bibliography: Current world literature. (no authorship indicated). (2003). *Current Opinion in Psychiatry*, 16(4), 473–493. Bibliography of literature published in *Current Opinion in Psychiatry* between early 2002 and early 2003. Items cover child and adolescent psychiatry and services research and outcomes.

6.53. Bibliography: Current world literature. (no authorship indicated). (2008). *Current Opinion in Psychiatry*, 21(4), 422–437. Bibliography of articles on child and adolescent psychiatry, services research and outcome, and medical comorbidity.

6.54. Pediatric psychosomatic medicine: An annotated bibliography. Pao, M., Ballard, E. D., Raza, H., & Rosenstein, D. L. (2007*). Journal of Consultation and Liaison Psychiatry*, 48(3), 195–204. Not represented as exhaustive or comprehensive, this bibliography covers clinical issues relevant to children and adolescents with medical illnesses; includes developmental issues, familial interactions, diagnostic categories, and pharmacologic concerns.

Disaster Psychology

6.55. Disaster research for the Hurricane Sandy impact area: A select bibliography. Piotrowski, C. (2012). *Journal of Instructional Psychology*, 39(3–4), 192–196. This study, based on a content analysis procedure, identified key articles on hurricanes indexed/abstracted in PsycINFO. Of the 1,408 references identified, this bibliography contains 61 citations to key articles, categorized across select topical areas, including but not limited to psychosocial, community, adult, and child recovery.

Educational and School Psychology

6.56. Annotated bibliography for the miniseries on assessment and treatment of children with autism in the schools. (no authorship indicated). *School Psychology Review*, 28(4), 621. Annotated bibliography of six books on assessment and treatment of children with autism in schools published from 1980 to 1999.

6.57. Annotated bibliography for the miniseries on lesbian, gay, bisexual, transgender, and questioning youth: Their interests and concerns as learners in school. (no authorship indicated). (2000). *School Psychology Review*, 29(2), 231–234. Special issue, Mini-Series: Lesbian, gay, bisexual, transsexual, and questioning youths. Annotated bibliography of twenty-two printed works and websites on the interests and concerns of lesbian, gay, bisexual, transgender, and questioning youth.

6.58. Annotated bibliography for the miniseries on multicultural and cross-cultural consultation in schools. (no authorship indicated). (2000). *School Psychology Review*, 29(3), 426–428. [Special issue, Mini-series: Multicultural and cross-cultural consultation in schools]. Annotated bibliography of eighteen empirical studies and books on multicultural and cross-cultural consultation in schools published from 1976 to 1999.

6.59. Annotated bibliography for the miniseries on promoting school success in children with chronic medical conditions. (no authorship indicated). (1999). *School Psychology Review*, 28(2), 264–265. Annotated bibliography

of nine works aimed at school psychologists and providing information about the relationship of chronic medical conditions in childhood to educational and behavioral issues in school.

6.60. Annotated bibliography for the miniseries on resilience applied: The promise and pitfalls of school-based resilience programs. (no authorship indicated). (1998). *School Psychology Review*, 27(3), 418–419. Annotated and selective bibliography of ten resources aimed at school psychologists to assist in designing school-based resilience programs. Materials cover program design, implementation, and evaluation and were published from 1982 to 1998.

6.61. An annotated bibliography of response to intervention studies. Johnson, K., Doggett, R. A., Paczak, H. A., Medley, M. B., Milton, M. H., Chandler, T. D., & Croft, L. L. (2011) *Journal of Evidence-Based Practices for Schools*, 12(1), 48–74. Research reviews in support of the Essential Element Matrices, generally from 2000 to 2008, focusing on areas that the school psychology literature may not heavily review and areas that the literature covers but does not assemble in a cohesive manner within a systems-level approach. The article is organized by Tiers 1, 2, and 3.

6.62. Gifted gay, lesbian, bisexual, and transgender annotated bibliography: A resource for educators of gifted secondary GLBT students. Treat, A. R., & Whittenburg, B. (2006). *Journal of Secondary Gifted Education*, 17(4), 230–243. A comprehensive resource for information regarding gifted youths who are gay, lesbian, bisexual, transgender, or questioning their sexual orientation and/or gender identity. It includes articles, brochures, books, lesson plans, staff development, video media, and web resources.

6.63. La ricerca-azione in Italia: spunti per una bibliografia (Action research in Italy: A bibliography). Galuppo, L., & Risorsa, U. (2006). *Rivista di Psicologia del Lavoro e dell' Organizzazione*, 12(2–3), 261–268. Brief Italian bibliography on action research published from the 1970s through 2006. Items are organized into methodological and epistemological studies, community psychology, educational psychology, and organizational studies.

6.64. Schoolyard bullying: Peer victimization: An annotated bibliography. Renfrow, T. G., & Teuton, L. M. (2008). *Community and Junior College Libraries*, 14(4), 251–275. Annotated bibliography of scholarly articles, books, and websites aimed at psychologists, teachers, school administrators, and parents. Materials cover statistics, attitudes toward school bullying, prevention, intervention, and research methodologies.

Ethics

6.65. *Annotated bibliography: Attitudes toward animal research (1998–2013)*. Yahner, E. (2014). Washington, DC: Humane Society of the United States Institute for Science and Policy. Annotated bibliography of books, chapters, and articles on attitudes toward animal research from a variety of disciplines. Downloadable from http://animal studiesrepository.org/hum_ed_bibs/8/.

6.66. A four-part working bibliography of neuroethics. Part 1: Overview and reviews: Defining and describing the field and its practices. Buniak, L., Darragh, M., & Giordano, J. (2014). *Philosophy, Ethics, and Humanities in Medicine*, 9(9). Part 1 of a four-part bibliography. This part includes a repository of international papers, books, and chapters that address the field in general and present discussion(s) of more particular aspects and topics of neuroethics. This first installment lists reviews and overviews of the discipline, as well as broad summaries of basic developments and issues of the field. This open-access article is located at https://www.ncbi.nlm.nih.gov/pmc/articles/PMC4047768/.

6.67. A four-part working bibliography of neuroethics. Part 2: Neuroscientific studies of morality and ethics. Darragh, M., Buniak, L., & Giordano, J. (2015). *Philosophy, Ethics, and Humanities in Medicine*, 10(2). Part 2 of a four-part bibliography. This part covers works from 2002 through 2013 addressing the "neuroscience of ethics"—studies of putative neural substrates and mechanisms involved in cognitive, emotional, and behavioral processes of morality and ethics. Covers 397 articles, 65 books, and 52 book chapters that present empirical/experimental studies, overviews, and reviews of neural substrates and mechanisms involved in morality and ethics, and/or reflections upon such studies and their implications. This open-access article is located at https://www.ncbi.nlm.nih.gov/pmc/articles/PMC4334407/.

6.68. A four-part working bibliography of neuroethics. Part 3: "Second tradition neuroethics"—Ethical issues in neuroscience. Martin, A., Becker, K., Darragh, M., & Giordano, J. (2016). *Philosophy, Ethics, and Humanities in Medicine*, 11(7). Part 3 of a four-part bibliography. This part includes 1,137 papers, 56 books, and 134 book chapters published from 2002 through 2014, covering ethical issues in neuroimaging, neurogenetics, neurobiomarkers, neuro-psychopharmacology, brain stimulation, neural stem cells, neural tissue transplants, pediatric-specific issues, dual-use, and general neuroscience research issues. This open-access article is located at https://www.ncbi.nlm.nih.gov/pmc/articles/PMC5028939/.

6.69. A four-part working bibliography of neuroethics. Part 4: Ethical issues in clinical and social applications of neuroscience. Becker, K., Shook, J. R., Darrah, M., & Giordano, J. (2017). *Philosophy, Ethics, and Humanities in Medicine*, 12(1). Part 4 of a four-part bibliography, a work in progress. This part focuses on clinical and social applications of neuroscience, including treatment-enhancement discourse; issues arising in neurology, psychiatry, and pain care; neuroethics education and training; neuroethics and the law; neuroethics and policy and political issues; international neuroethics; and discourses addressing "trans-" and "post-" humanity. This open-access article is located at https://www.ncbi.nlm.nih.gov/pmc/articles/PMC5452349/.

6.70. *Scientific misconduct: An annotated bibliography.* http://www.teachpsych.org/resources/Documents/otrp/resources/keith-spiegel94.pdf. Keith-Spiegel, P., Aronson, K., & Bowman, M. (1994). Statesboro, GA: Society for the Teaching of Psychology (APA Division 2), Office of Teaching Resources in Psychology (OTRP), Department of Psychology, Georgia Southern University. Annotated bibliography of scholarly and popular articles and books on scientific misconduct, created as a resource for teaching in psychology.

Forensic Psychology

6.71. *Annotated bibliography: Juvenile justice risk/need assessment & juvenile justice websites.* National Institute of Corrections Information Center (NICIC). (2013). Aurora, CO: NICIC. Annotated bibliography of articles, reports, and websites on juvenile risk assessment, including recidivism risk, gender- and ethnicity-related risk, case studies of evidence-based juvenile justice programs, and risk factors related to various types of offenses. Also includes links to scales for juvenile risk assessment. Available at https://info.nicic.gov/nicrp/system/files/027615.pdf.

6.72. An annotated bibliography for the testifying child and adolescent psychiatrist. Ash, P., & O'Leary, P. J. (2011). *Child and Adolescent Psychiatric Clinics of North America*, 20(3), 577–590. Citing scholarly literature is often important in persuading fact finders that professional opinion has a scientific basis. This work is not comprehensive, but provides examples of literature that may be cited to bolster testimony.

6.73. Bibliography: Current world literature. (no authorship indicated). (2004). *Current Opinion in Psychiatry*, 17(5), 423–431. Selected bibliography of articles on forensic psychiatry, scientific communication, and developmental intellectual disorders, published from mid-2003 through mid-2004.

6.74. *Cognitive-behavioral therapy.* https://nicic.gov/library/package/cbt. National Institute of Corrections (NIC). Links to reports on and evaluations of cognitive-behavioral therapy (CBT) and evidence-based practice (EBP), CBT and female offenders, CBT and mentally ill offenders, CBT and probation, CBT and sex offenders, CBT program evaluations, CBT effectiveness with youth, moral reconciliation therapy (MRT), "Thinking for a Change" CBT programs, and general CBT effectiveness reports.

6.75. *Mental health services in criminal justice system settings: A selectively annotated bibliography, 1970–1997.* Van Whitlock, R., & Lubin, B. (1999). Westport, CT: Greenwood Press. 190 pp. Includes 1,264 citations to books and scholarly articles, about half of which are annotated. Most empirically based works are annotated; theoretical and practical works are annotated only if they are of major value. Items are from psychology, psychiatry, nursing, education, social work, and other related areas and are related to service provision to mentally ill and substance-abusing offenders in criminal justice settings.

Geropsychology

6.76. *Bibliography of research and clinical perspectives on LGBT aging.* David, S., Asta, L., Cernin, P., & Miles, J. (2006). Washington, DC: American Psychological Association. 43 pp. Comprehensive bibliography of books and articles on aging in the LGBT community. Available at http://www.apadivisions.org/division-44/resources/advocacy/aging-bibliography.pdf.

6.77. Work with older people: A bibliography. Kegerreis, P. (2012). *British Journal of Psychotherapy*, 28(1), 117–124. References to books and articles on psychodynamically oriented treatment covering general issues and individual, couples, family, group, and creative therapies.

Health Psychology

6.78. Annotated bibliography of life coaching and health research. Newnham-Kanas, C., Gorczynski, P., Morrow, D., & Irwin, J. D. (2009). *International Journal of Evidence-Based Coaching and Mentoring*, 7(1), 39–103. Annotated bibliography of articles classified into categories of aging, anxiety/stress/emotional health, asthma, attention deficit hyperactivity disorder, brain/head injury, breastfeeding, burn injuries, cancer, cardiovascular health, compromised urinary bladder syndrome, mental health, depression, diabetes, dialysis/renal failure, dyspnea, fitness/exercise/physical activity participation, health promotion, holistic medicine, labor, obesity, postoperative pain, and self-determination/self-efficacy.

6.79. Bibliography. Evans, W. (2005). *Health Communication*, 17(1), 105–113. Includes 141 empirical and theoretical publications related to health communication. Items cover topics such as how health information communication influences health behavior change, information-seeking behavior, and resistance to health messages covering many different health issues.

6.80. *Personalizing, delivering and monitoring behavioral health interventions: An annotated bibliography of the best available apps.* Simmons, K., Garcia, E., Howell, M. K., & Leong, S. (2016). Washington, DC: National Register of Health Service Psychologists. Annotated bibliography of applications ("apps") for smartphones and tablets aimed at assisting those with substance abuse issues or severe mental illness; in need of violence prevention, relaxation, or sleep; or suffering from PTSD, anxiety, mood tracking, and chronic pain. Annotations also indicate for which device type (e.g., Android, iPhone, iPad) the application is available. Available at https://www.nationalregister.org/pub/the-national-register-report-pub/the-register-report-fall-2016/personalizing-delivering-and-monitoring-behavioral-health-interventions-an-annotated-bibliography-of-the-best-available-apps/.

History of Psychology

6.81. *Chronology of noteworthy events in American psychology: Book sources.* https://www.cwu.edu/~warren/sources.html. Warren Street wrote the book *A Chronology of Noteworthy Events in American Psychology* in 1994 (American Psychological Association). The book is a general academic book, which lists significant dates and events from before 1892 through the early 1990s. This website is the bibliography of books, most of which are scholarly works in themselves, used in Street's research to create his book.

6.82. Contextualizing the history of psychiatry/psychology and psychoanalysis: Annotated bibliography and essays. Addenda A-F. Wallace, E. R. (2008). In E. R. Wallace and J. Gach (Eds.), *History of psychiatry and medical psychology: With an epilogue on psychiatry and the mind-body relation* (pp. 117–169). New York: Springer. Annotated bibliography with essays providing a broad interdisciplinary context for the general history of psychiatry. The chapter is divided into six major sections with topical subsections.

6.83. *Guide to manuscript collections in the history of psychology and related areas.* Sokal, M. M., & Rafail, P. A. (Comps.). (1982). Millwood, NY: Kraus International Publications. 212 pp. BF81. Annotated bibliography of more than 500 individual manuscript collections and major repositories, primarily in the United States. Includes manuscript collections in the areas of anthropology; child, clinical, educational, experimental, Gestalt, and industrial psychology; mental deficiency' mental health and hygiene; neurology; parapsychology; psychical research and spiritualism; philosophical psychology; phrenology; physiology; psychiatric hospitals; psychiatry; psychoanalysis; testing; female psychologists; psychology and art; race; sex; school psychology; social psychology; social work; university administration; and institutions of psychiatry and psychology.

6.84. *History of American psychology in notes and news 1883–1945: An index to journal sources.* Ludy, T. B., et al. (1989). Millwood, NY: Kraus International Publications. 591 pp. Z7201 or BF108. Alphabetical listing of appointments, publications, events, and programs listed in the "news" and "notes" sections of the early journals of psychology.

6.85. *History of psychology: A guide to information sources.* Viney, W., Wertheimer, M. & Wertheimer, M. L. (1979). Detroit, MI: Gale Research. 502 pp. Z7204 or BF81.

Selectively annotated bibliography of materials useful to scholars researching the history of psychology. It includes general works on history, major periodicals, development of psychology in specific countries and regions of the world, archives and manuscripts, historiography, systems and schools of psychology, specific content areas, and histories of related fields such as psychiatry, philosophy, sociology, and biology.

6.86. *History of psychology and the behavioral sciences: A bibliographic guide.* Watson, R. I. (1978). New York: Springer. 241 pp. Z7201 or BF81. Annotated bibliography includes guides to the literature, encyclopedias, bibliographies, biographical collections, archives, manuscript collections, and oral histories. Also included are historical accounts of psychology in general, branches, national psychology, school psychology, science, philosophy, psychiatry, psychoanalysis, physiology, neurology, anatomy, biology, medicine, anthropology, sociology, and readings. This work also covers methods of historical research, historiographic fields in psychology and other behavioral sciences, and historiographic theories.

6.87. *Psychiatry in Nigeria: A partly annotated bibliography.* Boroffka, A. (2006). Kiel, Germany: Brunswiker Universitätsbuchhandlung–Medizin. 560 pp. Bibliography of almost 2,500 papers, rare documents, articles, and books related to psychiatry and neighboring disciplines, written in and about Nigeria and other parts of Africa, including early history of psychiatry and related research, and covering most of the twentieth century. Approximately half of the items are annotated.

Industrial and Organizational Psychology

6.88. *Gender-based violence in the world of work: Overview and selected annotated bibliography.* Cruz, A., & Klinger, S. (2011). Geneva, Switzerland: International Labor Organization. 80 pp. Working paper aimed at understanding gender-based violence in the workplace. Defines "gender-based violence" and "world of work" and presents human rights and business rationale for prevention initiatives. Includes risk factors for victims and perpetrators and covers child laborers, forced and bonded laborers, migrant workers, domestic workers, health services workers, and sex workers. The bibliography is on pages 23–69 and is organized by geography—international works, regional and country-based works—and tools, measures, and guides. Available at http://www.ilo.org/gender/Informationresources/WCMS_155763/lang-en/index.htm.

6.89. La ricerca-azione in Italia: spunti per una bibliografia (Action research in Italy: A bibliography). Galuppo, L., & Risorsa, U. (2006). *Rivista di Psicologia del Lavoro e dell' Organizzazione*, 12(2–3), 261–268. Brief Italian bibliography on action research published from the 1970s through 2006. Items are organized into methodological

and epistemological studies, community psychology, educational psychology, and organizational studies.

6.90. Police performance measurement: An annotated bibliography. Tiwana, N., Bass, G., & Farrell, G. (2015). *Crime Science: An Interdisciplinary Journal*, 4(1). Annotated bibliography includes works on overviews, methodological issues, and performance management in other industries; national, international, and cross-national studies; frameworks; criticisms (particularly unintended consequences); crime-specific measures; practitioner guides; performance evaluation of individual staff; police department plans and evaluations; and annotated bibliographies in related areas. This open-access article is available at https://crimesciencejournal.springeropen.com/articles/10.1186/s40163-014-0011-4.

6.91. Selected bibliography on diversity consulting: Supplement to the special issue on culture, race, and ethnicity in organizational consulting psychology. Leong, F. T. L., Cooper, S., & Huang, J. L. (2008). Special issue of *Culture, Race, and Ethnicity in Organizational Consulting Psychology*, 215–226. This bibliography is neither exhaustive nor comprehensive, but rather a collection of references that have been found to be helpful in multicultural consultation practice.

6.92. Sources and bibliography of selected human factors and ergonomics standards. Rodrick, D., & Karwowski, W. (2006). In W. Karwowski (Ed.), *Handbook of standards and guidelines in ergonomics and human factors* (pp. 569–589). Mahwah, NJ: Lawrence Erlbaum. Bibliography of selected human factors and ergonomics standards as of 2004 and books and articles on theoretical and empirical research on the standards.

Multicultural Psychology

6.93. Annotated bibliography for the miniseries on multicultural and cross-cultural consultation in schools. (no authorship indicated). (2000). *School Psychology Review*, 29(3), 426–428. [Special issue, Mini-series: Multicultural and cross-cultural consultation in schools.] Annotated bibliography of eighteen empirical studies and books on multicultural and cross-cultural consultation in schools published from 1976 to 1999.

6.94. *An annotated bibliography on children's development of social inclusion and respect for diversity.* Romero, M. (2010). New York: Columbia University–National Center for Children in Poverty. 8 pp. Annotated bibliography of books, articles, reports, and other resources on how children aged birth to ten years develop concepts related to social inclusion and respect for diversity. Available at https://academiccommons.columbia.edu/catalog/ac:135666.

6.95. Bibliography on multicultural issues (Bibliografía Sobre Temas Multiculturales). Cardalda, E. B., Rodríguez-Menéndez, G., Lozada-Lugo, A., Avilés, M., & Martínez,

J. V. (2009). *Revista Puertorriqueña de Psicología*, 20, 190–217. Selective bibliography on multicultural issues in psychology from databases and two psychology department websites and archives, from the United States and Puerto Rico.

6.96. Cultural identification and substance use in North America: An annotated bibliography. Beauvais, F. (1998). *Substance Use & Misuse*, 33(6), 1315–1336. Annotated bibliography on issues related to cultural identification and substance abuse. Includes items on ethnic identification in general, specific ethnic identities, and measurement issues. Reference list includes citations to related readings not annotated.

6.97. MMPI-2 and MMPI-A research with U.S. Latinos: A bibliography. Corrales, M. L., Cabiya, J. J., Gomez, F., Ayala, G. X., Mendoza, S., & Velasquez, R. J. (1998). *Psychological Reports*, 83(3, pt. 1), 1027–1033. Comprehensive listing of research conducted on US Latinos, including Puerto Ricans, with the MMPI-2 and MMPI-A, 1989 through 1998.

6.98. Principles of multicultural counseling and therapy: A selective bibliography. Gielen, U. P., Draguns, J. G., & Fish, J. M. (2008). In *Principles of multicultural counseling and therapy* (pp. 419–432). New York: Routledge. Selective bibliography includes books, book chapters, and journal articles classified under nineteen categories covering multicultural therapy and counseling, special populations and issues, therapy with children and adolescents, family therapy, care of refugees and immigrants, history of psychological healing in the West, psychopathology and mental health across cultures, transcultural psychiatry, culture and assessment, shamanism, altered states of consciousness, indigenous North American healing traditions, indigenous healing traditions in Latin America and the Caribbean, Asian and Oceanic healing traditions, Western psychology and Asian traditions, and African and Islamic healing traditions.

6.99. *Psychiatry in Nigeria: A partly annotated bibliography*. Boroffka, A. (2006). Kiel, Germany: Brunswiker Universitätsbuchhandlung–Medizin. 560 pp. Bibliography of almost 2,500 papers, rare documents, articles, and books related to psychiatry and neighboring disciplines written in and about Nigeria and other parts of Africa, including early history of psychiatry and related research, and covering most of the twentieth century. Approximately half of the items are annotated.

6.100. Selected bibliography on diversity consulting: Supplement to the special issue on culture, race, and ethnicity in organizational consulting psychology. Leong, F. T. L., Cooper, S., & Huang, J. L. (2008). Special issue of *Culture, Race, and Ethnicity in Organizational Consulting Psychology*, 215–226. This bibliography is neither exhaustive nor comprehensive, but rather a collection of references that have been found to be helpful in multicultural consultation practice.

Neurodevelopmental Disabilities

6.101. Intellectual disability, ethics and genetics—A selected bibliography. Meininger, H. P. (2003). *Journal of Intellectual Disability Research*, 47(7), 571–576. Bibliography of materials on the title topic found in psychology, medicine, philosophy, and education databases.

Neuropsychology

6.102. Ralph M. Reitan's bibliography. Hom, J., & Nici, J. (2015). *Archives of Clinical Neuropsychology*, 30(8), 774–783. Bibliography of Ralph Reitan's published works over the course of his more than sixty-year career.

Perception

6.103. *Perception: An annotated bibliography* Emmett, K., & Machamer, P. (Eds.). (1976/2017). Florence, Italy: Taylor and Francis. 190 pp. Z7204. Selectively annotated bibliography of literature on perception, focusing on literature from 1935 to 1974.

Personality

6.104. Bibliography: Hans J. Eysenck, Ph.D., D.Sc., 1939–2000. (no authorship indicated). (2001). *Personality and Individual Differences*, 31(1), 45–99. Bibliography of H. J. Eysenck's books and articles published between 1939 and 2000.

Research Methods and Statistics

6.105 Annotated bibliography of studies using consensual qualitative research. Chui, H. T., Jackson, J. L., Liu, J., & Hill, C. E. (2012). In C. E. Hill (Ed.), *Consensual qualitative research: A practical resource for investigating social science phenomena* (pp. 213–266). Washington, DC: American Psychological Association. Annotated bibliography of studies that used consensual qualitative research (CQR). Includes ninety-nine studies published through 2010 organized into seven topics: psychotherapy, psychotherapist/counselor training/supervision, multiculturalism, career development, trauma, medical/health-related topics, and same-sex relationships. Items were selected based on strict adherence to CQR method and include traditional CQR, consensual qualitative research-modified (CQR-M), and consensual qualitative research-case study (CQR-C).

6.106. The introduction of path analysis to the social sciences, and some emergent themes: An annotated bibliography. Wolfe, L. M. (2003). *Structural Equation Modeling*, 10(1), 1–34. Trends in the use of path analysis in the social sciences.

6.107. *Survey research methodology, 1990–1999: An annotated bibliography*. Walden, G. R., (2002). Westwood,

CT: Greenwood Press, 432 pp. Includes 617 detailed annotations on the application of cognitive psychology techniques and theories to understanding and reducing error in survey research and the application of computer and telephony technologies to data collection and analysis. Annotations are from monographs, journals, government documents, dissertations, and documents from business, criminology, education, health and medicine, law, library science, mass media, military science, political science, psychology, sociology, social work, religion, and women's studies.

Schizophrenia

6.108. Bibliography: Current world literature. (no authorship indicated). (2003). *Current Opinion in Psychiatry*, 16(2), 233–260. Bibliography based on literature published in the journal *Current Opinion in Psychiatry* between November 2001 and October 2002. Entries are annotated and cover schizophrenia and behavioral medicine.

Sexuality and Gender

6.109. Annotated bibliography for the miniseries on lesbian, gay, bisexual, transgender, and questioning youth: Their interests and concerns as learners in school. (no authorship indicated). (2000). *School Psychology Review*, 29(2), 231–234. [Special issue, Mini-series: Lesbian, gay, bisexual, transsexual, and questioning youths.] Annotated bibliography of twenty-two printed works and websites on the interests and concerns of lesbian, gay, bisexual, transgender, and questioning youth.

6.110. *Bibliography of research and clinical perspectives on LGBT aging*. David, S., Asta, L., Cernin, P., & Miles, J. (2006). Washington, DC: American Psychological Association. 43 pp. Comprehensive bibliography of books and articles on aging in the LGBT community. Available at http://www.apadivisions.org/division-44/resources/advocacy/aging-bibliography.pdf.

6.111. Gifted gay, lesbian, bisexual, and transgender annotated bibliography: A resource for educators of gifted secondary GLBT students. Treat, A. R., & Whittenburg, B. (2006). *Journal of Secondary Gifted Education*, 17(4), 230–243. A comprehensive resource for information regarding gifted youths who are gay, lesbian, bisexual, transgender, or questioning their sexual orientation and/or gender identity. It includes articles, brochures, books, lesson plans, staff development, video media, and web resources.

6.112. HIV/AIDS prevention through changing risky sexual behavior among heterosexual college students: A 1990's bibliography. Livingston, M. M. (1998). *Psychological Reports*, 83(3, pt. 1), 781–782. Bibliography of 126 citations to works on AIDS prevention among college students.

6.113. *An interdisciplinary bibliography on language, gender and sexuality (2000–2011)*. Motschenbacher, H.

(2012). Amsterdam, Netherlands: John Benjamins. 294 pp. P120. Comprehensive bibliography covering recent research activity in the field of language, gender, and sexuality. The main part of the bibliography lists 3,454 relevant publications (books, book chapters, and journal articles) that were published from 2000 to 2011.

6.114. A selective bibliography of transsexualism. Denny, D. (2002). *Journal of Gay & Lesbian Psychotherapy*, 6(2), 35–66. Transsexualism, codified in DSM-IV-TR as Gender Identity Disorder, first appeared in DSM-III in 1980 with the name Gender Dysphoria, but its history in the psychiatric profession dates back more than a hundred years. This article discusses the history of influential publications, treatment centers, and paradigms, including the sex reassignment of Christine Jorgensen, the Johns Hopkins University–affiliated clinic, and other gender clinics, their closure, transsexual support groups, literature written by transsexuals, and diverse conceptions of transsexuality and treatments, as well as alternative, nonpathological models of transsexualism.

6.115. *Sexual violence and individuals who identify as LGBTQ: Annotated bibliography*. Enola, PA: Pennsylvania Coalition Against Rape and (PCAR) and Pennsylvania Coalition Against Rape and the National Sexual Violence Resource Ctr (NSVRC). Annotated bibliography of articles, reports, and films that explore sexual violence against individuals who identify as LGBTQ from a variety of angles, including lifetime sexual victimization, intimate partner violence, sexual violence as hate/bias crimes, and service provisions for survivors. Available at http://nsvrc.org/sites/default/files/Publications_NSVRC_Bibliographies_Sexual-Violence-LGBTQ.pdf.

6.116. Sexuality and disability: A SIECUS annotated bibliography. (no authorship indicated). (2002). *Sexuality and Disability*, 20(3), 209–231. SIECUS (Sexuality Information and Education Council of the United States) annotated bibliography on issues of sexuality, physical and mental disabilities, and chronic illness.

Sleep and Dreaming

6.117. Recent bibliography of sleep, dreams and hypnosis. (no authorship indicated). (2002). *Sleep and Hypnosis*, 4(3), a4–a14 and 4(4), a7–a18. Recently published works in sleep and sleep disorders, dreams and dreaming, and hypnosis and hypnotherapy.

Sport Psychology

6.118. Bibliography on the Profile of Mood States in sport and exercise psychology research, 1971–1998. LeUnes, A., & Burger, J. (1998). *Journal of Sport Behavior*, 21(1), 53–70. Bibliography of 194 items on the use of the Profile of Mood States (POMS) related to sport and exercise and 63 articles on the use of POMS related to athletic injury, disabled athletes, intramural sports, overtraining, psychometric issues, and steroid use.

6.119. Updated bibliography on the Profile of Mood States in sport and exercise psychology research. LeUnes, A. (2000). *Journal of Applied Sport Psychology*, 12(1), 110–113. Fifty-seven citations from the literature on the use of the Profile of Mood States scale in sport and exercise psychology research.

Stress

6.120. Bibliographie française sur l'expérience post-traumatique (French bibliography on post-traumatic stress). Brillon, P., & Martin, M. (2002). *Revue Québécoise de Psychologie*, 23(3), 271–279. List of French-language articles on post-traumatic stress. Citations are classified into ten categories: neurobiological aspects of post-traumatic stress, comorbidity, theoretical concepts, description of symptoms, epidemiological factors, evaluation, trauma experience in children, factors associated with the development of post-traumatic stress, reports on post-intervention in the field, and intervention strategies and treatment. A list of book chapters, books, and specialty reviews on post-traumatic stress is also included.

Teaching of Psychology

6.121. Annotated bibliography on *The Teaching of Psychology*. Johnson, D. E., Schroder, S. I., Erickson, J. P., & Grimes, K. N. (2007). *Teaching of Psychology*, 35(4), 376–384. The thirty-fifth and last version of this title to be published, it is an annotated bibliography of the year's publications on the teaching of psychology. Numbering is continued from previous bibliographies, and there are also some articles from 2006 that were not included in the previous year's bibliography. This annual bibliography was ended due to widespread use of database searching on the topic and fewer requests for reprints.

6.122. Behavioral contributions to *Teaching of Psychology*: An annotated bibliography. Karsen, A. M., & Carr, J. E. (2008). *The Behavior Analyst*, 31(1), 23–37. Summarizes behavioral contributions to the journal *Teaching of Psychology* from 1974 to 2006. Includes 116 articles of potential utility to college-level instructors of behavior analysis and related areas that have been annotated, and organized into nine categories.

6.123. A bibliography of articles of interest to teachers of psychology appearing in *Psychological Reports* 1955–2010. Abramson, C. I., Curb, L. A., & Barber, K. R. (2011). *Psychological Reports*, 108(1), 182–212. A bibliography of 605 articles classified into twenty-one sections, including, among others, history, psychology of the scientists, teaching tips, textbook evaluation, and evaluation of students and professors.

6.124. *Scientific misconduct: An annotated bibliography*. http://www.teachpsych.org/resources/Documents/otrp/resources/keith-spiegel94.pdf. Keith-Spiegel, P., Aronson, K., & Bowman, M. (1994). Statesboro, GA: Society for the Teaching of Psychology (APA Division 2), Office of Teaching Resources in Psychology (OTRP), Department of Psychology, Georgia Southern University. Annotated bibliography of scholarly and popular articles and books on scientific misconduct, created as a resource for teaching in psychology.

Tests and Measures

6.125. *Annotated bibliography of measurement compendia: Reliable, valid, and standard measures of substance abuse and mental and behavioral health indicators and outcomes of interest*. Substance Abuse and Mental Health Services Administration (SAMHSA). Selected, annotated bibliography of seventeen compendia mostly containing full text of instruments; the others describe available instruments. Most are compendia of measures used with individuals, but several are for institutions to measure outcomes. Available online at https://www.samhsa.gov/capt/tools-learning-resources/annotated-bibliography-measurement-compendia.

Verbal Behavior

6.126. An annotated bibliography of verbal behavior articles published outside of the analysis of verbal behavior 2016. Lechago, S. A., Jackson, R. E., & Oda, F. S. (2016). *Analysis of Verbal Behavior*, 32(1), 60–68. Annotated bibliography of thirty-nine journal articles on verbal behavior published outside of *The Analysis of Verbal Behavior* in 2016. **NOTE:** This bibliography is created for each publication year.

Violence/Aggression

6.127. *Annotated bibliography: Cruelty to animals and violence to humans (1998–2013)*. Yahner, E. (2014). Washington, DC: Humane Society of the United States Institute for Science and Policy. Annotated bibliography of books, chapters, and articles on the relationship of animal cruelty to violence against humans. Downloadable from http://animalstudiesrepository.org/hum_ed_bibs/5/.

6.128. *Gender-based violence in the world of work: Overview and selected annotated bibliography*. Cruz, A., & Klinger, S. (2011). Geneva, Switzerland: International Labor Organization. 80 pp. Working paper aimed at understanding gender-based violence in the workplace. Defines "gender-based violence" and "world of work" and presents human rights and business rationales for prevention initiatives. Includes risk factors for victims and perpetrators and covers child laborers, forced and bonded laborers, migrant workers, domestic workers, health services workers, and sex workers. The bibliography is on pages 23–69 and is organized by geography—international works, regional and country-based works—and tools, measures, and guides. Available at http://www.ilo.org/gender/Informationre sources/WCMS_155763/lang-en/index.htm.

6.129. Marital rape: A selected bibliography. Harmes, R. (1999). *Violence Against Women*, 5(9), 1082–1083 [Special section: Wife rape]. Selective bibliography of citations to rare, international, and lesser-known articles on wife rape.

6.130. References examining assaults by women on their spouses or male partners: An updated annotated bibliography. Fiebert, M. S. (2014). *Sexuality & Culture: An Interdisciplinary Quarterly*, 18(2), 405–467. Includes annotations of 343 scholarly investigations (270 empirical studies and 73 reviews) that indicate that women are as physically aggressive as, or more aggressive than, men in their relationships with their spouses or male partners.

6.131. References examining assaults by women on their spouses or male partners: An annotated bibliography. Fiebert, M. S. (2004). *Sexuality & Culture: An Interdisciplinary Quarterly*, 8(3–4), 140–177. Includes annotations of 155 scholarly investigations (126 empirical studies and 29 reviews and/or analyses) that indicate that women are as physically aggressive as, or more aggressive than, men in their relationships with their spouses or male partners.

6.132. References examining assaults by women on their spouses or male partners: An annotated bibliography. Fiebert, M. S. (2010). *Sexuality & Culture: An Interdisciplinary Quarterly*, 14(1), 49–91. Includes annotations of 271 scholarly investigations (211 empirical studies and 60 reviews) that indicate that women are as physically aggressive as, or more aggressive than, men in their relationships with their spouses or male partners.

6.133. *Sexual violence and individuals who identify as LGBTQ: Annotated bibliography*. Enola, PA: Pennsylvania Coalition Against Rape and (PCAR) and Pennsylvania Coalition Against Rape and the National Sexual Violence Resource Ctr (NSVRC). Annotated bibliography of articles, reports, and films that explore sexual violence against individuals who identify as LGBTQ from a variety of angles, including lifetime sexual victimization, intimate partner violence, sexual violence as hate/bias crime, and service provisions for survivors. Available at http://nsvrc.org/sites/default/files/Publications_NSVRC_Bibliographies_Sexual-Violence-LGBTQ.pdf.

6.134. *Teen dating violence: A literature review and annotated bibliography*. Offenhauer, P., & Buchalter, A. (2011). Washington, DC: Library of Congress Federal Research Division, National Criminal Justice Reference Service (NCJRS). Literature review and annotated bibliography of materials from 1999 to 2011 on dating violence among high school and middle school youths. Covers quantitative and qualitative literature on the definition and prevalence of dating violence and risk factors for adolescent dating violence, also called teen relationship abuse, including demographic and community-level factors and proximate family-level, individual-level, and situational risks. Includes longitudinal research on the effectiveness of prevention programs and on responses to the issue of dating violence in the law and legal systems. Available at https://www.ncjrs.gov/pdffiles1/nij/grants/235368.pdf.

Well-Being

6.135. *Well-evolved life: Well-being, evolution and personhood; An annotated bibliography*. Moore, K., & Minchington, L. (2014). Canterbury, NZ: Lincoln University. 186 pp. This annotated bibliography of 347 sources focuses on the overlap in the literature on human well-being, evolutionary (including biological) perspectives on human behavior, and person (including "the self"). It includes articles, books, and reports.

Miscellaneous

6.136. *Annotated bibliography: Interaction with animals (1998–2013)*. Yahner, E. (2014). Washington, DC: Humane Society of the United States Institute for Science and Policy. Annotated bibliography of books, chapters, and articles on the interactions of children (with and without developmental disabilities) with animals. Downloadable from http://animalstudiesrepository.org/hum_ed_bibs/2.

6.137. Annotated bibliography of cochlear implant research and publications. Easterbrooks, S. R. (2002). *Communication Disorders Quarterly*, 24(1), 28–31. Covers recent research and publications on efficacy of cochlear implants as treatment for children with hearing loss and on controversies about this treatment.

6.138. Benefits of interacting with companion animals: A bibliography of articles published in refereed journals during the past 5 years. Barker, S. B., Rogers, C. S., Gurner, J. W., Karpf, A. S., & Suthers-McCable, H. M. (2003). *American Behavioral Scientist* [Special issue: Human-animal interaction & wellness], 47(1), 94–99. Bibliography of eighty-four citations from a literature search of psychology and medical databases. Items were published from 1996 through most of 2001 and focus on the benefits of interacting with companion animals, including animal- and/or pet-assisted therapy; human-animal bonds and animal behavior were not a focus of this search.

6.139. *The concept of time in psychology: A resource book and annotated bibliography*. Roeckelein, J. E. (2000). Westport, CT: Greenwood Press. 335 pp. This work addresses the concept of time in psychology from ancient history through the prescientific era and up to the scientific account of time in psychological literature through 1999, with more than 900 annotated entries.

6.140. *Grandparents: An annotated bibliography on roles, rights, and relationships.* Strauss, C. A. (1996). Lanham, MD: Scarecrow Press. 560 pp. Z7164 or HQ759. Bibliography of more than 1,000 citations to books, chapters, journal articles, theses and dissertations, and selective newspaper articles. Items are organized into categories of grandparental roles, minority group grandparents, the grandparent-parent relationship, the grandparent-grandchild relationship, grandparents and divorce/remarriage, and the legal rights of grandparents. Appendixes include demographic data and selected legislation affecting grandparents.

6.141. *Political psychology (annotated bibliography).* Haas, I. J. (2016). Faculty Publications: Political Science. Annotated bibliography of general overviews in political psychology, ambivalence, attitudes, authoritarianism, biopolitics, candidate perception, cognition, emotion, identity, ideology, intergroup conflict, morality, neuroscience, personality, stereotyping, prejudice, and discrimination and system justification theory in political psychology. Available at http://digitalcommons.unl.edu/poliscifacpub/72.

6.142. *The psychology of humor: A reference guide and annotated bibliography.* Roeckelein, J. E. (2002). Westport, CT: Greenwood Press. 579 pp. BF575. Traces the origins and evolution of the concept of humor in psychology from ancient to modern times, with an emphasis on an experimental/empirical approach to the understanding of humor and sense of humor. Includes more than 3,000 citations pertaining to the history, theories, and definitions of the concept of humor, and 381 annotations to empirical works published after 1969. Items are classified into ten categories, including bibliographies and literature reviews, cognition and humor, methodology and measurement, and social aspects of humor.

6.143. A resource on behavioral terminology: An annotated bibliography of "On Terms" articles in *The Behavior Analyst.* Carr, J. E., Briggs, A. M. (2011). *The Behavior Analyst*, 34(1), 93–101. Summarizes thirty-five articles published between 1979 and 2010 in the "On Terms" section of this journal. Articles are classified using common behavior analysis course content frameworks.

6.144. Scientometric analysis and bibliography of digit ratio (2D:4D) research, 1998–2008. Voracek, M., & Loibl, L. M. (2009). *Psychological Reports*, 104(3), 922–956. Scientometric analysis of research on the second-to-fourth-digit ratio (2D:4D), a putative marker for prenatal androgen action, and comprehensive bibliography of over 300 works published from 1998 to 2009.

6.145. Toward a core bibliography of presence. Ijsselsteijn, W. A., Lombard, M., & Freeman, J. (2001). *CyberPsychology & Behavior*, 4(2), 317–321. Bibliography of more than ninety books and articles in the field of presence research published between 1964 and 2000.

7

United States Government Agencies

INTRODUCTION

This chapter lists US government agencies that are related to various aspects of psychology. Descriptions are generally quoted directly from the agencies' websites; in some cases (e.g., the Census Bureau) the information has been condensed here to avoid duplication and create consistent formatting in entries. Where there are omissions within a description, the ellipsis (. . .) is used to indicate them; formatting changes are not indicated. Where additional information is provided, it follows the URL in a "**NOTE**."

Agency website URLs are provided at the end of each entry; contact information and other more detailed information can be found through the agency websites. Federal agencies were identified and selected from the alphabetical list of these agencies located at https://www.usa.gov/federal-agencies/.

PSYCHOLOGY-RELATED GOVERNMENT AGENCIES

7.1. Administration for Community Living. The Administration for Community Living (ACL) was created around the fundamental principle that older adults and people with disabilities of all ages should be able to live where they choose, with the people they choose, and with the ability to participate fully in their communities. By funding services and support provided by networks of community-based organizations, and with investments in research and innovation, ACL helps make this principle a reality for millions of Americans. . . . The aging and disability networks include national, state, and local organizations that support community living options for older adults and people with disabilities. In some cases, ACL grants funds to specific programs or initiatives operated by independent organizations. In others, like those found in this section, ACL funds organizations, or networks of organizations, to provide a range of programs to meet the specific needs in their local communities. https://www.acl.gov/.

7.2. Agency for Healthcare Research and Quality (AHRC). The Agency for Healthcare Research and Quality's (AHRQ) mission is to produce evidence to make health care safer, higher quality, more accessible, equitable, and affordable, and to work within the U.S. Department of Health and Human Services and with other partners to make sure that the evidence is understood and used. https://www.ahrq.gov/.

7.3. Census Bureau. The Census Bureau's mission is to serve as the leading source of quality data about the nation's people and economy. We honor privacy, protect confidentiality, share our expertise globally, and conduct our work openly. What Data We Collect & When—Decennial Census of Population and Housing (. . . counts every resident in the United States . . . takes place every 10 years); Economic Census (. . . official five-year measure of American business and the economy); Census of Governments (identifies the scope and nature of the nation's state and local government sector including public finance and public employment and classifications); American Community Survey (ACS) (. . . the premier source for information about America's changing population, housing and workforce). Census data informs how states and communities allocate funding for: neighborhood improvements, public health, education, transportation. https://www.census.gov/.

7.4. Centers for Disease Control and Prevention (CDC). The CDC is charged with detecting and responding to new and emerging health threats; tackling the biggest health problems causing death and disability for Americans; putting science and advanced technology into action to prevent disease; promoting healthy and safe behaviors, communities and environment; developing leaders and training the public health workforce, including disease detectives; taking the health pulse of our nation; . . . confronting global disease threats through advanced computing and lab analysis of huge amounts of data to quickly find solutions; . . . tracking disease and finding out what is making people sick and the most effective ways to prevent it; . . . bringing new knowledge to individual health care and community health to save more lives and reduce waste; . . . detecting and confronting new germs and diseases around the globe to increase our national security; . . . building on our significant contribution to have strong, well-resourced public health leaders and capabilities at national, state and local levels to protect Americans from health threats. https://www.cdc.gov/. **NOTE:** The CDC has a web page for virtually every physical and mental disorder, syndrome, and condition. One can browse disorders, syndromes, and conditions alphabetically at https://www.cdc.gov/DiseasesConditions/. These web pages will typically have a menu or links to basic facts, symptoms, diagnosis, and treatment; free materials (print or order free materials); research; data and statistics; scientific articles and key findings; and recommendations.

7.5. Centers for Medicare and Medicaid Services (CMS). The Centers for Medicare and Medicaid Services (CMS) provides health coverage to more than 100 million people through Medicare, Medicaid, the Children's Health Insurance Program, and the Health Insurance Marketplace. The CMS seeks to strengthen and modernize the Nation's health care system, to provide access to high quality care and improved health at lower costs. https://www.cms.gov/.

7.6. Department of Education (ED). ED's mission is to promote student achievement and preparation for global competitiveness by fostering educational excellence and ensuring equal access. . . . [Developing] policies on federal financial aid for education, and distributing as well as monitoring those funds, collecting data on America's schools and disseminating research, focusing national attention on key educational issues, prohibiting discrimination and ensuring equal access to education. https://www.ed.gov/.

7.7. Department of Health and Human Services (HHS). It is the mission of the US Department of Health & Human Services (HHS) to enhance and protect the health and well-being of all Americans. We fulfill that mission by providing for effective health and human services and fostering advances in medicine, public health, and social services. https://www.hhs.gov/. **NOTE:** The HHS has a very broad mission and authority and is the parent agency for many of the other federal agencies in this chapter.

7.8. Department of Veterans Affairs (VA). The Department of Veterans Affairs (VA) is responsible for providing vital services to America's veterans. VA provides health care services, benefits programs and access to national cemeteries to former military personnel and their dependents. The department carries out its duties through three main administrative divisions: Veterans Benefits Administration; Veterans Health Administration; and National Cemetery Administration. All three divisions have run into trouble while carrying out their missions, including controversies involving VA hospitals and long-standing delays in providing services. VA offers a full range of mental health services for veterans, including outpatient, residential and inpatient services and readjustment services. Available outpatient services include assessment and evaluation, medication management, and individual and group psychotherapy. Specialty services are available to target problems such as PTSD, substance abuse, depression, and homelessness. In addition, they provide specialized services to women veterans, including service-related sexual abuse, veterans involved in the criminal justice system, older veterans, veterans at risk for suicide, and veteran family services. https://www.va.gov/.

7.9. Food and Drug Administration (FDA). The Food and Drug Administration is responsible for protecting the public health by ensuring the safety, efficacy, and security of human and veterinary drugs, biological products, and medical devices; and by ensuring the safety of our nation's food supply, cosmetics, and products that emit radiation. FDA also has responsibility for regulating the manufacturing, marketing, and distribution of tobacco products to protect the public health and to reduce tobacco use by minors. FDA is responsible for advancing the public health by helping to speed innovations that make medical products more effective, safer, and more affordable and by helping the public get the accurate, science-based information they need to use medical products and foods to maintain and improve their health. FDA also plays a significant role in the Nation's counterterrorism capability. FDA fulfills this responsibility by ensuring the security of the food supply and by fostering development of medical products to respond to deliberate and naturally emerging public health threats. https://www.fda.gov/.

7.10. Health Resources & Services Administration (HRSA). The Health Resources and Services Administration (HRSA), an agency of the U.S. Department of Health and Human Services, is the primary Federal agency for improving health care to people who are geographically isolated, economically or medically vulnerable. HRSA programs help those in need of high quality primary health care, people living with HIV/AIDS, pregnant women and mothers. HRSA also supports the training of health professionals, the distribution of providers to areas where they are needed most and improvements in health care delivery. HRSA oversees organ, bone marrow and cord blood donation. It compensates individuals harmed by vaccination, and maintains databases that protect against health care malpractice, waste, fraud and abuse. https://www.hrsa.gov/.

7.11. Indian Health Service (IHS). The Indian Health Service (HIS) . . . is responsible for providing federal health services to American Indians and Alaska Natives. The provision of health services to members of federally recognized tribes grew out of the special government-to-government relationship between the federal government and Indian tribes. The IHS is the principal federal health care provider and health advocate for Indian people, and its goal is to raise their health status to the highest possible level. The IHS provides a comprehensive health service delivery system for approximately 2.2 million American Indians and Alaska Natives who belong to 567 federally recognized tribes in 36 states. https://www.ihs.gov/.

7.12. National Council on Disability (NCD). NCD is an independent federal agency charged with advising the president, Congress, and other federal agencies regarding policies, programs, practices, and procedures that affect people with disabilities. . . . NCD's mission is to be a trusted advisor, in collaboration with people with disabilities to the president, the Congress, federal entities, state, tribal communities, and local governments, and other entities and organizations. NCD fulfills its advisory roles regarding disability policies, programs, procedures, and practices that enhance equal opportunity by convening stakeholders to acquire timely and relevant input for recommendations and action steps, gathering and analyzing data and other information, engaging and influencing current debates and agendas, identifying and formulating solutions to emerging and long-standing challenges, and providing tools to facilitate effective implementation. https://ncd.gov/.

7.13. National Institute of Mental Health (NIMH). The National Institute of Mental Health (NIMH) is the lead federal agency for research on mental disorders. . . . NIMH envisions a world in which mental illnesses are prevented and cured. The mission of NIMH is to transform the understanding and treatment of mental illnesses through basic and clinical research, paving the way for prevention, recovery, and cure. For the Institute to continue fulfilling this vital public health mission, it must foster innovative thinking and ensure that a full array of novel scientific perspectives are used to further discovery in the evolving science of brain, behavior, and experience. In this way, breakthroughs in science can become breakthroughs for all people with mental illnesses. https://www.nimh.nih.gov/. **NOTE:** NIMH fulfills its mission through various offices and divisions:

- 7.13a. The Office of the NIMH Director contains the Office on AIDS, Office of Autism Research Coordination, Office of Clinical Research, Office of Constituency Relations and Public Liaison, Office of Genomics Research Coordination, Office for Research on Disparities and Global Mental Health, Office of Management, Office of Rural Mental Health Research, Office of Science Policy, Planning, and Communications, and the Office of Technology Development and Coordination
- 7.13b. The Division of Neuroscience and Basic Behavioral Science (DNBBS) provides support for research programs in the areas of basic neuroscience, genetics, basic behavioral science, research training, resource development, technology development, drug discovery, and research dissemination. The Division has the

responsibility, in cooperation with other components of the Institute and the research community, for ensuring that relevant basic science knowledge is generated and then harvested to create improved diagnosis, treatment, and prevention of mental and behavioral disorders. Through the various programs housed in its branches and offices, the Division offers support for a spectrum of relevant extramural activities. By reviewing the program descriptions, investigators should be able to identify an appropriate contact. For the Division and each program we also provide Areas of High Priority and Areas of Emphasis. In addition, [it] continue[s] to encourage innovative applications in any area relevant to the mission of the Institute. Components of DNBBS include the Behavioral Science and Integrative Neuroscience Research Branch, Genomics Research Branch, Molecular, Cellular, and Genomic Neuroscience Research Branch, Office of Research Training and Career Development, and Small Business Innovation Research (SBIR) and Small Business Technology Transfer (STGTR)Programs.

- 7.13c. The Division of AIDS Research (DAR) supports research to reduce the incidence of HIV/AIDS worldwide and to decrease the burden of living with HIV/AIDS. DAR-supported research encompasses a broad range of studies that includes basic and clinical neuroscience of HIV infection to understand and alleviate the consequences of HIV infection of the central nervous system (CNS), and basic and applied behavioral science to prevent new HIV infections and limit morbidity and mortality among those infected. DAR places a high priority on interdisciplinary research across multiple populations, including racial and ethnic minorities, over the lifespan.

The portfolio on the basic neuroscience of HIV infection includes research to: elucidate the mechanisms underlying HIV-induced CNS dysfunction in the setting of long-term antiretroviral therapy; understand the motor, cognitive, and behavioral impairments that result from HIV infection of the CNS; develop novel treatments to prevent or mitigate the CNS complications of HIV infection; and, minimize the neurotoxicity induced by long-term use of antiretroviral therapy. Critical approaches to this effort require molecular, cellular, and genetic studies to delineate the pathophysiologic mechanisms that lead to HIV induced CNS dysfunction, and to identify potential targets for therapeutic intervention. In addition, eradication of the virus from HIV-infected individuals to achieve a cure or a functional cure is a high priority. The behavioral science research agenda emphasizes developing and testing behavioral interventions that are effectively integrated with biomedical approaches to significantly impact the HIV/AIDS epidemic. The behavioral science agenda targets prevention of both transmission and acquisition of HIV, adherence to intervention components to reduce the burden of disease, and studies that address the behavioral consequences of HIV/AIDS. A strong component of integrating behavioral and biomedical approaches is expanding collaboration with other NIH institutes and federal agencies to leverage resources and broaden the impact of this research. DAR components include the HIV Prevention Science Branch, HIV Treatment and Translational Science Branch, HIV-1 Neuropathogenesis, Genetics and Therapeutics Branch, AIDS Research Centers Program, Training, Fellowship, and Health Disparities Programs, and Small Business Innovation Research (SBIR) and Small Business Technology Transfer (STTR) Programs.

- 7.13d The Division of Services and Intervention Research (DSIR) supports two critical areas of research: intervention research to evaluate the effectiveness of pharmacologic, psychosocial (psychotherapeutic and behavioral), somatic, rehabilitative and combination interventions on mental and behavior disorders—including acute and longer-term therapeutic effects on functioning across domains (such as school, family, peer functioning) for children, adolescents, and adults and Mental health services research. The interventions focus is broad and inclusive with respect to the heterogeneity of patients, the severity and chronicity of disorders, and the variety of community and institutional settings in which treatment is provided. It includes clinical trials evaluating the effectiveness of known efficacious interventions, as well as studies evaluating modified or adapted forms of interventions for use with additional populations (such as women, ethnic, and racial groups), new settings (public sector, pediatric primary care, schools, other non-academic settings, communities at large), and people with co-occurring disorders. Other foci include: identifying subgroups who may be more likely to benefit from treatment, evaluating the combined or sequential use of interventions (such as to extend effect among refractory subgroups), determining the optimal length of intervention, establishing the utility of continuation or maintenance treatment (that is, for prevention of relapse or recurrence), and evaluating the long-term impact of efficacious interventions on symptoms and functioning. Services research covers all mental health services research issues across the life span and disorders, including but not limited to: services organization, delivery (process and receipt of care), and related health economics at the individual, clinical, program, community and systems levels in specialty mental health, general health, and other delivery settings (such as the workplace), interventions to improve the quality and outcomes of care (including diagnostic, treatment, preventive, and rehabilitation services), enhanced capacity for conducting services research, clinical epidemiology of mental disorders across all clinical and service settings, and dissemination and implementation of evidence-based interventions into service settings. The Division also provides biostatistical analysis and clinical trials operations expertise for research studies; analyzes and evaluates national mental health needs and community research partnership opportunities; and supports research on health disparities. Components of DSIR include Adult Treatment and Preventive Intervention Research Branch, Child and Adolescent Treatment and Preventive Intervention Research Branch, Services Research and Clinical Epidemiology Branch, Office of Research Training and Career Development, Ethics of Mental Disorders Research Program and Small Business Innovation Research (SBIR) and Small Business Technology Transfer (STTR) Programs.

7.14. National Science Foundation (NSF). The National Science Foundation (NSF) is an independent federal agency created . . . to promote the progress of science; to advance the national health, prosperity, and welfare; to secure the national defense. NSF is the only federal agency whose mission includes support for all fields of fundamental science and engineering, except for medical sciences. NSF is tasked with keeping the United States at the leading edge of discovery in a wide range of scientific areas, from astronomy to geology to zoology. So, in addition to funding research in the traditional academic areas, the agency also supports "high risk, high pay off" ideas, novel collaborations and numerous projects that may seem like science fiction today, but which the public will take for granted tomorrow. And in every case, we ensure that research is fully integrated with education so that today's revolutionary work will also be training tomorrow's top scientists and engineers. Unlike many other federal agencies, NSF does not hire researchers or directly operate our own laboratories or similar facilities. Instead, we support scientists, engineers and educators directly through their own home institutions (typically universities and colleges). Similarly, we fund facilities and equipment such as telescopes, through cooperative agreements with research consortia that have competed successfully for limited-term management contracts. NSF's job is to determine where the frontiers are, identify the leading U.S. pioneers in these fields and provide money and equipment to help them continue. https://www.nsf.gov/. **NOTE:** A list of NSF organizations, each of which supports a different area in the sciences, is located at https://www.nsf.gov/staff/orglist.jsp. There is a link to each organizations website; there is a Directorate for Social, Behavioral & Economic Sciences and a Directorate for Education & Human Resources, as well as other directorates and offices.

7.15. Office of Juvenile Justice and Delinquency Prevention (OJJDP). OJJDP provides national leadership, coordination, and resources to prevent and respond to juvenile delinquency and victimization. OJJDP supports states and communities in their efforts to develop and implement effective and coordinated prevention and intervention programs and to improve the juvenile justice system so that it protects public safety, holds justice-involved youth appropriately accountable, and provides treatment and rehabilitative services tailored to the needs of juveniles and their families. https://www.ojjdp.gov/.

7.16. Office of National Drug Control Policy (ONDCP). ONDCP coordinates the drug control activities and related funding of 16 Federal Departments and Agencies. Each year, ONDCP produces the annual National Drug Control Strategy, which outlines Administration efforts for the Nation to reduce illicit drug use, manufacturing and trafficking; drug-related crime and violence; and drug-related health consequences. ONDCP also leads the development of the consolidated Federal drug control budget, which is published annually in the National Drug Control Strategy: Budget and Performance Summary. ONDCP also administers two grant programs: the High Intensity Drug Trafficking Areas (HIDTA) and Drug-Free Communities (DFC). The HIDTA program assists Federal, state, local, and tribal law enforcement operating in areas determined to be critical drug trafficking regions of the United States. HIDTA supports law enforcement efforts in 49 states, the District of Columbia, Puerto Rico, and the U.S. Virgin Islands. The DFC program provides grants to community coalitions to strengthen the infrastructure among local partners to create and sustain a reduction in local youth substance abuse. Currently, there are 698 DFC-funded coalitions across the country. DFC coalitions are made up of community leaders representing twelve sectors that organize to meet the local prevention needs of the youth and families in their communities. These twelve sectors are: youth (18 or younger), parents, businesses, media, schools, youth-serving organizations, law enforcement, religious/fraternal organizations, civic/volunteer groups (i.e., local organizations committed to volunteering, not a coalition member designated as a "volunteer"), health-care professionals, state, local, or tribal governmental agencies with expertise in the field of substance abuse (including, if applicable, the state agency with primary authority for substance abuse), and other organizations involved in reducing substance abuse. **NOTE:** On March 29, 2017, President Donald J. Trump signed an executive order establishing the President's Commission on Combating Drug Addiction and the Opioid Crisis. ONDCP provides administrative and financial support for the commission and its activities. https://www.whitehouse.gov/ondcp.

7.17. Office of Refugee Resettlement (ORR). The Office of Refugee Resettlement (ORR) provides new populations with the opportunity to achieve their full potential in the United States. Our programs provide people in need with critical resources to assist them in becoming integrated members of American society. . . . ORR's Survivors of Torture program provides rehabilitative, social, and legal services to individuals—regardless of immigration status—who have experienced torture which occurred outside the U.S. ORR also provides care and placement for unaccompanied children who enter the United States from other countries without an adult guardian. ORR's Six Guiding Principles . . . inform ORR's commitment to the populations it serves, and the partners with which it works. [The principles are] Appropriate Placement and Services . . . Client-Centered Case Management . . . Newly Arriving Refugees . . . Health and Mental Health Services . . . Outreach . . . Data Informed Decision-Making. https://www.acf.hhs.gov/orr.

7.18. Office of Special Education and Rehabilitative Services (OSERS). The Office of Special Education and Rehabilitative Services has two main components: the Office of Special Education Programs (OSEP) and the Rehabilitation Services Administration (RSA). The Office of Special Education Programs (OSEP) is dedicated to improving results for infants, toddlers, children, and youth with disabilities ages birth through 21 by providing leadership and financial support to assist states and local districts. The Individuals with Disabilities Education Act of 2004 (IDEA) authorizes formula grants to states and discretionary grants to institutions of higher education and other non-profit organizations to support research, demonstrations, technical assistance and dissemination, technology and personnel development and parent-training and information centers. The Rehabilitation Services Administration's (RSA's) mission is to provide leadership and resources to assist state and other agencies in providing vocational rehabilitation (VR) and other services to individuals with disabilities to maximize their employment, independence and integration into the community and the competitive labor market. More specifically, RSA is responsible for administering formula and discretionary grant programs authorized by Congress; evaluating, monitoring, and reporting on the implementation of Federal policy and programs and the effectiveness of vocational rehabilitation, supported employment, and other related programs for individuals with disabilities; coordinating with other Federal agencies, State agencies, and the private sector including professional organizations, service providers, and organizations of persons with disabilities for the review of program planning, implementation, and monitoring issues. More specific information about programs administered by RSA is located at https://rsa.ed.gov/. OSERS: https://www2.ed.gov/about/offices/list/osers/index.html.

7.19. Substance Abuse and Mental Health Services Administration (SAMHSA). The Substance Abuse and Mental Health Services Administration (SAMHSA) is the agency within the U.S. Department of Health and Human Services that leads public health efforts to advance the behavioral health of the nation. SAMHSA's mission is to reduce the impact of substance abuse and mental illness on America's communities. In order to achieve its mission, SAMHSA has identified strategic initiatives focused on leading change to better meet the behavioral health care needs of individuals, communities, and service providers. The goals of SAMHSA's strategic initiatives are to increase awareness and understanding of mental and substance use disorders, promote emotional health and wellness, address the prevention of substance abuse and mental illness, Increase access to effective treatment, support recovery, support the behavioral health field with critical data from national surveys and surveillance, build public awareness of the importance of behavioral health, support innovation and practice improvement by evaluating and disseminating evidence-based, promising behavioral health practices and engaging in activities that support behavioral health system transformation, collect best practices and developing expertise around prevention and treatment for people with mental illness and addictions, and help states, territories, and tribes build and improve system capacity by encouraging innovation, supporting more efficient approaches, and utilizing evidence-based programs and services to produce measurable results. Issues addressed by SAMHSA include alcohol, tobacco, and other drugs, behavioral health treatments and services, criminal and juvenile justice, data, outcomes, and quality, disaster preparedness, response, and recovery, health care and health systems integration, health disparities, health financing, health information technology, HIV, AIDS, and viral hepatitis, homelessness and housing, laws, regulations, and guidelines, mental and substance use disorders, prescription drug misuse and abuse, prevention of substance abuse and mental illness, recovery and recovery support, school and campus health, specific populations, state and local government partnerships, suicide prevention, trauma and violence, tribal affairs, underage drinking, veterans and military families, wellness and the workforce. https://www.samhsa.gov/.

8

Biographical Resources

Because the history of psychology is so intertwined with the individuals who created that history, the resources in this chapter illuminate not only the individuals they cover, but also the history of psychology. Two major types of sources are presented: substantive biographical sources that contain information themselves, and bibliographies that direct the user to substantive sources.

Most large encyclopedia sets on psychology and the social sciences include biographical entries; such works are not included in this chapter. In addition, there are a number of serial publications from before 1980 that were discontinued; these are not included, but can be identified in *Research Guide for Psychology* by Raymond McInnis (1982). In addition, because books on individual psychologists and other contributors to psychology are so numerous that they would merit their own annotated bibliography rather than a chapter in this book, they are also not included here. (One can easily identify them by searching on the individual as "subject" in any catalog, including WorldCat.)

SUBSTANTIVE SOURCES

8.1. *American Psychological Association member directory.* http://community.apa.org/home. This directory is an online resource in which APA members may enter their own profiles and search others' profiles, as well as communicate with other members. Members decide how much and what to enter, and may include name, credentials, photo, social media information, division membership, and other professional information.

8.2. *American men and women of science: A biographical directory of today's leaders in physical, biological, and related sciences.* Various editors. (1906–). Farmington Hills, MI: Gale. First published as *American Men of Science* by J. McKeen Cattell in 1906, the title was changed to its current form in 1971. The 2017 edition is the thirty-fifth. In recent years, each edition has consisted of approximately eight volumes, with the last volume

being the discipline section, which organizes scientists according to their area of activity. Entries include selected American and Canadian scientists and are alphabetically arranged. Recent editions have contained 30,000–40,000 entries on scientists living at the time of publication, with approximately 1,000 entries being new and the rest being updates of previous entries. Entries include the following information, if available and applicable: birthdate, birthplace, citizenship, name of spouse, name(s) or number of children, field of specialty, education, honorary degrees, professional experience, honors and awards, memberships, research information, addresses, facsimile numbers, and e-mail addresses. Generally, entrants are in the physical and biological sciences, public health, engineering, mathematics, statistics, and computer science.

8.3. *Biographical dictionary of psychology.* Sheehy, N., Chapman, A. J., & Conroy, W. A. (Eds.). (1997). New York: Routledge. 675 pp. BF109. This work includes biographical information and critical analysis of the influences, interests, and receptions of approximately 500 major figures, ranging from the emergence of experimental psychology in the 1800s through the late 1900s. It also includes a list of principal publications of each entrant.

8.4. *Educational psychology: A century of contributions.* Zimmerman, B. J., & Schunk, D. H. (Eds.). (2003). Mahwah, NJ: Erlbaum Associates. 490 pp. LB1051. This volume covers major figures in educational psychology. Individuals are captured in their own chapters, organized by period of educational psychology, including the founding period (James, Binet, Dewey, Thorndike, Terman, and Montessori), rise to prominence (Vygotsky, Skinner, Piaget, Cronbach, and Gagne), and the modern era (Bloom, Gage, Bruner, Bandura, and Brown).

8.5. *Eminent contributors to psychology.* Watson, R. I. (Ed.). (1974–1976). New York: Springer. 1628 pp. BF38. Two-volume set. Volume 1, *A Bibliography of Primary References*, covers approximately 500 individuals living between 1600 and 1967 who made an important contribution to the psychological literature. For each individual, it lists up to eighty important publications, for a total listing of approximately 12,000 citations. Volume 2, *A Bibliography of Secondary References*, contains more than 50,000 citations to selected secondary references to the works of individuals included in volume 1.

8.6. *History of psychology in autobiography.* (various editors). (serial, 1930–). Washington, DC: American Psychological Association. BF105. Originally edited by Edwin Boring and published by Stanford University from 1930 to 1989, the most recent edition is volume IX, published by APA in 2007. Like earlier volumes, this volume provides extensive entries on a small number of psychologists; this volume's 354 pages are dedicated to nine psychologists: Elliot Aronson, Albert Bandura, Gordon Bower, Jerome Kagan, Daniel Kahneman, Elizabeth Loftus, Water Mischel, Ulric Neisser, and Richard Thompson.

8.7. *Names in the history of psychology: A biographical sourcebook.* Zusne, L. (1975). Washington, DC: Hemisphere [Wiley]. 489 pp. BF109. This volume provides information on 526 psychologists deceased at the time of writing. Brief biographical information is provided; the focus is on the individual's contributions to psychology in philosophy, theory, discoveries, methodologies initiated, research conducted, books published, and influence on the field. **NOTE:** The 1984 *Biographical Dictionary of Psychology* by Zusne is a revised edition of this work.

8.8. *Portraits of pioneers in psychology.* Kimble, G. A., Wertheimer, M., & White, C. (serial, 1991–). (various authors). Washington, DC: American Psychological Association. BF109. As of August 2017, there are six volumes in this open series. Each pioneer is covered in an individual chapter, including a biography, contributions to the field, and a reference list.

8.9. *Psychologists defying the crowd: Stories of those who battled the establishment and won.* Sternberg, R. J. (Ed.). (2003). Washington, DC: American Psychological Association. 293 pp. BF75. This work covers sixteen modern psychologists who deviated from an existing theory, a research paradigm, a philosophical orientation, or subjects. The content of each individual's chapter is based on answers to questions such as how he or she defied the establishment, why, opposition encountered, response to opposition, what if anything he or she would do differently, personal and professional costs and benefits, and advice to others following a similar path.

8.10. *Women in psychology: A bio-bibliographic sourcebook.* O'Connell, A. N., & Russo, N. F. (Eds.). (1990). New York: Greenwood Press. 441 pp. BF109. This work has five major sections. There is an overview of women in psychology; thirty-six chapters devoted to thirty-six individual women; one chapter summarizing award-winning contributions as recognized by APA and APF; one chapter of bibliographic resources, including the most important books and other information resources on women in psy-

chology and autobiographical and biographical information on 185 specific women; and appendixes, including a chronology of birth years, places of birth, and the major fields of the thirty-six women featured in the book.

SELECTED BIOGRAPHICAL BIBLIOGRAPHIES

8.11. Bibliographic processes and products, and a bibliography of the published primary-source works of B. F. Skinner. Morris, E. K., & Smith, N. G. (2003). *The Behavior Analyst*, 26(1), 41–67. Reviews extant B. F. Skinner bibliographies created from 1958 to 2001. It then describes the methods used in constructing this new, comprehensive, and corrected bibliography of Skinner's primary-source published works, which includes 291 books, articles, chapters, monographs, book reviews, manuals, encyclopedia entries, letters to the editor, and so forth, from 1930 to 1999.

8.12. Bibliography. (no authorship indicated). (2004). *Psychoanalytic Psychotherapy*, 18(1), 139. List of references on therapist pregnancy.

8.13. Bibliography: Hans J. Eysenck, Ph.D., D.Sc., 1939–2000. (no authorship indicated). (2001). *Personality and Individual Differences*, 31(1), 45–99. Bibliography of H. J. Eysenck's books and articles published between 1939 and 2000.

8.14. A bibliography of mental patients' autobiographies: An update and classification system. Sommer, R., Clifford, J. S., & Norcross, J. C. (1998). *American Journal of Psychiatry*, 155(9), 1261–1264. Seven anthologies and forty-eight autobiographies of former psychiatric patients published between 1980 and 1998.

8.15. Bibliography of Michael Balint's related works. Hudon, M., & Haynal, A. (2003). *The American Journal of Psychoanalysis*, 63(3), 275–279. Bibliography of Michael Balint's related works, incorporating references from various sources, including the Balint Archives and the Balint Society website.

8.16. Carl Rogers bibliography of English and German sources. Schmid, P. F. (2005). *Person-Centered and Experiential Psychotherapies*, 4(3–4), 153–160. This bibliography lists all original publications of Carl Rogers from 1922 onward, including German translations. Following English-, German-, and Spanish-language introductory remarks, the chronological part lists unpublished papers and interviews, and, separately, films. The alphabetical part consists of both name and title indexes. The bibliography is also available online at http://www.pfs-online.at/1/indexbibliocrr0.htm, where it is updated.

8.17. *Jacques Lacan: An annotated bibliography.* Clark, M. (2014/1988). New York: Routledge. 893 pp. Z8469 or BF109. Two-volume set. Covers primary and secondary works by and about Lacan, including books, essays, seminars, interviews, and dissertations. Incorporates (and corrects where appropriate) information from all earlier published bibliographies of Lacan's work, including Joel Dor's *Bibliographie des travaux de Jacques Lacan*. Also includes all information about Lacan's published work on record in the Bibliotheque de l'Ecole de la Cause Freudienne. Includes items in English, French, Japanese, Russian, and five other languages.

8.18. Karen Horney: A bibliography of her writings. Paris, B. J. (2001). *American Journal of Psychoanalysis*, 60(2), 165–172. Bibliography of Karen Horney's books, articles, essays, lectures and talks, and other writings.

8.19. Multilingual bibliography of the works of Michael Balint. Haynal, A., & Hudon, M. (2003). *The American Journal of Psychoanalysis*, 63(3), 257–273. Multilingual and chronologically arranged bibliography of the works of Michael Balint.

8.20. Ralph M. Reitan's bibliography. Hom, J., & Nici, J. (2015). *Archives of Clinical Neuropsychology*, 30(8), 774–783. Bibliography of Ralph Reitan's published works over the course of his more than sixty-year year career.

8.21. Seventy-five years of Kleinian writing 1920–1995: A bibliography. Hinshelwood, R. D. (2000). *Kleinian Studies E-journal*. Bibliography of Kleinian writings by Melanie Klein and other authors from 1920 to 1995. Available online at http://ww.psychoanalysis-and-therapy.com/human_nature/ksej/hinbib.html.

8.22. A tribute to Bunky at 125: A comprehensive bibliography of E. M. Jellinek's publications. Ward, J. H., & Bejarano, W. (2016). *Journal of Studies on Alcohol and Drugs*, 77(3), 371–374. This comprehensive bibliography on Jellinek, considered the father of alcoholism studies, includes 165 original publications published between 1912 and 1982. Many of his works were reprinted; the original publications are included with the reprint information following that on the original work. Jellinek also published in other areas, and these works are included as well.

8.23. Viaggio attraverso la bibliografia di Jerome Bruner: Dagli anni della formazione alla psicologia culturale (Journey through the bibliography of Jerome Bruner: Toward the development of cultural psychology). Ornaghi, V., & Groppo, M. (1998). *Archivio di Psicologia, Neurologia e Psichiatria*, 59(2), 199–244. Includes an extensive bibliography, organized by date. J. Bruner's bibliography is discussed relative to the central themes of his works and outside influences. The works are analyzed by the period of formation: World War II (1939–1945), the influence of European Gestalt and the New Look movement (1946–1950), the influence of Piaget and Vygotsky (1956–1966), research on infancy and initial language studies (1967–1971), studies on the development of communicative and linguistic competence (1972–1979), interactionism and cultural roles (1980–1984), and autobiographical narrative and the construction of self (1991–1998).

9

Directories and Organizations

DIRECTORIES OF GRADUATE PROGRAMS

9.1. *Directory of graduate programs in applied sport psychology* (5th ed.). Sachs, M. L., Burke, K. L., & Schweighardt, S. L. (2011). Madison, WI: Association for Applied Sport Psychology. 318 pp. GV365.

9.2. *Graduate study in psychology*. American Psychological Association. (2016–). Washington, DC: American Psychological Association. 1385 pp. BF77.

9.3. *Insider's guide to graduate programs in clinical and counseling psychology 2016–2017*. Norcross, J. C., & Sayette, M. A. (2016). New York: Guilford Press. 442 pp. RC467.

9.4. *International handbook of universities* (13th ed.). International Association of Universities (2016–). Paris: International Association of Universities. 3 vols. L900.

DIRECTORIES OF ASSOCIATIONS AND ORGANIZATIONS

9.5. *Directory of divisions of American Psychological Association*. http://www.apa.org/about/division/index.aspx. Lists and provides links to the fifty-six divisions of the American Psychological Association. List is available by division number and topical areas.

9.6. *Directory of EuroPsy member countries*. http://www.europsy-efpa.eu/countries. EuroPsy was established by the European Federation of Psychologists' Associations (EFPA) and is the European qualification standard for psychologists. EuroPsy supplements national standards, credentials psychologists who meet educational and professional criteria, and helps the public to identify psychologist competencies in particular areas of practice.

9.7. *Directory of international and regional organizations of psychology*. http://www.apa.org/international/networks/organizations/international-orgs.aspx. Provides name, address, telephone number, and name of president of organization for international and regional associations of

psychology. Most entries also provide fax number, e-mail link, and other senior officer information.

9.8. *Directory of national associations of psychology*. http://www.apa.org/international/networks/organizations/national-orgs.aspx. Provides name, address, telephone number, and name of president of organization for national associations of psychology. Most entries also provide fax number, e-mail link, and other senior officer information.

9.9. *State, provincial & territorial psychological association directory*. (US and Canada). http://www.apa.org/about/apa/organizations/associations.aspx. Provides name, address, telephone number, and link to websites of state, provincial, and territorial psychological associations in the United States and Canada.

9.10. SELECTED NATIONAL ASSOCIATIONS

American Academy of Child and Adolescent Psychiatry. http://www.aacap.org

American Board of Assessment Psychology. http://www.assessmentpsychologyboard.org

American Counseling Association. http://www.counseling.org

American Psychiatric Association. http://www.psychiatry.org

American Psychoanalytic Association. http://apsa.org

American Psychological Association. http://www.apa.org. APA is the leading scientific and professional organization representing psychology in the United States. Its mission is to promote the creation, communication, and application of psychological knowledge to benefit society and individuals by advancing the development and application of psychology in the broadest sense; promoting research in psychology and the application of research findings; establishing high standards of ethics, conduct, education, and achievement for psychologists; and disseminating knowledge through meetings, professional contacts, reports, papers, discussions, and publications.

American Psychological Society. http://www.psychologi calscience.org. APS is a nonprofit organization committed to the advancement of scientific psychology and its representation at the national and international levels (previously the American Psychological Society).

Australian Psychological Society. http://www.psychology .org.au/

British Psychological Society. http://www.bps.org.uk/

Canadian Psychological Association. http://www.cpa.ca

National Academy of Neuropsychology. https://www.nan online.org/

National Academy of Sciences. http://www.nas.edu. The National Academies of Sciences, Engineering, and Medicine are private, nonprofit institutions that provide expert advice issued in their domains, with the goal of shaping sound policies; informing public opinion; and advancing the pursuit of science, engineering, and medicine.

National Association of School Psychologists. http://www .nasponline.org

9.11. GENERAL

Association for Psychological Science (APS). http://www .psychologicalscience.org/

European Federation of Psychologists' Associations. www .efpa.eu/

Society for General Psychology (APA Division 1). http:// www.apadivisions.org/division-31/

State, Provincial and Territorial Psychological Association Affairs (APA Division 31). http://www.apa.org/about/ division/div31.aspx

9.12. CLINICAL AND COUNSELING PSYCHOLOGY

Academy of Psychological Clinical Science. http://acad psychclinicalscience.org

American Association of Suicidology. http://www.suicid ology.org

American Society for the Advancement of Pharmacotherapy (APA Division 55). http://www.apadivisions.org/divi sion-55/

Association for Behavior Analysis International. http:// www.abainternational.org

Association for the Advancement of Gestalt Therapy. http:// www.aagt.org

Behavior Analysis (APA Division 25). http://www.apadivi sions.org/division-25/

Center for Quality Assessment and Improvement in Mental Health. http://www.cqaimh.org

National Center for PTSD. http://www.ptsd.va.gov

Psychoanalysis (APA Division 39). http://www.apadivisions .org/division-39/

Psychological Clinical Science Accreditation System. http:// www.pcsas.org

Psychopharmacology and Substance Abuse (APA Division 28). http://www.apadivisions.org/division-28/

Society for a Science of Clinical Psychology. http://www .sscpweb.org

Society for Clinical Neuropsychology (APA Division 40). http://www.scn40.org/

Society for Humanistic Psychology (APA Division 32). http://www.apadivisions.org/division-32/

Society for Research in Psychopathology. http://www.psych opathology.org

Society for the Advancement of Psychotherapy (APA Division 29). http://societyforpsychotherapy.org/

Society of Addiction Psychology (APA Division 50). http:// www.apa.org/divisions/div50/

Society of Clinical Child and Adolescent Psychology (APA Division 53). https://www.clinicalchildpsychology.org/

Society of Clinical Psychology (APA Division 12). http:// www.div12.org/

Society of Counseling Psychology (APA Division 17). http://www.div17.org/

Society of Group Psychology and Group Psychotherapy (APA Division 49). http://www.apadivisions.org/division-49/

Society of Pediatric Psychology (APA Division 54). http:// www.societyofpediatricpsychology.org/

Society of Psychological Hypnosis (APA Division 30). http://www.apadivisions.org/division-30/

Trauma Psychology (APA Division 56). http://www.apa traumadivision.org

9.13. COGNITIVE PSYCHOLOGY

Canadian Society for Brain Behaviour and Cognitive Science. http://www.csbbcs.org

Cognitive Science Society. http://cognitivesciencesociety .org/index.html

European Society for Cognitive Psychology. http://www .escop.eu

9.14. COMMUNITY PSYCHOLOGY

Society for Community Research and Action: Division of Community Psychology (APA Division 27). http://www .scra27.org/

9.15. DEVELOPMENTAL PSYCHOLOGY

Adult Development and Aging (APA Division 20). http:// www.apadivisions.org/division-20/

Developmental Psychology (APA Division 7). http://www. apadivisions.org/division-7/

European Association of Developmental Psychology. http:// www.esdp.info/Home.83.0.html

International Society for Developmental Psychobiology. http://www.isdp.org

International Society for the Study of Behavioural Development. http://www.issbd.org

International Society on Infant Studies. http://www.isisweb.org

Jean Piaget Society. http://www.piaget.org

Society for Research in Child Development. http://www.srcd.org

9.16 EDUCATIONAL AND SCHOOL PSYCHOLOGY

American Educational Research Association (AERA). http://www.aera.net/

Division of School Psychology (APA Division 16). http://apadivision16.org/

Educational Psychology (APA Division 15). http://apadiv15.org/

9.17. EXPERIMENTAL, ENGINEERING, AND COGNITIVE PSYCHOLOGY

Applied Experimental and Engineering Psychology (APA Division 21). http://www.apadivisions.org/division-21/

Experimental Psychology Society. http://www.eps.ac.uk

Psychonomic Society. http://www.psychonomic.org

Society for Experimental Psychology and Cognitive Science (APA Division 3). http://www.apadivisions.org/division-3/

9.18. HEALTH PSYCHOLOGY

European Health Psychology Society. http://www.ehps.net

International Society of Health Psychology Research. http://userpage.fu-berlin.de/~health/is.htm

Society for Health Psychology (APA Division 38). http://www.health-psych.org/

9.19. HISTORY OF PSYCHOLOGY

Society for the History of Psychology (APA Division 26). http://historyofpsych.org/

9.20. INDUSTRIAL AND ORGANIZATIONAL PSYCHOLOGY

European Association of Work and Organizational Psychology. http://www.eawop.org

Human Factors and Ergonomics Society. https://www.hfes.org

Institute of Ergonomics and Human Factors. http://www.ergonomics.org.uk

Society for Consumer Psychology (APA Division 23). http://www.myscp.org

Society for Industrial and Organizational Psychology (APA Division 14). http://www.siop.org

9.21. NEUROSCIENCE AND COMPARATIVE PSYCHOLOGY

Animal Behavior Society. http://animalbehaviorsociety.org

Cognitive Neuroscience Society. http://www.cogneurosociety.org

Federation of Associations in Brain and Behavioral Sciences. http://www.fabbs.org

Federation of the European Societies of Neuropsychology. http://www.fesn.eu

International Society for Comparative Psychology. http://www.comparativepsychology.org

Society for Behavioral Neuroscience and Comparative Psychology (APA Division 6). http://www.apadivisions.org/division-6/

Society for Neuroscience. http://www.sfn.org

9.22. PERSONALITY AND SOCIAL PSYCHOLOGY

European Association of Personality Psychology. http://www.eapp.org

European Association of Social Psychology. http://www.easp.eu

Social Psychology Network. http://www.socialpsychology.org/

Society for Personality and Social Psychology. http://spsp.site-ym.com

Society for Personality and Social Psychology (APA Division 8). http://www.spsp.org/

Society for the Psychological Study of Social Issues (SPSSI) (APA Division 9). http://www.spssi.org/

Society of Experimental Social Psychology. http://www.sesp.org

9.23. PSYCHOLOGY STUDENT ORGANIZATIONS

American Psychological Association of Graduate Students (APAGS). http://www.apa.org/apags/

Association for Psychological Science Student Caucus (APSSC). http://www.psychologicalscience.org/index.php/members/apssc

Psi Beta (Community College National Honor Society in Psychology). http://psibeta.org

Psi Chi, The National Honor Society in Psychology. http://www.psichi.org

9.24. RESEARCH METHODS AND STATISTICS

Quantitative and Qualitative Methods (APA Division 5). http://www.apadivisions.org/division-5/

9.25. SPECIFIC POPULATIONS

Intellectual and Developmental Disabilities/Autism Spectrum Disorders (APA Division 33). http://www.division33.org/

The International Psychology Network for Lesbian, Gay, Bisexual, Transgender and Intersex Issues (IPsyNet). http://www.apa.org/ipsynet/index.aspx

Society for the Psychological Study of Lesbian, Gay, Bisexual and Transgender Issues (APA Division 44). http://www.apadivisions.org/division-44/

Society for the Psychological Study of Men and Masculinity (APA Division 51). http://division51.net/

Society for the Psychology of Women (APA Division 35). http://www.apadivisions.org/division-35/

South Asian Psychological Networking Association (SAPNA) (South Asians and South Asian Americans). http://www.oursapna.org/oursapna.org/index.html

9.26. SPORT PSYCHOLOGY

Society for Sport, Exercise and Performance Psychology (APA Division 47).

http://www.apa.org/about/division/div47.aspx

9.27. TEACHING OF PSYCHOLOGY

Council on Undergraduate Research. http://www.cur.org

International Teaching of Psychology Network. http://interteachpsy.org/

Society for the Teaching of Psychology (APA Division 2). http://teachpsych.org

9.28. MISCELLANEOUS

American Psychology-Law Society (APA Division 41). http://www.apadivisions.org/division-41/

Cambridge Center for Behavioral Studies. http://www.behavior.org/index.php

Center for Open Science. https://cos.io/

European Brain and Behaviour Society. http://www.ebbs-science.org

http://www.apadivisions.org/division-47/

International Association for Cross-Cultural Psychology. http://www.iaccp.org/

International Association of Applied Psychology. http://www.iaapsy.org

International Psychology (APA Division 52). https://div52.org/

International Society for Ecological Psychology. http://www.trincoll.edu/depts/ecopsyc/isep

International Society for Research on Aggression. http://www.israsociety.com/

International Society of Political Psychology. http://ispp.org

International Union of Psychological Science. http://www.iupsys.net

Psychologists in Independent Practice (APA Division 42). http://division42.org/

Psychologists in Public Service (APA Division 18). http://www.apadivisions.org/division-18/

Rehabilitation Psychology (APA Division 22). https://division-rehabpsych.squarespace.com/

Society for Chaos Theory in Psychology and Life Sciences. http://www.societyforchaostheory.org

Society for Child and Family Policy and Practice (APA Division 37). http://www.apadivisions.org/division-37/

Society for Computers in Psychology. http://www.scip.ws

Society for Couple and Family Psychology (APA Division 43). http://www.apadivisions.org/division-43/

Society for Disability Studies. http://disstudies.org

Society for Environmental, Population and Conservation Psychology (APA Division 34). http://www.apadivisions.org/division-34/

Society for Judgment and Decision Making. http://www.sjdm.org

Society for Mathematical Psychology. http://www.mathpsych.org

Society for Media Psychology and Technology (APA Division 46).

Society for Military Psychology (APA Division 19). http://www.apadivisions.org/division-19/

Society for Psychophysiological Research. http://www.sprweb.org

Society for the Psychological Study of Culture, Ethnicity and Race (APA Division 45). http://division45.org/

Society for the Psychological Study of Social Issues. http://www.spssi.org

Society for the Psychology of Aesthetics, Creativity and the Arts (APA Division 10). http://www.div10.org/

Society for the Psychology of Religion and Spirituality (APA Division 36). http://www.apadivisions.org/division-36/

Society for the Study of Ingestive Behaviors. http://www.ssib.org/web

Society for the Study of Motivation. http://thessm.org

Society for the Study of Peace, Conflict and Violence: Peace Psychology Division (APA Division 48). http://peacepsychology.org/

Society for Theoretical and Philosophical Psychology (APA Division 24). http://www.theoreticalpsychology.org/

Society of Consulting Psychology (APA Division 13). http://societyofconsultingpsychology.org/

10
Style Guides and Related Resources

There is only one style manual used in psychology, which is currently in its sixth edition and commonly referred to as "the APA manual."

10.1. *Publication manual of the American Psychological Association* (6th ed.). American Psychological Association. (2010). Washington, DC: American Psychological Association. 272 pp. BF76.7 .P83 2010. The manual begins by covering writing for behavioral and social sciences, including types of articles, ethical and legal standards in research and publishing, and intellectual property rights. It also covers manuscript structure and content, concise writing, mechanics of style, results displays, crediting sources within text and in the reference list, and the publication process, and it contains many examples of correct and incorrect presentation. This and the other APA publications below are essential for undergraduates, graduate students, faculty, and beginning and advanced researchers writing in psychology.

10.2. *APA style guide to electronic references* (6th ed.). American Psychological Association. (2012). Washington, DC: American Psychological Association. 46 pp. Available only in electronic PDF format. Institutional purchases are made directly from the American Psychological Association. Individual purchases are made from Amazon Kindle. Covers online journal articles, data sets, measurement instruments, books, videos, apps, websites, podcasts, blog posts, and other social media.

10.3. *Concise rules of APA style* (6th ed.). American Psychological Association. (2010). Washington, DC: American Psychological Association. 280 pp. BF76.7 .C66 2010. This work targets only rules required for clear communication, including concise and bias-free writing; punctuation, spelling, and capitalization; italicizing and abbreviating; how to present numbers, metrics, and statistics; footnotes, appendices, and supplemental material; crediting sources; and reference examples.

10.4. *Displaying your findings: A practical guide for creating figures, posters, and presentations* (6th ed.). Nicol, A. A. M., & Pexman, P. M. (2010). Washington, DC: American Psychological Association. 191 pp. BF76.8 .N53 2010. Covers best practices in visual representations of data commonly used in presentations and poster sessions, including bar graphs, histograms, line graphs, plots, drawings, combination graphs, pie graphs, dendrograms, stem-and-leaf plots, charts, and photographs.

10.5. *Presenting your findings: A practical guide for creating tables* (6th ed.). Nicol, A. A. M., & Pexman, P. M. (2010). Washington, DC: American Psychological Association. 171 pp. HA31 .N53 2010. Provides guidance on the proper table format for a wide range of commonly used statistical analyses. Each statistic has its own chapter, and chapters are organized according to the complexity of the analysis.

10.6. *Reporting research in psychology: How to meet journal article reporting standards* (6th ed.). Cooper, H. M. (2011). Washington, DC: American Psychological Association. 137 pp. BF76.8 .C66 2011. Explains the need for transparent reporting and how to meet journal article reporting standards (JARS) and meta-analysis reporting standards (MARS). Examples from APA journals are included as illustrations of JARS and MARS.

The American Psychological Association (APA) also provides guidance on and examples of citations to print and electronic resources in its FAQs and blog on APA style. The FAQs page is located at http://www.apastyle.org/learn/faqs/index.aspx and covers general style information, references, punctuation, grammar and writing style, and formatting. The APA style blog is located at http://blog.apastyle.org/ and addresses style issues presented by guests that may or may not be covered in the APA manual and FAQs. Examples include how to cite Twitter, Facebook, and YouTube. Tags are on the right-hand side; once one clicks on a tag, a list of recent posts will appear beneath the tag list.

10.7. *Mastering APA style: Instructor's resource guide* (6th ed.). American Psychological Association. (2010). Washington, DC: American Psychological Association. 221 pp. BF76.8 2010. Provides guidance on how to incorporate student learning of APA style into the curriculum; includes multiple-choice assessments, correction keys and answer sheets on citation and references, grammar, headings, statistical presentation, italics, capitalization, number styles, and table formatting.

10.8. *Mastering APA Style: Student's workbook and training guide; [a hands-on guide for learning the style rules of the Publication Manual of the American Psychological Association]* (6th ed.). American Psychological Association. (2015). Washington, DC: American Psychological Association. 220 pp. BF76.8 2015. This student workbook can be used in a self-paced, self-taught manner or as part of organized instruction. Includes instruction exercises and practice tests on citation and references, grammar, headings, statistical presentation, italics, capitalization, number styles, and table formatting.

There are a number of print and electronic resources produced by other publishers that aim to simplify APA style, particularly for undergraduates.

10.9. APA style at OWL: Purdue Online Writing Lab. https://owl.english.purdue.edu/owl/section/2/10/. The OWL APA Overview and Workshop provides an overview of APA style and provides an annotated list of links to all of its APA material. The *OWL APA Formatting and Style Guide* offers examples of the general format of APA research papers, in-text citations, endnotes/footnotes, the reference page, and other components of an APA paper.

10.10. APA style essentials. Degelman, D. http://www.van guard.edu/psychology/faculty/douglas-degelman/apa -style/#title. This site covers a common core of elements of APA style that one can use as minimal standards for any assignment that specifies APA style (e.g., for an undergraduate course). It provides a link to a PDF; citation and reference examples; and links to images of format-related items such as title page, abstract, body, references, footnotes, tables, figures, and appendixes.

10.11. *Pocket guide to APA style* (5th ed.). Perrin, R. (2015). Stamford, CT: Cengage Learning. 181 pp. BF76.7 .P47 2015. Provides a concise treatment of the most common materials covered in the APA manual, but also includes advice on how to select a topic, components of the library, avoiding plagiarism, evaluating web resources, and citing various electronic resources. A particularly nice feature is the reference list entries for commonly used materials, conveniently located on the last page and back cover.

10.12. *Psychologist's companion: A guide to writing scientific papers for students and researchers* (5th ed.). Sternberg, R. J., & Sternberg, K. (2010). New York: Cambridge University Press. 366 pp. BF76. This work is aimed at undergraduates; graduate students; and more advanced researchers, faculty, and professionals who would like to improve their scientific writing. The fifth edition covers APA style and the entire research process, including the literature review, planning a study, and writing the paper/article. The sixth edition also contains new chapters on ethics and generating and selling ideas, writing book and grant proposals, and other new areas.

11
Diagnostic Manuals and Related Resources

INTRODUCTION

There are two diagnostic systems used in the classification of mental disorders. *The Diagnostic and Statistical Manual of Mental Disorders* (DSM), published by the American Psychiatric Association, has been used primarily in the United States. *The International Statistical Classification of Diseases and Related Health Problems* (ICD), produced by the World Health Organization (WHO), is primarily used in the rest of the world, although it has been used by Medicare and Medicaid in the United States for many years. In addition, mental health and disorders is only one component of the ICD; it covers all areas of health and disease. These manuals have been used by clinicians, researchers, psychiatric drug regulation agencies, health insurance companies, pharmaceutical companies, policy makers, and the legal system. In recent years, the US National Institute of Mental Health (NIMH) has also been engaged in early development of a biologically based system entitled Research Domain Criteria (RDoc).

11.1. *DIAGNOSTIC AND STATISTICAL MANUAL OF MENTAL DISORDERS*

As mentioned previously, the current version of the *Diagnostic and Statistical Manual of Mental Disorders* is DSM-5, published in May 2013.

11.1a. *Diagnostic and statistical manual of mental disorders* (5th ed.). American Psychiatric Association. (2013). Arlington, VA: American Psychiatric Association. 947 pp. RC455.2 C4 D54 2013. Highlights of changes from the DSM-IV-TR to the DSM-5 have been published by the American Psychiatric Association at http://www.dsm5 .org/Documents/changes from dsm-iv-tr to dsm-5.pdf.

What is the significance of changes in the DSM? In some instances, the changes are in terminology, rather than in criteria for diagnosis (e.g., "intellectual disability" replaces "mental retardation"). In other cases, there are changes in criteria, differentiation of a previous disorder into two or more disorders, collapse of two or more disorders into one disorder, and the addition and/or removal of entire disorders.

Previous versions of the DSM were IV-TR (2000), IV (1994), III-R (1987), III (1980), II (1958), and the original DSM (1952).

Although the ICD-10 was already in use in much of the world when the DSM-5 was published in 2013, the ICD-9 was still being used in the United States. Implementation of ICD-10 in the United States was not required until 2014, which was then extended to 2015. Cross-referencing between DSM-5 and the ICD, therefore, often includes both ICD-10 and ICD-9 codes.

The following are recent, well-reviewed, and noteworthy works on using the DSM-5:

11.1b. *DSM-5 essentials: The savvy clinician's guide to the changes in criteria.* Richenberg, L. W. (2014). Hoboken, NJ: Wiley. 116 pp. RC473.D54 R45 2014. Chapters cover the changes from DSM-IV-TR to DSM-5 in each diagnostic category and present tables with DSM-5, ICD-10, and ICD-9 codes.

11.1c. *DSM-5 guidebook: The essential companion to the Diagnostic and Statistical Manual of mental Disorders* (5th ed.). Black, D. W. (2014). Arlington, VA: American Psychiatric Association. 543 pp. RC455.2.C4 B52 2014. The appendix lists DSM-5 classifications with both ICD-9 and ICD-10 codes.

11.1d. *DSM-5 handbook of differential diagnosis.* First, M. B. (2014). Arlington, VA: American Psychiatric Association. 332 pp. RC473.D54 F554 2014. Appendix contains ICD-9 and ICD-10 codes for major disorders.

11.1e. *DSM-5 made easy: The clinician's guide to diagnosis.* Morrison, J. (2014). New York: Guilford Press. 652 pp. RC469 .M677 2014. ICD-10 and ICD-9 codes are presented with each diagnostic category.

11.1f. *Essentials of psychiatric diagnosis: Responding to the challenge of DSM-5* (rev. ed.). Frances, A. (2013).

New York: Guilford Press. 218 pp. RC473.D54 F74 2013b. The appendix cross-references diagnostic categories to ICD-10 and ICD-9.

11.2. *INTERNATIONAL CLASSIFICATION OF DISEASES AND RELATED HEALTH PROBLEMS*

The International Classification of Diseases and Related Health Problems (ICD) is the international standard used worldwide for morbidity and mortality statistics, reimbursement systems, and automated decision support in health care and is intended to enable international consistency in the collection, processing, classification, and presentation of health-care statistics. It is maintained by the World Health Organization, which is the directing and coordinating authority for health within the United Nations. As mentioned previously, the current edition is the ICD-10, which was released in 1992 but not required for widespread use in the United States until 2014 (later extended to 2015). The ICD-11 is expected to be available in 2018. The ICD is part of a "family" of guides that can be used together. The other two guides are *The International Classification of Functioning, Disability and Health* (ICF) and *The International Classification of Health Interventions* (ICHI). Minor updates to the ICD are made annually. The ICD-10 contains twenty-two "chapters"; mental and behavioral disorders are covered by chapter V and are available in print as *The ICD-10 Classification of Mental and Behavioural Disorders.*

11.2a. *The ICD-10 classification of mental and behavioural disorders: Clinical descriptions and diagnostic guidelines.* World Health Organization. (1992). Geneva, Switzerland: World Health Organization. 362 pp. RC455.2 .C4 I34.

11.2b An outline of chapter V can also be accessed at the following web address; the outline does not include the diagnostic guidelines provided in the print volume above: http://apps.who.int/classifications/icd10/browse/2016/en#/V.

Some countries have adapted the ICD to include more codes for classification of diagnostic and procedure codes. In the United States, the adaptation is created by the US National Center for Health Statistics (NCHS) to provide additional morbidity detail and is entitled *International Clas-sification of Diseases: Clinical Modification* (ICD-10-CM). It too is updated annually. A useful resource for US users of chapter V is *A Primer for ICD-10-CM Users.*

11.2c. *A primer for ICD-10-CM users: Psychological and behavioral conditions.* Goodheart, C. D. (2014). Washington, DC: American Psychological Association. 169 pp. RC455.2 C4 G662 2014.

11.3. RESEARCH DOMAIN CRITERIA

While the DSM has been recognized for standardizing diagnostic categories and criteria, it has also been subject to controversy and criticism, including criticism from the US National Institute of Mental Health (NIMH). Ongoing controversies and criticism include arguments that it is an unscientific and subjective system, questions about the reliability and validity of the diagnostic categories, its focus on superficial symptoms, arbitrary divisions among categories and from "normality," questions about cultural bias, and medicalization of human distress. An excellent review of these issues and those below can be found in *Making the DSM-5.*

11.3a. *Making the DSM-5: Concepts and controversies.* Paris, J., & Phillips, J. (Eds.). (2013). New York: Springer. 180 pp. RC438 .M35 2013.

In recent years, NIMH has been developing an alternative system to the DSM entitled Research Domain Criteria (RDoC). The strength of the DSM has been perceived as its diagnostic reliability, which is why it has been favored for clinical research, but it has been criticized regarding its validity. Unlike diagnostic systems in medicine, in which diagnoses are often based on objective laboratory or imaging technology, DSM categories are constructs based on consensus regarding clusters of clinical symptoms. The goal in developing the RDoC is to create a biologically valid framework for understanding mental disorders based on modern research in genetics, neuroscience, and behavioral science. At this time, the RDoC is in early development and is useful only in a research context. More information on the RDoC is located at https://www.nimh.nih.gov/research-priorities/rdoc/index.shtml and http://www.nimh.nih.gov/research-priorities/rdoc/rdoc-frequently-asked-questions-faq.shtml#1.

12

Career and Education Resources

INTRODUCTION

Students decide to major in psychology for many reasons, some evident, some not. But regardless of their reasons, at some point between declaring their majors and graduating with their baccalaureates, they start (or need to start!) thinking about what they will do with their degrees. If they plan to go to graduate school, it's important that they start planning for that in junior year in order to acquire the types of experiences and references that will make them competitive candidates for graduate programs. If they plan to enter the workforce, they will still want to acquire experiences and references that will make them competitive as new graduates in the workforce.

The purpose of many of the following resources is to guide undergraduates in exploring their education and career options, deciding what paths they wish to follow, and preparing them for success in reaching their goals. These are included in the first section.

Those who have decided to go to graduate school and have been successful in achieving that goal still have many tasks and choices before them. Most graduate programs in psychology require admission to the doctoral program in order to begin the master's program, and the culture, study, and work demands of these programs are often quite different than the student has experienced as an undergraduate. There is also the matter of navigating department politics, selecting an adviser, developing a thesis, selecting a committee, completing and defending the thesis, and then doing all of these steps again to complete a doctorate. Along the way, the student needs to make decisions that prepare him or her better for some career options than others.

Therefore, the purpose of other resources in this section is to provide graduate students with the information necessary to survive and thrive in their programs by identifying and providing guidance on the tasks and decisions involved in graduate work and to prepare them for success in their careers beyond graduate school. These resources are included in the third section.

There are also resources aimed at and/or useful to both undergraduates and graduate students. These are included in the second section, between sources aimed only at undergraduates and those aimed only at graduate students.

The fourth and last section covers major websites that list current openings; these are useful to both types of students to get a sense of what employers are looking for at any given time.

Resources included in this chapter are the latest edition available at the time of printing, generally were published after 2005, and are still in print. The few exceptions are unique in that their content or approach is not covered in more recent items. In addition, there are several resources for which new editions were scheduled for publication in late 2016 or in 2017; in these cases, the current edition is included, followed by a note indicating that a newer edition is scheduled and the expected year.

UNDERGRADUATE CAREER AND EDUCATION RESOURCES

Psychology as a Major

12.1. *Insider's guide to the psychology major: Everything you need to know about the degree and profession.* Wegenek, A. R., & Buskist, W. (2010). Washington, DC: American Psychological Association. 126 pp. BF80. A concise guide for the undergraduate student in psychology, this work begins by presenting information about psychology majors: common misperceptions among them, predictors of success, and where the previous year's graduates are one year after graduation. It goes on to cover making the most of resources and opportunities available to undergraduates, how one becomes a professional psychologist, occupations for those with a baccalaureate degree in psychology, and information about graduate school. A nice feature of this work is that each chapter contains "One Professional's Perspective" and "One Student's Perspective" exhibits and ends with "My

Proactive Plan Exercises." Appendix A lists major journals classified by the subdisciplines of psychology, which facilitates browsing journals of interest (electronically or in print), and appendix B presents major organizations hosting research conferences in the United States. A nice, concise, and readable work with some unique information for undergraduates.

12.2. *Psychology major's companion: Everything you need to know to get you where you want to go.* Dunn, D. S., & Halonen, J. S. (2017). New York: Worth. 238 pp. BF77. Designed for prospective and current undergraduates in psychology, the aim of this book is to help students map an education and career in psychology. It starts out with a nice chapter on what psychology is and is not, and chapters include "reality check" boxes to assist students in the decision-making process. It addresses what psychologists actually do, settings in which they do it, employment opportunities with the bachelor's degree, becoming a competitive applicant to graduate programs, and the advantages of being a psychology major beyond the curriculum and career.

12.3. *Psychology major's handbook* (4th ed.). Kuther, T. L. (2016). Boston: Cengage Learning. 276 pp. BF77. Now in its fourth edition, this book has become a must-have in the "psychology education and careers" literature for undergraduates in institutions with psychology undergraduate programs. In addition to covering the many subdisciplines of psychology and how to write a literature review and an empirical paper, which are covered elsewhere, this book asks pertinent questions of students and provides exercises to assist them in answering the questions for themselves. Examples include "Is Psychology Right for You?"; how to "Take an Active Role in Your Education"; "What Can I Do with a Bachelor's Degree in Psychology?"; and "What Can I Do with a Graduate Degree in Psychology?" Also included are "Finding a Job with Your Bachelor's Degree" and "Applying to Graduate School in Psychology." This book will be invaluable to undergraduates as well as to psychology faculty and should probably be required reading at some point in psychology undergraduate education.

12.4. *Student's guide to studying psychology* (4th ed.). Heffernan, T. M. (2016). London: Psychology Press. 223 pp. BF77. This work addresses how to optimize one's undergraduate experience as a psychology major. It provides an introduction to the field and the various perspectives within the discipline; a study guide on understanding the purpose of lectures, seminars, and tutorials; and a discussion of how to work and succeed in each. Also included is guidance to writing and referencing essay papers, research methods, research ethics, writing and referencing empirical reports, preparation for various types of examinations, and what to do after completion of the bachelor's degrees. A nice feature of this work is that it presents the full text of various types of papers, followed by a critical

assessment of the paper and specific strengths and weaknesses. It also explains what professors are looking for in papers and typical grading schemes.

12.5. *What psychology majors could (and should) be doing: An informal guide to research experience and professional skills.* Silvia, P. J., Delaney, P. F., & Marcovitch, S. (2009). Washington, DC: American Psychological Association. 167 pp. BF76. A concise, practical, and easy-to-read book that explains why it is important (and fun) for undergraduates to immerse themselves in psychology outside of the curriculum by getting involved in research as early as possible. It explains the challenges and enjoyment of working with faculty and graduate students and connecting their course learning to the practice of psychology as a science. It covers collecting and analyzing data, learning how to utilize primary research, and how to write research papers, as well as information on attending academic conferences, presenting a poster presentation, and giving a research presentation. A very useful book for undergraduates at any point in their education, but particularly in early years to give more focus to their education.

Employment with a Bachelor's Degree in Psychology

12.6. *Finding jobs with a psychology bachelor's degree: Expert advice for launching your career.* Landrum, R. E. (2009). Washington, DC: American Psychological Association. 158 pp. BF76. The purpose of this book is to advise students graduating with a baccalaureate in psychology on how to market themselves to employers using the knowledge, skills, and abilities (KSAs) they have developed through their undergraduate programs. Part I covers what KSAs the APA expects graduating psychology students to have and what employers want from such graduates. Also included are tools to classify job titles and personal preferences and the US Department of Labor, Employment and Training Administration's Occupational Information Network (O*NET) job titles. Part II presents profiles and interviews of psychology graduates describing their early, mid-level, and later career choices and a summary of themes and advice from the profiles. Part III provides general guidance on job searching as well as psychology-specific guidance, and Part IV presents the study that led to the creation of this book. This book will be useful to students graduating with a bachelor's degree and entering the workforce as well as to faculty and college/university career center advisers.

12.7. *Majoring in psych? Career options for psychology undergraduates* (5th ed.). Morgan, B. L., & Korschgen, A. J. (2014). Boston: Pearson. 144 pp. BF76. Provides answers to questions from many undergraduates in an easy-to-read, conversational style. Questions addressed include whether one should major in psychology, what careers are available for psychology majors, how to explore careers and enhance employability, salaries, whether one should apply to and how to prepare for graduate school, and how to do a job search. The chapter on careers includes information such as job titles, work tasks, work settings, salary potential and projected demand, qualities of the job that employees tend to like and dislike, and personal qualities that match the job best. Each chapter ends with a "Great Resources!" box, which typically includes print materials and at least one helpful website.

12.8. *Your undergraduate degree in psychology: From college to career*. Hettich, P. I., & Landrum, R. E. (2014). Los Angeles, CA: Sage. 289 pp. BF76. This work is aimed at students graduating with a bachelor's degree in psychology and seeking employment. It begins by providing recent information about the workplace, careers available to those with a bachelor's degree in psychology, and a number of brief questionnaires to assist the reader in determining what type of career best suits him or her. It then provides advice on understanding what unique knowledge, skills, and abilities (KSAs) the psychology graduate possesses that other majors don't and the various resources available to the graduate: career center, faculty, continuing education and skills training, job-shadowing, and workplace-specific courses and training. Also covered is how to organize oneself for job seeking, including résumés, organizing references, keeping track of applications and contacts, and what to do after one has landed the first job.

Career Opportunities in Psychology

12.9. *Careers in mental health: Opportunities in psychology, counseling, and social work*. Metz, K. (2016). Chichester, England: John Wiley & Sons. 180 pp. RA790. This work is organized by the types of degrees and/or other certifications one might acquire to work in the mental health field. It covers PhDs and PsyDs in clinical and counseling psychology, master's in social work (MSW), master's in counseling, master's in marriage and family therapy (MFT), substance abuse/chemical dependency credentials, and school psychology degrees. For each credential, it covers the overall history and philosophy of the profession, education, licensing, types of careers for which the credential qualifies one, and earning potential. It also addresses why one should or should not choose a mental health career, critical thinking skills required, ethics, how to increase the probability of getting into a graduate program, and postdegree issues such as continuing education and malpractice. This work is particularly valuable in that it includes nonpsychology programs and credentials that an undergraduate psychology major might pursue.

12.10. *Careers in psychology: Opportunities in a changing world* (4th ed.). Kuther, T. L., & Morgan, R. D. (2013). Belmont, CA: Wadsworth/Cengage Learning. 218 pp. BF76. The first chapter describes the overall discipline of psychology, then provides advice on selecting a major

and a checklist to determine if psychology is the right major for the reader. Each of the following chapters addresses subdisciplines of psychology (clinical, counseling, school, health, sport, experimental, cognitive, quantitative, social, consumer, and developmental psychology; law and psychology; biopsychology, cognitive neuroscience, and clinical neuropsychology; and industrial/organizational psychology and human factors). These chapters describe the subdiscipline, provide information on career opportunities with a bachelor's degree and opportunities with a graduate degree, salary information, a career profile of an individual working in that field, a "Is this area for you?" checklist, suggested readings, and websites. The last two chapters address "out of the box" careers for those with a graduate degree in psychology and getting into graduate school. This valuable work is primarily addressed to undergraduates, but also contains some information of interest to graduate students.

12.11. *Guidebook to human service professions: Helping college students explore opportunities in the human services field* (2nd ed.). Emener, W. G., Richard, M. A., & Bosworth, J. J. (Eds.). (2009). Springfield, IL: Charles C. Thomas. 264 pp. HV10. Explores human service professions in which undergraduate psychology students may be interested, including applied anthropology; audiology; speech-language pathology; case management; clinical, counseling, school, and industrial/organizational psychology; college student development; criminal justice; gerontology; marriage and family therapy; mediation; mental health, school, and rehabilitation counseling; public administration; social work; and special education. Each chapter includes an introduction to the field, history and development, mission and objectives, typical clientele, philosophical assumptions and theories, applications in the real world, salary information, professional preparation and development, work settings, professional organizations, future outlook for the profession, and references. As professional positions in these fields generally require postbaccalaureate degrees, part III also provides information on occupations in these fields that only require the baccalaureate.

12.12. *Life as a psychologist: Career choices and insights*. Oster, G. D. (2006). Westport, CT: Praeger. 159 pp. BF76. In this volume working psychologists describe the various career paths that they followed and what they learned along the way. Early chapters cover the expanding role of psychology in the twenty-first century and how to decide if psychology is the career that will meet one's personal and professional needs. It also covers the graduate school application process, including how to research graduate schools, practical considerations, and questions one should ask. It ends with essays by prominent psychologists on meaningful careers and lessons learned. This book would be useful to any undergraduate collection in psychology.

12.13. *Opportunities in psychology careers* (rev. ed.). Super, C. M., & Super, D. E. (2009). New York: McGraw-Hill. 149 pp. BF76. Aimed at high school students and undergraduates, this work provides a brief examination of psychology as a science, a profession, an academic pursuit, an instructional field, and a public debate. It describes the various areas of psychology; education and training in psychology; and employment prospects for those with bachelor's, master's, and doctoral degrees. It also lists professional organizations and licensing and certification boards and provides advice on planning a career in psychology.

12.14. *Psychology major: Career options and strategies for success* (5th ed.). Landrum R. E., & Davis, S. F. (2014). Boston: Pearson. 198 pp. BF76. This work begins by addressing very basic issues, such as who goes to college, student and employer expectations of graduates, and the benefits of going to college. It then covers the same issues regarding being a psychology major. Subsequent chapters cover careers with the bachelor's, master's, and doctoral degrees; the graduate admissions process; research and teaching assistantships; internships and organizations; sharpening library and research skills; APA style; study tips; ethics in psychology; and related fields for psychology majors. Some nice features of this work are the "success stories" boxes; sample résumés and action verbs for résumés; strategies for securing strong letters of recommendation and sample recommendation letters; interviewing advice, including questions likely to be asked in an interview and sample questions to ask a potential employer; top characteristics for graduate school success; salary information; how to decode graduate school information; how to narrow the list of potential graduate schools; writing the personal statement and samples of statements; and behaviors one should not engage in as an undergraduate.

12.15. *Your career in psychology: Clinical and counseling psychology*. Kuther, T. L. (2006). Belmont, CA: Thomson/Wadsworth. 134 pp. RC467. Provides an introduction to clinical and counseling psychology and the differences between them, as well as the distinctions among psychiatry, social work, and counseling. Covers the activities and employment settings of practicing clinical and counseling psychologists, including college and university counseling centers, community mental health centers, and hospitals. Also covers careers in public health, program development, military psychology, forensic and police psychology, consulting, and academia. It also covers graduate training at the master's and doctoral levels for such careers. Each chapter includes the advantages and disadvantages of that type of work and ends with suggested readings, web resources, and career profiles of one or two psychologists. Although not a very recent publication, this work provides undergraduates with a good overview of various careers in clinical and counseling psychology.

12.16. *Your career in psychology: Industrial/organizational psychology*. Kuther, T. L. (2005). Belmont, CA: Thomson/Wadsworth. 84 pp. BF76. Provides an introduction to three areas of work psychology: industrial psychology, organizational psychology, and human factors. Covers the activities and employment settings of practicing in these areas, including human resources, consulting, product development and environmental design, and academia and research. Each chapter covers different career paths within that area and ends with suggested readings, web resources, and career profiles of one or two psychologists. Although not a very recent publication, this work gives undergraduates a good overview of various careers in industrial, organizational, and human factors psychology.

12.17. *Your career in psychology: Psychology and the law*. Kuther, T. L. (2004). Belmont, CA: Thomson/Wadsworth. 88 pp. RA1148. Covers various careers in forensic psychology, including forensic evaluation, research and treatment in criminal and civil law, public policy and advocacy, correctional and police psychology, trial consulting, expert witness testimony, and social activism as a congressional fellow or staff member or as a political consultant. It also covers graduate training at the master's and doctoral levels for such careers. Each chapter includes the advantages and disadvantages of that type of work and ends with suggested readings, web resources, and career profiles of one or two forensic psychologists. Although not a very recent publication, this work provides undergraduates with a good overview of various forensic psychology careers.

Applying to Graduate School in Psychology

12.18. *Applying to graduate school in psychology: Advice from successful students and prominent psychologists*. Kracen, A. C., & Wallace, I. J. (Eds.). (2008). Washington, DC: American Psychological Association. 235 pp. BF77. This book is unique in that the chapters were written by nine current graduate students. Chapters begin with information about the graduate student (where born, where reared, current graduate program and university, previous degree[s], number of graduate schools to which he or she applied, age when starting graduate program, professional interests, and career aspirations). Chapters include an overview of psychology, life as a graduate student, financial considerations in pursuing a graduate degree in psychology, finding the right "fit" of graduate schools, the application process, strengthening the application, campus visits/interviewing, fielding offers and making a final decision, and what one should do if not accepted into a program. Each chapter is also followed by an essay written by contemporary professional leaders in the field of psychology. This book will be valuable to any student interested in applying to graduate school in psychology.

12.19. *Getting in: A step-by-step plan for gaining admission to graduate school in psychology* (2nd ed.). American Psychological Association. (2007). Washington, DC: American Psychological Association. 230 pp. BF80. A well-organized and direct presentation of useful processes and practices in which anyone considering graduate school in psychology should engage. Although some of the data in this book are outdated, the guidance about deciding if graduate school is even the right decision, whether one is a competitive candidate, the costs involved in applying as well as attending, and how to work through the multiple decision processes (should one apply, to what programs, and if one is fortunate enough to be accepted by several, which to attend) is useful. Invaluable worksheets provided throughout stand the test of time. There are worksheets for application timetables, checklists for each application, worksheets for listing program requirements, strengths and weaknesses of programs for the particular candidate, questions the candidate will likely be asked in interviews, questions the candidate should ask, and more. A valuable resource for anyone considering attending graduate school in psychology as well as other disciplines.

Directories of Graduate Programs in Psychology

12.20. *Directory of graduate programs in applied sport psychology* (5th ed.). Sachs, M. L., Burke, K. L., & Schweighardt, S. L. (2011). Madison, WI: Association for Applied Sport Psychology. 318 pp. GV365. Provides information on graduate programs in applied sport psychology in the United States, Canada, South Africa, Australia, and the United Kingdom. For each program, it provides a contact name, e-mail address, telephone and fax numbers, web address, and a list of faculty with their individual interests. Also included are the degree(s) offered, the number of students who apply each year and the number accepted, number of students in the program, admissions requirements, financial support, research and teaching assistantships, internship opportunities, and comments. The introductory chapters provide an overview of the field, covering careers in sport psychology, certification/licensure, different program models, and being a wise consumer in selecting programs for application and acceptance, and also include questions the applicant should ask himself or herself and the program(s) of interest. The appendices also provide valuable information such as related programs, internships, books and articles on applied sport psychology, references on professional and ethical issues, and quick charts of information located within the main body. A very useful work for anyone wishing to explore education and careers in this area.

12.21. *Graduate study in psychology*. American Psychological Association. (2016–). Washington, DC: American Psychological Association. 1385 pp. BF77. Published annually, this work provides comprehensive information about approximately 600 graduate programs in psychology in the United States and Canada. The following information is provided for all programs: number of applications received, number of individuals accepted, dates for applications and admission, types of information required for an application (GRE scores, letters of recommendation, documentation concerning volunteer or clinical experience, etc.), in-state and out-of-state tuition costs, availability of internships and scholarships, employment information for graduates, and orientation and emphasis of departments and programs. Other relevant information includes department demographics, housing and day care, special facilities or resources, and information for students with physical disabilities. This work should be in every library and be consulted by anyone considering graduate programs in the United States or Canada.

12.22. *Insider's guide to graduate programs in clinical and counseling psychology 2016–2017*. Norcross, J. C., & Sayette, M. A. (2016). New York: Guilford Press. 442 pp. RC467. This biennial guide offers comprehensive information on more than 300 APA- and PCSAS-accredited clinical and counseling programs and how best to prepare for graduate school in these areas. There is an excellent section on various types of accreditation as well as a chapter on choosing the PhD or the PsyD and the salient differences between the two types of education and training. Also covered is preparation for graduate school, including coursework, faculty mentoring, clinical and/or research skills, extracurricular activities, and entrance exams. The chapter on starting the application specifically addresses issues of potential interest to racial/ethnic minority, LGBTQ, disabled, and international applicants. Other topics covered include selecting schools to which one might apply, applying to programs, the interview, and making the final decision, as well as what to do if not accepted into any programs. The appendices, with timelines for the process, worksheets for choosing programs, assessing program criteria, and making final choices, will be very helpful to anyone going through this process.

Career and Education Resources for Both Undergraduate and Graduate Students

12.23. *Career paths in psychology: Where your degree can take you* (3rd ed.). Sternberg, R. J. (Ed.). (2017). Washington, DC: American Psychological Association. 523 pp. BF76. This work identifies thirty areas in which doctoral level (PhD, PsyD, or EdD) psychologists work and is divided into three major sections: academia, clinical and counseling psychology, and specialized settings. The section on academia includes teaching not only in psychology departments, but also in schools of education, business, medicine, law, and public policy. The section on clinical and counseling psychology covers practice in general, private practice, child and geropsychology, neuropsychology, and psychologists specializing in psychopharmacology and rehabilitation.

The section on specialized settings covers working in hospitals, public service such as policy research, government careers, school and industrial and organizational settings, media and publishing, business consulting, military psychology, health psychology, and test development. Each chapter covers the career itself, how to prepare for it, typical activities in the career, financial compensation, advantages and disadvantages, and opportunities for advancement.

12.24. *How to be a researcher: A strategic guide for academic success.* Evans, J. St. B. (2016). East Sussex, England: Routledge. 162 pp. BF442. This guide is aimed at advanced undergraduates, graduate students, and even early-career faculty. It focuses on topics such as scholarship and the origin of ideas, literature reviews, designing empirical studies, research support and funding, collaboration and supervision, communication of one's work, and how to publish in the best venues.

12.25. *Your practicum in psychology: A guide for maximizing knowledge and competence* (2nd ed.). Matthews, J. R., & Walker, C. E. (Eds.). (2015). Washington, DC: American Psychological Association. 256 pp. RC467. This guide is aimed at both undergraduate and graduate students to assist them in understanding the practicum experience. It addresses what one can expect in a practicum, characteristics of the helping relationship, rapport with clients, confidentiality and other ethical issues, psychopathology and the use of the *Diagnostic and Statistical Manual of Mental Disorders*, psychological assessment, evidence-based interventions, medication, and special issues involved in working with children and older persons. The last chapter addresses the various other types of mental health professionals with whom students may work in their practicum, such as social workers, psychiatrists, and counselors, and the role of each.

GRADUATE STUDENT CAREER AND EDUCATION RESOURCES

Graduate School

12.26. *Entering the behavioral health field: A guide for new clinicians.* Suffridge, D. A. (2016). New York: Routledge. 258 pp. RC454. This book is aimed at new clinicians in behavioral health as practiced in community-based organizations. It is also aimed at supervisors and faculty to assist them with teaching the application of theoretical and academic knowledge to clinical work as a therapist or case manager. Chapters focus on personal preparation, professional preparation, the first session, cultural issues, assessment and diagnosis, special situations in assessment, case formulation and treatment planning, the therapeutic relationship, case documentation and management, planned and unplanned termination, and the development of professional identity.

12.27. *Getting the most out of clinical training and supervision: A guide for practicum students and interns.* Falender, C. A., & Shafranske, E. P. (2012). Washington, DC: American Psychological Association. 304 pp. RA972. This work aims to help graduate students and interns optimize their clinical supervision experience through increasing understanding of both the therapy process and the supervision process. Part I covers competency-based supervision and both supervisor and supervisee expectations of supervision. Part II focuses on the therapeutic process, with "reflection activities" for the supervisee to contemplate and presumably discuss with the supervisor. Part III returns more specifically to the supervision process and is followed by competency benchmarks for readiness for practicum, readiness for internship and readiness for entry to practice, a practicum competencies outline, and a questionnaire on practices and beliefs vis-à-vis working with clients who are ethnically/racially different than the supervisee. Particularly valuable is the guidance on how to handle problems in supervision. For graduate students in or practitioners of clinical/counseling/school psychology as well as social work and other fields.

12.28. *Internships in psychology: The APAGS workbook for writing successful applications and finding the right fit* (3rd ed.). Williams-Nickelson, C., Prinstein, M. J., & Keilin, W. G. (2013). Washington, DC: American Psychological Association. 120 pp. BF77. This work breaks down into manageable parts and thoroughly covers the APPIC Uniform Application and how to carefully answer each question. It provides advice on matching; number of applications; tracking hours; writing the curriculum vita; interviewing; addressing autobiographical, theoretical orientation, diversity, and research experiences in the personal statement; creating a rank order list; recommendation letters; and the interview. The book ends with FAQs (frequently asked questions). A highly valuable resource for doctoral students applying to accredited internship sites.

12.29. *School psychology practicum and internship handbook.* Joyce-Beaulieu, D., & Rossen, E. A. (2016). New York: Springer. 233 pp. LB3013. Provides guidance to graduate students in school psychology on both basics of practica and internships and how to optimize both experiences. The first section deals with practica and includes professional issues vignettes, security procedures, student liability insurance, client-contact issues, demonstration of knowledge and skills, supervisor-supervisee conflict, peer mentoring, research considerations in practica settings, and classification systems other than the DSM. The second section deals with internships and includes writing the curriculum vita, the application process, personal statement, recommendation letters, documentation, time management, boundaries, transitioning to the professional role, evaluation measures and competencies, ethics, conflicts in laws or agency rules, report writing, and preparing for the postgraduate career. This work will be valuable to all graduate students in school psychology.

12.30. *Surviving graduate school in psychology: A pocket mentor.* Kuther, T. L. (2008). Washington, DC: American Psychological Association. 269 pp. BF77. Covers a range of topics on surviving graduate school: finding a residence, graduate assistantships, money and time management, understanding how graduate school is different from the undergraduate experience, peer and mentor relationships, department politics, personal relationships, practica and internships, teaching, dissertation work, and socialization as a professional. At the end of each chapter there are recommended readings. Valuable for graduate students in any area of psychology.

12.31. *Trainee handbook: A guide for counseling & psychotherapy trainees* (3rd ed.). Bor, R., & Watts, M. (Eds.). (2011). Thousand Oaks, CA: Sage. 382 pp. RC495. This work begins laying the groundwork for the trainee by defining "profession" and briefly covering professional ethics, cooperative inquiry between the clinician and client, statutory regulation, increased association of psychology with medicine, and rationing of services. It then goes on to cover effective writing; handling referrals; assessing new clients; case formulation; written communication; writing case studies and reports; optimizing the supervision experience and personal therapy; and planning, conducting, and reporting on research. It also includes a primer on psychopharmacology, a trainee's perspective and tips, and advice on job preparation. Each chapter contains boxes with helpful questions, checklists, and examples. This work will be helpful to students entering any form of traineeship. **NOTE:** the fourth revised edition is expected to be published in late 2016.

12.32. *Your graduate training in psychology: Effective strategies for success.* Giordano, P. J., Davis, S. F., & Licht, C. A. (2012). Thousand Oaks, CA: Sage. 326 pp. BF77. Twenty-five chapters offer current and incoming master's and doctoral students in psychology practical advice for surviving and thriving in graduate school. Section I covers settling in, relationships with peers and faculty, considerations for ethnic/racial minority, special needs, international and older nontraditional students, and self-care. Section II covers development and maturation in writing, teaching, research, presentation, and clinical/counseling skills and applying for research funding. Section III covers winding down in graduate school and winding up for professional employment: working with the dissertation committee, career planning, ABD status, and applying for clinical and academic positions. Valuable to graduate students in all areas of psychology as well as other disciplines.

The Dissertation

12.33. *Dissertations and theses from start to finish: Psychology and related fields.* Cone, J. D., & Foster, S. L. (2006). Washington, DC: American Psychological Association. 375 pp. BF76. A step-by-step guide to beginning, working through, and completing what can seem a monumental task. The first, brief chapter provides an explanation of the dissertation and its function. The remaining thirteen chapters address steps in the dissertation process, beginning with assessing one's preparedness to begin, time management, deciding upon a topic, advisers and faculty collaborators, literature review, methodology, measures, statistics, data collection and analysis, the committee, and further presentation. Chapters end with suggested further readings and a to-do list. The appendix contains selected ethical standards relevant to the conduct of research in psychology, which are adapted from APA's "Ethical Principles of Psychologists and Code of Conduct." This would be a useful book for any graduate student in psychology to keep on the desk while working on his or her dissertation.

Career after Graduate School

12.34. *Portable mentor: Expert guide to a successful career in psychology* (2nd ed.). Prinstein, M. J. (2013). New York: Springer. 370 pp. BF76. Although the book is aimed at graduate students and early career psychologists, part I covers the decision to apply to graduate school and becoming a successful applicant, so it also has some interest for undergraduates, who may be interested in both the early chapters and the later chapters. Part II ("Beginning Your Career") covers information that will be valuable during the graduate school career and afterward, including the scientist-practitioner model, cultural competence, developing and practicing ethics, and balancing career and family. Part III ("Your Research/Academic Career") also addresses issues of importance both in graduate school and afterward, including writing literature reviews, presenting and publishing one's research, writing reviews, and teaching in psychology. Part IV ("Your Career as a Practitioner") addresses issues particular to clinical, counseling, and school psychologists, including internships, supervision, licensing, and private practice. Part V ("Your Professional Service Career") covers involvement in professional organizations, career advancement, advocacy, and interactions with news media. Part VI covers postdoctoral fellowships, applying for NIH grants, the job search, and employment trends and salaries in psychology. This work will be highly valuable to both graduate students and early career psychologists as well as the more experienced psychologists who mentor them.

12.35. *Practicing psychology in primary care.* Searight, H. R. (2010). Cambridge, MA: Hogrefe. 159 pp. RC467. A practical guide for psychologists entering positions in primary care settings. The early chapters describe the patients and the culture of primary care, which is very different from the culture for which psychologists are trained and oriented. Subsequent chapters focus on the efficiency demands of primary care and population-oriented interventions, counseling for health risk behaviors, assessing and addressing patient motivation, motivational interviewing, primary care approaches to psychosocial problems, problem solving and acceptance and commitment therapy, and cross-cultural issues in primary care. The topics there are patients, physician colleagues, applied epidemiology, brief assessment, and population-oriented intervention. Then the author looks at specific interventions that are suited to the environment, among them brief counseling, motivational interviewing, primary care approaches to psychosocial problems, problem-solving therapy, and cross-cultural issues. A pragmatic and valuable source for psychologists considering or working in primary care settings.

12.36. *Psychology 101 1/2: The unspoken rules for success in academia* (2nd ed.). Sternberg, R. J. (2017). Washington, DC: American Psychological Association. 294 pp. BF77. This book is aimed at those considering or in early employment in academia. It consists of 101½ lessons, including how to deal with important issues such as deciding what is important, nipping problems in the bud, getting "it" in writing, avoiding defensiveness and making friends in the field, creating opportunities, not taking oneself too seriously, accepting losses graciously, loyalty, maintaining one's reputation, letting others do your bragging for you, realizing that this too shall pass, and redefining yourself (more than once!). Lessons are those learned through the author's long career and are described in a conversational tone. A helpful work for anyone in academia.

12.37. *Your career in psychology: Putting your graduate degree to work.* Davis, S. F., Giordano, P. J., & Licht, C. A. (Eds.). (2009). Chichester, England: Wiley-Blackwell. 306 pp. BF76. This work actually begins with advice to the beginning graduate student about issues to think about from the beginning of graduate school, dealing with student loans, and taking care of oneself. Advice on academic careers also begins in graduate school, focusing on relationships with the adviser and chair and moving on to the application and interview process and being a good member of the department after being hired at both teaching and research institutions. It then goes on to present special considerations for psychologists in clinical/coun-

seling/school, forensic, industrial/organizational, neuropsychology, and other specialties. Valuable to graduate students in all areas of psychology.

12.38. *You've earned your doctorate in psychology—now what? Securing a job as an academic or professional psychologist.* Morgan, E. M., & Landrum, R. E. (2012). Washington, DC: American Psychological Association. 190 pp. BF76. Providing advice based on evidence and best practices, this work covers identifying career options; utilizing one's network; preparing one's CV; securing strong recommendation letters; research, teaching, and practice portfolios; preparation for phone, video, and in-person academic and professional interviews; and examples of and strategies for dealing with illegal questions. A nice component is the "from the trenches" box, which appears throughout the book and features firsthand experience and advice from both applicants and employers. Sample recommendation letters and interview schedules as well as other illustrations add to the text. A valuable resource for graduate students in any area of psychology.

12.39. WEBSITES LISTING CURRENT POSITION OPENINGS

A good way to check out available careers is to explore position postings, even if one is not currently applying for a position. It provides a nice snapshot of what degrees and knowledge, skills, and abilities employers are seeking. Most of the positions posted at these websites required the doctoral degree or that one be all-but-dissertation (ABD).

APA online classified ads (PsycCareers). http://www.psyc-careers.com/. Contains advertisements from the monthly *APA Monitor.* Organized by state or country, it includes clinical, academic, business, and other opportunities. Most positions require a PhD, but it is useful for undergraduates to get a sense of career opportunities at that level.

Chronicle careers. http://chronicle.com/jobs/. Contains advertisements from the current edition of the *Chronicle of Higher Education.*

HigherEdJobs. http://www.higheredjobs.com/. Lists college and university positions, including academic, clinical/counseling, and miscellaneous positions.

13

Book Reviews

Book reviews can be highly useful to psychology faculty, students, general readers, and librarians responsible for collection development of psychology materials. There are a few issues to consider about any book review, but before addressing those, a major caveat in utilizing book reviews for any purpose is that *most books do not get reviewed*! This means that the user is more susceptible to negative error than to positive error. One is likely to be satisfied with a book about which one has read one or more positive reviews, particularly detailed reviews from credible sources, avoiding positive error (in this case reading, purchasing, or selecting a book erroneously). One is more susceptible, however, to negative error; in this case, the negative error being not selecting or even being aware of a book's existence, even though it would be highly useful to the user, because it hasn't been reviewed.

Some reviews are done for publications whose primary business is book reviews. Examples include *CHOICE*, *Book Review Digest*, *Kirkus Reviews*, and *New York Review of Books*. Most major newspapers also have a book review section, typically published on a specific day, often the Sunday edition. Scholarly journals often review books in their subject area, and particular disciplines may have a journal dedicated to reviewing books in the discipline.

BOOK REVIEW ORGANIZATIONS/PUBLISHERS

13.1. *CHOICE Reviews*. Association of College and Research Libraries (ACRL). (serial, 1964–). Chicago: ACRL, a division of American Library Association. Pagination varies. Z1035. Electronic subscription is also available at http://www.choicereviews.org. *CHOICE* is a publication of ACRL dedicated primarily to providing academic librarians with the reviews, tools, and services necessary to make optimal collection development decisions. It has been in existence since 1964, and is used by more than 18,000 librarians, faculty members, and key material decision makers. *CHOICE* reviews are as-signed and organized primarily by Library of Congress (LC) call number, but with broad topical headings as well (e.g., psychology), making it easy for faculty or others interested in a particular discipline to use. Reviews are typically done by academics with expertise on the topic and will often compare the title at hand with other similar or complementary titles published in the past or concurrently. Recommendation categories include recommended, highly recommended, essential, recommended with reservations, optional, and not recommended. Reviews also indicate the audience for the book, including general audience, lower-level undergraduate, upper-level undergraduate, graduate students, faculty, researchers, or all readers. *CHOICE* also reviews public and subscription websites and other electronic products. Approximately 600 titles are reviewed each month. In addition to books/websites/other electronic resource reviews, *CHOICE* also publishes "Outstanding Academic Titles" (OAT) for each year, covering about 10 percent of the approximately 7,000 titles reviewed each year. The award of "Outstanding Academic Title" is based on overall excellence in scholarship, importance in the context of other literature on the subject, distinction as a first work on a given topic, originality or uniqueness of approach, value to undergraduate students, and importance in building undergraduate library collections. *CHOICE* also publishes bibliographic essays, which may address a new topic, a topic about which interest has increased, an interdisciplinary area, or a topic in which there has been substantial growth in the scholarly literature. Book selection products/databases such as *Books in Print* and *GOBI* also have links to *CHOICE* reviews if available.

13.2. PsycCRITIQUES was an electronic book review continuation of the print journal *Contemporary Psychology*, a bimonthly periodical dedicated to book reiews of scholarly works related to psychology published from 1956 through 2004 (the journal was also known as *APA Review of Books*). PsycCRITIQUES was discontinued in December 2017. The archives of both PsycCRITIQUES and *Contemporary Psychology* are available via the Cummings Center for the History of Psychology at the University of Akron at http://cdm15960.contentdm.oclc.org/cdm/landingpage/collection/p15960coll21

13.3. *Doody's Reviews*. http://www.doody.com. (1993–). Book reviews on health-related books, including those in psychology. Each year subject experts review approximately 3,000 book and software titles from over 250 of the world's leading publishers of professional-level, health-care-related publications. Like *CHOICE* reviews, Doody's reviews are typically available through book selection products such as *Books in Print* and *GOBI*.

13.4. *American Reference Books Annual (ARBA)*. Various editors. (annual, 1970–). Santa Barbara, CA: Libraries Unlimited. Various pagination. Z1035 1. Chapters are organized by discipline, and it contains reviews of small numbers of selected dictionaries, encyclopedias, handbooks, and yearbooks on psychology published during the previous year. It is also available electronically by subscription at http://www.arbaonline.com/.

13.5. *New York Review of Books*. Silvers, R. B., & Epstein, B. (dec.). (serial, 1963–). Publisher varies. Pagination varies. Z1219. Also available by subscription at http://www.nybooks.com. This serial (aka NYRB) is published twenty times per year. In the area of psychology, it reviews scholarly works intended for a high-level general audience.

13.6. *Kirkus Reviews*. Kirkus Service. (serial, 1933–). New York: Kirkus Media. Pagination varies. Z477. Also freely available at http://www.kirkusreviews.com and by subscription via several database vendors. This serial is published biweekly and has undergone several title changes; it was previously known as *Virginia Kirkus Service*, *Kirkus Service*, and *Jim Koback's Kirkus Reviews*. In the area of psychology, it primarily reviews nonfiction, research-based books in psychology intended for a general and/or undergraduate audience.

INDEXES/ABSTRACTS/BIBLIOGRAPHIES OF BOOK REVIEWS

13.7. *Book Review Digest*. H. W. Wilson Company. (serial, 1905–). New York: H. W. Wilson Company. Pagination varies. Z1219. Electronic version also available from 1983 onward. Provides excerpts and citations to over 5,000 reviews from more than 100 American, Canadian, and British journals per year. *Book Review Digest* covers all topics, fiction and nonfiction, scholarly and popular,

adult and children's literature; as such, it would not be the first source for finding reviews of scholarly works in psychology.

13.8. *Book Review Index*. Gale Gengage. (serial, 1965–). Farmington Hills, MI: Cengage Learning. Various pagination. Z1035 A1. Available in print or as a subscription electronic product. Citations to over 5.6 million reviews of over 2.5 million titles published since 1965. Indexes book reviews from thousands of primarily North American, primarily general interest and book review publications. Like *Book Review Digest*, this would not be the first source for finding reviews of scholarly works in psychology.

13.9. *International Bibliography of Book Reviews* (*Internationale Bibliographie der Rezensionen geistes- und sozialwissenschaftlicher Literatur*) (*IBR*). http://www.degruyter.com/databasecontent?dbid=ibr&dbsource=/db/ibr. (serial, 1983–). Osnabruck, Germany: F. Dietrich. Contains over 1.57 million citations to book reviews from 1983 to the present. Some 60,000 new reviews from 6,200 primarily European academic journals are added each year. The print version extends back to 1971. This work has had a number of previous titles, including *Bibliographie der Rezensionen* (1921–1943), *Bibliographie der Rezensionen und Referate* (1915–1921), *Bibliographie der Rezensionen* (1911–1914), and *Bibliographie der Deutschen Rezensionen* (1900–1911).

13.10. *JSTOR*. https://www.jstor.org/. New York: Ithaka. *JSTOR* is a subscription full-text database of scholarly journals, starting with the first issue of the publication and continuing until a "moving wall" date, meaning that a number of the most recent years (typically three to seven) of the publication are not available. Many of these journals contain book reviews; in the advanced menu one can limit to book reviews and search on a particular topic or a particular journal.

13.11. PsycINFO, the premier database for psychology, indexes approximately 2,500 journals; about half are fully indexed and about half are selectively indexed, so not all reviews are necessarily indexed by PsycINFO. One can find book reviews in PsycINFO simply by limiting "document type" to "review-book" and clicking search. One can limit results to reviews from a particular journal by following the same steps and also entering the journal title in the search box and changing "Select a Field" to "Source." And of course one can limit to reviews of books on a particular subject by following the first steps and then entering one's search terms in the search boxes.

14
Major Museums and Archives of Psychology

The following are selected physical and online museums and archives of psychology; criteria for selection included quality and size of collection and having an English-language website.

14.1. APA History and Archives. http://www.apa.org/about/apa/archives/index.aspx. The American Psychological Association archive contains collections in APA governance, photos, historical tests, historical films, classic books, and coins, as well as APA materials at the Library of Congress (scroll down on the URL provided here for links to each archive). The governance collection is the official depository of APA records, including but not limited to agenda books of the APA Council of Representatives (1951–current) and the APA Board of Directors (1956–current), as well as agendas and minutes from other boards, committees, commissions, task forces, and other groups that together make up the governing body of the APA. The photo collection includes more than 2,300 photographs of people, institutions, and other items related to psychology. The historical tests collection contains tests that were used and developed in the United States and includes early versions of intelligence, personality, vocational interest, aphasia, motor skills, and other psychological or behavioral abilities, as well as the manuals for administration and scoring. Both well-known and more obscure tests are included. The historical film collection contains Louis Aarons's films on brain function; films on Piaget, Skinner Pavlov, Maslow, and others; and films on twin research, various mental disorders, and animal behavior, including ants, baboons, and monkeys. The classic books collection contains more than 3,000 classics dating from the 1800s through the 1900s. The coin collection contains eighty-three coins minted between 1799 and 2004 bearing images of psychologists, psychiatrists, and physiologists, as well as philosophers, biologists, and chemists who contributed to the field of psychology by influencing the thoughts of later scientists, who in turn used these ideas to form the field of psychology. There is also a collection of APA materials at the Library of Congress; more than 270,000 items from the APA central office, divisions, and state and provincial psychological associations from 1917 to1980 are located in the Manuscript Division of the Library of Congress.

14.2. Barnard College Psychology Department History of Psychology Collection. https://psychology.barnard.edu/museum/. This is a collection of digitized documents and images of apparatus that have been stored in the departmental archives for nearly 100 years.

14.3. Bethlem Museum of the Mind. http://www.museumofthemind.org.uk. Bethlem Royal Hospital was founded in 1247 and was the first institution in the United Kingdom to specialize in the care of the mentally ill. The museum is located within the hospital grounds, sharing a building with the Bethlehem Gallery. The museum contains the archives of Bethlem Royal Hospital, the Maudsley Hospital, and Warlingham Park Hospital. There is an online catalog (to which records are still being added), and selected documents are available online. In addition to object artifacts, the archives include, but are not limited to, minutes of governing bodies and committees, annual reports, hospital magazines, accounts, ledgers, salary books, staff records, patient admission and discharge registers, medical records, correspondence, maps and plans, title deeds, and photographs. The collection includes staff and patient records, but does not include personal diaries. A small part of the collection is available for viewing online, including minutes of the Court of Governors of Bridewell and Bethlem Hospital from 1559 to 1800 (with some gaps); Bethlem Hospital's patient admission registers from 1683 to 1902; Bethlem's annual reports for 1825 and 1842 only; photographs of several dozen mid-Victorian patients at Bethlem Hospital; sale particulars for the Monks Orchard Estate, to which Bethlem relocated in 1930; and a lantern slide collection maintained by Bethlem Hospital's chaplain in the early twentieth century.

14.4. Drs. Nicholas and Dorothy Cummings Center for the History of Psychology. http://www.uakron.edu/chp/.

Located at the University of Akron in Ohio, this center is the home of the Archives of the History of American Psychology and the National Museum of Psychology. In 2002 the center became a member of the Smithsonian Institutions Affiliations program, which links the resources of quality cultural and educational organizations in the United States. The Archives was established in 1965. It is the world's largest repository of materials documenting the history of psychology and related disciplines from the 1800s to the present and is searchable online. It consists of manuscripts, artifacts, books, moving images, psychological tests, and special interest collections. The manuscript collection contains more than 2,000 linear feet of correspondence; research notes; manuscript drafts; and organizational records, which include correspondence, meeting minutes, reports, bylaws, and other materials from American psychological organizations. The artifacts collection contains more than 1,000 instruments and apparatus, including kymographs, chronoscopes, ergographs, Skinner's baby-tender, a diathermy machine used in asylums to calm patients, and early models of home monitoring devices designed by psychologists. The book collection contains 50,000 rare and antiquarian books; autographed volumes; textbooks; professional and trade publications dating from 1533 to the present; and asylum reports, journals, and newsletters. The moving image collection includes films, VHS tapes, DVDs, and other formats containing footage of Freud, psychological treatment of war neuroses, very early research in child development and other key studies in psychology and related disciplines. The psychological tests collection contains more than 6,000 paper-and-pencil and object tests, including well-known achievement, aptitude, spatial, personality, religiosity, hostility, and spousal compatibility as well as lesser-known tests such as that on homemaking ability. The special interest collection contains US Air Force, Navy, and Army technical and research reports; newsletters of the Association of Veterans Administration Chief Psychologists; Neuropsychiatry Division of the Veterans Administration Information Bulletins; instruments, apparatus, manuals, and catalogs; popular psychology magazines; and small personal papers collections. The National Museum of Psychology was opened in 2010 and features documents, media, and artifacts from the center's special collections, including the simulated shock generator used in the Milgram obedience studies. As of August 2017, the museum was closed for installation of new exhibits. Museum status and contact information is located at http://www.uakron.edu/chp/contact-us/.

14.5. Freud Museum—London. https://www.freud.org.uk/. Freud Museum—Vienna. http://www.freud-museum.at/en/. The Vienna (Austria) museum is housed in Freud's former office and apartment at Berggasse 19. Its permanent exhibition documents the life and work of Freud, the founder of psychoanalysis, who lived and worked in this house from 1891 until 1938, when he was forced by the Nazis to flee with his family into exile in England. Original furnishings include the waiting room; a selection of Freud's antiquities; and signed copies and first editions of his works, which allow insight into Freud's life, his cultural environment, and the development of psychoanalysis. The museum also contains Europe's largest library on psychoanalysis and has an online catalog, psychoanalysis database, and other research tools available via its website. The London museum is housed at 20 Maresfield Gardens in Hampstead. This was the home of Sigmund Freud and his family from when they escaped Austria in 1938 until Anna Freud died in 1982. The centerpiece is Freud's study, preserved as it was during his lifetime and containing his collection of almost 2,000 Egyptian, Greek, Roman, and Oriental antiquities. Almost 2,000 items fill cabinets and are arranged on every surface. The largest collection of Freud's personal library is also housed here, as is the famous couch. The museum also has a large photo collection; an online catalog; and the Sigmund Freud Archive, which contains approximately 10,000 letters, 1,600 documents, and 1,500 press cuttings

14.6. Glore Psychiatric Museum. http://stjosephmuseum.org/museums/glore/. This award-winning museum chronicles the 130-year history of the State Lunatic Asylum No. 2, founded in 1874 in St. Joseph, Missouri. It is a physical museum located on the adjoining grounds of the original state hospital and also documents centuries of mental health treatment. Surgical tools, treatment equipment, furnishings, nurse uniforms, personal notes, and other items from the hospital are on display, as well as drawings, paintings, pottery, needlework, and other artwork done by patients.

14.7. Museum of the History of Psychological Instrumentation. http://tomperera.com/psychology_museum/. Originally developed out of Montclair University in New Jersey, this online museum presents images, descriptions, and uses of the apparatus listed in the 1903 Zimmerman firm catalog (E. Zimmermann, *XVIII. Preis-Liste über psychologische und physiologische Apparate* [Leipzig: Eduard Zimmermann, 1903]).

14.8. Museum Psychiatric Hospital Aarhus, Denmark (Museet, Psykiatrisk Hospital i Århus). http://museum-psyk.dk/eng/the_museum.htm. This museum is part of the psychiatric hospital in Aarhus, Denmark, and part of Aarhus University Hospital. One section is dedicated to the history of the hospital and the history of psychiatry and the other to art created by psychiatric patients. Researchers with appropriate qualifications have free and ready access to collections and exhibitions as well as to the extensive archives of files, hospital charts, and registers of the hospital and of the Danish Society of Psychiatry (Dansk Psykiatrisk Selskab). Parts of the collections on the history of the hospital and of psychiatry are available online, but as of August 2017 in Danish only.

14.9. Oregon State Hospital Museum of Mental Health. https://oshmuseum.org/. This is both a physical museum and an online collection. The physical location is in Salem, Oregon, and is located in the oldest building on the Oregon State Hospital campus. The museum is dedicated to telling the stories of the Oregon State Hospital and the people who lived and worked there; it includes permanent and changing exhibits. Permanent physical and online collections include a timeline, recordings of "why I am here," treatment modalities and equipment, work and play life, education, a ward room, and life on the ward. The film *One Flew Over the Cuckoo's Nest* was filmed here, and there is also a collection of artifacts from that film.

14.10. Science Museum. http://www.sciencemuseum.org.uk. This museum, located in London, has previously hosted exhibitions of items related to psychology; it contains many psychological tests, objects, and web pages on famous people, hospitals, and treatments in Britain, particularly institutions and programs for "shell shock" or PTSD. Entering "psychology" in the site's search box yields 323 links to its psychology holdings as of August 2017.

14.11. University of Sydney Psychology Museum. http://www.psych.usyd.edu.au/museum/. Held by the School of Psychology at the University of Sydney, this collection is the oldest and largest psychology collection in Australia. The collection contains more than 1,000 early laboratory and mental testing artifacts as well as documentary, photographic, and audiovisual materials. It also houses a large collection of historical psychology-related cartoons featured in British and American satirical periodicals from 1841 through 1980. Further information about the cartoon collection is located at http://www.psych.usyd.edu.au/museum/cartoons/.

14.12. University of Toronto Scientific Instruments Collection, Psychology Collection. https://utsic.escalator.utoronto.ca/home/. Housed at the University of Toronto, this collection contains thousands of objects from various departments at the university, including the Psychology Department, and there are special collections of psychology and engineering psychology objects. The physical collection is not open to the public, although one may make an appointment to visit, and objects and their descriptions and uses are available in the online collection. Each spring the collection hosts an exhibition of selected objects that is open to the public.

14.13. Wellcome Museum. https://wellcomecollection.org. The Wellcome Collection is a free museum and library. Its large collections focus on the connections among science, medicine, art, and life. It is a physical museum, with large parts of its print and image collections also available online; it also hosts many events on all aspects of the above. The library catalog of manuscripts, images, and other materials is available at http://wellcomelibrary.org/search-the-catalogues. Those interested in psychology materials are best served by searching "psychiatry" as well as "psychology."

Index

Notes about using this index:

1. Indexing is to item numbers, not page numbers. Some numbers also refer to section headings which contain conceptual content and instructions.
2. For ease of use, some items are duplicated under several major headings in the text, particularly in chapters 2,4, and 6. In such cases, only the first or most relevant item number is indexed.
3. When an entire work is devoted to the indexed term, that item number is in **bold** type. For multi-volume works, the item number is in **bold** if an entire volume is devoted to the topic.
4. Some works may be *correctly* attached to a subject in the index, but the subject term may not appear in the work's annotation due to space and readability considerations.

About the Author

Deborah Dolan is associate professor of library services and subject specialist for psychology, speech-language-hearing, and disabilities studies at Hofstra University. She has an MA and doctoral credits in clinical psychology from the University of Maryland–College Park and an MLS in library science from City University of New York–Queens College. She has taught various psychology courses at University College of Maryland, State University of New York at Old Westbury, and Nassau County Community College. Since 2001 she has been teaching information literacy and conducting research consultations in psychology and speech-language-hearing with undergraduates, doctoral students, and faculty at Hofstra University. She has published articles in both library science and psychology.

9 781442 276017